ACCOUNT *and* EX?

OF THE

MANUSCRIPTS

IN THE

Library of the King of France.

PUBLISHED UNDER THE

INSPECTION OF A COMMITTEE

OF THE

Royal Academy of Sciences at Paris.

———————

TRANSLATED FROM THE FRENCH.

————————————

VOL. II.

════════════════

LONDON:

PRINTED FOR R. FAULDER, NEW BOND-STREET; T. AND J. EGERTON,
WHITEHALL; AND E. AND T. WILLIAMS, STRAND.

———

M,DCC,LXXXIX.

C O N T E N T S

B O O K

WANDERING STARS,

CONTAINING

The Hiftory of Egypt and Cairo.

By the Sheik *Schemfeddin Mohammed ben Abilforour al-Bakeri al Sadiki.*

Arabian Manufcript, No. 784, Quarto, 175 Leaves.

By M. SYLVESTRE DE SACY.

SCHEMSEDDIN Mohammed, the author of this work, was as diftinguifhed by the noblenefs of his origin, as by his literary merit. He was defcended from Mahomet by Ali, and reckoned among his anceftors, Mohammed Bakeri and Diafar Sadiki, (fons of Bakeri) the fifth and fixth imams; on which account he bears the furnames of Bakeri and Sadiki. It appears that he was born at Cairo, in the year 1005 of the hegira, of Jefus Chrift 1596-7, under the government of Seïd Mohammed Pacha; if it was on account of his birth, (as there is reafon to believe) that his father fheik

VOL. II.   B   Abil-

Abilforour, gave in that city a magnificent feaft, which lafted forty days, and to which the pacha was invited. He informs us of this circumftance in his works, where he contents himfelf with faying, that this feaft was given on this occafion, without entering further into the fubject.

His grandfather fheik Mohammed ben Abilforour Almefri Albakeri Alfadiki Altëimi, was author of a book called, "The Sources of Hiftory, and the Delight of the Eyes." It is an univerfal hiftory from the beginning of the world. He has alfo made an abridgement of this work, under the title of "Collection of the moft curious Relations relating to the Hiftory of the Kings and the Kalifs." Hadji Khalfa, who makes mention of it in his library of Arabic, Turkifh, and Perfian writers of the century in which he wrote, fay, "This author bore alfo the furname of *Sebt Albaffan*, the "outcaft of the family of Haffan;" and it is by this name that he is ufually cited, as M. de Herbelot has remarked.

Another writer, who ftill bears the name of Sadiki, is the fcheik Delaleddin Mohammed ben Afad Alfadiki, who died in the year 907, of Jefus Chrift 1501-2. He was alfo of the fame family as our author, who mentions him in the work of which we are now going to give an account. Djelaleddin has compofed for fultan Mahmoud, an introduction to the fciences, under the title of "Enmou-"ded Aloloum."

Schemfeddin,

Schemfeddin, author of this hiftory of Egypt and Caïro, compofed feveral other works. In many places he cites a more extenfive chronicle, to which he refers for the particulars of events peculiar to the reign of each of the Ottoman fultans. This chronicle, which is unknown to me, does not really extend beyond the reign of Muftafa II. depofed for the fecond time in the year 1032 (1622-3); and it is doubtlefs for that reafon that the author has inferted in his hiftory of Egypt, a circum-ftantial recital of the principal events of the reign of his fucceffor, fultan Merad, (Amurath IV.)

The other works of Schemfedden are, a hiftory of the conqueft of Egypt by the Ottomans; a fmall ef-fay on the abolition of the contributions the military of Egypt compelled the labourers to pay, and which the vizir Mohammed Pacha abolifhed in the year 1017 (1608-9): laftly, a collection, whofe object is alfo the hiftory of the moft remarkable revolu-tions which have happened in Egypt.

The hiftory contained in this manufcript ends the firft day of the year 1063, of Chrift 1652-3; but the latter years have been afterwards added by the copyift. We even faw fome blank pages which were defigned to receive the recital of events in the reign of Mohammed IV. crowned 1058, (A. D. 1648); and of what paffed in Egypt under the government of the pacha Mohammed and his fuccef-fors. This manufcript, as the note which ends it proves, has been finifhed in the month of Dhoul-hadja 1055, (February 1646.) We may conclude

from

from hence with certainty, that the detail of events posterior to that date, has been afterwards added: but that is not sufficient to determine precisely where the work of the author ends.

The different writings, and the difference in the intervals of the lines, which is seen in two places, makes me think that the history of the sultans did not originally extend beyond the coronation of Ibrahim, in the month of Schawal 1049, (February 1640,) and that the history of the Beglerbegs of Egypt ended at the nomination of Ayoub Pacha in 1054 (1644). At the end of the conquest of Egypt by Selim I. the author remarks that this country has remained from that time to the year in which he wrote, which was the 1055th of the hegira, under the Ottoman dominion; but it is possible that the copyist has substituted the year in which *he* wrote, in the place of that which the author had expressed.

The stile of this work is simple, and rather diffused, than concise: the only difficulty that appears, arises from a great number of words which we have sought in vain in the dictionaries, and which are either peculiar to the Arabs of Egypt, or introduced into the language by the mixture of the different nations who inhabit that country. There are many whose signification I have not been able to determine with precision. Such as the names of the different kinds of stuffs made by the Egyptians, and which they manufacture in that country, or formerly manufactured there: and the names

of

of the monies. We find many which appear to have been entirely unknown to our lexicographers, and which I do not recollect to have read in the relations of travellers. I have thought myself obliged to preferve the original terms : perhaps fome other work will one day furnifh an explanation. I have met with ftill more difficulty in the part which refpects the natural hiftory and the rural œconomy. The fame name being often common to many plants, where, defcribing in any country ; in Arabia for example, a plant different from that which he defcribes in Egypt ; I have taken for my guide the *Flora Egyptiaco-Arabica* of the learned Forfkal, and particularly that part of the work which treats of Egyptian plants. But to avoid in a fubject to which I am a ftranger, running a rifk of confounding the fpecies or the genus, in adopting one denomination in preference to another, I have been careful to add to the French word which I have thought beft to ufe, the original term, and the name by which every plant is called in the work of the celebrated Philologus, who has adopted the fyftem of Linnæus. I have obferved the fame rule for the names of fome few animals.

All the names which refpect government, the detail of the finances, of military difcipline, all the names of offices or employments, are borrowed from the Turkifh language, or derived from the Arabic roots, but fufceptible of various fenfes. I have in general followed the interpretation of Me-

ninfki

ninſki, although often too indeterminate; and for
the ſmall number of thoſe of which I have not been
able to diſcover a preciſe ſignification, I have
thought myſelf obliged to preſerve the original appellation.   I think this is the beſt means to render
this work the moſt uſeful to thoſe who ſtudy the
eaſtern languages.

This hiſtory of Egypt and of Caïro, is divided
into twenty chapters. I ſhall give in the ſame
order, an idea of the ſubjects treated of in each of
them; but from the third chapter I ſhall preſent a
particular extract, which will contain the hiſtory of
the governors of Egypt, ſince its reunion to the
Ottoman empire by the conqueſt of Selim I. to our
author's time; and I ſhall likewiſe tranſlate the
greater part of the thirteenth, which contains
ſome particulars of the natural hiſtory of that
country.

The firſt chapter treats of the ancient inhabitants of Egypt, and of the etymology of the
names they bear among the Arabs. The different
opinions of writers, from whom the author has extracted what he ſays on that ſubject, all unite in
opinion that Egypt is called *Miſtr*, from the name
of Miſrim, one of their firſt kings, or the chief of
the firſt colony.

The ſecond chapter has for its objects the extent
and limits of Egypt. Beſides the names of *the
ſea of Kolſom* and *the ſea of Hedjaz*, the Arabian
gulph is alſo called the *Salt Sea*, Bahr almelh: this
denomination, which is alſo uſed by other Arabic
writers,

writers, has not, I believe, been hitherto obferved. It is alfo proper to remark, that in the defcription of the frontiers of Egypt, the author includes a part of the coaft of Hedjaz, and of the Red Sea. Thefe are his words: " After having croffed the Nile at " Afwan, we pafs to the eaft of that city as far as " Aïdab, fituated on the coaft of the fea of Hed- " jaz, and fifteen days journey diftant from Afwan. " From Aïdab we muft crofs the Salt Sea to come " to the coaft of Hedjaz. Haura is the firft city " of Egypt on that coaft; it borders on the terri- " tory of Medina. This fea, which comes within " the limits of Egypt, is the fea of Kolfom: its " territory, as well eaftern as weftern, and maritime, " form part of Egypt. In the eaftern parts are " Hama, Taïba, Neïl, Medyan, Aïela, and all " above, to the mountain of *Almokattam**. The " weftern territory is the fea coaft from Aïdab to " that part of the fea which wafhes the foot of the " above mountain. In the maritime part are the " city of Kolfom and mount Tor: from Kolfom " to Farma, is a day and a night's journey. This " is the country which feparates the fea of Hedjaz " from the Mediterranean."

The third chapter has this title: *Of the kings of Egypt before the deluge, and during all the ages pre- ceding the eftablifhment of the Mahomedan religion in that country: of the kalifs and governors the of Egypt under their empire; of the princes who have fucceeded*

---

* See the chart of the Arabian gulph by M. D'Anville.

them;

*them; and, laſtly, of the governors who have exerciſed
authority there until the year* 1060* *of the begira.*

I ſhall content myſelf with giving a liſt of the
governors of Egypt for the kalifs, from the conqueſt of Amron ben Alâs to that of the Fatemites,
without dwelling on what concerns the hiſtory of
the Fatemite kalifs, of the Auoubite ſultans of the
two dynaſties of Mamlucs; and I ſhall paſs immediately to the conqueſt of Selim I. and to the
hiſtory of Egypt under the Ottoman dominion.
This extraƈt will contain the recital of the moſt
remarkable paſſages for more than thirty years,
and ſome tranſaƈtions foreign to Egypt, and
which belong to the general hiſtory of the Turkiſh
empire.

Selim Khan, ſon of Abouyezid, (Bajazet II.)
and grandſon of Mahomet II. whoſe name is celebrated in hiſtory by the taking of Conſtantinople,
was at war with Shah Iſmael, who then filled the
throne of Perſia, and who was the firſt king of
the dynaſty of the Sophis. Selim was not ignorant
that the ſultan of Egypt, Canſou Algouri, was by
intereſt conneƈted with the king of Perſia, and that
while Selim carried on the war againſt Iſmael,
Canſou had prevented the caravans of Aleppo from
joining his army. Being determined to take his revenge for this, Selim prepared to attack the dominions that Canſou poſſeſſed in Syria, with a deſign
afterwards to invade Egypt. Canſou informed of

---

* This date has been ſubſtituted in the room of another which
had been omitted.

his

his intention, haftened to affemble his troops, made them confiderable prefents, and advanced feveral months pay. Saturday, Kabial-akher 922, (17th May, 1516,) he began his march for Syria at the head of five thoufand men, a confiderable army, but too weak to refift the numerous troops of Selim.

Saturday the 22d of the fame month he nominated Emir Toumanbey, governor of Egypt in his ·abfence, and took his way to Damafcus. He arrived there on the eighth of the month Dgioumadial-akher, (the 7th of July, 1516,) and after having remained there nine days, he marched for Emeffa, in his way to Aleppo, where he arrived on the 20th of the fame month. He left that city to go in fearch of the enemy's army, and encamped the 20th of Redgib,· (the 15th of Auguft,) in the plain named Mardg da Cegh. The firft day of the week, the 27th of the fame month, in the morning, they difcovered the army of Selim; and after prayers, Canfou, at the head of his army, advanced towards the enemy: the onfet was very violent, and the troops of Selim were firft broken by thofe of Canfou; but the Ottoman army having made a new effort, overthrew that of Egypt. A great number of Canfou's troops were killed on the fpot, others took flight and difperfed. Canfou, with a fmall number of his foldiers, remained with the ftandard, the Emir, who bore it, reprefented to him, that the troops of Selim would not delay to make themfelves mafter of it, and advifed him to

fly

fly for fafety to Aleppo; at the fame time he folded up the ftandard. Canfou, affected with the defeat of his army, was fuddenly ftruck with the palfy, which deprived him of the ufe of one fide, and his mouth remained open and motionlefs. He made figns for water, and after having tafted it, attempted to fly, but fell from his horfe, and expired fome minutes after, under the horfes feet. All the baggage of the army fell into the hands of the conqueror. Thus, in one inftant, an end was put to the power of this prince.

After this victory, Selim marched towards Aleppo; took poffeffion of that city, and went from thence to Damafcus. He made himfelf mafter of Canfou's treafures, of the arms, and provifions for his army, and fubftituted his own name in the place of that of the fultan, in all the mofques. Selim ftill continued to advance into the dominions of Canfou, and took poffeffion of all the countries which had obeyed him, as far as Birket-alhady. Wednefday the 28th of Dhoulhadja, (the 21ft of January, 1517,) the army of Selim attacked that of Toumenbey, who had taken poffeffion of the throne as foon as he had received the news of Canfou's death, and defeated them. On the morrow, the laft day of the year, Selim moved his camp from Reidania to Boulac: he made his entry into Caïro; went afterwards to Alexandria, and returned again to Caïro. He quitted that place Thurfday the 20th of Schaban, 923, (the 27th of Auguft, 1517,) to return to Romania. He left in Caïro a garrifon

of

of 5000 horfe, and 500 fufileers, and gave the command of the citadel to Kaïreddin pacha, one of his officers, with orders not to go to it, or to fet his foot in the city. This officer is now called the Aga of the Janiffaries. When Selim quitted Egypt, he carried with him 1000 camels, loaded with gold and filver, without reckoning the reft of the plunder and the prefents which he had received. " The Ottoman family has remained in poffeffion of Egypt from this conqueft of Selim, unto the time I write this, in the year 1055, (1645-6) which is a fpace of 133 years."

Khaïrbeg Pacha, to whom Selim, (when he quitted that province) had entrufted the government of Egypt, the principal emir, under the reign of Canfou, ill-treated the people, and loaded them with every kind of vexation. After his death, Soliman, who fucceded Selim on the throne of Conftantinople, named Muftapha Pacha, to fucceed him, who took poffeffion of that government the 6th of Dhoulhadja (the 28th of October, 1522). He was fucceeded the following year by Soliman Pacha: the latter endeavoured to render himfelf independent in his government, and coined money in his own name. The Emirs affembled the troops, and furprifed him in a bath, at the time they were fhaving his head. When he found himfelf attacked, he fled half fhaved, and took refuge with an Arabian fhiek. The Emirs demanded, that he fhould be delivered into their hands, which, being granted, they cut off his head and fent it to
Conftantinople:

Conftantinople: he had governed Egypt about a
year. He was fucceeded under the reign of
Soliman by Khaffem Pacha and Ibrahim Pacha,
who made many regulations concerning the troops
and the divan. By Soliman Pacha and by Khafraf
Pacha, the fame Soliman who had governed before,
and after him by Dawood Pacha. The latter was
a man full of mildnefs, noblenefs, and generofity.
He loved and protected the learned: he had been
educated in the emperor's palace, and paffed from
the place of Khazendar of Soliman (grand treafurer) to the government of Egypt. He loved
ftudy, and applied himfelf to the reading of Arabic
books, of which he made a great collection : befides
thofe he purchafed, he employed a great number
of writers, to procure copies of thofe he could not
purchafe. By this means he formed a confiderable library.

Under his government, learning flourifhed; he
did not give himfelf up to pleafure and diverfions.
He loaded the learned of Egypt with benefits; the
people were happy, and they experienced neither
enaction nor injuftice. Ali Pacha fucceeded him.
He built or repaired many public edifices at Caïro,
at Foué, and at Rafched, and made himfelf beloved by his good conduct. Mahomet Pacha, who
fucceeded him, rendered himfelf odious. He was
depofed and put to death, on his arrival at Conftantinople, by order of the emperor. After him, Ef-
cander Pacha, Ali Pacha Alkhadem, Muftapha
Pacha, Ali Pacha Alfoufi furnamed Kiloun, and
Mahmoud

Mahmoud Pacha, were fucceffively nominated by Soliman to the government of Egypt. Ali Pacha Alfoufi had been formerly pacha of Bagdad. He carried with him fome inhabitants of Aleppo, and was entrufted with the receipt of the money for the public revenue, to be remitted to the emperor's treafure. Thefe people well underftood the pacha's intention, and took upon themfelves the coining of money, which they confiderably adulterated; fo that upon an hundred drams, they had a profit of thirty *nisf**; fince that time the adulteration of money has been conftantly increafing. Under his government, troops of robbers infefted the environs of Caïro; they came as far as the mofque Alabyadh, where my great grandfather lived; the virtue and fanctity of that refpectable man attracted the protection of heaven, and the thieves did no injury. The pacha came on the morrow to vifit that place, and ordered a wall to be built from the bridge Alhadjel to the mofque, to fecure that place from all furprife. This wall remains to this day. Mahmoud Pacha was the laft governor of Egypt appointed by Soliman. He took poffeffion of his government in the month of Schawal 973, (May 1566). He came with a great retinue, received a confiderable number of prefents on his journey from Alexandria to Caïro. At his

---

* This word fignifies *half*; it really means that the money which the Turks at prefent call *yaremlec*, which fignifies the fame thing in Turkifh as *nisf* in Arabic, is a filver coin, which is equivalent to half a piafter, or groufche, that is, twenty paras, or one livre; 2 st. 1d, French money.

arrival

arrival in that city, he found there emir Mohammed ben Omar, intendant of Saïd, or the Upper Egypt, who came to meet him with a large barque, loaded with prefents of all forts, and 50000 pieces of gold. He crucified him, and took poffeffion of all he had brought; he put to death in the fame manner the cadee Youffouf Alebadi, becaufe Youffouf had not met him with the other emirs, and had not given him prefents fome years before, when he paffed through Egypt in his way to Yemen. Many other diftinguifhed perfonages fell alfo victims to his cruelty. He pointed out to the Soubafchi, an officer, by motion of his hand, and without fpeaking of the perfons he doomed to death, and the kind of torments by which he would have them deftroyed. Yet this pacha was more generous and magnificent in his attendance, than any of his predeceffors, or minifters of his age. He was always richly cloathed, and only veffels of gold and filver were brought to his table.

The emir Ibrahim, who was then defterdar, (treafurer) and who had been nominated by the fultan to prefide at the religious ceremony on mount Araphat, dying the 3d of redgeb 974, (the 14th of January, 1567,) the pacha was much rejoiced at it: he vented the whole of his animofity againft him; but before the end of the year, he underwent the punifhment due to his injuftice. He had no fooner heard of the death of Ibrahim, then he fent fome people on his part to take poffeffion of his houfe and flaves. Ibrahim had amaffed immenfe

menfe riches and many precious things. Mahmoud at firft feized upon all he found, which he caufed to be fold at a low price; he afterwards tortured the flaves to oblige them to difcover the treafures which Ibrahim had fecreted in his houfe. The chief of the flaves revealed, and Mahmoud feized upon it; he found there an hundred thoufand pieces of gold, which he made ufe of to form the *treafure** which he was obliged to fend to Conftantinople.

He entrufted Mohradbeg, one of his flaves, with the carriage of the treafure. This perfon arrived afterwards to the dignity of grand vizier, under the reign of Ahmed, and at the fame time fent rich prefents to the fultan and his minifters. While he waited with a flattering hope the effect of his prefents, and the protection of the great, the decrees of Providence were accomplifhed. Wednefday, Dgioumadi Loula, 975, (5th December, 1567), as he appeared in public with his train, as he was accuftomed to do every Wednefday, an affaffin, pofted, according to the recital of fome credible perfons, by the emirs Hamzabay and Mamaibeg, mortally wounded him by a fhot from a mufquet, in a narrow ftreet between the walls of two gardens. The affaffin had made a hole in one of the walls, through which he levelled his mufquet, loaded with ball, without being feen by any one;

* By this word is meant the fum which the fultan annually receives from the impoft of the provinces and other public revenues. It is fent every year by the pacha, under the conduct of an officer charged to convey it to the general treafury of the empire.

Pocock's Voyages.

he..

he applied his lighted match, fired at the pacha, and ftruck him under the left fhoulder; he left his piece in the hole he had placed it, went out in the garden, and mixed among the croud, fo that they could not difcover him. The pacha, after having endeavoured in vain to continue his way, was obliged to alight from his horfe; they fpread on the ground fome filk carpets on which they placed him, and the emirs continued with him. The flaves entered the garden, faw the mufquet which the affaffin had left, and no one there, except two men who were at work, whofe heads they cut off, although they were entirely innocent, and had heard the report without feeing from what part it came. They caufed a covered litter to be brought for the pacha, who was carried back to his houfe in the greateft torments. The news of this fpread terror through the city, and the fhops were fhut up; but tranquillity was foon reftored by an amnifty which was publifhed. Neverthelefs the emirs and fandjacs patrolled the city all night leaft the pacha fhould moleft any perfon on account of this affaffination. Mahmoud having made his will, the cadec, the defterdar, the emirs, and the fandjacs retired, and he removed to his apartment, where he died furrounded by his women. His tomb is in the fquare of Romeïlé.

Beglerbegs

Beglerbegs of Egypt under the reign of Sultan Selim, fon of Sultan Soleïman.

Selim II. having afcended the throne in the month of Rebi-alakher 974, held it during eight years, one month, and fourteen days, and died the 17th of Ramadhan 982*.

Sinan Pacha was the firft governor that Selim gave to Egypt. He paffed from the government of Aleppo to this province, where he remained but nine days, having been deftined by the fultan to the command of the army he had fent into Arabia Felix. When he had made all the neceffary pre-, parations for this expedition, he departed the 4th of Schawal, 976, (23d of March, 1569), accompa- nied by Hamzabeg, Mamaïbeg, and feveral others of the principal emirs of Egypt. He conducted this expedition with much prudence and fkill, and after having been fuccefsful in the conqueft of Ye- men, he returned in triumph to Egypt. During his abfence Egypt had for governor Djerkes Ef- cander Pacha. He freed the poor, fick, lame, and the greateft part of men of letters from taxes. He was reputed a learned man himfelf. Sinan Pacha, on his return from his expedition, refumed his government the firft of Saphar, 979, and pof- feffed it till the month of Dhoulhadja, 980. This pacha undertook important works: he caufed the canal of Alexandria to be dug again and repaired; he alfo built a mofque, a market, and baths, in

---

* Thefe dates are not exact, and contradict one another.

that city; and a great mofque, a market, ftore-houfes for merchandize, and caravanferas for travellers at Boulac. He alfo erected a monaftery (Tekkié) on the road of Romania, in a retired place, to accommodate travellers with fubfiftence. Hoffaïn Pacha fucceeded Sinan. He poffeffed excellent qualities; was affectionate to men of learning, of a mild and modeft difpofition, and highly averfe to all cruelty. In his time troops of robbers fpread themfelves abroad in great numbers and committed many depredations.

Beglerbegs of Egypt under the reign of Sultan Mo-rad, (Amurath III.) fon of Sultan Selim.

Morad afcended the throne the 10th of Ramadhan, 982, (24th of December, 1574,) and died the 6th of Ramadhan, 1003, (15th of May, 1595). The firft governor of Egypt, under the reign of Sultan Morad, was Meffih Pacha Alkhadem, who was khazendar (grand treafurer) in the time of Sultan Selim. This pacha was of a ferocious and cruel character. It is faid, that during the continuance of his government, which lafted five years, he put to death about 10,000 perfons, but they were moftly malefactors, for the robbers had multiplied extremely under the government of Hoffaïn Pacha. Meffih almoft totally exterminated them, and from that time to the prefent, there has been known a very fmall number of robbers and thieves. He never accepted prefents from any one, which rendered Egypt very flourifhing. He built a great mofque

mofque at the gate of the fuburb Karafa, in favour of Scheikz Zoureddin Alkarafi, and gave to
him and his pofterity the fuperintendance of this
mofque, and the free difpofal of the revenue with
which he had endowed it. He ordered that the
catebs (clerks) fhould henceforth begin the firmams
and decrees with this formule: " Praife to God;
health and peace to our prophet, to his defcendants,
and to all his companions; maintain peace and
union among your brethren, and fear God; perhaps one day you will be converted unto him.
Servants of God, ftrive faithfully to fulfil the pre-
cepts of his religion, and conform your actions to
his laws."

Haffan Pæha Alkhadem fucceeded Meffih. He
had been before Khazendar to Sultan Morad.
He governed Egypt during two years, and was
wholly employed in amaffing wealth by every method. He revived the cuftom of receiving prefents, which his predeceffor had abolifhed. When
he quitted his government, he went out fron
Caïro by the quarter of the tombs, not daring to
fhew himfelf to the people. The fultan, informed
of his tyranny, caufed him to be ftrangled on his
return to Romania.

The vizir Ibrahim Pacha was appointed in his
room. He vifited all the depa tments of Egypt,
even to the utmoft extremity of Saïd: he came to
the place called *the Wells of the Emeralds*, (Bir Elzu-
murrud) whence he drew a great quantity of them.
When he arrived at Caïro he began to make ftrict

enquiries

enquiries into Haffan Pacha's extortion, and appointed an officer to receive the complaints which the fandjacs had to prefent againft him. Thefe informations were taken in the mofque of Faradi ben Barkouk. They began the 10th of Redjeb, 991, (30th of July, 1583, new ftyle,) and lafted to the end of Ramadhan of the fame year, (Oct. 1583). There was not a man in office, farmer or receiver of the public revenues, or an Arabian Scheikh, from whom Haffan had not exacted confiderable fums. They alfo enquired into the quantity of grain he had taken from the public granaries, and it was found that he had fold 100,442 ardabs. Thefe informations were reduced to writing, with the proof that had been produced, and the whole were tranfmitted to the emperor, who confifcated all the effects of Haffan Ibrahim, and nominated Sinan Pacha, who was defterdar, (treafurer) to fucceed him. The latter held this government during a year and an half. He took flight and quitted Egypt, when Awis Pacha, who fucceeded him, was fent to examine into his conduct. Awis was a fevere man, and of ftrict probity. He was firft eadi, afterwards defterdar of the province of Romania, and was promoted from that place to be Beglerbeg of Egypt. Having propofed to reform the difcipline of the troops, they revolted againft him, and attacked him in the divan, the 2d of Schawal, 997, (14th of Auguft, 1589). The foldiers expofed him to all kind of infults: they entered into his harem, and took what they found moft valuable,

valuable; among other moveables, a grand clock, which pointed out the days. Awis efcaped, but three of his attendants were killed. The foldiers entered likewife the houfe of the cadhilafker, and killed Othman, commander of the tfchaoufcks. They feized two cadies, and kept them prifoners at Kharafa; the next day they cut off their heads. Several emirs took flight and concealed themfelves. The rebels plundered the merchants ftores, and took the moft precious merchandizes and ftuffs. They caufed a prohibition to be publifhed againft the Arabians having any white flaves, and againft the Jews having girls for flaves; they even enjoined them to fend all they then had of them within three days, under pain of death. Thus armed they entered by troops into the houfes of the great, carrying off what they chofe. In vain did the defterdar and feveral other emirs endeavour to bring them back to duty. Awis was obliged to fend to the cadi an order to grant them all they fhould afk. This did but augment their infolence; they feized the children of the pacha as hoftages, in order to fecure the execution of what they required. The pacha confented to all their demands. From that time they never ceafed, from time to time, to renew their exceffes, to the time of Mohammed Pacha, who remedied thefe abufes, when he was nominated governor of Egypt under the reign of Ahmed.

Ahmed Pacha Hafedh Alkhadem fucceeded Awis; he had been previoufly beglerbeg of Cy-

C 3. prus.

prus. He had great talents for government, and loved the learned and the poor. He eftablifhed a diftribution * of water in favour of the poor pilgrims to Mecca; he conftructed at Boulac two ftorehoufes, (okals) with caravanferas and houfes, and fet apart a fourth of their revenue for this diftribution. He was the laft governor of Egypt, nominated by Sultan Mohrad.

Beglerbegs of Egypt under the reign of Sultan Mohammed, (Mohamet III.) fon of Sultan Morad.

Mohammed was crowned the 17th of Ramadhan, 1003, (26th of May, 1595,) and died on Saturday, 16th of Redgeb, 1012, (20th of Dec. 1603,) after a reign of eight years and eleven months.

He named for governor of Egypt Kourd Pacha, who made himfelf beloved by his mildnefs, and the liberality with which he diftributed abundant affiftance to men of letters, to the poor, and to all thofe who had recourfe to his beneficence.

The Seïd Mohammed Pacha, who fucceeded him, did not lefs diftinguifh himfelf by the wifdom of his government, and by the protection he granted to the learned. He re-eftablifhed the mofque Djame Alazhar, and founded a daily diftribution of lentils, in favour of the indigent; he alfo repaired the Mefchhed Hoffaïni. My father held in his pre-

---

* The Arabian word is Sehabat; perhaps it is a diftribution of water for the neceffitous pilgrims. The author fpeaks, lower down, of a like foundation, which confifted in a fupply of water of forty loads of camels, and implies the fame expreffion.

fence

fence a public lecture, of which he went out well satisfied. It was alfo under the government of this, pacha, that my father gave, on my account, a great feaft, for which he expended five thoufand pieces of gold, without reckoning the diftribution of prefents of all kinds, the value of which amounts to a fum equally confiderable.

The beglerbeg came and paffed three days in a houfe of my father, fcheik Aboulforour, which was fituated near Berketarrotli, and known by the name of Schadherwan. During his refidence there, he gave confiderable prefents to the people, and to the muficians who repaired thither from all parts. The feaft continued forty days, and during that time a great part of the inhabitants took no reft. Mohammed Pacha found himfelf expofed to a great danger, from which God delivered him. In the beginning of the month of Radjib, 1006, many bodies of troops affembled from different parts of Egypt, and repaired to Caïro. Mohammed being then at his country houfe at Djizé, according to the cuftom of former beglerbegs. He had with him a part of the troops of Caïro, and many emirs and fandjacs. When he returned to Caïro, although he was furrounded with emirs who accompanied him, fome malcontents fired at him: the janiffaries abandoned him, and it was with difficulty he faved himfelf. The rebels kept him befieged all that day, in the houfe to which he had retired. He afked them what they wanted: they required that feveral officers fhould be delivered up to them, of

C 4   which

which number was Dali Mohammed, one of the principal emirs, who gave away confiderable alms; the emir Djelad Sembafchi, and the emir Khedher, cafchef (governor) of Manfoura. The pacha demanded a parly of three days. They anfwered, *God fhall judge between us and our mafter Mohammed Pacha*; and they addreffed themfelves to the cadalifker, Abdarrawouf Arabzadé, who confented to receive their complaints, and examine their demands. While this paffed, a violent wind arofe, which raifed fo great a cloud of duft that the air was darkened. Mohammed availed himfelf of this circumftance to efcape under favour of the obfcurity: he haftened to mount his horfe, and entered the caftle, the gate of which was immediately fhut. He quitted his horfe, and was going to enter his apartment, when his foot being engaged in the extremity of his caftan, he fell on the ground. All this was a miraculous protection of the prophet from whom he drew his origin; for in that moment a man, who had entered the caftle with him, fired at him, and he efcaped only by the motion occafioned by treading on his robe. Haffan Pacha Alfekrani, who was beglerbeg of the army, and biribeg, emir elhadj, (conductor of the caravan) prefented themfelves to the mutineers, and remonftrated with them, which produce no other effect but to increafe their infolence. They proceeded to the houfe of the emir Dali, and on their way, meeting with the emir, Mohammed Beg, who was going up to the caftle, and who reproached them

with

with their revolts, and exhorted them to return to their obedience, they cut off his head, saying, *You are also one of those whose death we required.* Mohammed Dali had secured himself in his house near the bridge *Alfiba* with some brave men: the muti-neers attacked him there and forced the gate. The emir retired into the interior part of his house, and shut himself up in a very fine kiosk. Some soldiers mounted on the minaret of an adjoining college which commanded the kiosk and fired at him; he was killed by a ball which struck him on the head. The seditious party entered his house, and cut off his head, which they suspended at the gate Zuweila, and plundered the moveables, arms, precious stones, and horses; the loss was estimated at thirty thousand pieces of gold. The other emirs, whose death they had demanded, fled secretly into the province of Romania. They then attacked the Arabs, killed and plundered all those who they found dressed in the manner of the Greeks. The tumult was at last appeased, but the troops preserved the same spirit of insolence and mutiny, which continued during the government of Seid Mohammed Pacha.

His successor was the vizir Rhedher Pacha, who had been beglerbeg of Bagdad. He wanted, at the beginning of his government, to take away the distribution of corn which the learned received, under a pretence that the greater part of those who had a share of these distributions were merchants, and not men of letters. My father remonstrated with him on this subject, and promised to furnish him

him with an account of the learned who received
thefe diftributions. He accepted this propofal, and
charged the mocatadji (receiver general of the
revenue of the cuftoms) to regulate this affair with
my father, but my father took care to make his
court to him, and obtained of him that he would
make no alteration in the ordinary deftributions.
The firft day of the week, 20th of Ramadhan, 1009,
(26th of March, 1600), the troops having the cada-
lafker at their head, went up to the divan and demanded the ketkhoda (or lieutenant) and fome
other officers. They required of the cadi that he
fhould confent to examine their complaints on the
fubject of provifions and other grievances. The
ketkhoda was then with the beglerbeg: he attempted to efcape, but the foldiers attacked him
near the quarter of the Tfchaoufchs, and cut off
his head. They treated many other emirs in the
fame manner. On the next day the beglerbeg
granted their demands, and the tumult was appeafed.

The vizir Ali Pacha, who was felahdar, (an officer who carries the fultan's arms) was nominated
in the room of Khedher. He was a brave, generous, and equitable man: he treated his troops with
goodnefs, but he delighted in fpilling blood. He
never appeared in public with his retinue, without
killing at leaft ten perfons, in the blood of whom
he paffed with his horfe. There was a great famine during his time in Egypt. A meafure of corn,
called wabya, was fold as high as thirty-fix nefs:
this

this fcarcity was attended with a dreadful plague, fuch as has never been experienced before, if we except thofe that defolated Egypt in the time of the beglerbeg's, Djafar Pacha and Macfoud Pacha, of whom we fhall fpeak afterwards. This mortality extended over all Egypt. A man, who lived near the gate Elnafr, told me that he had feen above three hundred bodies carried in one day to the *meflat*, (chapel) fituated near that place. We may conjecture from thence how many there muft have been brought into the other chapels and mofques. The pacha prohibited the carrying in public the bodies of thofe who died. Ali Pacha, leaving Caïro, appointed for caïmacan, (lieutenant) the emir Biribeg. This emir dying, the fandjacs elected in his room the emir Othmanbeg, who exercifed the functions of caïmacan till the arrival of the beglerbeg Ibrahim Pacha.

Beglerbegs of Egypt under the reign of the Sultan Ahmed, (Achmet I.) fon of Sultan Mohammed.

Ahmed afcended the throne, Sunday the 17th of Rhedjeb, 1012, (21ft of December, 1603,) and died, Wednefday, 23d of Dhoulcaada, 1026, (23d of November, 1617).

The firft governor of Egypt, named by this fultan, was the vizir Ibrahim Pacha, who was killed by the troops, as we are going to relate. This pacha had formed the defign to reprefs the infolent demands of the troops, but his project proved abortive. Friday the laft of Rebialakher, 1013, (24th of

Sep-

September, 1644,) he quitted Caïro, and repaired
to Bouilac with a numerous retinue.   He embarked at this place, and went down to Schebra,
near the bridge built over the canal of Aboulmenedja.   The troops having heard that the pacha
had abandoned Caïro, met in the suburb of Kharafa, obliging themselves by oath to put him to
death.   The next day, early in the morning, they
departed for Bouilac, in order to attack him on his
return, and having heard that he then was in the
caftle of Doulab, near the bridge Aboulmenedja,
they refolved to go in fearch of him.   The pacha
was informed of their proceedings, and the fandjacs advifed him to embark quickly for Bouilac, before the rebels would have arrived at Doulab, but
he did not embrace this counfel.   He had with
him the cadhihafker, Muftapha Effindi Garmizadé,
Othmanbeg who difcharged the office of caïmacan
after the retreat of Ali Pacha, the emir Bayazid-
beg, and feveral other begs and cadis, with a
guard of tfchaoufchs, and of mutefarrakas *.
The rebels being arrived, furrounded the caftle,
and fifteen fpahis entered it fword in hand.   *What
do you want?* faid Ibrahim, on feeing them coming in;   *Have not I given you your pay, and the ufual
gratifications for my inftallation?   We afk nothing,* anfwered they;   *we come but to take away thy life.*
Ibrahim faw that he could not avoid death;   he
arofe;   one of the foldiers ftruck him with his fword
on the face, and the others falling upon him in the

* They are the two firft corps of the fpahis, or cavalry.

fame

fame inftant, he was pierced with wounds, and his head cut off. The emir Mohammed ben Khafraf, who reproached them for their unworthy conduct, underwent the fame fate. In the mean while an innumerable army furrounded the caftle: the murderers defcended, and fhewed their comrades the heads of Ibrahim and Mohammed. The emirs and cadies, who were in the caftle, took flight. The army returned to Caïro, and after having carried in triumph, into all the quarters of the town, the head of pacha and that of emir Mohammed, the foldiers fufpended them at the gate of Zuveïla, like thofe of people of the vileft condition. The fame day the army beftowed the command on Othmanbeg, and on his refufal on cadhihafker Muftapha Effendi. The two heads were buried. The whole town was in confternation and affright, and they generally bewailed the unfortunate fate of Ibrahim, who had formed the project of delivering the people from the vexations and infolence of the foldiery.

After the murder of Ibrahim, the vizir Mohammed Pacha Alkhurdji Alkhadem was nominated governor of Egypt. He conducted himfelf with much wifdom toward the troops, and he fucceeded in ridding himfelf of the great number of thofe mutineers he wifhed to punifh. When he arrived at Caïro, he received orders from the Porte, addreffed to all the fandjacs, and to the army, which were brought to him by the djufchneghirbafchi, (great cup-bearer); the object of thefe orders were

to

to enquire into what had given room to the demand of the troops; into the caufe of the death of Ibrahim, and after the authors of this wicked attempt. The fandjacs met in the place called *Carameïdan*, with the greateſt part of the army. The pacha was in the caftle; he fent for fome fandjacs, but they refuſed to obey, unlefs they fhould be firſt acquainted with the fubjeƈt which they were called ʾor. This conteſt gave room to feveral other meſfages, and at laft the emirs, who had been charged with the orders to the fandjacs, told them, *There are among you profligates who deſerve puniſhment; if you wiſh to obtain pardon for your crime, give up the names of the guilty.* The fandjacs accepted the propoſition, and they wrote down the names of the moſt mutinous. The bouluc agas, (commanders of different military corps) came to take thoſe whoſe names had been given; the moſt part were ſeized, and had their heads cut off in the divan. Mohammed Pacha continued difpatching by fuch means the moſt infolent; he put to death about two hundred. If he had continued longer in this poſt he would have totally exterminated them; but he was only feven months and eight days in his government. In his whole conduƈt he had no view but that of the public welfare, and the relief of the fubjeƈts.

The vizir Haffan Pacha fucceeded him; he always carefully fpared the troops, on account of his fon, who was beglerbeg of the army; all was quiet under his government. Haffan had for fucceffor

the

the vizir Mohammed Pacha, who entered in poffeffion of that place the 7th of Safar, 1016, (3d of Jan.
1607,) and held it four years, four months, and
twelve days. This pacha was a prudent and able
man; he fucceeded in re-eftablifhing peace and
tranquillity in the whole province, and he delivered
the people from the vexations to which they had
been fo long victims. The very firft day he held
a divan, which was the 15th of Safar, (11th of June,
1607,) he affembled the fandjacs, the tfchaoufchs,
the mutefarrakas, and the bouluc agas; and
afked them whether they had been prefent at the
murder of the pacha Ibrahim. As the others remained filent, the tfchaoufchs, and the mutefarrakas, took the word, and faid, in fhewing the fandjacs, *it is from thofe that the whole evil originally
fprings.* It was ordered at laft, that all thofe who
had any fhare in Ibrahim's murder fhould appear,
and that the beglerbeg would decide about the punifhment which they merited, as well as all thofe
who had extorted contributions. He fent in confequence the neceffary orders to all the rifs, or departments of the Lower Egypt, and the exactions
were ftopped for fome time. But towards the end
of Schawal, of the following year, (January, 1609,)
all the troops which were in the rifs affembled in a
town of Santon * Seïd Ahmed Albedawi, and fwore

---

* There is in the original, aref billah teâla ; that is to fay,
he that knows God; thus the Muffulmans call their contem-
plative perfons; they call contemplation, *marifat*, or *marifat
allah*, the knowledge of God.

not

not to suffer the abolition of the contributions, and
to put to death the emir Muftapha, ketkhoda of
the tfchaoufchs, and feveral fandjacs.   The rebels
chofe themfelves a chief, whom they proclaimed
fultan; they nominated vizirs, and diftributed the
departments of Egypt among themfelves, affigning
to each the diftrict where he was to give fcope to
his robberies.   They then diffolved, and quitting
the town of Seïd Ahmed, fpread themfelves in
feveral diftricts, and exacted from the inhabitants
fuch contributions as they were pleafed to fet on
them.   They caufed one hundred fheep, and a great
number of oxen and buffaloes, to be killed for
themfelves in every town, and if they met with any
foldier, they conftrained him to follow them: they
continued this robbery as far as Kalyoub.

When Mohammed Pacha was informed of the
commotions, he haftened to affemble the fandjacs,
the tfchaoufchs, and the mutefarrakas, and afked
them, if they were difpofed to obey the orders of
the fultan; they declared their fubmiffion. *My intention,* faid the pacha to them, *is to make you take
up arms againft thofe rebels of whofe fedition you have
heard.*   They anfwered him, that they would not
hefitate to execute his orders.   Mohammed then
put a caftan on Muftafabeg, who was ketkhoda of
the tfchaoufchs; he caufed the ftandard to be difplayed, and erected it in Carameidan.   Friday following, he caufed to be publifhed, that all thofe
who were faithful to God and the prophet, and difpofed to obey the imperial orders, fhould repair to
the

the ftandard, and remain there the following night. The whole army affembled, and the next day they marched with the ferdar, (general); they had fix cannons with them. All the tfchaoufchs and the mutefarrakas repaired with a part of the janifaries, of the Azabs (fecond corps of infantry), and of the lawends, (volunteers who receives pay). At the firft news of the revolt, the pacha had fummoned all the fcheiks of the Arabians. They repaired in a fhort time to him, and departed with the fandjacs who were in the city, Saturday, 9th of Dhoulcaada, 1017, (14th of February, 1609). The army encamped the following night at Birket-elhadj, and the next day they came up with the rebels at Khankah; a battle enfued, and they made ufe of their cannon and the whole artillery. When the rebels came to know the forces of the enemy, they were ftruck with terror. Some emirs availing themfelves of their panic, fummoned them to furrender. They all confented, and the ferdar began with requiring that their bouluc-bafchis, (commanders) fhould be delivered up: they all furrendered at difcretion, and were put into irons: they were twenty-three in number. One of the rebels having attempted to kill the ferdar, was prevented by the janifaries who cut him to pieces. The ferdar next ordered to be brought before him all thofe who ferved in the army of the rebels, though they were not of the body of the militia, nor did receive pay; they were about fifty, and he ordered their heads to be ftruck off. The whole army of the

rebels furrendered themfelves by degrees under the
ftandard, and were all difarmed. Monday following the ferdar entered the city with his army and
went to the pacha. The bouluc-bafchis and fifty
of the leading men of the army were put to death
by order of Mohammed. No amnifty was granted
to the rebels, and, as they were found, they were
put to death. A great number perifhed by this
means. Thofe who took to flight, fell into the
hands of the Arabians, who killed and ftripped
them, and thofe who concealed themfelves were
taken and punifhed with death, as foon as they
were difcovered, and the faubafchi or the kelkhoda
of the tfchaoufchs acquainted with it. Thurfday,
the 14th of the fame month, (19th of Feb. 1609),
the cadhilifker Mohammed Effidi Bakhlizadé advifed the pacha not to put to death the reft of the
rebels, but to fend them into Arabia Felix. This
counfel was approved by the pacha; he imprifoned
all thofe who were arrefted, and, towards the end
of this month, he caufed to be tranfported about
three hundred, loaded with chains, upon camels, as
far as Suez, where they were put on board a veffel,
which carried them to the coafts of Yemen. Such
is in abridgement the hiftory of this revolution.
The contributions we have fpoken of were called
tolbat. Thefe banditti addreffed themfelves to a
cafchef, and demanded of him an ordnance on fuch
or fuch a village, for the contributions they wanted
to exact. The cafchef gave them an ordnance, fetting forth, that fuch a perfon afked and obtained
a con-

a condemnation against such an inhabitant of the village whom they had described. They obliged him to write all they wanted, and for the most part what they acquired by this means was without reason. I was possessed of an estate at Menoukhead, that might have been worth a hundred thousand nisfs; I was taxed this year, with the inhabitants, two hundred thousand nisfs.

Mohammed Pacha, freed of this affair, carried his attention to other objects. He occupied himself about the pensions and salaries, and examined the rights of those who enjoyed them. He preserved all those which he found grounded on an ancient possession, or a valid title, and assigned the payment thereof on the revenue of the fund of the divan. He imposed, in proportion, new taxes on such places as they had been before levied on. These augmentations amounted to about 800 purses *. He would not permit the custom of the time of the Circassian Mamelucs to be followed any longer, but those that had been established in the year 932, under the reign of the Ottoman sultans. He afterwards settled the taxes of each department with the greatest equity, and took care to exact from every district such articles as they could most conveniently furnish. He observed the same method with respect to the distribution of the public works both summer and winter, and for all the ordinary contributions. If a department was loaded with an impost it could not satisfy, on ac-

* Purse is a sum of 500 piasters.

count

count of its poverty, and the fmallnefs of its revenues, he difcharged it, and levied it on fome weal-
thier diftrict, whofe charges were eafy, and which
could bear an augmentation. He caufed regifters
to be kept of all thofe regulations, and fent copies
into the different parts of the province. He
diftributed pay to the foldiers, and to all thofe who
had been accuftomed to receive it, on the 28th of
each month: he did not examine the rights of thofe
who received them, and he made no innovation in
this refpect.

Mohammed Pacha was trufted with the adminiftration of a moft confiderable legacy, which confifted in the revenues of feveral villages, and of
fome ftorehoufes (okals) fituated at Rafchid, and in
other towns: the annual revenue of thefe funds was
more then 20,000 pieces of gold. He employed
a part in eftablifhing a foundation for the pilgrims
of Mecca, which confifted in furnifhing annually
to the caravan, as much water as forty camels could
carry.

He founded alfo feveral other places for the
reading of the Alcoran, and made other fimilar
eftablifhments in Egypt. What remained of the
revenue, after the difcharging of thefe foundations,
was fent into Romania, to be employed in pious
works. The fultan Othman afterwards changed
thefe difpofitions. Hoffaïn Pacha, beglerbeg of
Egypt, fold, by his order, the funds of thofe lega-
cies, and collected the money for them, which he
fent into Romania.

When

When Mohammed Pacha quitted Egypt, hè enjoyed an honour which no beglerbeg of that province ever had after him; he left it without being divefted of his dignity, and nominated for caïmacam, Mohammed beg hadji tefterdar, who became afterwards beglerbeg of Yemen. Mohammed Pacha remained thirty days at Adelia, without meddling with the government, though he was not deprived of it, and he continued that whole time to diftribute the pay, and other ordinary recompences.

His fucceffór was Mohammed Pacha Alfoufi, who protected the learned, and all good fubjects, and conducted himfelf in his poft with perfect integrity. He never accepted any prefent, nor did he commit any injuftice. If there was fometimes caufe to complain of his government, it was the fault of Youfferef, his confident, to whom he gave up the exercife of his authority, from the good opinion he had formed of his conduct and punctuality. In the time of this pacha, A. H. 1022, a body of troops, of ten thoufand men, fent by the grand vizir into Yemen to appeafe fome troubles, having entered Egypt, the pacha received orders from the Porte to fupply them with the pay neceffary for the execution of the commiffion with which they were charged, and to conduct them into Yemen. Mohammed ordered they fhould receive their pay, and prepare themfelves to depart immediately for the place of their deftination. The troops replied, that they were fent into Egypt to

remain

remain there, and refufed to obey. They quartered themfelves in the magazines at the gate Efnafr, and in the houfes of the inhabitants, after having driven out thofe that occupied them. Every
ftep the pacha took to bring them to obedience was
ufelefs. They nailed up the gates of the quarter
where they were cantoned, fhut the gate Efnafr, and
placed artillery upon it. The pacha caufed the
tfchaoufchs, the mutefarrakas, and other military
bodies, with cannon to advance againft them, and
they began to befiege them. The emir Abedinbeg
advanced to the gate Efnafr, and entered with his
attendants by fome walls, the entrance to which
was in the college named *Medreffa Djanbelatia.*
The rebels, alarmed at the danger they were now
in, were in hafte to fubmit. The pacha diftributed
their pay to them, which amounted to more than
twenty-four purfes, and they went out of the city.
When Mohammed was depofed he retired to Adelia,
and diftributed in corn and money very confiderable fums; thefe diftributions, according to the report of a cateb, amounted to 10,000 othmanis a
day, and 400 ardabs of corn per month. He did
not quit Adelia until his fucceffor had arrived at
Alexandria.

The pacha Ahmed had been tefterdar in Egypt;
when he made his entry into Caïro, with a train,
the magnificence of which furpaffed all that had
been hitherto feen, a ftone, thrown from the inner
part of a houfe, fell on his head, and broke one of
the plumes of his turban. I myfelf faw the ftone
fall;

fill; it weighed five pounds. Some officers entered the houfe but found no one there. After the pacha was arrived at the caftle, inquiries were made, and the culprit difcovered: it was Khodjah Ibrahim Almanfouri, my brother's fon. He confeffed his crime, and was crucified in the very place he had committed it.

The firft day Ahmed held the divan, he ordered the mocatadies, (receivers-general of the cuftoms) and the catebs, to prepare a ftate of all the diftributions made by his predeceffor, in corn, money, or otherwife. He afterwards made ftrict inquiries repecting him, and found that he was indebted to the treafury one hundred purfes. He fent the proceedings and proofs to the Porte; but I am ignorant if this affair has been carried further. In the month of Moharran, 1025, (January, 1616,) Ahmed received orders to fend a thoufand men of the troops of Egypt to march againft the Perfians. He difpatched them under the command of Salitbeg, then emir-elhadj, with fo good difcipline, that the people did not fuffer any damage. On this, and three other the like occafions, he caufed bodies of troops to march acrofs the province, without the inhabitants being informed of their paffage, whereas formerly a hundred men could not march through a canton without its being deftroyed. This difference arofe from the good difcipline he caufed to be obferved, and the extraordinary diftributions he made to the troops that he fent againft the Perfians. This is the order in which he caufed them to march. At

the

the head were the lawendi (volunteers) of Suez,
and Raïfa followed by the emir who had the fuperintendance of the arfenal; after them the djebedjis
(corps of artillery) and their commander; then the
azabs, the janifaries, the circaffians, the tefekdjis,
and the komlis, each corps followed by its aga.
After thefe marched the ketkhodas of the fandjacs,
each with the people and equipage of their mafters;
the emirs of the circaffians, the fandjacs, and laftly,
the ferdar. The army being arrived at Khankah,
the pacha repaired thither, and mounted a throne
prepared for him. He had a large quantity of
pieces of gold near him, the whole army defiled
before him, and each foldier received a gratification
proportionable to his wants; there was not any that
did not receive at leaft twenty pieces of gold.

Ahmed Pacha, during the whole time of his government, which was two years, ten months, and
twelve days, put to death only ten perfons, and
thofe after judicial proceedings, and for crimes de-
ferving death. He never paffed judgments but
after the ftricteft examination, and after he had
feveral times heard the defence of the party. When
he was difplaced, the troops raifed an infurrection,
becaufe he had reduced their pay, and obliged him
to reftore all he had retained. The fandjacs did
the fame, nor did they permit him to depart until
he had paid twelve fandouks *, which his predeceffor, .

* This word fignifies *trunks*; it certainly means a determi-
nate fum; perhaps it anfwers to what the Turks call *yok*, that
is, the expence of a horfe, and is equal to 20 purfes, or 10,000
afpers.

they

they said, had left in the treafury. After he had fatisfied their demand he departed from Caïro; but he made no diſtribution, as many of the former governors, and particularly Mohammed Pacha Alfoufi, had done.

Beglerbegs of Egypt under the reign of Sultan Muſtapha I. fon of Sultan Mohammed, and brother of Sultan Ahmed.

Muftapha was crowned on Tuefday the 4th of Dhoulhaada, 1026, (24th of November, 1617,) and depofed on Wednefday the 3d of Rebialewel, (28th of February, 1616,) after a reign of three months and eight days.

He nominated the vifir Muftapha Pacha Lefgheli as governor of Egypt. This pacha left the whole authority in the hands of his relations, who abufed the eafinefs of his difpofition to rule without controul. This conduct produced a general infurrection of the army, which openly appeared on Friday the 7th of Schawal, 1027, (28th of September, 1618). The cateb of the divan, the emir Ahmed Aladjemi, aga of the Komlis, and Mohammed Tfchaoufch, were killed the fame day by the feditious. On the next day the turdjeman, Youffouff, fhared the fame fate, and the principal emirs were conftrained to fly. Thefe feditious proceedings continued until the arrival of the vifir Djafar Pacha, fucceffor of Muftapha.

Beglerbegs

Beglerbegs of Egypt under the reign of Sultan Aboul-
nafs Othman, (Othman I.) fon of Sultan Ahmed.

Othman was elected on Wednefday the 3d of
Rebialewell, 1027, (28th of February, 1618,) at
the fixth hour of the night after the depofition of
Muftapha, and died Thurfday the 8th of Redjeb,
1031, (19th of May, 1622).

The firft governor of Egypt appointed by Othman, was the vizir Djafar Pacha, who had been
formerly beglerbeg of Yemen. He enjoyed that
poft only five months and an half. This pacha was
inftructed in various fciences, and during his refidence in Egypt he did nothing but what was for
the advantage of the province committed to his
care. Egypt, in his time, was afflicted with a terrible plague, which continued from the end of Rebialewell, 1028, (March, 1619,) to the end of
Djoumadilakhora of the fame year, (May, 1619).
The greater number of thofe who perifhed by this
malady were between fifteen and twenty-five years
of age. They reckoned all thofe who died in the
fhops, and the number was fix hundred thirty-five
thoufand, without reckoning thofe that died in
other places; there were alfo a great number of
perfons of the firft rank perifhed.

The vizir Muftapha Pacha fucceeded Djafar.
He put to death Muftaphabeg Albacdjeli, the principal author of the troubles that had been raifed
under the government of Pacha Muftapha Lefgheli. His death was a caufe of great joy to the
                                                    people,

people, but the pacha damped the joy by the vexations he exercifed againft many merchants. The complaint, occafioned by fuch conduct, reached the fultan, who depofed him, and fubftituted Hoffain Pacha in his ftead. This new governor fuppreffed all the innovations eftablifhed by Muftapha, and required of him the payment of twenty fandouks, for the value of what he was indebted to the treafury. He afterwards fummoned all the merchants who had any fubject of complaint againft Muftapha: it appeared by their depofitions, and his own confeffion, that he had extorted from them thirty-three thoufand groufchs*, and the proceedings were fent to the Porte.

Hoffain Pacha was eafy of accefs, and of a modeft character, but his manners were rough and unpolifhed. After being fick many months, he gave on his recovery a feaft to his children, which lafted many days, and during which time he ordered there fhould be public rejoicings. On this occafion he received an infinite number of prefents of all forts; carpets bordered with gold, horfes, fugar, ftuffs, and even money. He would not accept from any rich perfon, either oil, honey, or fheep; if they prefented any of thefe things, he caufed them to be fent back to the perfons they came from, and took in the room of them, things of a greater value. In his time there was fo extraordinary an

* This money takes its name from the German *grofch*; Mepenfki writes it *grafch*: it is a piece of filver, worth at prefent forty paras, or 3 livres, 11 fous, 4 defc. French money.

over-

overflow of the Nile, that the Egyptians began to despair of seeing an end of the inundation. This occasioned a great scarcity, and a measure of corn (wabya) was worth thirty nesfs. The plague also made great ravages this year. Haffain Pacha having been displaced, the defterdar Haffan, who exercised the functions of caimacan, pretended that Hoffain had confiscated a part of the revenues of the treasury, and that he carried away corn from the public granaries. Hoffain found means to appease him, and obtained permission to depart, on paying twenty-five thousand pieces of gold only; he promised that the remainder should be paid by a Jew, named *Aben amel Albehar*, who was indebted to him an equal sum. This Jew had drawn upon himself the resentment of Hoffain, by having used injurious words respecting him since he had been difmiffed. When payment was demanded of the sum directed by Hoffain, he answered that he had already paid him. This answer was communicated to Hoffain, who pretended he did not owe any thing now, and yet consented to pay the twenty-five pieces of gold, on condition that the Jew should be delivered up to him, to treat him as he pleased. The proposition was accepted, and the Jew delivered to Hoffain, who first made him pay the twenty-five thousand dinars, and put him to death in the most cruel manner; his death delivered the Muffulmans from his extortions and injuftice. Hoffain arrived in Romania, after the revolution of which I have given an account in my great

chron-

chronicle, under the reign of Othman *. All parties united to name him to the dignity of grand vizir. He re-eftablifhed good order, beftowed the government of the provinces on men worthy of fuch employ, and put an end to all troubles.

The vizir Mohammed Pacha fucceeded Hoffain. The time of his government, which was only two months and an half, was agitated by great troubles, occafioned by the revolution that deprived Othman of the throne. However odious he might be to the Egyptians, he gave them no caufe of complaint, doubtlefs by reafon of the fhort duration of his government; as his former conduct in Romania will not permit us to think otherwife.

Beglerbegs of Egypt under the reign of Sultan Muftapha, after his reftoration.

Muftapha was reftored, Thurfday the 8th of Redjeb, 1031, (19th of May, 1622,) at noon, and depofed again on Monday the 15th of Doulcaada, 1032, fultan Morad, fon of fultan Ahmed, having been crowned in his place.

Muftapha appointed the vizir Ibrahim Pacha for governor of Egypt. During a year which he enjoyed that place, he fucceeded by his dexterity and cunning in gaining the affections of the troops and the people. There was then a great fcarcity, and the ardab of corn was worth five groufchs: it was not until his fucceffor's time that the price of pro-

* This was doubtlefs the depofition of Othman, and the re-eftablifhment of Muftapha.

vifions

vifions was reduced. Ibrahim having been recalled, embarked to go down the Nile, inftead of travelling by land, according to the cuftom of the Pacha. The catebs of the divan reprefented to Muftapha Pacha, who fucceeded him, that he had not paid the accuftomed contribution to the treafury. Muftapha difpatched fome tfchaoufchs to demand payment of it, but Ibrahim having attempted to kill them, they took flight, and returned to Cairo. Muftapha then fent the caïmacam, Salihberg, with orders to prevent his going out of the province, if he refufed to pay it; the emir, Salihberg, only overtook it at Alexandria. Ibrahim had already put his effects on board veffels; he anfwered the caïmacam, that if he owed any thing, he would pay the fultan, to whom he was then going, and at the fame time he failed away, and happily continued his voyage. When he arrived in Romania, Sultan Muftapha had juft been again depofed, and Morad had been elected in his place; this affair therefore had no confequences.

Muftapha Pacha had taken poffeffion of his government on Tuefday the 22d of Ramadhan, 1032, (20th of July, 1623). Ali Pacha was nominated to fucceed him on Monday the 14th of Dhoulhadja, (9th of October,) in the fame year. When they heard at Cairo that Ali Pacha had been appointed beglerbeg of the province, and Iffabeg, caïmacam, until the arrival of Ali, the mutefillim of the new governor, and Iffabeg received Mufta

pha's

pha's caftan, and each returned to his own houfe. The troops affembled, and went to Iffabeg's houfe, to demand from him the extraordinary diftributions which it was cuftomary for them to receive in the like circumftances. Iffabeg put them off until the morrow, and promifed to examine their demand in the divan. He communicated to them, at the fame time, the orders he had received to fecure the perfon of Pacha Muftapha, and to make an enquiry after all his effects, as it was fufpected he had appropriated to himfelf one of the hangings belonging to the feraglio, which had been loft. The army refufed to execute his orders, and anfwered, " We cannot feize the perfon of a vizir, nor make " any enquiry after his effects; let them appoint " fandjacs for guards, and let them conduct him " to Alexandria. If Ali Pacha is already arrived " in that city, they will put him into his hands; if " they do not find him there, let them conduct " him to Conftantinople." The whole army afterwards recited the firft furate of the Alcoran, as a folemn engagement not to depart from the refolution they had taken: this paffed the evening of Monday the 15th of Dhoulhadja, 1032. On the morrow, the fandjacs, and all the army, repaired to the divan, whither they caufed Muftapha to come and read the orders of the fultan; but the army began by demanding the ordinary diftribution. The * Mutefellim and Iffabeg contented themfelves

* The deputy of a new governor, fent into the province to carry his orders, and take poffeffion of the government.

with

with reproaching them, that they renewed the fame demands every three months. "Why then," replied the foldiers, "does the fultan, our mafter, "change the beglerbegs of the province every "three months, to the great injury of the inhabi- "tants? If he chufes to nominate every day new "beglerbegs, we fhall alfo demand every day con- "tributions." The mutefellim anfwered that he could not fatisfy them until the arrival of his maf- ter. The army anfwered him only by bad lan- guage, and both him and Iffabeg would have been maffacred in an inftant, if they had not quickly efcaped from the fury of the foldiers. Then they all cried aloud at the fame time, *We will have no other governor than Muftapha; let Ali return to the place from whence he came:* they then took an oath to maintain their refolution, and to re-eftablifh Muftapha in his dignity. Prefents were given by Muftapha to the whole army, while he haftened to write to the fultan, afking of him a confirmation of what had been done. Many ulemas and cadies wrote alfo in his favour. Mean time they were informed of Ali's arrival at Alexandria, and they difpatched many ketkhodas to prevent the troops and the inhabitants from manifefting any difpofition to receive him. Ali delivered to the deputies, let- ters to the emirs and the troops full of flattery, but the army, after having heard them read, directed the fame deputies to carry him an anfwer, agree- able to their former refolution, and which was figned by the principal emirs. Ali, on receiving
this

this anſwer, became furious, cauſed one of the deputies to be ſeized, and loaded with chains. The troops who were in garriſon in the citadel releaſed him, overturned the tents of the pacha, and obliged him to re-imbark. A contrary wind having driven him back to port, the emir Muſtapha directed the cannon of the citadel to be fired at him; from that time, the emir was ſurnamed *topotan*, that is, cannonier. The wind and weather would not permit him to return to Conſtantinople; he was obliged to put in at Berant, and to paſs the winter there.

Mean time they did not receive any accounts from Conſtantinople; and reports, without foundation, began to cauſe alarms among the inhabitants of Cairo, when on Saturday, the 20th of Rebia-lakher, 1033, (16th of February, 1624,) a letter, brought by a pigeon, announced the arrival of the ſchater-baſchi, (chief of the footmen) of Muſtapha, charged by the ſultan to carry him the caftan, and the patents, to confirm him in the office of beglerbeg. When he arrived, all the ſandjacs and principal officers of the regency repaired to the divan: Muſtapha dreſſed himſelf in the caftan, and the letters of the ſultan were read, addreſſed to the army, in which he acquainted the troops, that in compliance with their deſires, he had continued Muſtapha in the government of the province.

In the year 1034, (1624,) there was an extraordinary overflow of the Nile. They began to apprehend that the waters would not retire ſoon enough to enable them to ſow their land. The wa-

ters

ters were rifen to 24 dhirâ, but having fallen in a little time, they fowed, and their harveft was very abundant. Muftapha fucceeded to the inheritances of a great number of rich people who died under his government. Even when there exifted lawful heirs, he caufed feals to be affixed on the effects of the deceafed, until he had taken away what he pleafed; in this manner he amaffed immenfe riches. During his government a dreadful plague defolated Egypt; it began to appear on the firft days of Rebialewell, 1035, (November 1625). In the beginning of Schaban, (April 1626,) the malady abated; but it did not intirely ceafe until the month of Ramadan. The alarm had never been fo general: old men, upwards of an hundred years of age, were fearful of being attacked by the malady, and their fears were not without foundation, for this plague carried off perfons of fixty years old and upwards; on the whole, more than three hundred thoufand perfons perifhed. In this fituation the pacha fuppreffed all funeral ceremonies; the cries, the tears, and the attendants of the poor and the dervifes, the drums and mourning habits, fo that the dead bodies were carried through the ftreets without caufing the leaft ceremony; thefe precautions diminifhed the confternation. The vizir Beïram Pacha having been named in the place of Muftapha, the fandjacs obliged him to ftay until the arrival of his fucceffor. Beïram, after having rendered an account of the ftate of the treafury, demanded of Muftapha the reftitution of twenty fandoucs; Muftapha

tapha pretended he was not able to pay that fum, and caufed his furniture, camels, horfes, and mules to be fold: this was a deception to cover his great wealth: Baïram did not leave him in peace until he had paid the whole. The fultan Morad put him to death in the year 1037, for fome action which was contrary to the law of God.

Hiftory of the Coronation, and of the reign of Sultan Morad, (Amurath IV.) fon of Sultan Ahmed.

Morad was crowned the 15th of Dhoulcaada, 1032, (11th of September, 1623,) and died the 16th of Schawal, 1049, (9th of February, 1640,) after having filled the throne fixteen years, one month, and one day: this was the fecond of Ahmed's fons who wore the crown. Sultan Muftapha abfolutely neglected the care of his affairs and of government, not to abandon himfelf to pleafures, but to give himfelf up intirely to his inclinations for the exercifes of piety and devotions. The neighbouring people of the frontiers had made incurfions into the territories of the empire, and had made themfelves mafters of many provinces. Under thefe circumftances, the vizirs and principal officers of the empire, with the troops, unanimoufly refolved to place the crown on the head of Morad. The troops, for this purpofe, addreffed themfelves to the vizirs and moulas, and faid to them, *The empire is threatened on all fides by the incurfions of the neighbouring nations, and the revolt of Abaza Pacha; we wifh to have an audience from the fultan, to make*

fuch

fuch reprefentations to him as the circumftances require.
They all met at the gate of the feraglio*, on the
14th of Dhoulcaada, (10th of September, 1623,)
and defired to fpeak with the fultan. They waited
at the door till the hour for afternoon prayers, and
thofe of the interior part of the feraglio durft not
difcharge their commiffion, becaufe they apprehended the fultan might reply to the troops, that
he had no pretenfions to the crown, for this was
his ordinary difcourfe. The mufti Yahya Effendi
at laft prefented himfelf; he declared to the troops
that they muft wait until the following day. The
foldiers confented to withdraw, provided the mufti
and the vizirs would pafs the night in the feraglio,
for they feared leaft the fultana, mother of Muftapha, fhould make an attempt on the life of the
children of Ahmet, as fhe was fufpected to have
planned the defign. The troops retired upon this
condition, and the mufti remained in the feraglio
with the vizirs. They all refolved to put the
crown on the head of Morad, and they placed him
upon the throne after the evening prayer. Early
the next day the troops repaired to the gate of
the feraglio, and again demanded of the mufti and
the vizirs that Sultan Muftapha fhould be produced, as they had promifed them. The great
vizir Ali Pacha entered the interior part of the
feraglio, and returned a moment after, faying that
the fultan was ill, and that it was impoffible for

* We muft recollect that it is the name of the palace, and
not the apartment of the women.

him

him to appear. This anfwer put the troops into a rage, and they defired the mufti to enter the feraglio, and to bring forth the fultan. The mufti entered and returned almoft in the fame time, followed by Sultan Morad, who had the crown on his head, and was cloathed with all his imperial ornaments, and directing his fpeech to the troops, he faid to them, *Here is your fultan, you have no other than Morad.* The whole army exclaimed unanimoufly, *We wifh no other; this was alfo our intention.* The troops fwore fidelity to him, and he was proclaimed throughout the city. The army was ignorant of his having been crowned the day before. The new fultan perfuaded the troops to promife him that they would not afk of him any extraordinary diftributions or gratifications for his acceffion to the throne, confidering the exhaufted ftate to which the treafury had been reduced by the rapine of the grand vizirs, fince the death of Sultan Othman; and that they would not folicit either the nomination or the difmiffion of any vizir or officer, as they were accuftomed to do with his uncle the Sultan Muftapha. All the troops engaged themfelves folemnly, and their promife was reduced to writing, and depofited in the hands of Hoffain Effendi, cadhilifker of Romania.

The reign of Sultan Morad was fatal to the enemies of the empire, and he knew how to render himfelf refpectable to all the kings of the earth. His firft care, as foon as he found himfelf fettled on the throne, was to punifh the murderers of his

brother

brother Othman. He began by putting to death
Dawoud Pacha and his fon, becaufe they had been
the principal authors of that action; Hoffaïn Pacha foon after fhared the fame fate, and all thofe
among the troops, who had contributed to the death
of Othman, received the punifhment of their crime:
the fultan put to death about 30,000 in this manner,

Mohammed Abaka Pacha, and Youffouf Pacha,
who had been formerly invefted with the office of
emir-elhadj in Egypt, but who had been compelled
to quit, that province on account of the revolt of
the troops, had united with them, and erected the
ftandard of rebellion in the Diarbekr. Thefe two
rebels falling out, Youffouf was killed by Abaza.
The latter was going to put himfelf at the head
of his troops, when Morad fent an army commanded by the great vizir Khafraf Pacha againft
him. Abaza offered to fubmit; the great vizir accepted the propofitions, and fent him to the fultan,
who received him with honour, but foon after put
him to death,

Morad having ftripped Yahya Effendi of the
dignity of mufti, he invefted Hoffaïn Effendi Ak-
hizadeh with it, who behaved in that office very
different from all thofe who had preceded him.
The fultan having gone out of Conftantinople, to
take the diverfion of hunting, when he was about
three days journey from that city, the mufti began
to plot an intrigue to place one of his brother's on
the throne. They were four in number; Orkhan,
Soleiman, Kaffem, and Ibrahim. The fultana-
mother

mother difcovered the confpirary, and difpatched a courier to her fon, informing him of it. Morad immediately departed unattended, and haftened his return to Conftantinople. His horfe falling dead at Scutari, he continued his road on foot to the feraglio. He entered it at the fide next the fea without being difcovered. Immediately he mounted the throne, fent for the mufti, and, after fome reproaches, killed him with his own hand, and caufed his body to be thrown to the dogs; he then drove out fome utemas who had taken part in the confpiracy. The fultan re-inftated Yahya Effendi in his dignity of mufti, and apologized for the wrong that had been done him, faying, *Providence has fuffered us to be expofed to fo great a danger, to punifh us for not having rendered you the juftice you merited.* This mufti was learned, religious, and of perfect integrity. Morad was defirous to punifh with death the Nakib-alafchraf, (chief of the fherifs, or defcendants of the prophet); but the fultana, his mother, oppofed him, and reprefented that this man drew his origin from the blood of Mohammed; and the fultan was contented with depofing him, and fent him to Mecca to exercife the functions of cadi; but he died at Djida, before he arrived at the place of his deftination.

Under the reign of Morad the Hungarians revolted; and the fultan, informed of their rebellion, put himfelf at the head of his army and advanced to Adrianople, with a defign to reduce them by force of arms. The Hungarians, acquainted with

E 4   his

his march, fent to aſk peace of him. He at firſt made many difficulties, but at laſt granted it to them, exacting from tnem double the tribute which they had formerly been taxed with. The fultan then returned to Conſtantinople.

A ſhort time after this tranſaction the army revolted on account of a favourite who enjoyed all the good graces and confidence of Morad; he was called Mouſſa Pacha. The diſcontent of the troops roſe to ſuch an exceſs that they ſlew Mouſſa. The fultan at firſt difguiſed his refentment, but he afterwards got rid of all thoſe who had a part in this murder, and he put to death near 10,000 of them.

Khaſraf Pacha was then veſted with the dignity of grand vizir; he was a man of diſtinguiſhed bravery. He marched againſt the Perſians, and ravaged a great part of their country; he carried his arms as far as the territory of the royal city, when he returned to paſs the winter at Arzerum. His enemies profited by his abſence, to do him ill ſervices with Morad; they fucceeded in rendering him fuſpected, and Morad ſent fome capigis, (doorkeepers) who killed him on his journey: Ahmed Pacha Hadfedh was nominated to fucceed him, but the army revolted on account of the death of Khaſraf. The troops threw all the blame on the new vizir, and demanded his execution, and the fultan could not appeaſe them but by confenting to their requeſt. His poſt was beſtowed on Mohammed Pacha, formerly beglerbeg of Egypt, who

repaired

repaired to the frontiers of Perfia, and kept himself in garrifon at Arzeroufn.

Morad refolving to march in perfon againft the Perfians, the imperial tent was erected at Scutari, the 15th of Ramadan, 1044, (the 4th of March, 1635). He marched from this place towards Erivan the 9th of Schawal, (the 28th of March, 1635), and laid fiege to that city; and having made himfelf mafter of it in the month of Rebialewell, he put to the fword the greateft part of the Perfians found there, and placed in it a garrifon of twelve thoufand men, commanded by Mortadhi Pacha. He afterwards took the road to Romania, and when he arrived in the Diarbeckr, he fent to Beïram Pacha, whom he had left at Conftantinople to command in his abfence, an order to put to death two of his brothers, Orkhan, furnamed *Abouyezid*, and Soleïman. This order was executed, but Soleïman defended himfelf valiantly: he killed fixteen perfons, and mounted on the wall to fave himfelf; but being thrown down, he broke his leg, was taken and ftrangled. The fultan had fcarcely returned to Conftantinople before Erivan was retaken by the Perfians, and the garrifon put to the fword: Mortadhi Pacha alfo perifhed there. This news excited a revolt in Conftantinople.

Under the reign of Morad, on the 19th of Schaban, 1039, (3d of April, 1630), a torrent overflowed the banks, and the water entered into the city of Mecca, and penetrated even to the facred temple. The violence of the torrent was fo great that

that almoſt the whole edifice was overthrown; the wall on the right ſide only remained. The Seïd Maſour, governor of Mecca, gave notice of this diſaſtrous event to Mohammed Pacha, beglerbeg of Egypt, who acquainted the ſultan with it. The ſultan directed him to cauſe what had been deſtroyed to be repaired, Mohammed ordered wood, iron, marble, and all neceſſary materials to be tranſported thither, He ſent maſons and officers to ſuperintend the work: the expence amounted to above 100,000 grouſchs. This work was finiſhed the following year: No prince ſince Abdolmelic ben Merwan, fourth kalif of the race of the Immiades, had the honour of re-eſtabliſhing the houſe of God, and it was an eſpecial glory for the Sultan Morad, and a ſignal favour granted to him by heaven.

Fakhreddin, ſon of Maan, was prince of the Druſes, in Syria; this man, religious in his exterior, was in truth a wretch deſtitute of religion and honour. The ſultans, predeceſſors of Morad, had in vain attempted to bring him to ſubmiſſion. Morad formed the reſolution of ſtripping him of his power; for that purpoſe he ordered Koutchouk Ahmed, pacha of Syria, to take up arms againſt him, and to purſue him until he ſhould be totally ſubdued, Ahmed aſſembled his troops, attacked Fakhreddin, killed a great number of Druſes, and took twenty-one ſtrong places which had formerly belonged to the Iſmaeliens, (or aſſaſſins). Fakhreddin ſhut himſelf up in the citadel of Schakif; Ahmed beſieged him,

him, and opened a subterraneous way to the foot of the mountain, on which the place was built. When Fakhreddin knew that the mine was nearly finished, he went off with his treasures, and the place of his retreat was never discovered. The pacha seized upon his children, and all he had left in that place, and sent the whole to the sultan. Thus finished in that province the power of the Drufes, during the time of the kalif's Abbaffides, which they always despaired of destroying. They were known in their origin by the name of *Bateni-ans.* The territory, which had belonged to them, formed the government of a more respectable pacha than that of Syria; Tripoli in Syria was the capital of it.

The conduct which Sultan Morad held with respect to the spahis who had revolted, does honour to his government. His soldiers carried their insolence to an excess unheard off: they sent to demand considerable sums of the citizens of the first rank, which, if refused, they entered by force into the houses, and plundered them, debauching the women, maffacring the masters if they could find them. They took the opportunity of a solemn feast, to send Alexandrian tapers into the principal houses of Conftantinople to the first officers of the empire, and the grand vizir. It was a way of exacting from those to whom they sent them, some gratification to regale themselves during the feast. They pushed their insolence so far, as even to send them to the sultan: the sultan gave orders to give

them

them a thoufand pieces of gold. They refuſed to receive them, and ſent them back to him, ſaying, " that it was not money they aſked, but military rewards* in Natolia and Romania." They had no right to the benefits of thoſe provinces. The ſultan defired them to ſend to him ſome of their leaders, and that he would grant them what they defired: he defcribed them by their names, and named above a thouſand. It was a ſnare the ſultan laid for them; they thought his promiſes to be ſincere, and they repaired to the ſeraglio. When they had entered, the ſultan ordered the gates to be ſhut, and cauſed them to be maſſacred by the guards of the ſeraglio.

There was not one that had eſcaped; and their bodies were thrown into the ſea. The other ſpahis, above two thouſand in number, fled into Vatolia; they choſe themſelves a chief, named *Roum Mohammed*, and began to commit hoſtilities. The ſultan ſent an army of janiſaries againſt him, and they were all made priſoners: Roum Mohammed was alſo taken and ſent to the ſultan, who ordered him to be crucified. This event freed Conſtantinople from the robberies exerciſed by thoſe inſolent troops.

The ſultan having reſolved to undertake the ſiege of Bagdad, which the Perſians had made themſelves maſter of eighteen years before, collected

---

* The Arabian term is Khidmah, (pl. Khidem) which anſwers to what the Turks call *Temar*. They cannot be compared to any thing better than our-fiefs, or commanderies.

troops from all the provinces of the empire. He left Conftantinople in the month of Schawal, 1047, (February 1658) and came to a place named *Bafch-doulab*, near the citadel of Bagdad, within two mufquet fhot from Makam Alimam Abou Hanifa. He encamped there the 8th of Redjib, 1048, (15th of November, 1638). Morad difguifed himfelf, and mounting one of his beft horfes, approached the place to fee where it might be attacked with moft advantage: he was not alarmed by the difcharge of the cannon, and the whole artillery of the enemy. He found that the attack was impracticable on the fide of Makam Alimam, and of Bab-alafwad, (the black gate) becaufe they had fifteen years been employed in fortifying that part of the wall; and thefe fortifications had been conftructed with the greateft folidity. He faw, on the contrary, that he could direct the attack with more fuccefs againft the other parts, from Bab-alabyadh, (the white gate) becaufe they had neglected to fortify it, perfuaded that they had nothing to fear on that fide. Morad ordered them to make the principal attack on that part of the walls: a body of janifaries entered the trenches, and after having fortified them, they planted cannons, and began to batter the citadel and the walls of the place. Thefe difpofitions were made before the opening of the covered way, called the *Rat-way*; for the Ottomans ufe to cut fubterraneous ways to enter into the trenches, without being perceived by the enemy: this way was not dug until the 20th day of the fiege.

ſiége. Mohammed Pacha, grand vizir, comᵐ manded the ſiege on the ſide of Bab-alabyadh, and of the great caſtle which is in the angle near his quarter, was that of the capoudan pacha (great admiral), the vizir Muſtapha, Hoſſaín Pacha, comᵐ mandant of the troops of Natolia, had his quarᵗ ters oppoſite to the Perſian tower, to cover the army againſt any nocturnal ſally; and Derviſch Mohammed, pacha of Diarbekr, was behind the intrenchment. The beſieged cauſed fifty cannons to be fired againſt the intrenchment of the Ottoman army, and broke them in three different places: a great number of ſoldiers periſhed. The ſultan then cauſed four cannons to be brought, of the largeſt ſize *, which Derviſch Mohammed planted on the intrenchment; and as ſoon as they were ſolidly placed, they were levelled againſt the artillery of the beſieged, which battered the entrenchments from the Perſian tower : they diſmounted them, and the army of the beſiegers were greatly relieved by it ; for they were upon the point of ſeeing their battery overthrown. The ſiege continued in this ſtate during twenty days. The Ottoman army began to make different works in form of terraces; the capoudan pacha erected one near the ditch, in the form of the veſſel called *Ravin*, in Romania. They fired from the top of this terrace,

* The author remarks, that the Turks give them a name, which ſignifies, *thoſe who eat no honey*. It is indeed the meaning of the word bal-yemez, which the Turks give to large pieces of caſting.

in

in the interior part of the town; so that none of the besieged dared to appear. The artillery continued to batter the forts and the walls, and destroyed the most elevated parts; but it was impossible to hurt the lower part, as the Persians had thrown all the earth from the ditch against the walls of the citadel; so that it lay, as it were buried in the dust; and when the cannon fired upon them, they broke down only that part which the ball struck, because of this heap of earth. However, when the cannon we have spoken of, had been brought and planted near the ditch, they began to give the enemy uneasiness. The sultan's army began to fill up the ditch, but the enemy carried off the earth as it was thrown in. The capoudan pacha, to put a stop to this manœuvre, caused the intrenchments to be opened in several places, and posted troops there to guard the entrance, at the same time he marched a detachment into the ditch, who charged the enemy with vigour. The Persians were then constrained to keep behind the wall of the citadel, and the Ottoman troops remained in the ditch. Such had been ten days the state of the siege, when the sultan ordered a general assault. The whole army moved, and approached the place with a generous intrepidity: the very servants took up arms, as also a body of troops, which had formerly been deprived of their pay, and which had just been restored to them: it was these who had constructed the terrace: this happened in the morning. The grand vizir was at that instant entering

tering into the tent of the fultan, to afk him for
orders. As he returned to the intrenchment, he
heard a thundering noife of the cannons, and the
whole artillery, and the cries of the army. He
thought the enemy had made a fally: it was
on the contrary two bodies of the Ottoman army,
who mounted up to the affault of the fort.
The grand vizir had not refolved to give the
great affault that day, he retired therefore from the
army. About five hundred men of the fultan's
army were engaged with an equal number of the
befieged in the citadel: they continued the combat
from the hour of the evening prayer, till the next
morning: there perifhed a great number of men on
both fides. The Ottoman troops having obtained
· a reinforcement from the capoudan pacha's quarter,
remained in poffeffion of the ramparts: a body of
troops from the quarter of Hoffain Pacha, made
themfelves mafter of half the great citadel. Things
remained in this pofition that day and the following night, without the combat being difcontinued.

The Perfians made altogether a violent effort,
and charged the Ottoman army with fury, without
being able to make them retreat an inch, for fear
of being put to flight. The army of the fultan
charged them in return, and drove them back to
the citadel; but they made a new effort, and the
combat was very obftinate. The grand vizir had
been killed by a mufket fhot; the capoudan pacha
was immediately appointed to fucceed him. He
entered the intrenchments, took a purfe full of

pieces of gold, and exhorted the foldiers to give him proofs of their valour, by rufhing altogether upon the walls and citadel: as any foldier was removed from the engagement, or having been wounded by a ftone, returned to the camp, he gave him ten pieces of gold. This conduct animated the foldiers, and many feemed defirous of being hit by a ftone, to intitle them to the fame gratification: this caufed the attack to be fo violent, that the Perfian troops were nearly being maffacred. The befieged men apprehended, that if they fhould delay until the next day, they would obtain no quarter: at the hour of the evening's prayer, they gave notice from the tops of the minarets that they wifhed to capitulate. Immediately the whole artillery ceafed firing, and every one remained in the place where he was until the next day. The morning being come Biknafchkhan went out of the citadel, and being fhewn into the tent of the fultan, he kiffed the ground before him. The fultan gave him a caftan adorned with furs and gilded feathers, and a khandjar. When the army faw that Biknafchkhan had obtained a capitulation, the Ottoman foldiers entered the citadel and mixed with the Perfian troops: fome Perfians however took refuge in the city; the victorious army fcattered itfelf in the towers and the walls, and erected the Ottoman banners. The fultan fent back Biknafchkhan, charging him to fignify to the khans and the other officers, that all thofe who fhould leave the place that day, would be fafe with their lives; but that after this time he would not spare any. Several among them could not then resolve to take this part, and formed the project to get secretly out by the gate called *Bab-alafvad*; the sultan sent several times to summon them, and at each message they disputed among themselves, and came to blows: there were even some who having escaped unhurt from the fight, were wounded on this occasion. They came out at last, when they saw the impossibility of effecting their design, appeared before the sultan, and kissed the ground in his presence. The fight lasted longer within the town: the same day there perished about five thousand Persians, and two thousand left the town, and fled by the quarter of the Egyptian troops. Othman Aga, Ketkhoda of Selahdar-bafchi (master of the horse) was in that quarter with his troops; also the pachas of Caramania and of Rarafch: they pursued the runaways. Othman Aga atchieved prodigies of valour: he received two wounds: a great number of soldiers of the Ottoman army were killed or wounded; the Egyptian troops fought with distinguished courage. None of the runaways escaped, they were all massacred to a man: this siege cost the Persians about 20,000 men. Fetahkhan one of the principal officers of the garrison, having drank some glasses of wine, began to weep; and being asked the cause of his tears, "How, (answered he) should I not bewail the " loss of so fine an army? Never has one equal " been seen. The flower of the troops of the " fchah were in garrison in this place, and yet it has . . " been

" been taken, and his troops put to the fword. Un-
" fortunate prince, he would not have hefitated to
" abandon ten of the beft fortified places in his em-
" pire, to preferve fo fine an army; but fate has de-
" cided otherwife." In fact, the garrifon of Bagdad
was compofed of brave foldiers and choice troops;
and the king of Perfia did not imagine it poffible to
take that town. He had fent thither the kizlar aga
(the chief of the black eunuchs), with the beft part
of his treafures, and he relied very much upon the
fortifications, and the garrifon of the place. Now,
according to the report of the Turkifh fpies, the
fchah has no more than 3000 men near his perfon,
and Roftamkhan, his general, had no more than
12,000. It had never been known before that the
Perfians had loft 20,000 men in a fingle day.

After this conqueft, the tent of the fultan was
erected near Bagdad, Monday the 11th of Schaban
(the 20th of December 1638), and he departed ten
days after for the Diarbekr. He gave orders for
the rebuilding of the walls and the fortifications
of the town, and left the grand vizir there to fuperintend the works. The fortifications were repaired, fo that this place was no longer expofed to
be taken by force. The grand vizir then entered
on the Perfian territories: after a march of ten days,
he received a deputy from the king, who made propofals of peace; which was concluded, on condition
that the king fhould deliver up two ftrong places
of his dominions; which was accepted, and the two
places put into the hand of the grand vizir, who left

there 12,000 men in garrifon, and exempted their territory from all taxes, during three years. He gave the command of it to the pacha Mohammed Dervifch.

Three of Sultan Morad's brothers had been put to death by his order, Abouyezid, Soleïman, and Kaffem ; the two firft where his maternal brothers. Muftapha, another brother of Morad, died on his return from the expedition againft Bagdad. Morad was feared and refpected by all the kings of the earth ; Khorrem Schah, the Mogul fovereign of India, fent him prefents twice, though his country was at the diftance of four months travelling : no other Ottoman prince had experienced a like honour.

Beglerbegs of Egypt, under the reign of Sultan Morad.

The firft governor of Egypt, nominated by this prince, was Beïram Pacha : he protected men of letters, and made fome lucrative undertakings and commercial fpeculations in various kinds of merchandizes, and even in foap : he alfo knew how to keep the troops in fubmiffion. When he quitted his poft, he had a conteft with his fucceffor with refpect to what he owed to the treafury : the fandjacs interpofed in the affair, and he was difcharged for nine hundred and five purfes. He left the province with a brilliant equipage and attendance ; and at his arrival at Conftantinople, the fultan gave him the third place of vizir in the divan.

He

He had for fucceffor the vizir Mohammed Pacha, a wife and intelligent man. He led a moft
fedentary life, and appeared but fix times in public
during the continuance of his government, which
was two years. Havîng been informed of the ill
ftate of affairs in Yemen, he gave advice thereof to
the fultan, and perfuaded him to fend into that
proyince Canfouhbeg, who was then emir-elhadj.
The fultan approved this advice, and fent to Canfouhbeg the patents of his government: he nominated him at the fame time vizir and beglerbeg of
the army. Canfouhbeg levied an army of three
thoufand men, of which above three hundred were
foldiers of the garrifon of Caïro, or the neighbouring places, whom the hope of making fortunes had
engaged to fell their houfes, lands, and the pay they
enjoyed in Egypt, to follow Canfouh. Mohammed Pacha denied nothing that Canfouh defired of
him. However, his army began to perpetrate all
kind of violence, murders, and robberies, on the
inhabitants, and to plunder the travellers on the
roads. Two thoufand men of the province of Romania, fent by the fultan to accompany Canfouh,
came to join him in Egypt; and far from being
burthenfome to the inhabitants, they reftored them
to tranquillity, by putting a ftop to the robberies of
the troops of that emir. Canfouh found always fome
new pretence to defer his departure, notwithftanding
the reiterated inftances of the pacha, who granted
him all the fums he demanded. At length he embarked the two thoufand men of the province of

Romania,

Romania, and fome other troops under the condud of the emir Djafar aga, who had been an officer in the Circaffian troops of Egypt, and himfelf took the road in the month of Moharram, 1039, (Auguft 1629). His expedition was not attended with fuccefs, and all Arabia-felix fell under the dominion of the Imam.

In the year 1040, the overflowing of the Nile was very moderate: the firft day of Tot, (1630-1) it was not yet at the 16th dhira: the fluices were opened, and the fame day it lowered fuddenly. This occafioned a great dearth, but the good conduct of the governor faved the people, by placing them out of the reach of vexation. Mohammed Pacha, on his return to Conftantinople, was nominated by the fultan to the fifth place of vizir in the divan.

The vizir Mouffa Pacha fucceeded Mohammed: he was received with the moft flattering teftimonials of joy and fatisfaction, and the troops went to meet him as far as Schebra. On the very firft day he held the divan, he ordered the head of a careb of Suez to be ftruck off, and confifcated his property, which amounted to feventy-five purfes. A few days after he crucified Morad, fon of Alaeddin Nakib, (chief of the fcherifs) of Beïtelhafba, and appropriated to himfelf his fucceffion likewife to the amount of the purfes. He beftowed all the offices on the people of his retinue; but this conduct having excited the murmurs of the fandjacs, he laid the fault on Ketkhodan Redhwan-aga; took

away

away his place, and reftored the employments to thofe who had been deprived of them. He alfo began to enquire into the diftribution of the pay and penfions, with intention of making retrenchments in this object. This operation gave great embaraffments: they reprefented to him the confequences, and he gave up his project. Nobody was exempt from his oppreffions; he watched the conduct of all the rich, to find out fome pretence of feizing upon their fortunes.

In the month of Schaban 1040, (March 1631,) the fultan demanded troops of him for the expedition againft the Perfians. Mouffa gave the command of thofe troops to the emir Kitafbeg, and laid a tax on the province, for the furnifhing the camels neceffary for this expedition. He received an hundred purfes, the produce of this tax, and twenty-two others from Kitafbeg; and when all thefe difpofitions were complete, he fent a written order under his own hand, to Kitafbeg, by which he fignified to him that it would be ufelefs to march, that the treafure was exhaufted, and could not fupply the payment and maintenance of the army. The remonftrances of Kitafbeg were to no purpofe; he could not prevail upon Mouffa. Wednefday the 9th of Dhoulhadja, 1040, (the 9th of July 1631,) the day of the feaft of the victims, (the little Beïram *Id Alkarabin*) on which it was a cuftom for all the fandjacs to go up to the caftle to compliment the pacha, Kitafbeg prefented himfelf with the other emirs. He firft intended not to appear,

pear, becaufe he was confcious of the pacha's unfavourable difpofition towards him: but by permiffion of God, who was willing to accomplifh his eternal decrees, he was prevailed upon to go up to the caftle. Mouffa received him with marks of honour and friendfhip; but when he rofe to go out, the cateb of the treafure came before him, feized him by his legs, and threw him down. The mutefellim ran up immediately, and cut off his head with one blow of an axe: forty men threw themfelves on his body, and pierced it with wounds. The emirs Canaanbeg and Alibeg, who had come to the pacha after Kitafbeg, fhuddered with horror, and ftood motionlefs. , he body of Kitafbeg was carried back to his houfe, and this news fpread terror throughout the garrifon. A great number of fandjacs, having Kaffembeg at their head, affembled to attend the funeral of Kitafbeg: they turned out an aga who was come to put the feals on his houfe, and after having paid him the laft duties, they made known to all the garrifon, to the ketkhoda of the tfchaoufchs, and the turdjeman, that whofoever fhould be found prefent at the feaft, which the pacha was to give that day, would be punifhed with death. Mouffa gave orders for the feaft. After having expected the fandjacs for a long time in vain, he went to the mofque of fultan Naffer Mohammed ben Calaoun, to make the prayer, as was the cuftom on that feaft. On his return from the mofque, he eat with the people of his houfe, and diftributed to the poor the remains of the repaft.

The

The fame day, the troops repaired to the houfe of the emir Kaffembeg, and went with him to fee the cadhilafker Seïd Mohammed. He was charged to go on the part of the army, to *that man* (as they called the pacha) to demand a reafon for his having committed a murder on that folemn day, with injunction to bring forth the orders of the fultan if he had received any, or to give up the murderer into the hands of the troops to be tried. The pacha anfwered, that he had done nothing but in conformity to the orders of the fultan, but that he could not confent to any of the demands of the army. This anfwer excited great murmuring, but the affembly diffolved without coming to any refolution.

The troops, when they withdrew, met four men of the pacha's attendance; they put them all to death. Friday, the 11th of Dhoulhadja, the troops affembled again with all the fandjacs, in the place of Romeïlia: the principal officers met in the Medreffa of the Sultan Hoffan, and fummoned the cadhilafker, the nakib alafchraf, and Ahmed Effendi Alfadiki, my relation, who was mufti of the mofque Sultania. They were deputed to the pacha, charged with the fame propofitions as before, if we except their demanding eight accomplices, who were defcribed by name. The pacha replied, that the execution of the orders of the fultan refpected himfelf alone; and he offered to put himfelf into the hands of the troops, or to confent to the army's nominating in his room a caïmacam, if they thought themfelves empowered fo to do. This anfwer

anfwer excited a general indignation. Some were willing to get up to the caftle, and flay the pacha; others propofed to feize the eight men the army required, and to throw them into prifon. Several oppofed the nomination of a caïmacam, and reprefented that the army had no right to depofe a governor, or to nominate another without a delegation from the fultan. This was, however, the advice that prevailed. Haffembeg, an ancient defterdar, was created caïmacam, and vefted with the caftan by the nakib. Mouffa Pacha haftened to inform the fultan of this revolution; the army addreffed alfo two petitions to the fultan; the one written in Turkifh, which was figned by the fandjacs, the agas, and the principal officers of the garrifon; and the other in Arabian, fubfcribed by the cadies and the utemas. The caïmacam and the emirs required from Mouffa four hundred and thirty-feven purfes for the payment of what he owed to the treafury, and he fold his horfe, camels, mules, and all his moveables, to pay that fum. The fultan having received the different petitions, gave the government of Egypt to Khalil Pacha alboftandji. The mutefellim of the new governor, arrived at Caïro, Saturday the 16th of Safar 1041, (13th of Sept. 1631,) and brought an order to Haffanbeg to continue to exercife the functions of caïmacam, until the arrival of khalil.

Khalil Pacha took poffeffion of his government in the month of Rebialeweł, 1041, (October, 1631.) He received intelligence in the month of Ramad-
ham

him of the fame year, that the 25th of Schaban, (17th of March, 1632,) a numerous army was coming from Yemen to invade Mecca, that the army of the Scherifs had marched to meet the enemy with the garrifon, and the emir Muftaphabeg fandjac of Djidda, that after a long and obftinate combat it had been routed; that the emir Muftaphabeg, and the Seïd Mohammed, governor of Mecca, had loft their lives, and that the enemy had entered the town in triumph, and facked it, without any regard either to the fanctity of the places confecrated by religion, or the honour of the women. At the fame time they were informed that the chief author of that revolution was a fcherif named Nami, to whom the conqueror had given the government of the city. Khalil Pacha communicated this news to the troops of Caïro, and the emir Kaffembeg voluntarily offered himfelf to march againft thefe ufurpers. Khalil appointed him ferdar of the army deftined for this expedition. He diftributed caftans to the emirs, whom he nominated to accompany him, and appointed the officers of the different military corps of cavalry and infantry who were to be employed in that war. The emir Redhwanbeg alzulafcari departed at the head of the troops who were to repair to Arabia by land; he was vefted with the dignity of emir-elhadj. Five hundred men embarked under the conduct of the emir Youffoufbeg alafrandj, and of the capoudans of Suez and of Damietta, and landed at Djidda. The land army found at Yanboa the

Seïd

Seïd Zeïd at the head of a troop of Arabians who had joined him. After the death of the Seïd Mohammed, who, as we have said, had been killed in the combat, the government of Mecca devolved on Zeïd, The Arabians, who had then took poffeffion of Mecca, fent a deputation to Kaffembeg, to afk to be eftablifhed in garrifon at Mecca, on condition that the regency of Caïro fhould pay them their ftipends. Their deputies met the army of Egypt in the valley of Merou, called *Wadi Fatima*, and Kaffembeg anfwered them, that the fword alone could decide that quarrel. Cour Mahmoud, chief of thefe banditti, fecretly approached behind the mountains to view the ftrength of the army of Egypt. He faw that he was incapable of withftanding it, and returned quickly to Mecca, making the utmoft hafte he could to fly with all his troops. They retired towards Wadi abbas, and fhut themfelves up in a fort called *Turbet*. The army of Kaffembeg having approached to Mecca, entered the city without meeting with any refiftance; an hundred men of the enemy's army, who had remained for want of means to fly, were put to the fword. The army difcharged firft the ceremonies of the pilgrimage, and then difpofed themfelves to go in queft of the enemy. The troops who had embarked for Djidda landed there, and likewife took poffeffion of that city without any refiftance. After feven days march the army of Kaffembeg difcovered the enemy, whofe tents were placed at the foot of the fort Turbet, at the

entry

entry of the province of Nedjid. After the firſt
combat, in which the Arabians loſt about one hun-
dren men, they ſhut themſelves up in the fort, and
the conquerors plundered their tents. There were
near that fort five wells which ſupplied the Arabians
with water, and each of thoſe wells was defended by
a detachment of their army. Kaſſembeg the next
day ordered his troops to attack them; four of
theſe wells were carried, and the army formed an
intrenchment oppoſite to the fifth, which lay on
the foot of the walls of the fort. As ſoon as the
Arabians approached to draw water, the Egyptian
troops, ſheltered behind their intrenchments, fired
upon them, and killed a vaſt number: above two
hundred of the enemy's army periſhed with thirſt.
Ali, one of their chiefs, made a vigorous ſally, but
he was repelled, and obliged to re-enter the place.
Kaſſembeg was making a general aſſault, but one
of his emirs adviſed him to plant a ſtandard oppoſite to the fort, and to ſummon the beſieged to repair to the ſtandard; this advice was followed, and
the beſieged did not heſitate to ſubmit. As faſt as
they arrived they were conducted to Kaſſembeg,
who offered them the choice, either to remain with
him, or withdraw where they ſhould think proper.
Curd ali deſired alſo to capitulate: he addreſſed
himſelf to ſeveral emirs of the army of Egypt,
and when he had ſecured their conſent, he pre-
ſented himſelf to Kaſſembeg, without diſcovering
his perſon, or acquainting him who he was, till after the ratification of the engagement which the
emirs

emirs had contracted with him. Kaffembeg required only that the fcherif Nami and his brother fhould be given up to him, as alfo Cour Mahmoud and his brother. Curd Ali entered the place, perfuaded them that he had obtained for them the fame capitulation as for himfelf, and engaged them to come over and fee Kaffembeg, who loaded them with chains. The Arabians all left the fort; there remained but three hundred of the thoufand that had been there at firft. The victorious army returned immediately to Mecca, where the four chiefs of the rebels were put to death by different kind of torments. Public rejoicings were made in the city during feven days. The army returned from Mecca in the month of Safar, 1042, (Aug. 1632); when they arrived at Caïro, the pacha teftified his fatisfaction to the emirs, and diftributed caftans, and rejoicings were made, which lafted five days.

There was great plenty in Egypt under the government of Khalel, and the ardab of corn, which coft eight groufchs before, was reduced to two. A Jew, named *Yacoub*, had for fifteen years exercifed in Caïro the functions of farraf-bafchi, (chief of the exchangers). He had always been known to cultivate the favour of the governors; all the places and offices of the city were in his hands, and the Mufulmans groaned under the preffure of his odious vexations. The khalif refolved to punifh this criminal; he did not fuffer either his prefents, or the folicitations of the great who protected him, to effect a change in his refolution, becaufe he was indebted

debted to them for large fums; on the contrary, having been informed that this was the reafon of the concern they took in the fate of this profligate, he paid them what the Jew owed them, and put him to death. When Khalil quitted his government the fhops were fhut up from the 22d of Ramadhan, (1ft of April, 1633), to the end of that month: No beglerbeg had received fo flattering a teftimonial of gratitude from the citizens. None had been punifhed with death under his government, but after a judicious inquiry. Three robbers having been prefented to him one day, who had been ftopped juft before, he ordered them to be tried: one of the officers of the divan reprefented to him that all kinds of affairs were not to be fubjeded to the ftrict rules of proceeding, and that it would be eligible to make ufe of his authority, and to fentence them to death. The governor, for anfwer, directed the cateb of the divan to draw up an order to demolifh the houfe of the officer who had held that difcourfe, and charged fome of his attendants to put it into execution. That perfon, furprized at fuch a ftrange order, came to the pacha, and afked him the motive thereof. " How that " houfe which thou has built affects thee with " anxioufnefs; and fhall not God be offended, if " the edifice of his own hand fhould be deftroyed?" The officer, confounded, kiffed the lower end of the pacha's robe, loading him with bleffings, and Khalil revoked the order he had given, and fet the three robbers at liberty: from that time the greateft

fecurity

fecurity reigned in the town. Khalil returning to Conftantinople, the fultan confifcated his whole fortune, and banifhed him into the ifland of Cyprus with two flaves only; however, he afterwards reftored him to his favour, returned him his whole fortune, and promoted him to the government of Romania.

Khalil Pacha had for his fucceffor the Vizir Ahmed Pacha Alkurdji, who was before vefted with the dignity of emir-akhour, (chief of the ftates): In the month of Safar, 1043, he received an order from the fultan to fend into Syria 2000 men of the troops of Egypt for an expedition againft the prince of the Drufes, with 5000 quintals (kantar) of bifcuit, and 4000 quintals of powder. He fulfilled the orders of the fultan, but inftead of 2000 men he contented himfelf to fend 500, of which he gave the command to the emir Haffanbeg Defterdar.

Haffanbeg having opened to Ahmed Pacha that there was a great fcarcity of copper in Egypt, for the coining of fmall money, and that the fultan had a vaft quantity in Romania, the pacha wrote to the fultan, and afked of him 1000 hundred weight of copper for the coining of fmall money. The fultan fent him 12,000 hundred weight, and afked him for the value of that copper, a return of 300,000 pieces of gold. The pacha affembled the fandjacs on this fubject, who were of opinion, that thofe materials fhould be converted into obols: in confequence, he fent for all workmen of the hammer

mer, fmiths, founders, and others, and eftablifhed
furnaces in the edifice called *Akberdi*. The workmen betook themfelves to the fabrication, but the
pieces they made were hardly intrinfically worth
half the value of thofe that had been formerly
coined, fo that each of thofe ancient pieces would
have made two of this new coinage. This dimi-
nution excited a general difquiet, the price of the
goods augmented, and they became extremely
fcarce: befides this, the fultry heat of the work-
houfes caufed a great number of workmen to perifh. The pacha, informed of thefe inconveniencies, came to vifit the work-houfes, and, being convinced himfelf of the extreme fatigue the workmen were overwhelmed with, he put a ftop to the
bufinefs, and permitted them to return to their
homes. Some days after he affembled the emirs
and the cadies of the boroughs and villages, and
confulted them on the ufe he fhould make of that copper; one of the cadies counfelled him to diftribute it
among the inhabitants of Caïro, by authority, and
to employ it in the eftablifhment of religious foundations. The pacha was not of the fame opinion at
firft; his project was to convert it into wedges, and
to fend it to Tecrour, and into the country of the
negroes, and to reimburfe the fultan the value out
of his own money: unfortunately this advice met
with his approbation, and the very fame day he
appointed Muftaphabeg to fuperintend the diftribution of the copper; he honoured him with a caftan, and gave him a lodging in the building where

the coinage had been carried on. This diftribution began the 16th of Dhoulhadja, 1043, (Jan. 13th, 1634), and did not finifh until the middle of Rebialewel, 1044, (October 1634); no perfon, either high or low, was exempted from this fcourge; the moft indigent were conftrained to take their fhare; as the players on inftruments, thofe who wafh the dead, the grave-diggers, the gardners, the people of the markets, and the failors. They received the value in fpecie, except in the latter days of the month of Schaban 1044, (February 1635); when they took eighty groufchs for one hundred weight of copper.

The fame year, 1044, the rife of the Nile did not exceed nineteen dhira; yet, notwithftanding the drynefs, the harveft was more plentiful than in the years when the land had been more overflowed. In the month of Schaban, the fultan demanded of the pacha 3000 men of Egypt, and 3000 quintals of powder, for the expedition againft the Perfians; he at the fame time defired the pacha to give the command of the troops to the emir Redhwanbeg Alzulafcari and to Alibeg. The pacha anfwered, that Redhwanbeg was abfent with the caravan of pilgrims, in quality of emir Elhadji, and as Alibeg was withheld by his poft of governor of Djirdje, and by his fuperintendance of the fupply of the corn from Upper Egypt, he could not poffibly give him the command of the troops. Upon the fultan's anfwer he fent off about 2000 men, under the conduct of the emir Dilowerbeg, and had taken

care

care leaſt the troops ſhould do any damage to the province. Ahmed Pacha manifeſted, during the whole time of his government, an exaɗ vigilance; knew how to command reſpeɗ from the troops, and to render himſelf beloved by the poor citizens. In leaving Egypt he refuſed to account for what he owed to the treaſury, but ſubmitted himſelf to the judgment of the ſultan; when he arrived at Conſtantinople the ſultan ſtruck off his head. The diſſatisfaɗion of the ſultan aroſe from the pacha's having diſtributed the copper for eighty groufchs per hundred weight, which he had ſold to him at forty-five. He alſo reproached him with having ſent him an army compoſed of poor only, and having taken money of the rich to grant them exemptions.

The vizir Hoſſaïn Pacha was nominated to ſucceed Ahmed; he rendered himſelf deteſtable by his rapines and cruelties. The emir Redhwanbeg, who had before his arrival exerciſed the funɗions of caïmacam, had cauſed ſeveral tents to be prepared for him, among which were thoſe of the defterdar, the ketkhoda, the tſchaoufchs, and his own; Hoſſaïn Pacha took them for himſelf, without indemnifying the proprietors. He had brought with him a great number of Drufes, who committed all kinds of exceſs and robberies. At the end of the month Ramadhan, the people of his train over-run the city, and carried to every ſhop one or two tapers of Alexandria, for which they exaɗed five groufchs of every merchant, as a gra-

G 2 . tification

tification for the approaching feaſt. The ſhops were ſhut, and it was only upon the repreſentations of the emir Redhwanbeg that the pacha put an end to this kind of extortion. Nobody received any inheritance while he governed; he invaded the fortune of all thoſe who died, whatſoever the number of their heirs might be. It was ſufficient to procure one's revenge on an enemy, to denounce him to the pacha as guilty of having received a ſucceſſion, or ſecreted his treaſure; upon this bare accuſation he was thrown into priſon, and came out from it only by paying what it was thought proper to aſk of him. There was no day Hoſſaïn did not ride through the town on horſeback and maſſacre one or two perſons; if he ſaw a great concourſe of people in ſome place, he run up, ſword in hand, and cleared the way, hewing down all he found on his paſſage, men or animals. He compelled the inhabitants to receive adulterated gold for ſilver, or adulterated ſilver for gold, which he took only by the weight, and this exaction was renewed every month. He invaded the foundations, and the rights of thoſe who were in legitimate poſſeſſion of them, and he appointed them another deſtination; finally, there was hardly any kind of vexations or cruelties he did not practiſe, delighting in the ſpilling of blood, and making even a ſport and diverſion of it. During the continuance of his government, which was one year and eleven months, he put to death twelve hundred perſons, not including thoſe he ſlew with his

own

own hand. Notwithftanding thefe bad qualities, he knew how to keep his troops in awe, and to protect the citizens from their unjuft exactions. In the divan he examined affairs with the moft fcrupulous attention, he reprefled the arrogance of the bold and audacious, and, as long as he was at the helm, no robbery was ever heard of. The tidings of his depofition was accompanied by an order of the fultan, for him to give an account of the ftate of the treafury, and of other public revenues: on his refufal to pay the fum for which he was taxed, the caïmacam ordered him to a prifon, and he was fet free only by paying four hundred and eighty purfes.

The vizir Mohammed Pacha fucceeded Hoffaïn: he was fon of Achmed Pacha, who was the fon of a daughter of the fultan Selim II. He received an order in the month of Schawal, 1047, (February, 1638), to fend fifteen hundred men to the Sultan Morad for the expedition againft Bagdad. This army began to move in the month of Moharram, 1048, (May, 1638), and caufed no damage on its march; it returned from Egypt after the taking of Bagdad, at the end of Safar, 1049, (June, 1639.) This pacha reaped a great number of rich fucceffions by the death of the emirs, and of the moft diftinguifhed ulemas. He did not content himfelf with appropriating to his own ufe the revenues of the foundations, to enrich his fervants; he called before him all the farmers charged with the receipt of the funds deftined to

thofe

thofe eftablifhments, and put them into irons until they had paid the fums to which they had been taxed, which exceeded by far their abilities; and he did not deliver the revenues of the foundations to thofe that were entitled to them, until he had extorted from them an equal fum, and fometimes double the value. He reprefented to the fultan, that among thofe who received pay from the public treafury, there was a great number of women; the fultan deprived them, and ordered that no woman fhould receive more than ten othmanis, and that thenceforward no allowance fhould be made to them. This reform excited great complaints, becaufe thofe women were for the moft part widows, or in reduced circumftances.

From the time Mohammed Pacha had taken poffeffion of his government there had always reigned a ftrong enmity between him and the emir Redhwanbeg Aboulfchewarib, emir Elhadji. When the fultan demanded of the pacha a detachment of Egyptian troops, he ordered him at the fame time to give the command to Redhwanbeg. This emir gained the favour of the pacha* by a promife of forty purfes, but he always deferred fulfilling this engagement until the departure of the caravan. The pacha improved this circumftance by withholding thofe forty purfes of the fum deftined for the difburfements of the caravan, when it was paid

* It was moft affuredly to be excufed accepting this commiffion, which was not fo advantageous as the office of emir Elhadj.

in

in the camp of Birket-elhadj, into the hands of Redhwanbeg; the latter claimed his whole fum, and expoftulated with the pacha in terms of the higheft indignation. Mohammed ˙ fent him the forty purfes he had withheld, and waited for an opportunity of taking his revenge: he was not long before he found it. Muftaphabeg, nominated a fhort time before beglerbeg of Habefch died at Coufs, when he was going to enter upon his government; Mohammed wrote to the fultan to nominate Redhwanbeg in his ftead, and made him a promife of five hundred purfes out of the value of the fortune that emir was poffeffed of in Egypt. Having received an anfwer agreeable to his defire, he difpatched a courier to Redhwanbeg, with an order immediately to repair to his government, and to refign the conduct of the caravan into the hands of Soleïman, aga of the janifaries of Djida. Redhwanbeg was then at Medina, and was going to obey the orders he had received; but the aga of the janifaries excufed himfelf from undertaking the conduct of the caravan, and it was generally agreed, that Redhwanbeg fhould re-conduct them into Egypt. After the departure of the courier, Mohammed appointed emir Wellbeg in the room of the emir Elhadj, and difpatched him to take the conduct of the caravan. He met at Bender-alwoudjh, the emir Redhwanbeg, who furrendered to him all that was annexed to that office, and departed with a fmall train for Romania; as foon as the caravan was returned, Mohammed haftened to

lay

lay hold on all that belong to Redhwanbeg. The latter being arrived at Conftantinople, the fultan was much inclined to put him to death, for having difobeyed his orders, in not coming to join him at Bagdad, and then for procraftinating the affuming of his government. All his protectors could obtain for him, was the favour of his life; but he was caft into prifon, and recovered his liberty only a few days before the fultan's death. He returned to Egypt, and was re-inftated in his poft of emir-elhadj, under the reign of fultan Ibrahim. The viciffitudes and the difgraces this emir experienced, are fimilar to thofe of the Barmecides, whofe hiftory fills a great number of volumes.

Mohammed Pacha feized upon all fucceffions, even of thofe who left legitimate heirs behind them, and how powerful protectors foever a man might have had near his perfon, one half was the utmoft that could poffibly be obtained. When the Sultan Ibrahim afcended the throne, after the deceafe of Morad, he did not fend Mohammed the cuftomary prefents, which the pachas commonly received at the coronation of a new prince, and he took away from him the government of Egypt, to appoint him to that of Medina and Mecca. Mohammed apprehended he had incurred the difpleafure of the new fultan, and for a while fufpended his exactions; but he had no fooner heard that the cuftomary prefents had re-ingratiated him with the fultan, and that he had confirmed him in his government, than he abandoned himfelf with frefh vigour to his former
                                         tyrannical

tyrannical inclinations. He suppressed all the female muficians and players on instruments, and permitted them to exercife their profeffion, only on paying an enormous contribution. He ordered an account to be drawn up of the trades of all the different workmen in filk, and levied a tax on each branch: there were found 17,000 of them in Caïro, Ambaba, and Djize, not including thofe of other diftricts. Mohammed gave no ear to any reprefentation on that fubject, and alledged that this tax was indifpenfible for the coronation of the Sultan Ibrahim: the like impofition never had been heard of before in Egypt. The pacha appropriated to himfelf above one fourth of the produce of that impoft. He alfo levied a ftamp-duty on the balances and meafures (dhira).

Mohammed Pacha having been bereft of his government, refufed to pay the debts owing to the treafury until the arrival of Muftapha Pacha his fucceffor: the latter fettled his accounts, and required 700 purfes from him. A fhort time after, the emir Redhwanbeg returned into Egypt, and re-entered in the poffeffion of the place of emir El-hadj. All the citizens vied to felicitate him on this happy event, and proceeded to meet him as far as ↳Boulac. The fultan in re-inftating him in his dignity, permitted him to re-take the poffeffion of all the property of lands, the revenues of which had been annexed to his poft, and deftined for the expenditure of the caravan, and to difpofe of them with an unlimited licence.

Hiftory

History of the coronation, and of the reign of Sultan Ibrahim; beglerbegs of Egypt, nominated by this prince.

Ibrahim mounted the throne on Thurſday the 16th of Schawal 1049, (9th of February 1640): he was dethroned the 17th of Redjeb 1058, (8th of Auguſt 1648), and ſtrangled the 23d of the ſame month.

When the great vizir and the mufti came to take him from the place of his retreat, to put him in poſſeſſion of the throne, he refuſed, fearing his brother Morad might take away his life, as he had done by his other brethren. He placed no confidence in what theſe officers ſaid to him, and did not conſent to go to the ſeraglio until after the ſultana-mother aſſured him that Morad was dead. Towards the end of his life he gave himſelf up to the love of women, and laid aſide intirely all the cares of government. This conduct gave birth to a revolution which precipitated him from the throne, and placed his ſon Mohammed in his room. His mother herſelf favoured this revolution, convinced that his indolence was fatal to the ſtate. In the third year of his reign, Sunbul, aga of the ſeraglio, whom the ſultan had ſent to Caïro, after having deprived him of that poſt, was taken at ſea by the Franks with all his property. The ſultan in revenge ſent two hundred veſſels to Allack, in the iſland of Candia; it was the fineſt poſſeſſion of the Venetians. Canea, the ſtrongeſt place of the iſland, fell into the hands of the Muſulmans. Every year

year the fultan fent frefh troops thither, until he became mafter of all the ftrong and inhabited places, which were 14,000 in number. Hoffaïn Pacha, who had heretofore been governor of Egypt, commanded the Ottoman army, the fecond year after the taking of Canea. He left the enemy but one place in the whole ifland; it is that we call *Cafr*.

The vizir Muftapha Pacha alboftandji was nominated by the fultan Ibrahim to the government of Egypt after Mohammed Pacha. The citizens had much to fuffer under his government by the injuftice and odious depredations of his ketkhoda, as well as by his cateb of the divan. The pacha was ignorant of their conduct; they alone had accefs to his perfon, and they held him, if I may fo exprefs it, befieged in the caftle. Under the government of Muftapha, the increafe of the Nile having been very fhort, the drought was general all over Egypt, and grain became exceedingly dear: a meafure of corn (wabya) was fold at the price of thirty nisfs *.

In the month of Schawàl 1051, the tfchaoufchs revolted againft their ketkhoda the emir Ali, and the pacha was conftrained to yield to their requifitions and threats, and to deprive him of his place. He gave it to emir Abedinbeg, who was turdje-

* I muft notice here that the calamity with which Egypt is afflicted, when the increafe of the Nile is not fufficient to cover it, is always expreffed in the Arabian text by the word *Scharaki*. This word, which is not to be found in the Dictionaries, cannot fignify any thing elfe but drynefs, and properly a drynefs affected by the heat of the fun.

man.

man. The emir Ali had drawn this difgrace upon himfelf, for having conferred military promotions by his own authority, on whom he pleafed, inftead of making the diftribution in the divan.

Robbers had fo much multiplied under the government of Muftapha, that there was not any night but fome quarter of Caïro was plundered, which forced the inhabitants to abandon their dwellings. The pacha contented himfelf, when fome of them were feized, to give them up into the hands of the wala, (an officer charged with the police) without fentencing them to any punifhment, and the wala fet them at liberty for fome prefents. Five-and-twenty of thefe robbers, who lay concealed in a fubterraneous place near Djize, were taken and carried before the cafchef of that town. The cafchef accepted prefents from feveral, and difmiffed them; he fent the others to the wala, who fet them free, after having received from them a fum of money. The excefs of thefe robberies, and the conduct of the wala, excited general murmurs, and the pacha was obliged to difplace him, appointing in his room the emir Canaanbeg. The latter began immediately to make enquiry refpecting the robbers: feveral were taken and led before the pacha, who paffed no fentence on them. The wala kept them in prifon till the arrival of Makfoud Pacha, who fucceeded to Muftapha in the government of Egypt. This new pacha ordered fome to execution, and condemned the others to the gallies, to labour at the oar.

Muftapha

Muftapha Pacha was afterwards expofed to a great danger, by a general commotion of the troops. They complained that the public granaries were unprovided, and that above one year's ratio were due to them, and they compelled the cadhilafker Mohammed Effendi to come and view the ftorehoufes, to take an account of the quantity of grain he found there. They found the granaries empty, and that the greateft part of the grain had been fold to the Chriftians. Thefe enquires having been made, proved that it was Ahmed Effendi, cateb of the divan of Muftapha, who had fold the grain without the participation of the pacha: his place was taken from him to comply with the defire of the troops: a few days after the emir Ahmedbeg prefented himfelf before the pacha, promifing to pay the troops their due, and to fill the granaries: the pacha accepted his offers, and gave him the neceffary authority to accomplifh his promifes. Ahmed acquitted himfelf fo well in this commiffion, that in lefs than a fortnight he ftored more than 30,000 ardabs of corn in the granaries, and began to pay off the arrears of the army. The troops were appeafed, and the price of victuals was lowered. The cateb of the divan fucceeded in re-conciliating the favour of the tfchaoufchs and in re-eftablifhing himfelf in his port; he behaved ftill worfe than before: the pacha depended entirely on him, and did nothing without his advice. Muftapha reaped, during his government, feveral opulent *fucceffions*; but they were all abforbed by his ketkhoda or the cateb.

After

After the death of emir Muftaphabeg two hundred thouſand ardabs óf corn were found in his poſſeſ-ſion which were all fold to the people at the rate of four groufchs the ardab. The doctor Moham-med Effendi left alfo a confiderable fucceffion behind him, confifting chiefly in curious books, and in pre-cious china ware: he had above 5000 volumes in his poffeffion. The cateb put into chefts, and fent to Conſtantinople, what he could find moſt valuable.

When Muftapha left his government of Egypt, his fucceſſor, the vizir Makſoud Pacha, demanded 1700 purfes of him, as the fum he was indebted to the treaſury. Muſtapha refuſed paying that fum; he alledged that the drought of 1051, had brought on the treaſury a loſs of five hundred purfes on the leaſe of the lands, and that his predeceſſor, Mo-hammed Pacha had, in quitting Egypt, retained five hundred purfes on the land revenues of the treaſury of the preceding year. Makſoud anſwered him: " You have kept 470 purfes on account of " the drought which has diſtreſſed that province " under the government of Mohammed: this fum " ought to make good what the dryneſs you com-" plain of has coſt you. As to the five hundred " purfes you have given up to the pacha Moham-" med, he was accountable, and you ought to have " compelled the payment." Muſtapha lamented that he had been deceived by Mohammed. Mak-foud repreſented to him, that if he had been duped, it was by the men of his own houſe, who had pre-vented

vented him from having the cognizance of his own affairs. The fandjacs and the agas attempted in vain to bring them to an agreement: Makfoud fent the ketkhoda and the cateb to prifon, and kept Muftapha in his houfe, under a clofe guard of two emirs. He wrote to the fultan, who enjoined him to exact from Muftapha and his people, the payment of all that remained due to him, and, in cafe of refufal, to put all their goods to fale, and to fend them to Alexandria, to be kept in the fortrefs until he fhould order them to Conftantinople. Makfoud, encouraged by thefe orders, after having fecured the confent of the troops, fent feveral emirs and the bouluc-agas, to give notice thereof to Muftapha. All the reprefentations and inftances of thefe officers were fruitlefs, and Muftapha conftantly refufed to pay what they requefted of him. Makfoud ordered him to be fhut up in a building of the caftle; and threatened the ketkhoda and the cateb to have them baftinadoed if they did not undertake to pay the fum at which they fhould be taxed. The executioners had already fummoned them, and they were upon the point of being punifhed, when they at laft fubmitted to what was required of them. Makfoud caufed Muftapha to be conveyed to Boulac, into a houfe where he was kept prifoner; he took ftill feveral fteps refpecting him, and it was at laft agreed upon, that he fhould be fet free, paying only 250 purfes over-and-above the fum that was to be furnifhed by the ketkhoda and the cateb. Muftapha fubfcribed to this agreement,

ment, and an account was drawn out of all the fums for which he had remained debtor to the treafury, beyond what had heen exacted from him: it amounted to 450 purfes. Hoffaïn aga Emirakhour, (chief of the ftables) who had brough the orders from the fultan, was charged to convey to Conftantinople the writings containing thefe depofitions, and it was agreed that the ketkhoda of Muftapha fhould difburfe the promifed fums to the fultan, and that Hoffaïn Aga fhould bring the acquittal for them. After this agreement, the ketkhoda and the cateb, accompanied by feveral perfons of the fuite of Makfoud, repaired to Conftantinople, to collect the fum at which their mafter had been taxed and the two hundred purfes, to the payment of which they had been perfonally affeffed, and to put the whole at Scudari into the hands of the chief officer of the treafury, who departed from Caïro at the fame time they did. Makfoud received afterwards an order of the fultan, to fend without delay the Pacha Muftapha to Conftantinople. Makfoud communicated this order to him, and fupplied him with all he could want in his voyage. The fultan contented himfelf with obliging him to pay two hundred purfes to Muftapha, and difcharged his fucceffor, the pacha Makfoud, of the four hundred and fifty, for which Muftapha remained ftill indebted. He gave him a place afterwards among the feven vizirs, who fit in the divan of Romania, in confideration of his being his brother-in-law.

The

The vizir Makfoud Pacha had been beglerbeg of Diarbekr before he had been nominated governor of Egypt. In his time the province was afflicted with a plague more fatal even than thofe which wafted it under the government of the beglerbeg's Ali Pacha and Djafar Pacha: this fcourge was general, and the adult people were no more exempted from it then the younger. Never was the terror fo great: every one was in expectation of death every inftant, and thirty carcafes might often have been feen carrying in the ftreets at one time. Old men of above eighty years died on this occafion, which had never been remarked before. The diftemper began to manifeft itfelf at Boulac, from the beginning of Schaban 1052, (Nov. 1642); it was not until two months after that its fymptoms appeared at Caïro; it raged in full force from the firft days of Dhoulcaada of this year to the end of Safar 1053, (Feb. 1643): it then began to abate, but did not intirely ceafe until the end of the following month. The number of dead bodies that were brought to the five principal mofques (djame) of Caïro, from the beginning of Dhoulcaada to the end of Moharram, that is, during about three months, was 962,000. A great number of citizens preferred the difcharging in their own houfes the laft duties prefcribed by religion, to the carrying the bodies to the chapels or mofques neareft to their dwellings, and the number of thofe that were interred in this manner muft be at leaft equal to the former. They counted the infants of both

Vol. II.   H   fexes

fexes that were loft on this occafion, and they were found about 5000 in number. The governor at laft iffued a prohibition not to carry in public the bodies of thofe who died, and he ordered them to be buried without any ceremony. At the end of Safar, the value of the falaries, which proved vacant by the deceafe of thofe who had the right to them, amounted to 160,000 othmanis a day, and the number of the rations to 12,000 ardabs of corn per month. Two hundred and thirty villages were alfo vacant by the death of thofe to whom they had been granted.

Makfoud was the author of feveral public works, that proved burthenfome to the people, and interrupted commerce, which caufed an increafe in the price of all commodities. He fuppreffed all kind of unjuft exactions and extortions, and abolifhed the tax on female fingers and players of inftruments. He left the fucceffions to the legitimate heirs, and contented himfelf with taking as much as was due to the treafury. He ordered ftrict enquiries againft thofe robbers who had done fo much damage under the government of Muftapha: he punifhed them by the fevereft torments, and re-eftablifhed by that meafure the fecurity of the country.

On Friday the 20th of Dhoulcaada 1053, (29th of Jan. 1644), the capoudan of Alexandria defigning to launch a veffel newly conftructed; the Chriftian flaves, who were diftributed in feveral other fhips, were affembled; they were about fix hundred in number. When they had been freed of their

fetters,

fetters, an hundred and fifty united, forced the gate of the arfenal, feized the arms, and having entered Alexandria, at the time the people were in the mofques, they broke open the fhops and plundered them; they then got on board one of the veffels that was in the port and efcaped.

A general confpiracy was formed of all the fandjacs againft the Pacha Makfoud, and Friday the 12th of Ramadan 1054, (21ft of Nov. 1644), they met at the emir Redwhanbeg Aboulfchewarib's. Their difcontent originated from the pacha's having demanded of them the third of what they were indebted to the public treafury, in proportion to the military employments they were in poffeffion of, to raife the funds for the pay of the troops for the month Ramadan. They gave for anfwer, that the Nile had retired forty days later then ufual, which had been an obftacle to the earlier fowing; and moreover, that there was ftill above one month wanting to the ordinary expiration of the firft payment. The pacha perfifting in exacting this payment, they met, and declared to him, by their agas, that they would not fubmit to payment before the proper time. They alfo demanded the fuperceding of feveral officers, which they confidered as the inftigators of the pacha: Makfoud gratified them, and confented even to fend into exile thofe whofe removal they had defired. The fandjacs addreffed then a petition to the fultan, in which they fpoke to this purport: " The vizir Makfoud Pacha has folicited " us to fubfcribe a petition to the fultan, in which

H 2   " he

" he fets forth that the lands have fuffered by
" drought, and that they have been obliged to
" take five hundred purfes on the revenues of this
" year, to make good the funds of the treafury of the
" preceding year. We have abfolutely refufed that,
" becaufe we were informed, that he has had a fur-
" plus of feven hundred purfes on the public reve-
" nues of the laft year: the lands have befides been
" watered enough, and there has exifted no drynefs.
" We have therefore ftated the condition of the
" public treafury, and we have reprefented to him,
" that we were but depofitaries of the revenue of
" the fultan, and that we could not impofe on
" him. You muft have received that petition
" figned by the emirs Canaanbeg and Youffouf-
" beg, and of the Roudhnamedji *." The fandjacs next reprefented in their memorial what concerned the anticipated payment the pacha had required of them. They complained that the rents
on military tenures had increafed one-third fince
the year 1040, and they intreated the fultan to fupprefs this augmentation: laftly, they fupplicated
him to order, that the pay and the public leafes
may pafs from parents to children by right of fucceffion. They charged fome officers of the garrifon with the conveyance of their memorial. After
the departure of their deputies, the pacha received
a letter from the fultan: he obferved to him, that
he had been informed of the revolt of the troops,
that he was ignorant of the caufe, and furprifed

* An officer who keeps the regifter of the daily expences.

that

that the pacha fhould not have given him information of it. Makfoud anfwered the fultan, that there
exifted no revolt, but that the army having complained of fome abufes, fanctioned by cuftom, he
had reformed them, A fhort time after, new orders
of the fultan, directed to the pacha, and to the
corps of mutefarrakas, tfchaoufchs, janifaries, fpahis and azabs, were brought by the great aga: the
fultan enjoined them to make enquiry after the authors of the revolt, and to deliver them to the
pacha to be tried. Makfoud afked the fandjacs
whether they had any thing to oppofe to thofe orders. The emir Mamaïbeg arofe, and faid, "We
" have excited no uproar, and we do not oppofe,
" in any thing, the pleafure of the fultan, whofe
" flaves we are. We have had juft matter of dif-
" content; we have laid our complaints before him,
" and we expect his anfwer."

The pacha however continued to purfue this
affair, under pretence that he could not avoid
fending an anfwer to the fultan. He wifhed to
get the emirs Alibeg and Mamaïbeg, and of the
defterdar Schaban Effendi, out of the divan: he
had fuborned men to kill them, but the defterdar having come into the divan alone on that
day, the pacha was aware that it would prove of
little fervice to him to free himfelf of a fingle
man. Tuefday the 21ft of Dhoulhadja 1053, (the
1ft of March 1644), the whole army refolved to
depofe Makfoud, and to appoint for caïmacan the
defterdar Schabanbeg. Makfoud received with plea-

fure

fure the news of this refolution, which was notified to him by the agas; he put a caftan on Schabanbeg, and withdrew to his own houfe. The fandjacs directed a new petition to the fultan, giving an account of what had happened, and protefting their readinefs to accept any governor the fultan might be pleafed to fet over them. Soleïman Aga, the bearer of the petition, returned at the end of forty days with the fultan's anfwer, who granted them all their requefts, and informed them of the nomination of Ayoub Pacha in the room of Makfoud. When the new pacha arrived at Caïro, warm altercations took place between him and Makfoud, for the payment of what the latter remained indebted to the treafury. Ayoub having fummoned him, he furrendered himfelf at the caftle, and entered, of his own accord, the place where the pachas ufed to be kept in cuftody, confcious that the only intention of the pacha was to fhut him up in prifon; this affair was terminated by the mediation of the fandjacs. Makfoud, on his return to Conftantinople, was fharply reproached by the fultan, and put to death by his order, for having affented to the nomination of a caïmacan, and for abandoning the caftle, without being conftrained by open force.

Ayoub Pacha had employments in the feraglio, when the fultan Ibrahim, hearing of the depofition of Makfoud, and meeting him at the fame time, nominated him governor of Egypt notwithftanding his refufal. During the fpace of about two years he he occupied that poft, his good conduct, and that of the officers who fhared his confidence, kept up in every quarter tranquillity and good order. When he quitted his government, he refigned his dignity of vizir, gave up to the fultan all he was poffeffed' of, and embraced the profeffion of dervifch in a monaftery of Romania.

The vizir Mohammed Pacha ben Haïdar fucceeded to Ayoub Pacha: he maintained himfelf in that place near two years and an half, and the whole time of his government was only a feries of confufion and revolutions.

The 10th of Redjeb 1057, (11th of Aug. 1647,)' fome janifaries carried off a woman, and brought her by force to ancient Mifr; the wala of that city, who knew her, came to take her out of their hands. The janifaries refolving to be revenged, went up to the pacha to demand the death of the wala. This officer was fent for, and his affair having been difcuffed in the divan, in prefence of the cadhi Seïd' Mohammed Effendi Hanifizade, the pacha fentenced him to be ftrangled: this wala was of the corps of the tfchaoufchs. The pacha, feeling that this affair could not be long undifcovered by the fultan, determined to draw up a memorial on this fubject, and took the advice of Canfouhbeg. The latter perfuaded him, to reprefent in the memorial, that this affair originated with a band of people whom the emir Redhwanbeg emir-elhadj had brought' with him from Mecca; that thefe adventurers, who formerly exercifed the trade of robbers on the lands

'H 4 of

of Yemen, were now attached to the fervice of Redhwanbeg, and Alibeg, governor of Djirdje. He alfo advifed him to add, that if he was fomewhat flow in fending the treafure, it was by the fault of thefe two emirs and their partifans, who were to furnifh the major part of the money, and that the pacha was not powerful enough to compel them to make payment; that laftly, if the fultan would check their exceffes, and facilitate the reception of the rents, he knew no other means than to give the place of emir-elhadj to Mamaïbeg, and to appoint Canfouhbeg to the government of Djirdje. This requeft, drawn up by the advice of Confouhbeg, was figned by a great number of perfons; among thofe who underwrote it, was one of the friends of Redhwanbeg, who haftened to inform him of it. The emir Redhwanbeg alfo drew up a petition, wherein he fet forth the truth of the facts, and unveiled the black intention of thofe who drew up that of the pacha; he obferved that the principal of the treafure were in the hands of the emirs Mamaïbeg and Canfouhbeg: he concluded by declaring his intire fubmiffion, and that of Alibeg, to the orders of the fultan. By a juft difpofition of Providence, it happened that the petition of Redhwanbeg arrived before that of the pacha, and the great vizir made report to the fultan. *I know,* faid the fultan, *the emirs Redhwanbeg and Alibeg, they are incapable of what is imputed to them; and it is perhaps only the effect of a dangerous intrigue.* The next day he received the memorial from the pacha, and he

sent

sent orders to the emirs Redhwanbeg and Alibeg, to make enquiries, in conjunction with the pacha, against those who detained the rents of the treasury, and to try both them and the pacha if they should refuse to pay. The two emirs having received these orders, repaired to Caïro the 21st of Djoumadi-loula 1057, (24th of June 1647). Monday the 26th in the morning, the emir Alibeg went up to the castle; the pacha expected him in the Cara-meïdan, and Alibeg entered the place, accompanied by all his troops. The pacha set two caftans on him, and distributed others to several of the officers of the emir's train, and to fourteen cafchefs, whose departments depended on the government of Djirdje. As often as a cafchef entered the cara-meïdan the drums were beat: never before did a pacha leave the castle, and descend in the cara-meïdan, to receive a governor of Djirdje. Tues-day the 27th, all the military corps, the emirs and the fandjacs, assembled in the place of Romelia; Canfouhbeg and Mamaïbeg were the only men who were not present. They were summoned several times, and refused to come; but at length, by an effect of the eternal decrees, Mamaïbeg went to fee Canfouhbeg, and he persuaded him, notwithstand-ing his reluctance, to accompany him to the place of assembly. After having declared their submif-sion to the orders of the sultan, they answered the emir Alibeg, who summoned them to furnish the funds of the treasury, that they had never been en-trusted with them, and that the pacha must know

to

to whom he had committed them. The fame moment they received an order of the pacha to come
up to the caftle, and to treat with him on the affair
of the treafury: they faw that this was but a fnare
laid for them to fecure their perfons. Canfouhbeg
was going to refift, but Mamaïbeg diffuaded him,
exhorting him rather to facrifice himfelf to the intereft of the citizens, and to the prefervation of
public tranquillity. As foon as they had entered
the caftle, the azabs and the janifaries barricaded
the paffage with their mufkets, to hinder their attendants from following them. In the court of the
caftle they met Mohammed, aga of the janifaries,
charged with an order of the pacha to put them
into prifon; they were difarmed, and fhut up in a
tower of the caftle. Canfouhbeg vented reproaches
againft Mamaïbeg, whilft the latter entreated him
to fubmit to the will of heaven. The next day
they were ftrangled in prifon, (the 1ft of July 1647).
Canfouhbeg attempted to defend himfelf, and it was
with difficulty they could get the better of him;
the other emir on the contrary continued his prayer
with great compofure, till the moment the executioners came up to ftrangle him. Their bodies
were expofed in the place of Romelia, in the fight
of the army, and interred the fame day. Several
other emirs were alfo apprehended at the fame time,
and punifhed in like manner. The tranquillity which
had been re-eftablifhed by this revolution was again
interrupted fome time after by the cabals of the
emir Muftapha-alfchefchnir, ketkhoda of the tfchaoufchs.

6ufchs. The place of fandjac of the emir Canfouhbeg had been promifed to him, and as they deferred
fulfilling this engagement, he fell out with the emirs
Redhwanbeg and Alibeg, and irritated the pacha
againft them.

Monday the 8th of Ramadhan, (7th of October
1647,) Alibeg received an order from the pacha to
quit Caïro, and to fet out without delay for his government of Djirdje. Friday the 12th of the fame
month the pacha gave a great feaft, and fent re-
peatedly for Redhwanbeg to affift; this emir, fuf-
pecting fome furprife, conftantly refufed attending it. The pacha, to have his revenge, took away
from him the place of emir-elhadj, and gave it to
the emir Haffenbeg, fon-in-law of Nakib. Redhwanbeg refolved immediately to quit Caïro and to
go in queft of Alibeg; the fame evening he fet off,
and departed with about two hundred men, among
whom there were fome emirs and feveral cafchefs:
they left the town furrounded by a crowd of people,
and repaired to the fuburb Carafa. The next day
the pacha vefted with a caftan the emir Youffouf-
begdefterdar, named him emir of Djirdje, and ordered two thoufand men of the garrifon to hold
themfelves in readinefs to march againft the emirs
Redhwanbeg and Alibeg, under the orders of Abedibeg. The emir Abedibeg, confcious of the injuftice of this enterprize, employed the whole night,
with fome friends of Redhwanbeg, in intrigues to
prevail on the fandjacs to oppofe the execution.
The next day the whole army repaired to the place
of

of Romelia, the fandjacs went up to the caftle, and proteſted that they would not execute the orders of the pacha, unlefs he produced the orders of the fultan, and fet himfelf at the head of the army: all the troops teſtified they were of the fame refolution. In that moment the emir Ibrahim, ketkhoda of Redhwanbeg, arrived from Conſtantinople; he was charged with a caftan from the fultan Redhwanbeg, and with an order, conferring on him the place of emir-elhadj for his life: the fultan had alſo entruſted him with a like prefent for Alibeg, and likewife confirmed him in his government of Djirdje for the remainder of his days. The pacha having taken cognizance of the fultan's orders, fent the caftans to the two emirs, joined two others in his own name, and begged of them to return to Caïro. The emir Muſtapha, ketkhoda of the tfchaoufchs, was then fearched for, and fome other officers who took part in the affair. Friday the 19th of Ramadhan, Redhwanbeg and Alibeg returned to Caïro, and after having reciprocally fworn inviolable union, Alibeg returned to Djirdje, and Redhwanbeg to his own houfe.

The 6th of Dhoulhadja 1057, (2d of Jan. 1648,) it was reported at Caïro, that the vizir Muſtapha Pacha had been nominated governor of Egypt inſtead of Pacha Mohammed ben Haïdar; but the 26th of the fame month they were informed that the fultan had taken away from him that government to nominate the vizir Pacha. This pacha totally negleſted affairs to give himſelf entirely up

to

to pleafure; yet the government was not difturbed by any revolution. When he left Egypt, Ahmed Pacha, his fucceffor, fettled his accounts: he was found indebted to the treafury feven hundred puffes. Ahmed affented to his paying them at Conftanti-nople; but at his return to that city, the fultan con-fifcated his whole fortune, and thofe of the people of his houfehold.

Coronation of the Sultan Mohammed (Mahomet IV.) Son of Ibrahim: Beglerbegs of Egypt, under the Reign of this Prince.

Mohammed was crowned the 17th of Redjeb 1058, (the 8th Auguft,) and the account of it was received at Caïro, at the beginning of Ramadhan, of the fame year. Mohammed nominated to the government of Egypt, the vizir Ahmed Pacha, who had been formerly ketkhoda of the capidjis. The whole time of his government, which lafted two years, was agitated by great difturbances. In the year 1060, (1650) the Nile did not rife higher than fixteen dhira, which brought on a great cala-mity: fcarce any land of the Lower Egypt could be watered; and in the upper part, there was fcarcely one-third that could be laid under water. Although the Ahmed Pacha had amaffed greater fums than any of his predeceffors, he informed the porte, that he could not fupport the expenditures, and fent but two-thirds of the ufual treafure. The emir Kedhvanbeg having departed the fame year, with the caravan, the pacha, who had always entertained

tertained an averſion to him, wrote to the ſultan to
diſpoſſeſs him of his place of emir-elhadj, and to
transfer it on Alibeg, who had no knowledge of
his intrigue. The ſultan ſent him orders agreeable
to his requeſt ; and as ſoon as he had received them,
he ſummoned the emir Alibeg, and put him in poſſeſſion of this dignity. His intention was to divide
thoſe two emirs, and he reſolved to make Kedhwan-
beg feel the weight of his power, as ſoon as he
would be returned : but the night of the Saturday,
6th of Safar, it was reported that the ſultan had
taken away the government from Ahmed Pacha.
Redhwanbeg heard thoſe different accounts without
teſtifying any emotion, either of indignation or joy,
and the people conceived ſuch a high idea of his
virtue, that they gave him no other appellation but
that of Scheïkh Redwan. Alibeg having ſet out
to meet him, Redhwanbeg teſtified to him, that his
intention had been to reſign that place even in the
preceding year; they jointly entered the city, in the
night of the acclamations of the people, and ſur-
rendered themſelves at the carameïdan, where the
caïmacam received them with every kind of diſtinc-
tion, and made preſents to them and the men of
their retinue.

Wedneſday the 10th of Safar, the emir Alibeg
re-aſſembled all the troops, and diveſting himſelf
in their preſence of the caftan, which he wore as
a mark of his new dignity, put it on Redhwanbeg.
The ſandjacs ſettled the accounts of Ahmed Pacha,
and aſked payment of him for what he remained

indebted

indebted. At the fame time the commiffaries of the receiver of the revenue diftined for Mecca and Medina, charged him with having fold the graih that was deftined for the fupport of thefe two places, and claimed of him 3600 ardabs of corn, and the expences of the tranfportation. Ahmed refufed payment, and was fhut up in the caftle of Jofeph. This affair was concluded by an agreement; Ahmed went out of prifon, and made his way to Romania.

The vizir Abdervahman Pacha fucceeded him: he occupied this place till the beginning of Schawal of the year 1062, (1652), when he was difpoffeffed: he had many contefts with his fucceffor, for the payment of what he was owing to the treafury, and was fhut up in the caftle of Jofeph, alfo called *Carfar alablak.* This conteft was terminated by the interference of the fandjacs; Abdervahman was reftored to liberty, and departed with a numerous train.

His fucceffor, the vizir Mohammed Pacha was appointed to the government of Egypt, the 5th of Schawal 1062, (19th of September 1652,) and made his entry at Caïro, Tuefday the 8th of Moharvam 1063, (10th of December 1652).

The fourth chapter of the work of Schemfeddin, treats of the different diftricts of Egypt, and the number of the towns and villages in both.

Egypt is divided in two parts, the higher called Kibli, that is fouthern, and the lower which is called Bahri, that is maritime: it contains at this time

fix-

fix-and-twenty departments (amel). In the Lower
Egypt are the following departments: Scharkie,
Rihaïyé, Dekehlié, where writing paper was formerly manufactured, the trade for which, extended
to all countries where the Mahometan religion is
profeffed; the ifland of Kavifnas named to this day
Garbié, whofe capital is Mehalea, the diftricts of
Semenoud, Rikawié, Menouf, Nefterawié, Four,
the two Mazahamé, of Djeziré-beni-Nafr, Baheïré,
Alexandria and Djauf-Ramfis. The meridional
part includes the department of Djizé formerly fo
famous for the abundance and excellence of its
fruits, and by the beauty of the flowers it produced;
thofe of Atfih, of Aboufir, of Faïoum, a town built
by Jofeph; of Belineffa almoft in ruins at this time,
where formerly fine wrought carpets were manufactured; of Manfelout and of Ofyout. This latter
town was renowned anciently for its manufactory of
all kind of fine ftuffs; it alfo carried on a great
commerce in flax with all countries muffulman or
infidel. At prefent its commerce is entirely reduced, and it is from Faïoum that the fineft flax is
drawn. At Oyfout bitter oranges are to be found,
and geefe of an extraordinary fize, fome which
weigh one hundred and twenty pound (rotl). The
department of Akhmin belongs ftill to Upper
Egypt: this city is remarkable for its many ancient
monuments, for its fheep, and for its talifmans.

There were here formerly two kinds of myro-
boluns, called *citrinum* and *chebulenfe*, (ihliledj asfar,
myrobal citrinum, ihliledj cabuli,, *myr chebulenfe)*
and

and the hyofpiam* (fchedjer albendj *byofciamus datura*) which is fo fcarce. Several kinds of fluffs were made at Akhmim, known by the name of *motraf*, *motarraz*, *molam abyadb and molam mulawan*: a coat of the latter ftuff, or of motraf, coft fifty pieces of gold. The other departments of Upper Egypt are thofe of Coufs, of Afwan, and of Alwahat, (the Oafis).

The reft of the chapter contains only extracts of different authors, relative to the fertility of Saïd, and chiefly of the territory of Coufs and Afwan: fome accounts of the ancient Memphis, of little importance, and an enumeration of feveral cantons of Egypt, with the number of villages in each of them.

The fifth chapter contains the texts of the Alcoran, of the traditions, where Egypt is mentioned, and the excellencies of that country.

In the fixth chapter, the author fpeaks of the prophets who have preached the worfhip of one. God.

The feventh chapter contains fome eulogia on Egypt, and the names of the princes and prophets who have chofen it for their refidence.

The eighth chapter treats of the hiftory of the prophets, fages, and moft celebrated princes of Egypt: this is but a compound of fables.

---

* It feems that the Arabian name is alfo given to the *ftramonium*, or *dalura methel*. It is even given, though improperly, to the preparation of leaves of hemp, which the Arabians make ufe of, to put themfelves in a kind of intoxication. See the Dictionary of Meninfki.

The ninth chapter fuccinctly treats of the conquest of Egypt by the Muffulmans. The author defcribes Babylon under the names of *Omm-dcnin* and *Almaks*, which names are unknown to me, and which I do not recollect ever having read in any other writer.

The tenth chapter contains an account of the fortified towns of Egypt; of the commercial ones of the *mefcheds*,* the moft famous one of Caïro, of Alexandria, of Djidze, and of Carafa. We alfo find fome fables refpecting mount *Mocattam*.

In the eleventh chapter are found collected, the remarkable fayings by which feveral princes or philofophers have celebrated the fertility and excellencies of Egypt. About forrages we read the following article:

The meadows in Egypt begin to thrive at the end of the month Paopi, and are fit for mowing in the month of Choïac†: then the beafts go out to graze. Thofe meadows are overgrown with a kind of trefoil (kort, *trifolium Alexandrinum*), the feed of which is called *berfim*; it is fown in Paopi, and the crop is gathered in the months of Choïac and of Zobi‡: it is a moift forage which purges the

* Chapels built over the tomb of perfons who have diftinguifhed themfelves by a pious conduct, and a life confecrated to religion, or who died in its defence.

† Paopi is the fecond month of the year of the Cophtes, and anfwers to October: Choïac is the fourth, and anfwers to December. Lower down may be found an abridgement of the calendar of the Cophtes.

‡ Fifth month of the Egyptian year, which anfwers to the month of January.

horfes,

horfes, keeps them free from diftempers, and at
length fattens them.   Thefe forages are preferable
to the paftures of Syria and Irak; they alfo contribute to the affording a honey of a fuperior quality
to that of all other countries.   In general there is
no foil more fertile than that of Egypt.   This chapter ends with verfes of feveral poets, on the charms
and excellencies of the fpring.

The twelfth chapter enumerates the produce of the
taxes at different periods.   According to the report of
fome catebs of the divan, the impofts of all Egypt
in the year 1035, (1625) produced 1,800,000 dinars, of which 600,000 only had been fent to Conftantinople; the reft ferved for the fupport of
Mecca and Medina, and for the payment of the
fandjacs and the troops.   In this fum is not in-
cluded the value of what the beglerbeg receives
from the income of the military tenures, and of the
prefents of every defcription, camels, horfes, mules,
ftuffs, and fugar.

In the thirteenth chapter the author treats of all
that relates to the natural and œconomical hiftory
of Egypt.

We find in Egypt, horfes, affes, and excellent
mules.   There are two kinds of horfes peculiar to
that province; the one called *fafrani*, the other
whofe hair is of a cornelian colour.   Studs was formerly erected, to whofe fupport the funds of land
had been appropriated, which annually produced
300,000 pieces of gold.   The mines of Egypt are
mines of gold and filver, a mine of emeralds higher

up than Afwan, mines of nitre, of allum and of *baram**; quarries of black marble in the mountain near Suez, yellow marble and red marble in Upper Egypt, and mines of grey and white salt: the latter called *fultani* is found in the environs of the lake Menzalé. Mines of natron are also seen in Egypt†: whatever is thrown into those mines, is converted into natron. After drawing from a pit several hundred weight, it continually fills itself up again, and no vestige can be perceived the next day, of the void made in it. These mines contain a kind of stone called maffawic‡, that is, toothpicker, in the inside of which there is something which, if moved, produces a noise. These stones are an ex-cellent prefervative to women subject to miscarri-ages; it suffices that they carry any about them to efcape those accidents: Thus they prevent the abor-tion of mares, and the untimelinefs of the fruits of the palm tree. Lime stone (felfidadj§) are also found in a lake near Afwan; and at Okfor they make pottery of a peculiar earth called *fikaa*‖.

---

* This the name of a stone drawn from the mountains of Upper Egypt, and of which they make kitchin utensils, kettles, and the like veffels. It hardens by the fire : I fancy it is the kind of stone, known by the name of serpentine.

† Forfkal. Fl. Æg. p. xlvi.

‡ Thofe are Eagles stones. Pocock's Travels, Book I. chap. ii.

§ This name is common to lime, to a kind of parget stone, and to cerufe or lead lime. It must be taken here in one of the first acceptations.

‖ It feems to be a kind of clay. Defcer. Æg. Abulfedæ, page 15.

That

That kind of wheat which they call *Joseph's wheat*, is peculiar to Egypt, as also the oil of turnips (fidjel, *rafanus sativus*) both sweet and hot, and that which is used in the composition of medicines. It also produces the speckled ebony (ebnous ablak) and the balm oil (balsam, *amyris opobalsamus*). It was at Aïnschems, particularly (Keliopolis) near Materea, that this tree was formerly found. On this the Christian kings set a great value, and ranked it among the number of the most precious things: there is no more at present in that canton, and that used for medicines comes from Hedjaz. Egypt furnishes opium also, which is an object of commerce; we find here the various coloured orange, and a species of red peach called Zehri. It is the only country where the sirup of honey is extracted, and it has always been one of the tributary acknowledgments which the governors were obliged to make to the vizirs and califs. We find in Egypt the mullet, a kind of fish known to the ancients under the name of *abermis*, and which is called to this day *bouri* (*mugil cephalus**). It is exported salted from Egypt, and is also one of the obligations imposed on the governors. There is likewise in that province the palm tree *berni*, the dates of which are gathered before their maturity. Wax and honey are better there than any where else, They make various kinds of cheese, and a vinegar of wine better than any one known. Egypt produces also lu-

* It is the fish, which are employed in the making of botargos. Pocock's Travels, Book I. chap. iii.

pins,

pins (tirmis, *lupinus*), peafe of a fpecies peculiar to that country (djulban†); the fummer melon, the melon abdali (bitikh abdelawi, *cucumis chate*); fugar canes during feven months of the year; the caffia (khiar fchenbar, *caffia fiftula*) of which the phyficians recommend the ufe to give a fofter dif. charge to the bile, the *fcinc* (fkinkour,) the ichneumon (nims, *viverra ichneumon*) and a kind of weafel named *ris*, which are both of great utility, as they eat up the vipers; laftly, the ferpents which are employed in the compofition of theriaca, and the wild ox, of whom a fingle limb is worth as much as a whole ox of another country. There are in Djauf fome, from which feven hundred pounds of fat may be drawn. This fat is carried to Kolzom, Djidda, Eden, and to the coafts of China and of India, it ferves to pay the fhips. The giraf (ziràfà) and the rhinoceros (kerkend) are alfo found in Egypt, as alfo a kind of wild cow, which may be milked, but is not fit for tillage. The acacia

---

* Some authors tranflate this name by that of peafe of India, *Pifa Indica*. Mr. Forfkal defigns, under this name, a kind of trefoil, *trifolium melilothus diffufus*. I have followed the interpretation of that of our dictionaries, which I thought to be moft correct. It may be that the Egyptians give alfo this name to a kind of trefoil: it is known that there is relation between thefe different plants. Pocock's Travels, Book IV. chap. iii. fpeak of a kind of vetch or peafe, in ufe among the Egyptians; they call it *baum*. This word is not found in our author. It is perhaps the kind of peafe he calls *bimmifs* or *bommofs*, and which I have rendered by chick peafe.

(fount),

(fount*), is alfo one of the productions of this country: it is a wood that burns without leaving any afhes; there is no harder wood, nor any that keeps up a longer fire: an hundred weight of this wood yields hardly a pound of afhes: it produces but very little fmoak: they make a hard kind of coal out of it. Egypt is the only country where chickens are hatched in the dunghill. The fale of thefe chickens defrays every year the taxes of a moft extenfive canton, and they ferve befides to maintain the inhabitants.

Aftrological, Aftronomical, and Œconomical Calender, of the Egyptians.

The firft month of the Egyptian year is Thoth. In this month it is not good to lay the foundation of a building; the twenty-firft days are in no degree favourable to commerce; nor is it then proper to make long leafes. They may avenge, with fuccefs, againft their enemies during the firft part, and of their neighbours in the fecond. It is in this month that they begin to raife flax, and to few

* See Pocock's Travels, Book IV. chap. viii. the Egyptians call it *fcont.* There is great room to believe that this kind of wood is that which the Scripture defcribes under the name of *Setim,* in Hebrew *Schittim.* The re-duplication of the *Tetb,* in this word points out, as in feveral others, the abfence] of the *radical noun.* See Forfkal Flora Ægypt. This learned, man defigns this fhrub by the names of *mimofa nilotica* ; the Arabian name is fpelt, page 77 of his work, badly. This fpe- cies is not found among the fpecies of the *mimofa,* which he has given a defcription of in his fixth century.

lucerne

lucerne, (berfim). The earth chops or breaks in all parts of Upper Egypt. The greateft crop of frefh dates is made in this month, and they are better than thofe at any other time. The fpecies of pomegranites, named *feferdjel pyrufhadienfis*, and the winter raifin, are in abundance. This is the time for clarifying by the fun Oil of Séfame, and other liquors. There are great numbers of fmall fifh, and the larger fort are fatter at this time than at other feafons. The firft day of this month is the beginning of the year of the Cophtes; the fourth anfwers to the firft of the month Elul; the feventh, olives are gathered; the twelfth, Venus enters the conftellation *Sarfa*; the feventeenth is the feaft of the crofs; the eighteenth, the fun enters Libra, which is the firft fign of the autumnal quarter; and the twenty-fifth, Venus enters the conftellation *Awa*. They may yet bathe during this month in the cold water, but they ought to ceafe afterwards until the return of the fummer. This is alfo the time when they begin to prepare food for the winter, fuch as that called *beriffa*, and others of the like nature; likewife they make firup of honey, which is only a compofition of honey and water. They alfo choofe this time for treating difeafes of the reins and bladder.

The fecond month is Paopi. According to the opinion of philofophers, commerce is advantageous in the firft third part of this month; in the two latter, merchandize is difficult to be fold. People ought not to contract bonds during this month;

they

they ought alfo to avoid beginning a building in
the firft part, but there is no danger in doing it in
the fecond. This month is good·for fermenting
liquors, to confume corrupt humours, and purge old
men; it is favourable for marriage; the enmities
which take their beginning at this time are of long
duration. The fifh named *benni* (*cyprinus*) and
aberfnis, at the fame time fatten; the pomegra-
nates (rimman, *punica granatum*) are now in the
higheft perfection; the rofes begin to blow; the
fheep, fhe-goats, and wild bulls, generate. They
falt the fifh *bouri*, prepare oil of myrrh, and that of
niloufar, (nymphæa lotus). The time of budding
now approaches. The fheep, the fhe-goats, and the
bulls, become more temporate, but their flefh is not
good to eat. The fourth of Paopi is the firft of
Tifchrin-ewel; the eighth, Venus enters the conftellation *Sémac*; the nights are then at the longeft duration; the eighteenth, the fun enters Scorpio; the
twenty-firft, Venus enters the conftellation *Gafra*.

The third month is named *Ator*. Philofophers.
choofe the two firft thirds of this month for laying
the foundation of a building, undertaking expeditions, and contracting bonds, but they do none of
thefe in the laft third. They make choice of this
time for marriages, and undertaking the treatment
of humours produced by the wind, the hemorrhoids,
melancholy, the gall, and infanity. They prohibit the ufe of the baths this month, and forbid
children learning the firft elements of writing and
the occult fciences. After the middle of this month
they

they begin to fow wheat, and they continue fowing till part of the following month. The flefh of the fheep is good to eat. The narciffus (nerdjes *nar-ciffus tazetta*) are plentiful; the violet (benefsedj *viola odora*) begins to blow; likewife a great number of other flowers, and the moft part of culinary herbs, and in general all thofe which are watered; as the melongéne, (badhindjan, *folanum melongena*) and fimilar plants. The herbage of the meadow is then moft abundant in the territory of Coufs. The fifth of this month is the firft of Tifchrin-thani, and the fame day Venus enters the conftellation *Zubaniât*; the feventeenth, fhe enters *Iclil*; the eighteenth, the fun enters Sagittarius.

The fourth month named *Choïac*, is proper for intrigues, and for all thofe enterprizes which require fecrecy: it is not favourable for marriages, nor for defigns of inferiors and flaves againft their fuperiors and mafters. The bean *abaffi* (bakilla) begins to grow in this month: they then fow fennigreek, (halbé *trigonella facum græcum*), the lupine, and moft fort of feeds. The firft day of *Choïac* is the beginning of the firft of the quarantines in Egypt; the fifth is the firft of Canoun-éwel; the thirteenth, Venus enters the conftellation *Schaula*; the feventeenth, the fun enters Capricorn, which is the firft of thofe of winter; the twenty-fixth, Venus enters the conftellation *Naâim*; the twenty-ninth is the feaft of Chriftmas.

The fifth month is named *Tobi*. The wife men will not travel in this month, but regard it as fatal. The

The wind blows fo fierce that life is often endangered: the green beans, (bakilla) are good to eat: they plant palm-trees, move the paſtures of their horſes, aſſes, and oxen: they begin to extract the fugar from the canes. The water is fweet and drinkable, and fuffers no change in the veſſels in which it is inclófed; it is the period for making provifion for all the year; the fiſh *benni* (*cyprinus*) is good to eat; the fodder is good and purges the horſes. The fixth is the firſt of Canoun-thani; the ninth, Venus enters the conſtellation *Beléda*; the tenth is the faſt of the eve of Epiphany; the eleventh they celebrate the Epiphany; the feventeenth the fun enters Aquaries; the twenty-fecond, Venus enters the conſtellation *Saadoddbabik*.

The fixth month is called *Mikbir*. The philofophers confecrate it to ſtudy and travelling, and feek the aſſembly of wife men, and men of fpirit. Maſters ought to be on their guard againſt their flaves. The ufe of baths at this time is advantageous. They prepare the pitchers and vaſes of earth which ferve to keep the water throughout the year. It hails more in this month than in any other; this is the time of planting trees and pruning vines: they yet keep the horſes, aſſes, and oxen ſhut up. The fifth, Venus enters the conſtellation *Saadoboula*; the fixth is the firſt of Schebât; the fixteenth the fun enters Pifces; the eighteenth, Venus enters the conſtellation *Saadoſſoud*.

In the feventh month, named *Faménot*, is the commencement of the ſpring. This is the time

that

that they may form focieties with fuccefs, undertake perilous enterprizes, and run fome danger for
diftinguifhing themfelves and gaining honour. They
ought alfo to choofe this month for travelling, to
procure the neceffaries of life, and applying themfelves to their bufinefs and occupation. It is good
for taking medicines proper to procure evacuations.
The fociety of young people are now more advantageous than of the old. The trees begin to be
covered with leaves, and moft part of the fruits are
fet on the trees. They fow the fefame (fimfem,
fefamum indicum) and pull up flax. The milk is
abundant and wholefome. The firft of Faménot,
Venus enters the conftellation *Akhbia*. The fhowry
days, named *adjouz* and *boffoum*, commence the fourteenth, and ends the twentieth; the fourteenth, Venus enters the conftellation Fargolmokaddem; the
fixteenth they navigate the fea of Roum, (the Mediterranean) and the fun enters Aries, which is the
firft fign of fpring; the twenty-feventh, Venus enters
the conftellation *Fargolmoakhar*.

The eighth month is named Farmoudi: the philofophers then treat all kinds of difeafes; they confecrate it to affemblies of pleafure, rendering reciprocal fervices, and reftoring peace between thofe
which were at variance; it is found to be proper for
intrigues, cunning, and initiating young girls into
the myfteries of love: they fay that all their good
actions have a happy fuccefs. It is in the month
of Farmoudi they begin to collect their honey;
they alfo gather their beans, (bakilla) peafe, (djulban)

ban) and reddifh feed; they beat the cods of flax for cleanfing of its fhell: there is at this time a large quantity of red rofes, which are fuperior to thofe of other feafons. The fixth is the firft of Nifan; the tenth, Venus enters the conftellation *Refcba*; the feventeenth the fun enters Taurus; the twenty-third, Venus enters the conftellation *Schartin:* it is the head of Aries, and the firft houfe of the moon.

The ninth month is called Pafchons. The wife men forbid, during this month, all kind of familiarity; they believe that the fpirits were evil-difpofed; they employ their cunning and ftratagems, and prefer the commerce of old people to that of young ones. This month gives birth to many enmities, which are generally lafting. They at this time gather the apple, *kaffemi*, and thofe which are red and named *feroudi*; the melon, *abdali* and *khazefi*; the muza, (*muza paradifiaca;*) the apricot, (mifchmifch, *prunus Armeniaca;*) and the fruit of the fycamore, (djummeïz, *ficus fycomorus vera;*) they likewife have the red and white double rofe; during the firft part of the month they fow coriander, (kofbura, *coriandrum fativum;*) it is the time of the harveft of wheat and barley: at the end of the month they gather the apple named *fchouba*, and they prefs the juice from the apples for making of cyder. The fixth of Pafchons is the firft of Iyyar; the fame day Venus enters the conftellation *Batin*; the eighth is the firft of the Martyr; the eighteenth the

the fun enters the fign Gemini; the nineteenth, Venus enters the conftellation *Thoreya*.

The tenth month is named *Paoni*. The philofophers, during this month, affect outwardly an humble and fubmiffive behaviour: they prefcribe for the epilepfy, and make thofe who are fick wear the bone of the cramp-fifh, (riâda) for protection againft evil fpirits. This is the time when the Nile begins to increafe: they then gather the four grape, (hifrim) the fig *bouni*, the red peach named *rebri*, and the white known by the name of *mofcher*; the pears *boutic* and *arfi*, the pruens, (idjafs) and the mulberries (tout). The green dates, named *balb ramekh* begin to appear. This is the period of the greateft collection of honey. There is now little wind, but much duft. Life is more pleafant at this time than any other: on the fecond, Venus enters the conftellation Debaran; the 12th is the feaft of St. Michael. It is in this night that the dew *(nokta)* falls; the 15th, Venus enters the conftellation Haya; the 20th the fun enters Cancer, which is the firft fign of fummer; the 27th they publifh the number of fingers that the Nile has increafed till that time.

The eleventh month is named Epiphi. The wife men confecrated it to doing of good works; they affift the poor, and diftribute great alms: they believe that God facilitates the payment of debts contracted in this month: they take the beft advice for purging themfelves, and procuring
evacuations:

evacuations: the peach at this time is very abundant: the figs are in their greateft perfection: the
melons begin to lofe their fweetnefs. This is the
time for gathering the pear *fuccari*, and the dates
named *balb ramekb*: they now finifh collecting of
honey. This month is the proper time for mil-
ling the cloths called *dibiki*: this is the crifis of the
greateft increafe of the Nile. The feventh is the
firft of Tammuz: the eleventh Venus enters the
conftellation Dhira; the twenty-firft the fun enters Leo: the 25th, Venus enters the conftellation
Nethra: the twenty-fixth is the rifing of the ftar
Scharialyemania, (the Great Dog).

The name of the twelfth month is *Mefori*. This
was according to the opinion of philofophers the proper time for travelling, and to make court to princes; they employ themfelves in doing good to their
inferiors, and avoid reviving their enmities. In the
firft part of this month they prefs the raifin, and
particularly that which is intended to make vinegar;
it is alfo the period of preparing the raifin jelly
called *akid*: the waters now retire, the dates of the
palm *berni* begin to appear: the fruit of the muza
is now in its perfection. The tafte of the fruit
alters on account of the great humidity of the earth
during winter. They plant the vine and moft
other trees. It is principally in this month that
they make ufe of the enchantments of Mercury;
the feventh, Venus enters the conftellation Tarfa;
the eighth is the firft of Ab; the twentieth, Venus
enters

enters the conftellation Djebha; the twenty-firft, the fun enters Vigo.

Of the Order and Manner of fowing in Egypt.

Iba Wakhfchia remarks, in his book intituled, *Alfelabat Alnabatia*, the agriculture of the Nabatheans, that in the year 806, (1403-4) the waters having withdrawn from a part of the pond of Faïoum, called at prefent the Sea of Jofeph, it was fowed, and that it produced an extraordinary plentiful crop. Each faddan* of land yielded feventyone ardabs of barley, Faïoum meafure. The ardab of Faïoum contains nine wabias; at Caïro the ardab contains but fix.

At the time of the Fatimite califs, a faddan of corn paid three ardabs duty, but this tax was afterwards reduced to two ardabs. In the loweft ground of Egypt, they fow barley with wheat and other feeds: the lands having been watered, they begin to fow whilft they are ftill moift; and the fowing of barley precedes that of wheat, a few days. It is the fame with carrots (djezer *daucus carota*); their fowing is made in the month of Farmoudi. The bean harati (foul harati), is fown at the beginning of Paopi; they eat it green in the month of Choïac. About three wabias of feed are requifite for each fadden; it is gathered ripe in Farmoudi: one fadden

* Lower down may be found an eftimate of the faddan : the meafure called Wabia is, I believe, the fame which Mr. Niebuhr calls ufehbeh. The firft Volume of his Travels, page 119, affords fome more light on this fubject.

yielding

yielding about twenty ardabs. They fow the lentils (adefs *ervum lens*), and the chick peafe (himmis
cicer arietinum), in the month Ator, as alfo the
fpinage (elbanakh, *fpinacie oleracia*), which continues fowing till Choïac. Peafe are fown only on
rifing ground: they employ for fowing of one fadden, from an ardab to eight wabias of chick peafe,
from four wabias to an ardab of peafe (djulban),
and two wabias only of lentils. The lands which
have been tilled feveral times are the beft for the
cultivation of flax; when this is gathered they cover
it over with earth taken in the marfhes. After having remained a long while in this ftate, they make
bottoms of it called fchodad, and leave it on the
ground till it is dry; then they take it away to pluck
the grain from it, called flax nuts: this grain yields
a warm oil. Flax is fown in the month of Ator:
about an ardab and a third is wanted for a faddan.
The crop is gathered in the month Farmoudi: a
faddan yielding about thirty bottoms, and of grain
about fix ardabs and a third. At prefent in
Saïd, a faddan of flax pays between three and five
pieces of gold duty; at Dilafs, it pays thirteen
pieces of gold. The clover called *kort*, and whofe
feed is called *berfim*, is fown when the waters of the
Nile begin to fubfide, but they muft not defer fowing
to the time the wind Meriffi begins to blow: they
begin to fow it in the month Paopi, and fometimes
even at the beginning of the year: each faddan requires about two wabias and an half; it is gathered
green at the end of Choïac.

They fow the onion, (baffal *allium cepa*) and the garlic (thoum *allium fativum*) from the month Ator to the middle of Choïac; they employ for one faddan from a fixth to one half a wabia of onions; it is in the month of Farmoudi they gather it: the onion deftined for the production of the feed is fown from the beginning of Choïac to the end of Tobi; it requires an ardab of feed for a faddan; it is gathered in Farmoudi, and each faddan yields about twenty ardabs.

Thefe are the fpecies fown in the winter; thofe that are fown during the fummer, are melons, cucumbers, and gourds; (bittikh, khiar, kara;) they are fown from the middle of Famenot to the middle of Farmoudi, in proportion of a fourth of a wabia for a faddan: the crop is made in the months of Epiphi and Mefori. They fow the cotton (kotn *goffypium herbaceum*) in the month of Farmoudi; they ufe for one faddam four wabias of feed; the crop is gathered in the month Thoth; a fadden producing eight hundred weight, or thereabouts, clear. They plant the fugar-cane (kaffab fuccar, *facharum officinarum*) in the middle of Famenot, the ground having been broken up feven times. The beft cane ·is that which has been covered three times with water before the end of Pafchons; an excellent ground is required for this plant, and which has been entirely covered by the waters of the Nile; fome content themfelves with plowing the ground fix times. When they plant the canes each ought to have three whole buds; they make choice of

thofe

thofe that are *leaft* open, and have a greater number of buds. After the cane is planted, that is from the beginning of the fpring, they water it every fixth day; when it fhoots, and begins to bear leaves, they muft be cleared of the weeds which grow about them, and are a kind of rufh, called (halfa, *arundo epigeios*) and the purflain, (redjlé, *portulaca oleracea*); when it is ftrong and thick, they water it eight times with buckets. They ufually plant the fugar-cane along the river; when the Nile flows high, the cane is moiftened by a ftagnant water, until it has rifen above the ground the height of a palm-tree, then they deprive it entirely of water. The cane will profper better if it happens to be treated in the above-mentioned method; but if any of thefe precautions fhould be neglected, a part of it will be loft. Before the canes rife they muft be covered with pitch to fcreen them from vermin. They break the cane in the month of Choïac; the remains of the canes muft be burnt, and a fecond fprout will fucceed, which is called *khalfa*; the former is known by the name of *rafs*; this firft crop is fit to be gathered in the month of Tobi; the lateft it can be fafely put to the prefs is the commencement of the new year. A faddan of cane produces between forty and fifty *ebloudje* of fugar-candy; what they call *ebloudje** goes alfo by the name of *mahirât*.

* This word is either Turkifh or Perfian; it fignifies, according to the dictionaries of Meninfki, Richardfon, &c. fugar-candy. He feems to defign here a fixed meafure; perhaps it anfwers to what we call a fugar-loaf, fuppofing there fhould exift no moulds of different fizes. Pocock's Travels, Book IV. Chap. viii.

The colocafe (kolkas, *arum colocafa*) is fown at the fame time the fugar-cane is planted; ten hundred weight of feed is required for one faddan; it is gathered in Ator. The melon feed is fown in the months of Famenot, Farmoudi, Pafchons, and Paoni; and it may be gathered from Paoni till Mefori. The indigo plant (nilé *indigofera tinctoria*) is fown from Pafchons to Epiphi; they take a wabia of feed for a faddan. The turnip may be fown at any time of the year; each faddan requires as much feed as may be contained in one of thofe veffels called *kadah*; it is gathered at the end of forty days. The lettice (khafs, *lactuca fativa*) is fown in the month of Tobi; it is eaten at the end of two months: they fow their cabbages (kurumb, *braffica oleracea*) in the month of Thoth. The mallows*, (meloukia) and the ibifcus, (bamia *bibifcus*) are fown in the month Farmoudi; the grain of the gourd, when the fun enters the fign of the Ram; and they are gathered in the months Pafchons, Paoni, and Epiphi.

As to what concerns trees, they plant the vine in the month of Mekhir, at the time of pruning; this is alfo the time of planting the fig-tree and apple-tree. The mulberry-tree is pruned in the month Farmoudi, and it is planted by flips; they plant likewife the almond, the peach, and the apricot trees by flips in the month Tobi. The articles that have been fown in winter, are taken up and tranfplanted

* Mr. Forfkal tranflates this noun by that of *corchorus fativus*; according to our lexicons, it is the Greek word μαλαχꝰ, *malva*.

in

in Tobi. The narciffus onion is put into ground in the month of Mefori: the jaffmin is fown in the Epagomena, called *Niffi*, or in Mekhir: the myrtle (merfin, *myrthus brafilienfis*) is fown in the month Tobi, and is planted in that of Mekhir: the bafilic (rifan, *ocymum bafilicum*) is fown in Farmoudi: the winter gilliflower (menthour *cheiranthus chuis*) is fown in Tobi, and that of fummer in Mekhir: the caffia tree is fown in the month Famenot.

The vines are pruned from the time the north wind begins to blow to the month Famenot when the buds begin to thrive; the pruning of the other trees happen in the months Tobi and Mekhir, except the willow-tree called *fidr**, which is the fame as that called nabac, (*rhamnus nabeca*) which is pruned in the month Farmoudi. They water the trees *once* in Tobi; this watering is called *maolhayat*, that is, *water of life*; they are watered a fecond time in Mekhir, when the flower begins to appear: finally, in the month Famenot, they give them two waterings, which are the laft, until the fruit begin to appear. In Paoni, Epiphi, and Merofi, they are watered once every week; in the months of Thoth and Paopi they content themfelves with watering them *once* by laying the whole ground under water.

The meafure of land in Egypt is by faddans: this meafure confift of four hundred fakemite yards in length by one in breadth; the yard is about fix dhira of government meafure.

* Forfk. Fl. Æg. Ar. p. 204.

K 3   The

The fourteenth chapter treats of the canals and bridges which are built in that country. Here is what the author fays of the canal of Caïro, called *the canal of the prince of the faithful.*

The canal of Caïro owes its origin to an ancient king of Egypt, named *Tarfis ben Malia:* it was under his reign that Abraham came into Egypt. This canal comes almoft to the town of Rolfom, in paffing near Suez, and the waters of the Nile difcharge themfelves at that place into the falt fea. The veffels, loaded with grain defcended through this canal into the Arabian gulph, to the port of Jamboa, where they unloaded their merchandize for Mecca and Medina. Omar caufed this canal to be cleared and reftored, and it was called from that time *Khalidj emir Almoumenin,* the canal of the prince of the faithful. It continued in this ftate for about one hundred and fifty years, till the reign of the Abbaffide khalif Aboudjafar Almanzor, who clofed up the mouth of the canal in the fea of Kolzom. Nothing was left of it but what may ftill be feen at this day: they give it now the names of Khalidj Hakemi, Khalidj Allouloua, Khalidj Almorakkham, and feveral others.

The canal of Abou-menedja draws its name from a Jew, who was employed to open it under the reign of the fultan Alafdhal ben emir-adjloyoufch the Toulonid.

In the fifteenth chapter the author fpeaks of the wonders and antiquities of Egypt, and gives fome

detail

detail of the Nile. Here is what appeared to me worth extracting.

Among the curious monuments of Egypt, we must place that of the berbis * which are seen at Akhakmim, at Enfena, at Coufs, on its territory at Aboufir, and at Semenoud. We fee the figures of men and horfemen completely armed, and veffels of different fizes. It is faid, that if anciently fome foreign prince marched to make war in Egypt, they were warned by the moving of fome of thofe figures. In the berbi of Semenoud, a multitude of figures and ftatues may be feen, among which are thofe of the ancient kings of the country. It is reported that a learned man remarked thefe figures of men, who wore on their heads fchafs, (caps) after the Arabian cuftoms, and that under thofe figures, it could be read: *thofe will make the conqueft of Egypt.* At Deudira in the Saïd, a berbi can be feen, in which there is a dome that has as many windows as there are days in the year. Each day the fun makes its

---

* By this name the Arabians call the ancient temples of the Egyptians; this word has puzzled feveral learned men. M. Michaelis has expounded it by a paffage in the Travels of Pocock. This traveller fpeaks of a village fituated three miles weftward of Girge, called, fays he, *Alberbi*, (the temple). But he feems to have been ignorant of the origin of this word, as were alfo the tranflators of the Arabian Geography, known by the name of *Geogr. Nubienfis.* It is a Coptic word, compofed of the article Mafcul. ⲛ or ⲡ, and of the word ⲣⲡⲏⲓ, temple. It ought not to be furprifing that the Arabians fhould exprefs the letter φ by β: it has often the fame pronunciation in the Egyptian language: they fpell equally Barmoudi for Farmoudi. I have made ufe of Greek characters to fupply the want of Egyptian.

K 4   entry

entry by one of thofe windows, and it does not return before the fame day in the following year.

The Nile is itfelf one of the greateft wonders of
Egypt; it begins to rife in the month Paoni, and
continues in the month of Epiphi and Mufori, and
fometimes even to the end of Thoth. Formerly,
when the overflowing attained the elevation of fixteen dhira, and the harveft was good, Egypt paid
the whole tribute. The beft elevation by which the
whole country could be watered was that of feven-
teen dhira; when it came up to the eighteenth, one
fourth part of Egypt was totally drowned, which was
prejudicial to fome diftricts. At this time, on the
contrary, the elevation is infufficient, 'till the waters attain three-and-twenty dhira, becaufe of the
raifing of the lands, and becaufe the fluices are not
exactly fhut. Ebn Zoulac remarks, that each of
thefe meafures (dhira) to the twelfth, is eight-and-
twenty fingers, but above the twelfth they are only
twenty-four fingers. When the water rifes to nine
dhira, it makes its way into the canal of Menhi,
and in thofe of Favium and Serdous.

The fixteenth chapter has for object the nilome-
tres or mikias, conftructed in feveral places of Egypt,
but it contains no defcription of thefe edifices.

In the feventeenth chapter the author treats particularly of the two principal mofques of Cairo
Djame-alazhar and Djame-alhakem: we find the
date of their conftruction, and the names of thofe
who have contributed to the reparation, or the em-
bellifhment of thefe buildings.

The

The eighteenth chapter has for object the general excellencies of Egypt over all other countries: the whole of this chapter contains nothing remarkable, or that is not to be met with in some other part of his work.

The nineteenth chapter is divided into forty-eight paragraphs: it contains several details on all remarkable places of Caïro; of the ancient mifr of Djirdee and of Boulac; of the mosques, the birkets or ponds; the tombs and other public or private monuments. We find some remarks on the temperature of the climate; of the character of the inhabitants; their feasts, customs, commerce, manufactures; in fine, all that can attract attention, or claim the curiofity of a stranger. The obfervations contained in this chapter cannot be indifferent to a traveller, who should wifh to compare the actual ftate of Caïro and the environs, to that in which the town ftood at the time of the author; but they are not of the fame value with refpect to thofe who have not thofe objects in view; I fhall therefore content myfelf with extracting fome particularities.

In the fifteenth paragraph we find the detail of the ceremonies which anciently accompanied the opening of the fluice of the great canal. When the elevation of the Nile reaches fixteen dhira, they begin to open the fluices to introduce the water on the land, and into all the canals of Egypt; that day is a feftival. Formerly, before they had dug the canal Hakemi, the opening was made at the canal

Khalidj

Khalidj aleantara; there was in this place a turret in which the khalif or the prince placed himfelf for the opening of the canal. This day being arrived, the fultan or his lieutenant went out of the caftle on horfeback, and repaired to the ancient Mifr, on the fhore of the Nile, at the place called *Darelnobas*, where he alighted. He found two boats, both decorated with the name of the fultan, and fet off with various ornaments; he entered with the moft diftinguifhed perfons of his retinue in the firft of thefe boats called *barraka*; the other, which wore the name of *dhabbia*, was for the reft of his train. At the fame place a vaft number of other barks of different fizes were ready, and fumptuoufly decorated for the reception of the emirs and officers to which they belong. The boat of the fultan, attended by all the others, repaired to the ifland of Roudha: this ifland, fituated over againft Mifr-elatik, between the great arm of the river and that which paffes at the foot of this city, was filled with houfes and palaces. The fultan having landed on this ifland, re-mounted on horfeback, and prefented himfelf at the nilometer placed in the middle of the bed of the river; he entered it with his attendants, and fcattered faffron fteeped with mufk and rofe-water, and after having faid his prayers, a magnificent repaft was ferved before him. The repaft being over, the boat was drawn near to the grate of the nilometer, which was covered with its gilt hangings; he entered it, and returned with all the other boats that had accom-

panied

panied him, with the found of cannon and mufical inftruments. Arriving near Mifr, he caufed his boat to be conveyed towards the mouth of the canal which enters Caïro. On his whole route by land as well as on the river, in going and returning, he threw about golden pieces, and diftributed to the people fruits, confectionary, and fuch like. The fluice he was to direct to be opened was a kind of earthen wall raifed oppofite the bridge. The fultan, or he that reprefented him, gave the fignal with a napkin to the people charged to open them, who held fhovels in their hand; immediately they fell to work on the fluice, which was thrown down in an inftant: the fultan remounted his horfe and returned to his caftle. Since Egypt has been under the Ottoman fceptre, it is the beglerbeg who difcharges this ceremony; he comes out of the citadel in the morning, and repairs to Boulac, where he finds boats ornamented and prepared for him, and for the emirs and fandjacs oppofite to the arfenal. He fails attended by all the barks, and during that time a great number of cannons are difcharged: the beglerbeg goes up the river to the nilometer, in the ifland of Roudha; that happens when the elevation ftill wants twenty fingers of fixteen dhira, and he remains in the nilometer until it reaches this degree of height; if the elevation goes on flowly, he continues there one or two days after this term. Mean while boats are prepared, they expofe thofe figures which the people call *aroufs*, (or betrothed) and which they fet up with
care,

care, and they give themfelves up to all kinds of plays and diverfions. On the day when the beglerbeg is to prefide at the opening of the fluices, he gives, before fun rife, a great banquet to the fandjacs, to the tfchaoufchs, to the mutefarrakas, and to other troops in the garrifon: after the repaft, he diftributes caftans to the cafchef, to the fcheikh of the Arabians of Djidze, to the intendant of provifions, and to feveral other officers of the military and police. He then enters the boats with all his attendants, repairs to the fluice with the beat of drums, which he orders to be opened, and paffes through the opening on his return to the caftle.

In the twenty-fixth paragraph the author remaiks, that the emir Caracoufch-alaffedi, who had the fuperintendance of the public buildings under the reign of Saladin, deftroyed a part of the pyràmids of Djidze, to re-eftablifh the bridges of that city, the walls of Caïro, of Mifr-elatik, and thofe who are between that city and the caftle built on the mountain.

In the twenty-feventh paragraph he difcourfes about the preparation of the leaves of hemp, of which the Egyptians make ufe to deliver themfelves of a kind of intoxication*; it is chiefly near the bridge called the *new bridge,* (cantara djedida) that thofe meet who make ufe of it; it is alfo called for this reafon *cantarat-alhafchaifch.* They begun,

* See Gol. Lex. at the word Nafchifch. Travels of Pocock, Book IV. chap. v. Dict. of Meninfki, at the word Bendj; and Flora. La Egypt. Arab. of Forfkal p. 55 and 67.

fays

fays our author, to know this plant in Egypt only towards the end of the fixth, or the beginning of the feventh century of the Hegira; it was the fcheikh Karendal who firft made known its properties. This plant goes by feveral names, almoft to eighty diffe-rent ones; among others they give it that of *zib* and *karendalia*, becaufe of the fcheikh Karendal. It is prepared in feveral ways; one confifts in baking the leaves of the hemp, and threfhing them until they have taken the confiftence of a plaifter; next they are crufhed in water, and when they approach to the preparation of hinna*, they are fit for ufe. The author relates feveral fingular effects of the alienation of mind † caufed by the ufe of this plant, but among the facts he relates, there are fome which I do not think worth credit.

At the twenty-ninth paragraph he makes men-tion of the pond called *Birket-arrotli*. The name of this birket comes, fays our author, from a workman who fabricated weights of iron, (rotl) and whofe dwelling was near this fpot. Feaft and diverfions are given at the time it is filled up by the waters of the river; a multitude of boats go up and down, and afford the moft delightful profpect to the houfes that lie difperfed round it; when it has dried, they

* A kind of *cyprefs*; a plant which the Arabians make ufe of to paint their nails, or other parts of the body.

† He calls this intoxication *infital* and *iftital*, and thofe that are affected by it *maftoul*, pl. *mafatil*. Thefe words, whofe root *fatal* is not known to us, feems to fignify, after the expreffions of the author, the ftate of a man, who knows neither what he is faying or doing.

fow

fow flax and trefoil. Formerly they gave, at the firft day of Thoth, a ridiculous farce, which reprefented the marriage of the canal Haferi, with this birket that received the water of the Nile through this canal; an act was drawn up in prefence of a man dreffed in the habit of a cadhi, and in the prefence of two witneffes, at the beginning of the eighth century of the Hegira.

The forty-firft and forty-fecond paragraphs have for object the police eftablifhed at Caïro; even in night time there is no danger from thieves; the ftreets and the places are always crowding with a multitude of people; the whole town is lighted at night-time by two rows of lights on the right and left fide, in all the places and ftreets of the city. This cuftom dates its beginning from 835, (1431-2.)

In the twentieth and laft chapter the author treats of Alexandria, its origin, revolutions, pharos, and of the other ftupendous works; on all thefe matters he does but copy the fables which are to be found in every Arabian author.

Governors of Egypt for the Khalifs, from the conquest of Amrou-ben-alâs, to that of the Fatemites.

Names of the Khalifs.	GOVERNORS.
Omar.	Amrou ben alâs was nominated to the government of Egypt, after he had conquered that province the twentieth year of the hegira, and quitted his government in the year A. H. 25 A. D. 645-6
	Abdallah ben Saad, died at Afcalon, in the month Redjeb 35—Jan. 656
Othman.	Kaïs ben Saad, died a fhort time after.
Ali.	Mohammed ben Aboubecr alfiddik, killed by Moavia, in 38—658-9
Moavia.	Amrou ben alâs, for the fecond time, he died in - 42—662-3
	Akaba ben Amer, to whom fucceeded in the year - 45—665-6
	Moflema ben Mokhalled; who died in - - - 62—681-2
Yézid.	Saad ben Yézid elazdi, who has for fucceffor, in the month of Redjeb - - - 69—688-9
Abdallah ben Zobaïr, ufurper of Egypt, and of feveral other provinces, after the death of Yézid.	Abderrahman ben Atba, depofed by the khalif Merwan, in 75—694-5

The

Names of the Khalifs.	GOVERNORS.
Merwan.	The khalif Merwan gives the government of Egypt to his fon Abdalaziz ben Merwan, to whom fucceeds in - - - 96—714·5
Abdelmélic.	Abdallah ben Abdelmélic ben Merwan, he had for fucceffor,
Wélid.	Korra ben Schérik, Abdelmélic ben Réfaâ.
Omar ben Abdalaziz.	Ayoub ben Scharhabil, depofed in - - - - - 101—719-20
Yézid ben Abdelmélic.	Bafchar ben Safwân alkelbi.
	Scharhabil Khantala ben Safwân, to whom fucceeded, in 104—722-3
	Mohammed ben Abdelmélic ben Merwan, depofed in 105—723-4
Hefcham ben Abdelmélic.	Alharr ben Youffouf ben Yahya, had for fucceffor, in 108—726-7
	Hafs ben Alwélid alhadhrami, to whom fucceeded, in 109—727-8
	Abdelmélic ben Refaâ, governor for the fecond time, who died the fame year.
	Alwélid ben Refaâ, died in 118— - - - - 737
	Abderrahman ben Khaled, depofed in - - - - 119—737
	Khantala

Names of the Khalifs.	GOVERNORS.
Hefcham ben Abdelmélic.	Khantála ben Safwân; nominated for the fecond time to the government of Egypt, he had for fucceffor, in - - - - 124—741-2 Hafs ben Alwélid, who had already governed that province; the following year - 125—742-3
Wélid ben Yézid.	Iffa ben Abou Ata fucceeded him, and had for fucceffor, in 126—743-4
Merwan ben Mohammed.	Haffan ben Atahiya

Hafs ben Alwelid, nominated for the third time to this government in the year 128, (745-6) had for fucceffor

Ebn Sohail aladjlani, who was depofed in - - - 131—748-9

Almogaïra ben Abdallah who fucceeded him, and died the fame year.

Mouffa was the laft governor of Egypt under the khalifs Ommiades, to whom fuccęęded in the year 132— (749-50) the khalifs Abaffides.

Note. Schemfeddin fays, that the governors nominated by the Ommiades are in number twenty-fix; we find but twenty-five here. But we do not find in this lift Mouffa ben Nowaïr, who governed Egypt under the khalifat of Abdelmélic.

Abbaffides.

Salch ben Ali ben Abdallah ben abbas.

Names of the Khalifs.	Governors.
Aboulabbas alfaffàh.	Abouawn Abdelmélic ben Yézid,
	Mouffa ben Caab.
	Mohammed ben Afchhath alkhozaï.
	Hamid ben Kahtaba.
	Yézid ben Hatem, died in 152— - - - - 769-70
Almanfor.	Abdallah ben Abderrahman, died in - - - - 155—771-2
	Mohammed, , died in 156— - - - - 772-3
	Mouffa ben Ali, fucceeded in - - - 159—775-6
Almahdi ben Almanfor.	Abou dhomra Mohammed ben Salman.
	Mouffa ben Ali, a fecond time depofed in - - - 160—776-7
	Iffa ben Locman, to 162—778-9
	Wadheh.
	Manfour ben Yézid, to 163— - - - - - 779-80
	Aboufaleh Yahya, depofed in 164 - - - - - 780-1
	Aboukotaïfa Ifmaïl, depofed in 165 - - - - - 781-2

Ibrahim

Names of the
Khalifs.

G O V E R N O R S.

Ibrahim ben Saleh, depofed in
167 - - - - - - 783-4
Motreb, killed in the month Schawal, 168 - - - - May 785
Alfadhl ben Saleh, depofed in 169
- - - - - - - 785-6

Hadi.

Ali ben Soleïman alabbaffi, to
which he fucceded in 170—786-7

Haroun
arrafchid.

Mouffa ben Iffa, depofed in 172—
. - - - - - - 788-9

Mofléma Yahya.

Mohammed ben Zohaïr, depofed
in - - - 173—789-90

Dawoud ben Yézid, depofed in
175 - - - - 791-2

Mouffa ben Iffa, for the fecond
time.

Ibrahim ben Saleh, for the fecond
time.

he had for fucceffor, 177—793-4
Omar ben Mahran.

Ibrahim ben Saleh, named for the
third time, this fame year, governor
of Egypt, died almoft immediately;
he had for fucceffor,

Abdallah ben Zohaïr.

L 2   Ifhak

Names of the
Khalifs.

G O V E R N O R S.

Iſhak ben Soleïman, depoſed in
178   -   -   -   794-5
Harthéman ben Aayan.

Abdelmélic ben Saleh, depoſed in
179   -   -   -   795-6
Obaïdallah ben Almahdi, and brother of the khalif Haroun arraſchid.

Mouſſa ben Iſſa, for the third
time, depoſed in the year 180—
-     -   -   -   -   796-7
Obaïdallah ben Almihidi, for the
ſecond time, depoſed in 181—797-8

Iſmaïl ben Saleh, to the year 182—
-     -   -   -   -   -   -   798-9
Allaïth ben Abſadhl, to 187—
-     -   -   -   -   -   -   802-3
Ahmed ben Iſmaïl, to 189—804-5

Abdallah ben Mohammed alab-
baſſi

Alhaſſan ben Djemil alazdi, de-
poſed in 190   -   -   -   -   805-6
Alhadhib ben Abdalhamid, de-
poſed in 191   -   -   -   -   806-7
Alhaſſan ben Djemil, to 192—
-     -   -   -   -   -   807-8

Malec

Names of the Khalifs.	GOVERNORS.
	Malec ben Dalhem, depofed the fame year
	Alhaffan ben Altahtah, depofed in 194 - - - - - - 809-10
Alamin.	Hatem ben Harthama ben Aayan, to 195 - - - - - - 810-1
	Djaber ben Alafchhath, depofed in 196 - - - - - 811-2
Almamoun.	Harthama ben Aayan, nominated governor of Egypt, eftablifhed to govern there in his name
	Abad ben Mohammed, to 198— - - - - - - 813-4
	Almotleb ben Abdallah alkhozaï.
	Alabbas ben Mouffa alabbaffi, depofed in 199 - - - 814-5
	Almotleb, for the fecond time, depofed in the fame year.
	Alforri ben Alhacam, died in 204 - - - - - - 819-20
	Mohammed ben Alforri, died in 206 - - - - - - 821-2
	Ebn Alforri, brother of Mohammed, was difpoffeffed by Abdallah ben Taher, who appointed as governor of Egypt in his name, in the year 211 - - - - - 826-7

L 3   Ibrahim

Names of the
Khalifs.

GOVERNORS.

Ibrahim whom he difpoffeffed, and
to whom he gave for fucceffor in
212 - - - - - - 827-8
Iffa ben Yézid aldjéloudi. Al-
mamoun having driven from the government of Egypt Abdallah ben
Taher, he gave it, together with
Syria, to his brother Aboulifhak almotaffem; the latter nominated to
govern Egypt,

Kender, who died in 219—834-5

Almodhaffar, fon of Kender, fucceeded him, and died in 220—835-6

Almotaffem.   Mouffa ben Aboulabbas alfchami,
depofed in - 224—838-9

Malec ben Kender, to the year
226 - - - 840-1

Afchnas, died in 228 842-3

Ali ben Yahya alarméni, depofed
in 229 - - - - - 843-4

Wathek.   Iffa ben Manfour.

Almotéwekkel.   Anah, depofed in 233 847-8

Almontéfer ben Almotéwekkel,
to 241 - - - - - 855-6

Yézid ben Abdallah, in the name
of Almontéfer, depofed in 252—
- - - - - - - 866-7

Mozahem

Names of the Khalifs.	GOVERNORS.
Almotazz.	Mozahem ben Khacan, died in 254 - - - - - - - 868

Ahmed ben Mozahem.

Ahmed ben Touloun, nominated to the government of Egypt, rendered himfelf independent, and was the chief of the dynafty of Toulounides. After the extinction of this dynafty, in the month Safar 292, (Jan. 904) Egypt returned under the dominion of the khalifs, and had for governor,

| Almoctafi. | Iffa Alnoufchéri, who died in the month of Schaban 297   Apr. 910 |
| Almoctader. | Mekni Almotadhédi, depofed in 302 - - - - - - 914-5 |

Aboulhaffan Zéki alawar alroumi, died the fecond of Rebialewel, 307—
- - - - 2d of Aug. 919

Mekni, for the fecond time: after him, Ikhfchid took poffeffion of Egypt, and received in 324, (935-6) the inveftiture of the khalif Radhi; he was the author of the dynafty of the Ikhfchidites, which was put an end to by the Fatimites.

L 4

Inſtructions given to Moreau de Wiſſant, Chamber-
lain; Peter Roger de Lyſſac, Maſter of the Houſhold
of the Duke of Anjou*; and Theobald Hocie, or Ho-
cre, Secretary to the King, ſent by Loys I, Duke of
Anjou, to Henry King of Caſtile, reſpecting the King-
doms of Majorca and Minorca, and the Counties of
Rouſſillon and of Cerdaigne, poſſeſſed by the King of
Arragon, with the anſwers of the King of Caſtile.
Relation of the Embaſſy of Arnold d'Eſpagne, Lord of
Monteſpan, Seneſchale of Carcaſſone; Raymond Ber-
nard le Flamenc, and Jehan Foreſt, ſent by Loys
Duke of Anjou, to Henry King of Caſtile, and John I.
King of Portugal, touching the Kingdoms of Mail-
lorque *and of Minorca; in the Month of Janu-*
ary 1377.
Relation of the Embaſſy of Migon de Rochefort, Lord de
la Pomerade, and of William Gayan, Counſellors of
the Duke of Anjou, ſent into Sardinia by Loys I.
Duke of Anjou, to judge of Arborea, to conclude an
Alliance with that Prince againſt the King of Ar-
ragon, in the Month of Auguſt, 1378.
Taken from the Manuſcript in the King's Library, No. 8448,
Folio, in Calf, lettered on the back " EMBASSIES."
No. 32, of the Manuſcripts of Baluze.

By M. GAILLARD.

THESE different negociations, all relative to
the ſame objects, are ſo much the more worthy of our notice, as they appear to have been little
known to hiſtorians. Dom Vaiſſette had however

* In the room of P. R. de Lyſſac, John of Bergnetes
chamberlain to the king, was ſubſtituted.

know-

knowledge of them, and speaks of them, but very concisely in the fourth volume of his "General History of Languedoc," pages 358, 360, 364, 366. The Balearic islands, or the islands of Majorca and Minorca, which in 799, had surrendered to Charlemagne, had both before and since that period, been many times taken, lost, and retaken, by the Saracens; when the king of Arragon, James I. conquered Majorca from them in 1229, and Minorca in 1232. Roussillon and Cerdagne had been long united to the crown of Arragon. James I. by his will, left these different estates to James his second son, who formed the branch of the kings of Majorca. There were five successive monarchs of this younger branch of the house of Arragon, in the space of a century, from 1270 to 1375. The elder branch that reigned in Arragon, and this younger branch that reigned in Majorca, were almost always rivals and enemies, whether because the elder beheld with pain the partition that had been made in favour of the younger branch, or whether it was for other political reasons. The kings of Majorca were more than once deposed by the kings of Arragon. James I. king of Majorca, had been so by Alphonsus III. king of Arrogan, his nephew; but on the death of this prince, in 1291, he was restored. James II. king of Majorca, his grandson, was likewise dispossessed in 1343, by Peter IV. called the Ceremonious, king of Arragon, his brother-in-law; and having in 1349, attempted to recover his dominions, he was defeated in battle the 26th of October, and perished.

James

James III. his fon, was wounded, and made prifoner in the fame battle: he remained twelve years
in captivity; at laft he efcaped from his prifon, in
1362. He was the third hufband of the celebrated
Joan I. queen of Naples, who was pleafed to beftow a crown on him, an unfortunate prince, and
an illuftrious adventurer. When du Guefclin, in
1366, conducted into Spain *the great companies* to
dethrone Peter the Cruel king of Caftile, the king
of Majorca paffed alfo into Spain, and went to
ferve under Peter the Cruel, the conftant enemy
of the king of Arragon, in hopes that the war
would afford him an opportunity to return to his
kingdom of Majorca. He was again made prifoner. Joan of Naples, his confort, immediately
ranfomed him; he might afterwards have reigned
peaceably with her, but he chofe rather to continue
wandering from country to country, ever neglecting a crown within his reach, to run after another
that always efcaped him. He died in 1375.

He left by his will all his title to the kingdoms
of Majorca and Minorca, to Ifabella of Arragon,
his fifter, wife of John Palealogus, marquis of
Montferrat.

This title remained intire. " The two laft
" kings," fays our Manufcript, " loft their lives in
" purfuing their valid and juft claim upon it by
" deeds and arms, without having made any re-
" nunciation, act, compofition, or treaty whatfo-
" ever, to the prejudice of their claim."

The

The laſt king had given by an act during his life, the county of Rouſſillon to Lewis I. duke of Anjou, and he had confirmed this donation by his will.

The Marchioneſs of Montferrat, his ſiſter, ceded and made over all her rights to the kingdoms of Minorca and Majorca, to the county of Cerdaigne, and as much as in her lay, to the county of Rouſ-ſillon, to this ſame Louis of Anjou; our Manuſcript aſcribes three different motives for theſe donations and conceſſions.

Firſt, *The effects, profits, and honours*, which the laſt king of Majorca had recieved from the duke of Anjou. Second, the *family relation* which exiſted between the marchioneſs of Montferrat and the duke of Anjou; and third, certain large conſiderations as well in lands as in ſums of money, which the duke had given to the ſaid lady, in compenſation of the ſaid aſſignment.

The duke of Anjou, who is here mentioned, was the ſecond ſon of John king of France, and brother of Charles the Wiſe. It is he who was regent of France during the minority of Charles VI. his nephew, and who having been called to the kingdom of Naples, by this ſame Joan, widow of the laſt king of Minorca, did not arrive to her aſſiſtance in time, and died miſerably in 1384, in his expedition to Naples; he was the head of the ſecond branch of Anjou, who were never able to eſtabliſh themſelves on this foreign throne.

It

It appears that this prince's ambition was always to procure an establishment out of France, and to raise himself to the rank of a king: it was during the reign of Charles, his brother, that he acquired the title to the kingdom of Majorca, and that he endeavoured to render it effectual.

He easily foresaw that the king of Arragon, who had been long in possession of these estates, would not consent to resign them, and would pay no more respect to the claim of a foreign purchaser, than he had to the hereditary right of his brother-in-law and nephew.

It was by force then, that the duke of Anjou designed to gain possession of the estates and dominions that had been ceded to him " by the consent, and with the will of the king, who is pleased, out of his benign favour, to heed and esteem the act as his own; and, with the help of God, Monf. d'Anjou has an intention, and proposes to pursue his claim, first by mild and friendly measures; and if by these he cannot succeed, by way of deeds and arms, in the most quick, expeditious, powerful, and efficacious manner he is able."

Having need of allies to carry on his design, he first addressed himself to the king of Castile, the natural enemy of Arragon, by his situation alone, and who had besides the most intimate connection with France.

This king of Castile was Henry de Tranftamare, who, by the protection of Charles V. the money of France, and the arms of du Guesdin, had been recently

cently feated twice on the throne of Caftile, in which he was now eftablifhed by the death of Peter the Cruel.

Henry, either through gratitude or neceffity, was faithful to his alliance with France; on this the duke of Anjou founded his application and hopes: he afks of the king of Caftile counfel and affiftance; he will do nothing without his advice; he prays him to direct him in his enterprize, to trace the plan of it; from his hands he expects to receive allies and friends; he enjoins him, he prays him, to make a good ufe of the friendly difpofitions towards him; to procure him affiftance from the other fovereigns of Europe, particularly the kings of Portugal and Navarre. He flatters him, he praifes him, he preffes on his remembrance, that, for his very great virtues, and perfonal valour, he had chofen him for brother, and his particular and efpecial friend, which feems to us to mean, *the fellowſhip in arms*, formerly fo common: he adds, that *he has put his truſt and firm hope in him, above all the kings and princes of the world, next to the king, his very redoubted lord and brother.*

It is the intereft of Caftile, and particularly of Henry, that the duke of Anjou fhould fucceed in his enterprize, and make a conqueft of thofe eftates which have been ceded to him. Firft, this conqueft will in the fame degree diminifh the power of a neighbouring enemy, ambitious and dangerous, at whofe expence it will be made. Secondly, Henry will acquire, a neighbouring friend, always ready from gratitude, from intereft, for every reafon, and

by

by every method,. in the time of need, to furnifh him with every fuccour he may defire, and which a vicinity will enable him to do. He calls to his remembrance, not as fervices for which he afks a reward, but as proof of an unequivocal friendfhip, all he had done to fecond the expedition of Henry and du Guefclin into Caftile; he had beftowed on them, *favour, counfel, and aid*; had permitted a paffage through his government of Languedoc; had furnifhed money: and when Don Pedro, driven from Caftile, had come to Guienne, to afk affiftance of the Black Prince, and when the latter affembled his troops to reftore Don Pedro to Caftile, *Monfieur counteracted the faid prince and king Peter with all his power, and caufed his people to fight at the Ville Dieu, to hinder the faid prince's enterprize; it was attended with great expence to Monfieur, and to the kingdom of France, which amounted to more than three millions.*

Henry defeated in his turn by the Black Prince, and by Don Pedro, at the battle of Navarrette, the third of April 1367, had retired to the duke of Anjou, who had received him with every kind of honour, had given him the queen of Caftile for wife, and the caftle of Pierre Pertuife, on the confines of Rouffillon, and of the diocefe of Narbonne, as an habitation to his children; and feeing the mercenary troops of Henry ready to abandon him for want of pay, he retained them in the fervice of France, and had employed them in the war of Guienne, with a view to draw the prince of Wales thither,

thither, and to make a diverfion: the prince of Wales, to have his revenge, had fent troops into Anjou, who had there taken many cities, and done damage to the duke and his fubjects to the amount of more than four millions.

Afterwards, when Henry returned to Spain under more favourable circumftances, the duke of Anjou again gave him a paffage, covered his march, and caufed him to be accompanied by his braveft cavaliers.

Since Henry had mounted the throne of Spain by the affiftance of Charles V. and the good offices of the duke of Anjou, this laft prince had never ceafed giving him proofs of his friendfhip; the year before alfo, he had fent to the fame king of Arragon, now his enemy, fome minifters, in the number of which was Thibaut Hocre, whom he had fent at that time to the king of Caftile. The object of this embaffy of the preceding year had been to perfuade him from making war againft Henry, *which was an embaffy of great expence to Monfieur.*

In confideration of fo many marks of attachment, of fo many proofs of friendfhip, the duke of Anjou prays the king of Caftile, as king Charles V. himfelf alfo intreats him, and affectionately requires by his letters,

Firft, Not to make any alliance with the king of Arragon, his fons, or his allies.

Secondly, That if the faid duke fhall determine in council, to caufe the faid king of Arragon to be fummoned, by letters or meffages, to do him juftice,

or

or to reftore his kingdoms, countries, and lands, beforementioned; that the faid king of Caftile will alfo caufe him to be fummoned, and require him, by folemn meffengers, as often as Mouſieur d'Anjou ſhall give him notice: and if the faid king of Arragon ſhall be backward to do juſtice to the faid Monſieur d'Anjou, and to render and reſtore to him his own, that the faid king of Caftile ſhall, in his own name, fend a defiance to the faid king of Arragon, as his affiftant and ally, and ſhall make war on him in chief, and ſhall caufe the faid war to be proclaimed through all his kingdom.

Thirdly and laftly. In cafe he ſhould join battle, or undertake any fiege of importance, or do any notable feat of arms, he demands an affiftance of three thoufand men at arms, one thoufand genetaires, and a thoufand crofs-bowmen, *for a third or a fourth part of the year, if the duke ſhall require it; and all thefe aids the faid king of Caftile ſhall give the faid Monſieur, at his own proper charge, trouble, and expence, without the faid king of Caftile making any demand on Monſieur, the duke, for the fame.*

The king of Caftile anfwers in the moſt fatisfactory manner to moſt of the articles of the demand; he promifes not to make any alliance, either with the king of Arragon, his fons, nor his allies, but in concert with the king of France and duke of Anjou; he confents to join thefe princes in the demands they ſhould make on the king of Arragon, and to make and declare war againſt him, both by fea and land. He confents alfo to negociate

with the kings of Portugal and Navarre, to engage
them in the common caufe: he thinks he can anfwer for the king of Navarre, *and we juftly think he
has good inclination to do this; for he has always told
us, that he defired much to do all things which fhould be
for the honour of the king of France, and of our faid
brother.* But let us obferve that the king of Navarre was Charles the Bad, on whofe word it was
very imprudent to depend.

The moft delicate article, and which was attended
with the greateft difficulties, is that which concerns
the three thoufand men at arms, the thoufand genetaires, and the bow-men, to be furnifhed in a certain
cafe. The king of Caftile obferves, in that refpect,
that he is actually at war with England: in fact,
the duke of Lancafter, one of the fons of Edw. III.
having efpoufed Conftance, eldeft daughter of Peter the Cruel, had taken the title of king of Caftile, and was endeavouring to affert his right. He
was ftill at war with the greater part of the Moorifh
kings, and he obferves, that the king of Grenada
would not omit falling on Caftile, as foon as he
fhould fee him embarraffed. He alfo makes another
remark not lefs important: " Know alfo the faid
duke, our brother, (fays he) that the day we fhall
begin the war againft the king of Arragon, we
fhall have immediate employment for two thoufand
lances to ftation on the frontiers, which extend
more than one hundred and twenty leagues along
the frontiers of the kingdom of Arragon; and thefe
two thoufand lances we muft firft ftation there, in
order

order to guard our country from injury, and that they may make war continually on Arragon; thefe muft every day receive their pay."

In the like conjuncture, the king of Caftile contents himfelf with promifing the duke of Anjou generally, to furnifh him *fuch aid as ought to be fatisfactory to him.* " If he fhould fucceed in concluding a peace, or a truce of fome length with England, in that cafe, *it is our pleafure,* (fays he) that when the faid duke fhall do any of the three things contained in the faid article, (that is to fay, join battle, undertake any important fiege, or any notable feat of arms) to affift him with one thoufand men at arms, payed at our expence for three months."

But Henry de Tranftamere, much more anxious to prevent this war between France and Arragon, than attentive to furnifh his allies with forces which he ftood in need of for his own affairs, concluded by offering his mediation between the king of Arragon and the duke of Anjou; he defires the latter to fend ambaffadors to him, with fufficient powers to conclude a treaty, relative to the eftates and dominions which he claims; he alfo defires him to inform him of the precife fituation of the negociations which muft have been entered into on thefe affairs.

The duke of Anjou anfwers thefe queftions in a very affectionate difpatch; and here follows, in fubftance, the recital he makes to Henry of what had

paffed

paſſed between France and Arragon reſpecting his claim.

" The king of Arragon, preſſed by the king of France to do juſtice to the duke of Anjou, as to his claim and demands, anſwered by his ambaſſadors, that the marchioneſs of Montſerrat had not any title to the eſtates claimed, and conſequently could not diſpoſe of any by donation, ſale, ceſſion, or conveyance; in ſupport of theſe pretenſions, the ambaſſadors did not alledge any will or other inſtrument, nor produce the certificate of the exiſtence thereof. The duke of Anjou continuing to maintain that the king of Arragon had no title, but a violent uſurpation, Charles V. propoſed to ſubmit the affair to the arbitration of the pope and cardinals; (the pope was then at Avignon). The king of Arragon conſented to all; they ſettled the time at which the plenipotentiaries were to meet at Avignon; the duke of Anjou ſent his plenipotentiaries; the king of Arragon was in no hurry to ſend his, and fifteen days elapſed, after the time appointed, before any one appeared on his part. At laſt his ambaſſadors arrived, but without any power: they declared that they would not ſubmit *the judgment of their cauſe either to the pope or any others*, but that they would willingly communicate, in a friendly manner, their titles to the pope and cardinals. The examination of their reſpective titles was entered into before the pope and cardinals. This pope was Gregory XI. who removed the Holy See from

Avignon

Avignon to Rome. In hafte to depart for Italy, he could not determine this affair, but directed the cardinal Therouenne to bring about a treaty between France and Arragon: the duke of Anjou offered either to abide by the arbitration of the pope and cardinals, either at Rome or Avignon, or to fubmit himfelf to the decifion of Charles V. or of the king of Caftile, or of that king of Hungary, Lewis, who was then fo famous: *and the faid cardinal was of opinion, that we fubmitted ourfelves as far as we could, and as far as we or any other perfon could do*. The cardinal went to Barcelona, to carry the king of Arragon thefe propofitions, which he thought fo reafonable. The king of Arragon did not think them fo; he declared he would not fubmit either to litigation, or to compromife a title fo certain as his; but if the duke of Anjou would come to Narbonne, he would come to Perpignon, and thefe two cities being only a day's journey from each other, the cardinal mediator might eafily confer with the two parties. The king of Arragon did not come to Perpignon; he contented himfelf with fending thither his fon, the duke de Gironne, on whom he faid he had conferred all his authority, and given him unlimitted powers. Thefe powers, fo extenfive, did not however permit him to grant any thing, and to every propofition made by the cardinal, the duke de Gironne was obliged to write to his father, and wait for his anfwers from Barcelona: thefe anfwers were always evafive; inftead of the eftates demanded of him, he offered money:

firft,

firſt, *to one hundred thouſand florins, afterwards five hundred thouſand, and at other times two hundred thouſand, and then one hundred thouſand, without keeping to one propoſal.* The treaty therefore was abandoned, and cardinal de Therouenne returned to Avignon. The king of Arragon then required that the negociations ſhould be renewed: he aſſured them he was in the beſt diſpoſition, and that they ſhould perceive it by the more advantageous offers which he had to make: he accuſed the firſt negociators at the court of Avignon of too little zeal for the ſuccefs of that affair; that he ought to ſend new ones to the ſame court of Avignon, and required that the duke of Anjou ſhould alſo ſend them on his part. The duke, notwithſtanding ſo many proofs of bad faith in the king of Arragon, ſent thither, on the appointed day, to avoid the reproach of having refuſed peace; but as he had foreſeen, the king of Arragon wanted only to gain time: his ambaſſadors had no power to grant any thing, nor even to treat, *but only ſo far as to hear and report. The ſaid king has thus lead us on for two years and more, and we have not found either truth or loyalty in him;* yet out of reſpect to the prayer of the king of Caſtile, the duke of Anjou conſents to new negociations, although he does not hope any thing from them, and that he expects nothing but new delays and new evaſions on the part of the king of Arragon; *but I would rather,* ſays he to Henry, *that the buſineſs was finiſhed, and was brought to concluſion, and to effect, by you, than by any*

any other king in the world, except my lord the king; since we have more affection and confidence in you, as we also trust you have in us, rather in any other, after my lord the king, and for no other prince in the world, except my lord the king." This difpatch was dated at Thouloufe, Nov. 29, 1376.

The fecond embaffy announced in the title, was fent by the fame duke of Anjou, to the fame Henry, king of Caftile, and to John I. king of Portugal; the ambaffadors were Arnaut d'Efpagne, lord of Montefpan, fenefchal of Carcaffone, of Raymond; Bernard le Flamenc, and of John Foreft. The relation of this embaffy was in Latin; here is an extract from it:

" The ambaffadors left Thouloufe the 26th of January, 1376. They arrived the 30th, at the court of the count de Foix, when they brought over, or found him brought over, to the party of the duke of Anjou, who promifed to affift him as much as was in his power, if the treaty could not be concluded, and if it was neceffary to have recourfe to arms againft the king of Arragon. They arrived the 3d of February at Pampeluna; the king of Navarre made there a thoufand offers of fervice, whether in negociations or in war, and declared to them, in fpeaking of the duke of Anjou, that he was ready to do every thing for him, which he expreffed in a very fingular manner; *et plus fibi faceret et ferviret quam Deo.* This king of Navarre, as we have already faid, was Charles the Bad; he appeared

*fo

fo zealous in the caufe, as to be willing to take upon himfelf the mediation; but the ambaffadors, in loading him with thanks, declared that the king of Caftile was in poffeffion of that mediation, and their orders were to proceed to treat under his eyes, and by his means. They departed from Pampe-luna the 6th of February; they found near Burgos, a lord Ferrand, Fernand or Ferdinand du Guaftes, *dominum Petrum Ferrandi de Valbafto,* fo powerful, that they had credentials for him: he anfwered as the count de Foix and king of Navarre had done, by promifing every fervice that could depend on him. His anfwer is dated the 10th of February. The 11th the ambaffadors continued their journey. As they advanced into the dominions of the king of Caftile, they learned that this prince, whom they had hoped to find at Burgos or Valladolid, was gone by way of Cordova and Seville, and that he might be already arrived at Toledo. They dif-patched a courier to him to make him acquainted with their arrival, and to afk his inftructions; the courier in fact overtook him at Toledo; the king contented himfelf with a verbal anfwer by the courier, that his health required him to make a-voyage to Seville; but that the ambaffadors would find at Toledo, the infant of Caftile, his eldeft fon, in whom he defired they would place the fame con-fidence as they would have in himfelf. They re-ceived this anfwer the 18th of February, and on the 19th arrived at Toledo, where they found the infant and his council, to whom they made known

the

the rights of the duke of Anjou to the kingdom of
Minorca, and the counties of Rouffillon and de Cerdagne, and recounted all that had been done in fupport of thefe rights. The infant declared that the
king his father, as foon as he knew of their arrival,
had notified the fame to the king of Arragon, and he
defired they would wait for the Arragonian ambaffador, who could not be more than twelve days
before he arrived. They ought to have arrived
before us, according to the letters of the king of
Caftile, replied the French ambaffadors; we are not
come here to attend them: thefe are the ordinary
fubterfuges of the king of Arragon; we are ufed
to them, and we know them again; and they talked
of retiring. The infant of Caftile had efpoufed the
daughter of that king, and had a defire to reconcile
his father-in-law to the king of France, and the
duke of Anjou. He reprefented that the ambaffadors of Arragon could not fail to arrive immediately, and very affectionately preffed the French
negociators to confent to ftay, out of reverence to
God, and love for the king of Caftile his father:
*ob reverentiam Dei, et amorem domini regis Caftellæ
ejus genitoris.* He had good hope to conclude a
treaty favourable to the two opponents, and advantageous to all chriftianity; but if he perceived that
the king of Arragon fought to amufe or ufe artifice,
the bonds of attachment which held him to that
prince, fhould not prevent him from declaring himfelf warmly for the duke of Anjou, nor from affifting

ing him with all the forces of the king his father."
They refolved to wait.

During this time, the archbifhop of Toledo, chief
of the infant's council, required, for his inftruction,
as he faid, a copy of all that had been faid and done
in that affair at the pope's tribunal in Avignon.
The French ambaffadors replied, that the duke of
Anjou's title was fo clear, that he would willingly
fhew it to all the world: *videbat quod omnes homines
mundi fcirent et viderant fuum jus.* On the morrow,
the copy the archbifhop required was delivered to
him; Feb. the 22d he fent to the ambaffadors, to fay
he wifhed to fpeak to them, and when they were come,
he confeffed to them, there was a point that gave
him fome trouble, or at leaft afforded fome doubt;
it was, that it appeared that James II. king of Majorca, father of the marquis of Montferrat, had acknowledged that he held in fee, his kingdom of.
Majorca from the king of Arragon, and that afterwards, having become guilty of felony, by carrying
arms againft his fovereign, he had incurred a forfeiture. The ambaffadors replied that, faving refpect, the affair was not as the archbifhop had conceived it: *quod falvá fui gratiá non erat ita ut fibi
datum fuerat intelligi;* that the kingdom of Majorca
had never been a fief of the crown of Arragon;
that James I. king of Arragon, the conqueror of
Majorca, in dividing his eftates between his two
fons, and giving to the youngeft the kingdom of
Majorca, had exprefsly ordered that this kingdom,

and

and that of Arragon, fhould be independant of each other; *ordi navit et inhibuit quod dicta regni nullo mado fub mitterantur unum alteri*; that the kings of Arragon and Majorca had made, at different times, according to circumftances, different treaties, con-taining the refpective ftipulations and obligations, more or lefs advantageous, according to the turn of their affairs and their fucceffes; but that no de-pendence, no vaffalage, of the kingdom of Minorca, to that of Arragon, could ever be inferred. The French negotiators went farther; they urged that, though even James II. forced by circumftances, fhould have confented to degrade his crown of Ma-jorca by fome act of homage, he would not have been empowered to do it, becaufe of the exprefs prohibition contained in the original and conftitu-tional act, to which ftrict attention ought conftantly to be obferved. The archbifhop of Toledo could not withftand thefe arguments; he anfwered, *quod cer fuum, quod antea erat obfcurum, nunc eft clarifica-tum propter evidentes rationes et refponfiones fibi dictas, et ad occulum oftenfas.*

The 25th of February, the French ambaffadors departed to vifit the king of Caftile at Cordova, as the infant had fuggeffed to them, the better to fup-port the delays which he forefaw they would be expofed to on the part of the king of Arragon. The Arragonians not being arrived at the end of twelve days, the king of Caftile requefted of the French a new delay of a fortnight; but as they ex-preffed their apprehenfion of incurring their mafter's

dif-

difpleafure, Henry took upon himfelf to apologize for them to the duke of Anjou. He left Cordova and went to Seville, whither the French ambaf-fadors attended him.

The 20th of March, further complaints were made on their part, for not having heard any thing of the king of Arragon; the king of Caftile con-feffed that their complaints were but juft, but he demanded eight days more.

The 28th, the fame complaints: " Well,(faid the king of Caftile, in a voice the moft affectionate) the wrongs of the king of Arragon only add confirma-tion to your right; but for heaven's fake, once more eight days for laft and final delay: *pro ultimâ et finali dilatione five expeSatione.*"

The 5th of April the French ambaffadors re-folved to take their leave, with the confent of the king of Caftile, (who agreed with them, refpecting the bad faith and ill difpofition, of the king of Ar-ragon,) and claimed the fuccour which had been promifed to them for the war of Arragon, which was now unavoidable. But France and Caftile were jointly carrying on hoftilities againft England. This was the excufe of Henry: I cannot at once con-tinue the war to England, and take upon me ano-ther in Spain. If the duke of Anjou defires me to affift him againft Arragon, let him prevail on the king, his brother, to difpenfe with the fuccour I am bound by treaty to furnifh him againft the Englifh. The French negociators did not reply, and in fact Charles the Wife, far more concerned

in

in the expulsion of the English from France, then in the settling his brother in Majorca, requested him, as will be seen afterwards, to defer the war with Arragon, till such time as that with England should be terminated.

But what am I to say to the Arragonian ambassadors, if they arrive after your departure? said Henry. Here the French ambassadors spoke of a treaty which had been proposed by the cardinal de Therouenne, which imported that the son of the duke of Anjou should marry the daughter of the duke of Gironne, to whom the countries in dispute should be given as a dower, together with fifteen hundred thousand livres. As the contracting parties were both in their infancy, the duke of Anjou did not particularly relish this proposal, and the ambassadors did not believe him disposed to accept it, insinuating, that if yet he should ever give his consent to it, it was solely in consideration of the king of Castile. This would be a very important contract, said Henry, but I doubt whether the king of Arragon will ever be brought to ratify it. I have heard some loose hints about an offer of six hundred thousand florins, for which he might engage himself. What shall I say then, if, persisting in keeping the lands, he should propose nothing but money?—That the duke of Anjou was not willing to sacrifice lands, neither for one million, nor one and an half.—O replied Henry, he will never be sufficiently rich to make a similar offer;— and he would make it in vain; therefore let us speak

no

no longer of it. I fee too plainly, that the duke'
of Anjou will never fet matters aright with the
king of Arragon: *quòd dictus dominus dux alias
non haberet rationem fuam de rege Arragonum nifi
cum baffineto in capite.* The ambaffadors took their
leave.

The fixth of April they departed for Portugal,
and arrived the 15th at Santaren, on the Tagus,
where the court was then fitting. Their embaffy
had its fuccefs; they found the king of Portugal
difpofed to unite his arms with the duke of Anjou
againft Arragon.

But whilft they were ftill at Santaren, they received letters from the king of Caftile, in which he
announced them that he had received an anfwer
from the king of Arragon, eight days after their
departure from Seville; he requefted them to pafs
through Caftile on their return, where the infant
would then communicate this anfwer. They left
Santaren the fecond of May, and arrived the twelfth
at Valladolid, where the infant of Caftile communicated to them the letters of the king of Arragon,
who afferted, that he had entrufted the archbifhop
of Saragoffa, his chancellor, with this affair, whofe
love for peace, and talent of reconciling interefts,
to the mutual fatisfaction of the refpective parties,
he was well acquainted with. The infant of Caftile reprefented that it was no more then fix day's
journey from Valladolid to Saragoffa; he was
going to fend a courier to the archbifhop, to invite
him to confer and treat with the French ambaffadors;

dors; he afked them no more than the requifite time for the archbifhop's arrival. The ambaffadors confented to a delay of twenty days, at the lapfe of which, the infant of Caftile having no report about the archbifhop of Saragoffa, nor even the courier who had been difpatched to him, and who was, in all probability, retained to gain time, the ambaffadors took the infant as witnefs of the evident perfidy of that king, and conjured him to perfevere in his alliance with France, notwithftanding the ties that united him to this faithlefs and perjurious prince; the infant promifed it; and the ambaffadors took their leave on the ninth of June.

In the mean while the negociations continued between the king and the infant of Caftile with the king of Arragon, for we find an anfwer returned the ninth of December, 1378, by the duke of Anjou, to the propofals which the infant of Caftile had made him. The king of Arragon had at laft fent ambaffadors to treat with the infant of Caftile, on the affair of the kingdom of Majorca, and on the demand of the duke of Anjou; the marriage of the fon of the duke of Anjou with the daughter of the duke of Gironne was brought anew upon the carpet. The duke of Anjou anfwered, that this propofal feemed to him becoming, but that he did not underftand that this marriage fhould debar him of his rights, and he was ready to fubfcribe to it, provided a fair compenfation be made to him for thofe his rights.

The

The infant required that the ambaſſadors ſhould be ſent again on the part of the duke of Anjou, ſince the king of Arragon had manifeſted a reſolute deſire to ſend others on his part; the duke of Anjou reminded him of the inutility of the frequent embaſſies and conferences ſent and held on that ſubject at the court of Charles V. at that of Avignon; at firſt before the pope and the cardinals, and then with the cardinal of Therounne, and again at the court of the king of Caſtile, and the infant himſelf; and inferring from the paſt to the future, and from the diſpoſitions of the king of Arragon by his intereſts, he did no longer think it becoming his dignity to expoſe his ambaſſadors to farther delays, circumventions, and ſubterfuges; but that he repoſed an unlimitted confidence in the friendſhip of the infant, and in his protection of his intereſts and rights, notwithſtanding the title of a brother-in-law, which he bore to the king of Arragon; that he truſted in this friendſhip with as much unreſervedneſs as in that of the dauphin, his own nephew! *habet et ſemper habuit plenum et ſingularem fiduciam qualem poſſet habere de ſereniſſimo principe domino Delphino Viennenſi, ne pote ſuo.*

It is obſervable, that he gives, throughout this writing, the ſame title of nephew to the infant of Caſtile; we cannot impute this to any other relation then that of the confraternity of arms, which ſubſiſted, as we have obſerved, between the king of Caſtile and the duke of Anjou; for it does no where appear that the infant of Caſtile had been

a real

a real nephew to the duke of Anjou: either by the duke of Anjou's having married a fifter of the king of Caftile, or the king of Caftile's having taken a fifter of the duke of Anjou in marriage; and the infant, as it has been hinted in fundry places, had efpoufed the daughter of the king of Arragon.

This king of Navarre, who had fhewn fo much forwardnefs for the intereft of the king of France, in fpeaking to the ambaffadors, had now attempted, about the fame time, to poifon Charles V; the plot being detected, his accomplices had been arrefted, convicted by their own confeffion, and executed in the public markets at Paris; at the fame time he treated with the Englifh about delivering into their hands all the places the king was ftill mafter of in Normandy. The king of France and the king of Caftile united to punifh him for fuch perfidioufnefs; the infant of Caftile conquered almoft all Navarre; the duke of Anjou congratulates him in the fame letter on his valour, good conduct, and on his prudence, fuperior to his age, by which he had fignalized himfelf in that expedition; he exhorts him to profecute and complete his conqueft, without entering on any terms of accommodation with this odious prince; *qui nunquam tenuit juramentum nec promiffionem quam fecerit . . . . cum et nequiffimus ille rex aliud nunquam cogitaverit quam bella fufcitare, vicinos dampnificare, populos quietos et pacem foventes commovere, et eft credendum quod adbuc fi poffet, deteriora faceret.*

VOL. II.   N   The

The duke of Anjou informs the infant of the conquefts the king had made on his fide over the king of Navarre; he had taken away from him all his places of Normandy, except Cherburgh, where the Navarians and Englifh were actually befieged by the French. He does not fpeak of the conqueft of Montpellier, which he had made himfelf from the king of Navarre, becaufe the infant muft have received early notice of it on account of its vicinity.

: In general, the duke of Anjou, in this difpatch, fhews much lefs animofity againft the king of Arragon, his direct enemy, but who, after all, is but like moft conquerors, willing to retain and keep his conqueft, than againft the king of Navarre, whofe attempts, more recent and more criminal, muft have excited a greater indignation. We fee this prince more inclined to enter into an accommodation with the king of Arragon, and that, drawn on by events, he relaxed in his project of recovering Majorca, and other places in difpute, from that prince by force. We fhall fee fome of the reafons of this relaxation in the relation of the third embaffy expreffed in the title, and which precedes fome months the difpatch we have given an account of.

: This embaffy is of the month of Auguft, 1378, that is, it begins at that epocha. It was compofed of Migon de Rochefort, lord of Pomerède, and of William Gayan, counfellors of the duke of Anjou, who fends them to Sardinia, to Hugh,

judge

judge of Arborea, to contract an alliance with him against the king of Arragon.

We shall first investigate who this judge of Arborea was, whose alliance is courted by great and powerful princes, who send him embassies, and even ask of him (as we shall see) his daughter in marriage. The historians of Italy and Spain acquaint us with a house of Arborea, a Sardinian family, whose rights have passed by marriage into the houses of Doria and Narbonne-Lara. That house in all probability derived its name from Arborea, an ancient city of the island of Sardinia, which is thought the same as Oristagni, which was in fact the residence of the judges of Arborea.

About the middle of the twelfth century, when the Pisans and Genoese, after having wrested from the Saracens the island of Sardinia, disputed among themselves the possession, Barissone, of the house of Arborea, availed himself of their divisions to make himself king of Sardinia. He brought over to his interest the emperor Frederick Barbarossa, receiving from him the investiture of this kingdom, and submitting to an annual tribute. Frederick consented, on this condition, to his being crowned king of Sardinia; he proved unable however to maintain his post: it was his daughter that espoused an Andrew Doria. Sardinia was again shared between the Genoese and the Pisans; the kings of Arragon made themselves masters of it towards the end of the thirteenth century, by virtue of the concessions of the popes; but the lords of the house of Ar-

borea,

borea, under the title of *judges* and of *princes*, (no longer of kings,) valiantly defended their country againft thefe foreign ufurpers: towards the middle of the fourteenth century, Mariano, judge and prince of Arborea, made a fuccefsful war againft the fame Peter IV. called the *Ceremonious*, king of Arragon, the enemy of the duke of Anjou; he died about the year 1376. Hugh, his fon, is this judge of Arborea, to whom the duke of Anjou fent this embaffy in 1378: he was the twenty-fecond judge and prince of Arborea: the titles he took upon him were; *Hugh, by the grace of God, judge and prince of Arborea, count of Gofiano, vifcount of Bofa.* It was Beatrice, his fifter, who by her marriage with Amaury III. vifcount of Narbonne, carried into the houfe of Narbonne-Lara, the rights of the houfe of Arborea; and the firft-born of that branch of Narbonne bore afterwards the title of *judge and prince of Arborea.*

Hugh continued his war with glory againft the king of Arragon; this is the motive which engages the duke of Anjou to court his alliance. This embaffy of 1378, was not the firft he had fent him; he had already opened a treaty with him, which came not to execution, as may be feen by an abftract of the relation of this embaffy of 1378.

The ambaffadors departed the 5th of Auguft from Avignon; the 23d from Marfeilles; and after a voyage which was not without dangers, as the pirates continually infefted the Mediterranean; they arrived the 28th at the port of Bofa, in Sardinia, whence

whence they sent to Oriftagni, the ordinary refidence
of the judge of Arborea, to announce to him their
arrival. It was too late, when they arrived, to enter
the city of Bofa; the podeftàt and the ancients
declared to them, that it was impoffible to introduce them into the city; and that the prohibition
of the judge of Arborea was too explicit to admit
of infraction upon any pretence whatever; that the
fear from the Catalonian corfairs, who cruifed un-
ceafingly in that latitude to annoy the inhabitants
of Sardinia, rendered this precaution neceffary.
The thirtieth they arrived at Oriftagni, where the
guards fhut the gates before them, declaring that
they could not be received without an exprefs order from the judge of Arborea. The gate being
opened more than an hour afterwards, they entered
and went to an inn, where, towards the evening,
an officer of juftice, named *Don Pal*, accompanied
by four mace-bearers, and about twenty men armed
with fwords, came to receive, and lead them to
the audience of the prince or judge; they found
him reclining on a kind of fmall bed, having half-
boots of white leather, after the Sardinian cuftom,
more Sardico on his feet; both the room and the bed
were naked of all kinds of ornaments: *nullis para-
mentis in camerâ feu lecto parvulo exiftentibus*. He
had with him a bifhop, his chancellor, whom he
defired to withdraw: this judge of Arborea was an
intrepid, wild iflander, who knew little of the poli-
ticks of our European princes, who looked upon
a treaty as a facred engagement, who did not know

N 3   that

that there were fome made by way of precaution
and all hazards, and on the execution of which
nobody relies, but after the turn of interefts and
circumftances; that treaties are made on one fide
with friends to obtain fuccours againft enemies, and
on the other with enemies to do without the fuccours of friends, and to be difpenfed from furnifhing them. The duke of Anjou had made fome promifes in former treaties which he did not keep; the
judge of Arborea feverely upbraided the ambaffadors with it: " I am very much diffatisfied with your
" mafter;" (faid he to them) " he is a perjured
" man; he has not kept his word. Is it not un-
" becoming, that the fon of a king fhould fail in
" his promifes and oaths? He has hurt me; he
" drew from my ifland, by virtue of our alliance,
" the crofs-bow-men and other warriors I wanted
" myfelf; he has no ways employed them for our
" common fervice, and he has been the caufe that
" I could not pufh the war againft the king of
" Arragon with that vigour I would otherwife
" have done. He treated with him whilft he was
" allying himfelf to me. That king of Arragon
" has alfo fent me ambaffadors to treat for peace;
" I did not even admit them to my fight. I do
" not underftand treating with my enemies, to the
" prejudice of my friends."

The ambaffadors, fomewhat difconcerted at a
tone they had been fo little accuftomed to, anfwered, that their inftructions contained anfwers
fatisfactory to thefe objections. " Well," faid he,

" let

" let me have a copy of it then, as also of your
" powers; I shall give you my anſwer in a few,
" words, and I ſhall diſpatch you in a ſhort time."

We find here theſe inſtructions in Latin and
French; their contents are as follows:

" The duke of Anjou had formerly ſent to the
judge of Arborea an embaſſy, compoſed of Meſſrs.
Gillaume Mauvinet and Pierre Gilbert. Theſe
ambaſſadors had concluded with the judge of Arborea a treaty of alliance, which the duke of An-:
jou had ratified *for the ſake and honour of the ſaid
lord judge, though fraught with ſome hard articles :.
more et honore dicte domini judicis, licet in eiſdem eſſent
articuli bene onerantes.* Theſe ambaſſadors returned
from Sardinia, had informed him, that the judge of
Arborea ought alſo to ſend to him in his turn, the
more to cement thoſe alliances; the ſame had been
confirmed by ſome Genoeſe merchants. The duke
of Anjou expected theſe ambaſſadors from Sardinia,
and this was one of the reaſons why he deferred
this ſecond embaſſy, which he ſent-in 1378.·· He
alſo aſſigned as reaſons for this delay: Firſt, The
negociations entered at Bruges, for the peace between France and England; negociations whoſe
iſſue he waited, the more freely and vigorouſly to
proſecute the affairs of Arragon, the object of his
alliance with the judge of Arborea. Secondly,
The negociations which the king of Caſtile had
obliged him to permit him to open conferences with
the king of Arragon on objects of the duke's demands; negociations which the duke would never

N 4   have

have carried on so far with the king of Arragon, without the judge of Arborea; but of which
he wished to draw the effect which has actually re-
sulted, that of interesting the kings of Castile and
Portugal in the common cause. This was what
he wanted himself to be able to announce to the
judge of Arborea, before he sent him this second
embassy.

If he had not yet begun the war against the Arragonians, these negociations of the king of Castile
were in great part the cause; but, beside that, the
king of France, his brother, had requested him to
engage in that war, as long as that with the English
should subsist. Obliged to obey his king, and to serve
his brother, the duke of Anjou had been taken up
last year with conquering a part of Guyenne from
the English; and the king of Navarre having since
seconded the enemies of the state, by his crimes
and treasons, the duke of Anjou had been employed this year in dispossessing him of Montpellier
and its dependencies; but that it was resolved at
length, whatever might be the consequence, to begin
the war against the king of Arragon, in 1380. If
he took so long a term, it was the better to prepare
himself; but he was ready to abridge it, and begin
the war the very next year, 1379, if the judge of
Arborea should wish it.

Lastly, he announced to him as his friend and
ally, that a son had been born to him the 7th of
October, in the interval of the two embassies,
and offered him that son for his daughter. He did
not

not conceal, that the king of Caftile had afked him for the daughter of the duke of Gironna, fon to the king of Arragon, and that he intended to make this márriage the pledge of the reconciliation of the duke of Anjou with the king of Arragon. Several other powerful princes had afked of him his fon for their daughters ; but that it was to the judge of Arborea he gave the preference. In fact, the new ambaffadors were vefted with powers, not only to confirm and renew the alliances, but alfo to contract this marriage. A propofal like this would have, in all appearances, flattered a petty prince, who was not even comprized in the catalogue of the European princes, and whom the kings of Arragon regarded as an adventurer, and as a rebel: it did not move him at all. He anfwered, " This " propofal is only a new impofture, and is in " itfelf but a mere derifion and mockery; my " daughter is marriageable ; your fon is not yet " one year old. I mean to marry my daughter " in my life-time, and to fee her offspring, which " will procure me joy and comfort, and not to " expect winds which are to blow hereafter, & *non* " *expectare futuros ventos.*" As to the other propofals contained in the inftructions of the new ambaffadors, he replied to the following purport :

" I have given order, that the new ambaffadors " fhould be fhewn the articles ftipulated and fworn " to by the former, in the prefence of the people, " in the cathedral of Oriftagni, that they may " have cognizance of the damages and interefts,

" to

" to which the duke of Anjou has submitted him-
" self, in cafe of retraction. I shall know how, in
" proper time and place, to vindicate these da-
" mages and intereft, and to prepare for him the
" punifhment which he has incurred. I have feen
" his falfe and frivolous new offers, of entering into
" war with Arragon, with whom he may have, or
" may not have any war; it matters not to me.
" Let every one tranfact his affairs after a better
" example. The Arragonians and Catalans are
" my enemies; I have made war on them thefe
" twelve years, like my father, without any help,
" but that of God and the bleffed Virgin, in pro-
" tection of my right, and that of my fubjects,
" I fhall continue it without any other affiftance.
" I deceive no body, and I am never twice de-
" ceived. I want neither the duke of Anjou, who
" having once fhewn himfelf perfidious, muft be
" fuppofed always fo; nor of any other power.
" Let princes deceive one another, fince this fport
" anfwers their purpofe, I wifh the alliance of none; I
" am fufficient alone for my defence and my revenge.
" Bid then the duke of Anjou not to ally with me;
" or to give an infant for a hufband to my daugh-
" ter; but to feek how to compenfate for the detri-
" ment done me by his breach of the treaty;
" otherwife I fhall make my complaints, and claim
" juftice of all princes, and in the face of all
" the univerfe; not to implore their fuccour, but
" exhibit this prince fuch as he is, and that all po-
" tentates

" tentates of the earth may know how he infolts
" the facrednefs of treaties."

The anfwer terminated by thefe words: *Et hæc
eft refponfio dicti domini judicis.*

To this anfwer was added a letter addreffed to
the duke of Anjou. " I have feen your ambaffa-
" dors; they have acquainted me with your friro-
" lous excufes, I have caufed my anfwer to be
" delivered to them, and I have taken the precau-
" tion to have the whole regiftered in my chan-
" cery."

To a fharp anfwer the judge of Arborea added
alfo a fharp conduct towards the ambaffadors. The
latter having delivered their papers to the judge,
quietly waited his anfwer at the epifcopal palace,
where the judge had affigned them apartments,
and very honourable treatment. On Wednefday
the laft of Auguft, two mace-bearers, and two ferjeants, or fervants *fervientes*, armed with fwords, and
in the prince's livery, came to tell them, in the
language of the country, *in eorum fardifco*, that my
lord the judge ordered them to come to him.
When they came into the great court of the palace,
they found it filled with an immenfe number of
people; in the midft of which they could diftinguifh a bifhop, a cordelier, furrounded by other
cordeliers, a multitude of priefts and monks, and
many fervants in the prince's livery. The ambaffadors wifhed to get out of the crowd, and, as they
had done the evening before, went into a fmall
inner

inner court, which led to the judges chamber: the
door was fhut fuddenly againft them, and they were
obliged to wait in the outer court, mixed among
the crowd. The door at laft opened; and they
faw the bifhop-chancellor appear, holding a paper
in his hand, and attended by a notary and fecretary,
who had alfo papers. There was alfo with them
Don Pal, the officer of the palace; who, the evening before, had introduced the ambaffadors into
the judges chamber, the podeftat, and attending
upon them a great number of mace-bearers, ferjeants, and other fervants of the judge. The bifhop
raifing his voice, fo as to be heard by the whole
affembly, called out, in the language of the country, *in eorum fardifco*, " Good people, *(bona gentes)*
" the judge has called you hither, to acquaint you
" with the fickle difpofition and unfaithfulnefs of
" the duke of Anjou, in prefence of thefe ambaf-
" fadors, who are equally capable with you, to
" make a comparifon between the paft and the
" prefent. Here is the treaty which you have
" heard the former ambaffadors fwear folemnly to
" the execution of, in the church of St. Mary. It
" is poffible thefe new ambaffadors are ignorant
" of this; therefore we are willing to read it in
" your prefence. Here alfo are the recent dif-
" patches of the duke of Anjou, brought by thefe
" new ambaffadors, which contains a formal con-
" feffion of the breach of the treaty, with new
" promifes, which only contain new falfehoods."

This

This was the anfwer which the judge made to fuch deceit.

At the fame time he caufed to be read, or read himfelf, all thefe documents, which he commented upon, to aggravate the injuries done by the duke of Anjou, and to make the infidelity they reproached him with, appear more confpicuous: then turning to the ambaffadors, he told them, on behalf of the judge of Arborea, that they muft quit that country, and retire on board their fhips; and that it was thus the judge difmiffed them. *People of our charaɛter ought not to be treated in this manner*, replied the ambaffadors: they requefted alfo of the chancellor a copy of the judge's anfwer, and permiffion to fee him to take their leave. *Wait a moment*, faid the bifhop, and he went to receive Hugh's anfwer. Don Pal, who went with him, returned in a moment after, and told them they could not fee the judge; but they might return to dine at the palace, and wait his orders. They dined forrowfully, *mæſti et dolentes modicum pranſi fuerunt*; and after dinner, which this account calls *prandium paſſimum*, not hearing any thing, they fent fome of the moft diftinguifhed perfons of their retinue twice to Don Pal, again to afk permiffion to fee the judge: the firft time they could not even procure an interview with Don Pal; the fecond time they faw him, and received a definitive anfwer, " that the judge would not fee the ambaffadors again." All kinds of affronts were put upon them, either by the judge's order; or, as

the

the people thought, they were fulfilling his wifht they withheld the provisions they had laid ih for their fupport, and which they had juftly paid for: they ftopped their baggage at the gate of the town, and fearched it very narrowly, to fee if they had no fecret or fufpicious papers; but they had taken proper precautions in that refpect.

The fame Wednefday, the 13th of Auguft, the ambaffadors being on board their fhips, Francis Pifani came from the judge of Arborea, to bring them a copy of his anfwer, which had been read in the affembly of the people, and his letter addreffed to the duke of Anjou.

Their return to France was not without danger; above all they were fearful of meeting with fome Catalan veffels. The fhips which brought the ambaffadors, had been hired at Marfeilles; the captain was of that place. The Provençals, then fubject to queen Jane I. of Naples, were at peace with the people of Arragon and Catalonia. This removed one danger. The fhip put into a port in the gulph of Algery, to take in water, ten miles from that place: Algery, and that part of Sardinia, belonged to Arragon. A bark arrived, bearing the flag of Marfeilles; many people came from on board her; among others, a conful, refident at Algery, for the Marfeillians and Provençals. They went on board the ambaffador's fhip, and addreffing themfelves to the mafter, faid, they were fent by the governor of Algery, who was furprized, confidering

dering the friendſhip which ſubſiſted between the
Provençals and Catalans, that the maſter had not
applied to him for refreſhments; he therefore prevented him, by ſending them to make the offer.

" We are well provided with every thing," ſaid
the maſter; and to convince them of it, he treated
them with excellent wine, in ſilver veſſels, and began
to drink with them. Thus drinking and talking,
they aſked him, in a friendly manner, where he came
from ? " I came," ſays he, " from cruiſing for
" ſome Sarracin cruiſers, who have been plundering
" in the ſea of Marſeilles."—" Oh, no !" replied
one of thoſe who were ſent from Algery, " you are
" returning from France, and have on board two
" French ambaſſadors." He then told him all their
names, ſurnames, titles, and qualities. " The go-
" vernor of Algery," added he, " is well informed
" of it, and is not a little uneaſy. How can you
" be ſo imprudent as to engage yourſelf here in an
" Arragonian port? Take my advice; do not
" ſtay here any longer; you will not be ſafe."—
The patron, who was a man of ſpirit, *qui magnanimus
exiſtebat alto corde*, replied, " Do you adviſe me ſo ?
" Well, then, what you ſay is true. I have the
" French ambaſſadors on board my ſhip; I deſign
" to land them ſafe and found at Marſeilles. I do
" not fear the governor of Algery; let him do the
" worſt he can; *faciat pejus quod facere poterit.* I
" will not depart from hence before to-morrow
" morning. I will ſup, I will ſleep here; if they
                                                    " wake

" wake me, they muſt take the conſequence, and
" know, that there is not in the port of Marſeilles
" a ſingle veſſel, which (ſaving the allegiance due
" to our ſovereign), is not at the ſervice of the
" duke of Anjou."

After this diſcourſe they went away; the maſter
remained, as he had ſaid he would, and did not fail
until next morning. The name of this brave man
was John Caſſe.

The ambaſſadors, in the other part of the paſſage, met with violent tempeſts, which ſtrained
their ſhip ſo much that ſhe leaked in every part,
and every one expected to periſh. They went
into port and caulked her. They were ſcarcely at
ſea again, when they ſaw two veſſels (corſairs), who
chaſed them, but their ſhip being the beſt ſailer,
eſcaped.

They did not arrive at Marſeilles until the 16th of
September. They were indebted to the maſter
one thouſand and ſeventy-five livres for paſſage, a
ſum they were not in poſſeſſion of; they therefore
offered him pledges. The generous Caſſe refuſed
them, and would take no other ſecurity than their
promiſe, and the patronage of the duke of Anjou.
They arrived the 18th at Avignon, where they remained ſome time, and it was not till the 11th of
October that they could ſend to the duke of Anjou, at Thouloufe, the anſwer and the letter of the
judge of Arborea, and to render an account of the
bad ſucceſs of their embaſſy.

This

This is all this manuſcript furniſhes us with relative to the claim of the duke of Anjou, on the kingdom of Majorca, and the counties of Rouſſillon and Cerdagne. It ſeems as if this affair was given up, the duke having always been employed about other objeĉts more preſſing; the war againſt England was prolonged; Charles V. died in 1380, and the duke of Anjou became regent of the kingdom of Francis. His being afterwards adopted by Jane of Naples, carried him to Italy, where he died; and the uſurpation of the king of Arragon ſeems confirmed by length of time.

This was the reſult of a multitude of pieces, of which we have only mentioned the three principal in the title. We think to give our readers a proper idea of this manuſcript, we ought to preſent them with a kind of inventory of all the pieces, in the order they ſtand in it.

The firſt of theſe pieces is without a title, this is not entirely foreign to the buſineſs we have juſt been ſpeaking of, but which has only an indirect and diſtant reference. It is the marriage contract, in Latin, of Blanch of Bourbon with Peter the Cruel, king of Caſtile, brother and predeceſſor of Henry of Tranſtamare.

The ſecond are the inſtructions given to the firſt ambaſſadors, by Henry king of Caſtile. This is the firſt piece mentioned in the title.

The third has for title, *The Cauſes and Motions which the Meſſengers of my Lord the Duke may make*

uſe

ufe of to the King of Caftile, to induce him to conde-
fcend to the prayer and requeft of my Lord the Duke.

The fourth is the anfwer of Henry king of Caftile to the requeſt of the duke of Anjou.

The fifth, a letter of the duke of Anjou to the
king.—The four laſt are in French.

The fixth is a relation of the fecond embaſſy from
the duke of Anjou to the king of Caftile. This
is the fecond piece announced in the title.

The feventh is an anfwer of the duke of Anjou
to the infant of Caftile, on fome propofals of accommodation with Arragon.—The two laſt in
Latin.

The eighth has this title: *Hic continentur qui
poſſunt facere guerram in Catalaunia et in regno Major.*
This piece, in Spaniſh, is only a liſt.

The ninth is the relation of an embaſſy to the
judge of Arborea. This is the third piece announced in the title, and is in Latin.

The tenth and eleventh are the fame pieces, in
French and in Latin, under thefe two titles: *Rotulus credentie in Gallico*; and *Rotulus predentie ex Gallico in Latinam tranflatus.* Thefe are letters of credit, and inſtruꜩions given to the ambaſſadors going
to the judge of Arborea.

The twelfth is a power to confirm alliances, and
to form new ones: *Procuratorium fuper allegantiis
jam faꜩis confirmandis, et de novo etiam faciendis.*

The thirteenth is a power to prevent the marriage between the fon of the duke of Anjou and

the

the daughter of the judge of Arborea : *Procura torium fuper matrimonio contrahendo.*

The fourteenth and laſt is the anſwer of the judge of Arborea, with his letter to the duke of Anjou.—Theſe three laſt are in Latin.

The other pieces contained in the ſame volume, and which are very numerous, will furniſh materials for ſeveral other accounts.

NAR-

NARRATIVE

OF THE

DEATH of RICHARD II.

KING of ENGLAND,

In the Year 1399.

Taken from the Manuſcript in the King's Library, No. 8448, bound in calf, and lettered on the back " EMBASSIES." No. 22, of the Manuſcripts of Baluze.

By M. GAILLARD.

THIS is the ſame volume that has already furniſhed us with ſo full an account of the negociations reſpecting the kingdom of Majorca and
Minorca, and the counties of Rouſſillon and Cerdagne, invaded by the king of Arragon, and re-
claimed by Louis I. duke of Anjou. We have no
clue to lead us to the author of this narrative, from
which we ſhall give an extract; but he appears to
be a man of information; his account is intereſting,
and he preſents us, in the minuteſt circumſtances,
with a juſt picture of the manners of the age, and
country of which he writes.

Richard II. king of England, whoſe melancholy
death we are about to relate, ſon to the Black
Prince, and grandſon to Edward III. was the con-

O 3   temporary

temporary of Charles VI. and as much the friend of that prince, as his father and his uncles had been the enemies of his predeceffors. Thefe two kings were of the fame age, both in their infancy when they began to reign, and both governed by three uncles, on the father's fide, who were ambitious and defigning. Fate feems even to have ftudied to give to the uncles of the king of England the fame difference of character as to the uncles of the king of France; and this difference of character took place in the fame order. The duke of Lancafter, regent of England, poffeffed the haughtinefs, ambition, and rapacity of the duke of Anjou; the duke of York in effeminacy and indolence refembled the duke of Berry; and the duke of Gloucefter had the audacity and turbulence of the duke of Burgundy.

Richard, though two years older than Charles VI. was his fon-in-law, having married his daughter Ifabella. The marriage could not be confummated, becaufe of the tender age of the princefs; but fhe was educated in England, where the eyes of the nation were offended at the fight of a French princefs.

It is remarkable that all the kings of England, who have efpoufed princeffes of France, have been hated by their fubjects, and have come to an unfortunate end: witnefs Edward II. Richard II. Henry VI, and Charles I. This is not our defcription of thofe hiftorical fingularities for which we are at a lofs to account; but the natural effect

of

of a very obvious caufe. It arifes from the rivalry and national hatred of the two countries, from the difference of conftitution, manners, and principles of government, and from the fear, whether founded or not, that a French princefs would inftil into a king of England the defire of rendering himfelf abfolute, and point out to him the way of becoming fo.

There could be no ground for this apprehenfion with refpect to the daughter of Charles VI. who left France at the age of fix years, and who was only ten when Richard died. But all the kings of England who have had a friendfhip for kings of France, have been accufed, or fufpected, of a defign of learning from them how to render themfelves abfolute, and of availing themfelves of their affiftance in order to attain their end. The attachment of Charles II. and James II. to Louis XIV. though they had not married princeffes of the houfe of France, was fufficient to expofe the former to continual oppofitions, and to drive the latter from his throne.

Henry V. is the only inftance of a king of England marrying a French princefs without bad confequences to himfelf; and this was becaufe he took advantage of the marriage to opprefs and invade France; a meafure highly pleafing to the Englifh, who faw not that the title of conqueror, rendered him much more abfolute than he would have been without his conquefts.

O 4　　　　　　　The

The reign of Richard II. has been conftantly torn by parties and factions; it is perhaps difficult to form a juft opinion of this prince. He has his cenfurers, and his panegyrifts. He had his favourites, whom he loaded with wealth. To one he gave the fovereignty of Ireland, as he would have given a houfe or a field; and this favourite dying in a foreign country, he caufed his body to be brought to England, and ordered his coffin to be opened that he might contemplate him at leifure, and take a final look at him, before he was depofited in the tomb he had erected for him. From thefe proofs of fo ftrong an attachment father Orleans praifes him as a king fufceptible of friendfhip. The Eng-lifh, more fevere, confidered thefe friends merely as minions, and Richard II. in this refpect as per-fectly fimilar to Edward II.

The readinefs with which he facrificed thefe favourites to the hatred of his parliament, whilft it feems to contradict the opinion of the Englifh, takes from Richard a part of the praife beftowed upon him by father Orleans, and proves him in all cafes to have been a weak and fickle prince. Troif-fart confidered thefe favourites in the fame light as the people of England, and calls them the king's dolls.

There are two fhining periods in the life of Richard. His uncle the duke of Lancafter, regent of the kingdom, having married Conftance, fifter to Peter the Cruel, difputed the crown of Caftile with

with Henry de Tranftamare, and burthened England with fubfidies for that expedition, as the duke of Anjou did France for the expedition of Naples. Thefe extortions were attended with the fame effect both in France and in England, that is, with infurrections. There was a violent one in London, excited chiefly by the lower claffes of people. One Wat Tyler, a blackfmith, was at the head of the infurgents. Superior in force, he treated with the king as his equal, or rather as his inferior; and the propofitions which the king made not being agreeable to him, he drew his poignard two or three times to ftrike him. Fired at this infolence, Walworth, mayor of London, threw himfelf before the king, and ftruck down Wat Tyler with his mace, who was foon difpatched by others of the king's retinue. The rebels, immediately crying " Wat " Tyler and Revenge," bent their bows. The king's troop, weak as it was, prepared for the combat, but was withheld by him, who advanced alone to the rebels and faid, " My friends, Wat " Tyler is dead; henceforth you fhall have no " chief but your king." The mob, changed by this fingle word, came over to the party of the king. Knolles, one of his generals, arriving to his affiftance with what troops he could affemble, afked permiffion to charge the rebels. " Rebels," replied the king, " there are none here; the perfons " whom you fee are my fubjects and my children." Richard was at this time only fixteen years old. Could any thing announce more ftrongly the fon

and

and fucceffor of the Black Prince and Edward III?
Other rebels having taken up arms in different
parts of the kingdom, Richard vanquifhed them in
perfon in two battles.

The other ftriking period in the life of Richard,
was when he declared himfelf of age. His pro-
fufion to his favourites had caufed meafures to be
taken to reftrain his authority. A council had been
impofed on him, without whofe confent he could
undertake nothing, and he had been compelled to
fwear fubmiffion in every thing to their decifions.
The king one day appeared in the parliament, and,
with the fame air with which he had difarmed the
rebels, exclaimed—" How old do you think me?"
He was anfwered, " Twenty-one."—" I ought
" then to begin to take the reins of government
" into my own hands; nor do I feel myfelf lefs
" able than my predeceffors." The firmnefs of
his manner awed them: they applauded and obeyed.
The king immediately began to exercife the authority he had re-affumed; took the chancellorfhip
from the archbifhop of Canterbury, who had fhown
himfelf an enemy to the favourites, turned many
others out of office, and forbid the duke of Gloucefter, whom of his uncle's he moft fufpected, to
enter the council. In all this he met no oppo-
fition.

But the reft of his life anfwered too little to thefe
two brilliant moments. Giving himfelf up to effeminacy and diffipation, he forfook the fteps of his
predeceffors. Weak and hafty, he was neither
capable

capable of avoiding prejudices nor diffembling them: he fubftituted peevifhnefs in the place of authority. When the parliament requefted him to difmifs minifters or favourites that abufed their credit, he anfwered with paffion that he would not difmifs the loweft fcullion in his kitchen to pleafe the parliament, and threatened to unite with the king of France to learn of him how to reduce rebellious fubjects to obedience: he was then frightened and yielded. He broke out at every oppofition, and very imprudently always againft his uncle's, whom he thus taught to unite and cabal againft him. The party of the king was diftinguifhed from that of the princes, and the latter appeared to be that of the nation. The duke of Lancafter was either gone to make war in Spain and claim Caftile, or remained in London without credit with the king, or the people. From his abfence or his inactivity the duke of Gloucefter became the foul of the league formed againft the king. The duke of York held the balance between the two parties, or rather was of no party, more from indolence than virtue.

The greateft complaint of the Englifh nation againft Richard was the reftoration of fome places of importance to France, and the truce of twenty-eight years which he concluded with that country, and which he confirmed by his marriage with Ifabella, then fix years old. Of all their ancient poffeffions in France, and of all the conquefts of Edward III. a few places only remained in the hands

of

of the Englifh before this truce concluded in 1395; but they were the keys of fo many provinces: Calais of Picardy, Cherburgh of Normandy, Breft of Brittany, Bordeaux of Guyenne. Cherburgh had been mortgaged to the Englifh by Charles the Bad, king of Navarre, for twenty-five thoufand livres. Charles the Noble, his fon, demanded the place on repaying the money. His demand was juft, as Richard always wanted money: this bufinefs therefore was concluded. Breft, which had alfo been delivered to the Englifh by the duke of Brittany, was for the fame reafon reftored for an hundred and twenty thoufand livres. A negociation was begun for Calais, but it was given up.

The reftoration of Breft completely alienated the minds of Richard's fubjects, and here the narrative of the MS. begins:

‘ The duke of Brittany remaining at Breft, agreeable to the treaty, difmiffed the Englifh garrifon, which returned to England. Richard, who loved feafts, gave one at Weftminfter: “ at this feaft arrived the foldiers who had held Breft for the king. They were received and came to dinner in the city of the king and in his hall. ...... Then began the duke of Gloucefter to fpeak to king Richard, faying: *Sire, did you not obferve the people who dined here?* The king replied, *Good uncle, who are they? They are your foldiers, Sire, arrived from Breft, who have ferved you faithfully, been badly paid, and know not what to do.*” The king, who began to feel difpleafed at this difcourfe, contented him-

self

felf with anfwering coldly; *they fhall be fully paid,*
and gave orders for that purpofe. The duke of
Gloucefter, who had thus begun, was not to be
ftopped by a fingle word. He replied *haughtily,*
" Sire, before you reftore or fell any of the cities
that your predeceffors, the kings of England, have
gained or conquered, you fhould with your own
arms have taken a city from your enemies." To
this the king anfwered haftily, " What fay you?"
The duke repeating his infolent fpeech, the king
flew into a paffion, and faid to the duke, " Am I
a merchant or a madman to fell my territories?
No by St. John Baptift: for our coufin of Brittany
has well and truly paid the fum my predeceffors
lent him on the city of Breft, and it is but juft that
the pledge fhould be reftored."

From this converfation the king and his uncle
were never truly reconciled.

The abbot of St. Alban's, who was godfather to
the duke of Gloucefter, fent to the prior of Weftminfter to be at St. Alban's on a certain day. The
prior on his arrival found the duke of Gloucefter
at table with the abbot. After dinner, when they
were alone, the abbot faid to the prior: " May
God and St. George help you as you fpeak the
truth; Have you not had a vifion this night?—
Yes, faid the prior. Then relate your vifion truly,
faid the duke. The prior then fell on his knees
before the duke of Gloucefter, in the prefence of
the abbot, and prayed them to pardon him for what
he fhould fay, adding he would much rather hold
his

his peace. Speak boldly, faid the abbot, his high-
nefs pardons you. Then the prior replied, By
God and St. George, I was warned this night that
the kingdom would be loft by our lord king
Richard."

The abbot declared that he had had the fame
vifion; and both having again demanded pardon
of the duke for having fpoken what he wifhed to
hear, the duke told them that *a fure remedy fhould
foon be applied*. He appointed a meeting with them
that day fortnight at the caftle of Arundel, where
were alfo prefent the earl of Arundel; the earl of
Nottingham his fon-in-law, marfhal of England;
his brother the archbifhop of Canterbury; the earl
of Derby fon of the duke of Lancafter; and many
other lords. " Thefe confpirators firft heard mafs
performed by the archbifhop of Canterbury, who
adminiftered the facrament to the duke of Gloucefter, the earl of Derby, the earl of Arundel his
brother, the earl marfhal, &c." They then refolved to fecure the perfons of the king and his
minifters, to put fome to death, and confine the
reft in prifon for life.

The earl of Nottingham pofted to the king to
difclofe to him the whole tranfaction. His treachery coft his father-in-law the earl of Arundel,
to whom he was in fecret an enemy, his head.
The king wifhed to enjoy the fight of the execution, and was accompanied by the earl of Nottingham, who exulted at the death of his father-in-law.
Arundel made them both blufh at fuch indignity.
He

He was of the firft confequence and more efteemed than any other Englifh nobleman.

Amongft the complaints made by Richard to parliament againft the earl of Arundel, was the following. The queen, (Anne of Luxemburgh, Richard's firft wife, daughter of the emperor Charles IV. and fifter to the emperer Venceflas, always ftiled by the Englifh, whofe hearts were gained by her beneficence and amiable qualities, *tho good queen*) fays the manufcript, " was at one time three hours on her knees before the earl of Arundel, to beg the life of a gentleman called John Carnailly, who not-withftanding had his head cut off: the earl faying to the queen, *Madam, you had better pray for your-felf and your hufband."*

. We relate this fact to remark that hiftorians attri-bute this infolent cruelty to the duke of Gloucefter, not the earl of Arundel, and inftead of Carnailly they all name *Simon Burleigh,* governor of Richard II. a perfon much more known than Carnailly.

The king, at the fame time that he fecured the earl of Arundel and the other confpirators whom Nottingham had pointed out, one day mounted on horfeback at fix o'clock in the morning, *at which the people of London were much furprifed,* having with him the earl of Huntingdon his natural bro-ther. He took the road to a country houfe of the duke of Gloucefter, near London, fending his bro-ther before him *with a few attendants* to apprife the duke of his vifit. " On his afking if the duke were at home, a damfel anfwered that *he and his lady*

lady were still in bed. Then the king, who had formed a small battalion of armed men, with abundance of archers, came riding into his uncle's court, his trumpet founding before him. Upon this the duke of Gloucester came into the court where the king was, and of a truth the duke had nothing on him but his shirt and a mantle over his shoulders: the duchess followed him attended by all her waiting women. The duke fell on his knees before the king, saying, " Sire, you are most " welcome: Why, my dear lord, came you so early " without acquainting me of your coming?" and the king answered, " Dear uncle, dress yourself and we " will then talk together." The duke being returned, the king said, " Dear uncle, you must go with me:" " Most willingly, answered the duke, and then " mounted on horseback." When the king and all his people were out of the gate of the court, he said to the earl marshal (Nottingham), "Convey my uncle " to our tower of London, I will speak with him there " and no where else." The duke would willingly have spoken with the king, but the king would not, nor did he ever after."

The manufcript says nothing farther respecting the fate of the duke of Gloucester. This omission we shall supply. Fearful of the partisan the duke had in England, the king removed him to Calais. Some time after, the parliament, believing this faction destroyed by the banishment or death of its principal leaders, resolved to bring the duke of Gloucester to trial, and ordered the governor of

Calais

Calais (this was Nottingham) to bring his prifoner
to England. Nottingham anfwered, that Gloucefter was juft dead of an apopleftic fit. It was
afterwards known that he was fmothered between
two mattreffes.

We have faid that the earl of Derby (Lancafter)
was at Arundel's cohference; but having fhewn lefs
violence there than the reft, the king pardoned him
on his full confeffron of his faults and promife to
make amends for them. He afterwards accufed the
earl of Nottingham (then duke of Norfolk), of being difloyal and a traitor to the king and kingdom.
It appeared that in faft he had been by turns
the accomplice and the betrayer of Richard's
enemies.

The earl of Derby having prefented to the king
the paper containing this accufation, the king communicated it to the earl of Nottingham, with thefe
words; " *What fay you to this, Thomas?*" He anfwered, " My dear lord, with your leave, if I may
" anfwer your coufin, faving your reverence, I fay
" that Henry of Lancafter, duke of Arnord (or of
" Hereford, a new title juft conferred on him), is
" a liar, and in what he has faid, and would fay of
" me, lies like a falfe traitor as he is." Nottingham was governor of Calais: the earl of Derby
accufed him of two things; of having applied to
his own ufe money deftined for the payment of the
garrifon, and of having murdered the duke of
Gloucefter. Nottingham appears to have fully

Vol. II.   P   juftified

juftified himfelf on the firft charge: on the fecond he was filent.

After all the denials, defiances, refufals of reconciliation, gages of combat thrown down and taken up again, and all the ceremonies and formalities of the trial by fingle combat, which are here related at large, the combatants made their appearance in the lifts at Coventry, on an appointed day, in prefence of the king and the whole court. The king having *fworn by Saint John the Baptift that he would never make peace between them:* the earl of Derby firft arrived, *and croffed himfelf as nimbly as if he had not been armed, and waited for his enemy in a gallant manner, as was fitting on fuch a day.* Nottingham entered the lift alfo, *after having heard three maffes,* faying, *God fpeed the right.*

The earl of Derby advanced his fhield, and figned himfelf with his hand, " making a crofs, and put his lance in the reft, the point towards his enemy, and advanced feven or eight paces to pay his compliments: the duke of Norvolt (Nottingham), neither ftirred, nor offered to defend himfelf. At this the king arofe, and cried out; ho! ho! and ordered the earl of Derby's lance to be taken away." Then a herald proclaimed aloud the judgment of the king and his council; which, while it beftowed eulogiums, and did juftice to the valour of the two adverfaries, of which they had elfewhere given proofs, banifhed the earl of Derby from the kingdom for ten years, and declared, that *if he returned*

turned before the expiration of that time, he should be
hanged, or lose his head. And when this proclamation was made, the people wondered much that
the duke of Arnord (Derby), should be banished
for having shewn himself so gallant in the performance of his duty, and they made so great a noise
that nothing could be heard, for every one thought
he had loft his honour." Silence however was obtained, and the fecond part of the fentence published, banishing the earl of Nottingham for ever,
and feizing his possessions till he had fully paid the
garrison of Calais.

This ftrange fentence, so contrary to all the laws
of trial by fingle combat, condemning and punish-
ing both the accufer and the accufed, without either
of them being convicted, is perfectly inexplicable.
Authors reafon differently on it. The king forbad
the two exiles to choofe the fame place of retreat,
to feek each other for the purpofe of fighting, or
even to fight if chance should bring them together,
under penalty of confifcation of all their poffeffions.
To this they gave him their words and departed,
each well pleafed, according to the manufcript, at
having efcaped the fate of the earl of Arundel.
Nottingham however died foon after of grief at
Venice.

The king alfo prepared for his departure to
make war in Ireland, where at that time were great
difturbances. The account of his domeftic arrange-
ments before his departure is curious, fimple, and
interefting. He left his uncle, the duke of York,

lieuteuant of the realm in his abfence. Ifabella of France, his wife, he recommended to him and Scroop, chancellor of the exchequer, *to fee that fhe and her people wanted nothing.* And the king ordered a phyfician, one mafter Pool, to take care of the queen as of himfelf, and gave orders to Philip la Vache, the queen's chamberlain, that mafter Pool and the confeffor were fupreme guar‑ dians of the queen.

He then took thefe three perfons to his clofet, and after having made them fwear to fpeak the truth to what he fhould afk, ordered them to tell him, whether they thought the dame de Courcy, the queen's governante, of whom he had apparently fome fufpicion, " was good, accomplifhed, and pru‑ " dent enough to be the guardian and miftrefs of " fuch a perfonage as the queen of England." To this Philip la Vache and mafter Pool replied, " Right worthy Sire, the confeffor knows foreign " ladies better than we; let him fpeak what he " thinks proper." The confeffor begged the king to make Philip la Vache or mafter Pool fpeak, as the lady might owe him a grudge for it.

This was faying enough, and, being preffed anew by the king, they all three declared fhe was unwor‑ thy fo noble an employ. The reafons they affign are very remarkable. " She lives in greater fplen‑ " dor, fay they, one thing with another, than the " queen, for fhe has eighteen horfes by your order, " befides the livery of her hufband, whenever fhe " comes or goes; and keeps two or three gold‑ " fmiths,

" ſmiths, ſeven or eight embroiderers, two or three
" cutlers, and two or three furriers, as well as you
" and the queen: and ſhe is alſo building a chapel
" that will coſt fourteen hundred nobles; this, if
" ſhe had remained in France, ſhe would have dif-
" penſed with." The king gave orders that ſhe
ſhould be ſent back to France, and that all her
debts ſhould be paid. He put the dame Mortimer
in her place.

The king and queen, before they ſeparated, af-
ſiſted at divine ſervice together, with the canons
of St. George. The king chanted a colleɛ̃t, then
made his offering, and taking the queen in his,
arms, very amorouſly kiſſed her more than forty
times, ſaying in a ſorrowful tone, " Adieu, madam,
" think of me till we meet again;" the queen began to weep, and ſaid to the king, " Alas, ſir, will
" you leave me here?" At this the king's eyes were
full of tears, and he could ſcarce forbear weeping.
The king and queen then took wine and ſpices together, ſtanding at the door of the church, and
afterwards the king ſtooped down, lifted the queen
from the ground, and, holding her a long time in
his arms, kiſſed her at leaſt ten times, frequently repeating, ' Adieu, madam, till we meet again.' He
then ſet her down and kiſſed her three times more,
and, by our lady, I never ſaw ſo great a lord make
ſo great a feaſt, nor ſhow ſo much love for a lady,
as king Richard did for the queen."

She

She was not then ten years old, *and it was great pity they parted, as they never saw each other again.*

It appears from this relation, that the author was a cotemporary and occular witnefs to feveral of the facts he mentions.

When the earl of Derby took leave of the king, he promifed him to fhorten the term of his exile to four years, and iffued letters patent to preferve to him whatever inheritances might fall to him, if the duke of Lancafter, his father, fhould die in his abfence; which actually happened.

The earl of Derby having retired to France, the king of England took umbrage at his apparently endeavouring to ftrengthen himfelf againft him, by a foreign alliance with a rival, he having demanded in marriage the daughter of the duke of Berry, uncle to Charles VI. Richard fent the earl of Salif-bury into France, to put a ftop to this negociation; and the marriage did not take place. He revoked the letters patent that he had granted the earl of Derby, and retained the poffeffions of the houfe of Lancafter.

The new duke of Lancafter (Derby) returned from his exile to reclaim his poffeffions. Circum-ftances were favourable to him, and he foon faw that he had it in power to deprive the prince of of his crown, who would have robbed him of his patrimony. He was not however the prefumptive heir; the duke of Clarence, younger brother to the Black Prince, but elder brother to the duke of

Lancafter,

Lancaster, had left a daughter married to Edmund Mortimer, earl of March. Roger Mortimer, the fruit of this marriage, had juft been killed in a battle in Ireland, leaving a fon, feven years old, to inherit his rights. It was to avenge the death of this Roger that the king went to make war in Ireland. Lancaster flattered himfelf, that the Englifh, already difcontented with too young a king, would prefer him to a king ftill younger, a prince like himfelf, capable of taking into his hands the reins of govenment. He faw that the very oppreffion under which he laboured would ftand him inftead of legal right. "He fent at leaft," fays our author, "an hundred and fifty pair of letters, invent-"ing falfehoods againft king Richard and his go-"vernment." He faid, that Richard fecretly drew to his court a crowd of knights and great lords from France, Brittany, and Germany; "and by "their affiftance, he would domineer and lord it "over the kingdom of England, more than any "of his predeceffors, and then he might impofe "what fubfidies, taxes, and impofts, he pleafed."

This was exprefsly mentioned in his letters, addreffed to the city of London. He added, that it was to free England from the yoke with which it was threatened he had returned to his country. Thefe letters did not fail to produce their effect. The king was not on the fpot to defend himfelf. The fon of the earl of Arundel, and the other mal-contents, emboldened by the king's abfence,

ranged

ranged themfelves under the ftandard of the duke
of Lancafter. Thefe mal-contents confifted of almoft
the whole nation. Lancafter foon faw himfelf at
the head of a formidable army : even the duke of
York, regent in the king's abfence, joined the duke
of Lancafter. The chancellor of the exchequer,
'(Scroop) more loyal, haftened to Ireland to inform
the king of the arrival and revolt of the new duke
of Lancafter. At this news, the king recollecting
what the late duke of Lancafter had often told him
of his fon, " Ha !" cried he, " dear uncle of Lan-
" cafter, God reward your foul; for had I be-
" lieved you, this man would not now have of-
" fended me : you told me truly that I did wrong
" to pardon him fo often, for he would ftill con-
" tinue to offend me. Three times have I par-
" doned his mifdeeds, and this is the fourth offence
" he has committed."

Richard haftened to England to defend his crown.
His army confifted of about thirty-two thoufand
men, Englifh and foreigners; but the firft were
not well difpofed towards him. Some days after
his arrival in England, " when the king arofe in
the morning, and was about to fay his orifons, as
ufual, he leaned on a window that looked to the
field where his army was encamped; and when he
faw the fmallnefs of the number, he was quite
difmayed." This army of thirty-two thoufand,
was reduced to fix thoufand; the reft having deferted during the night, and joined the duke of
Lancafter. This was the effect of the letters fent

to

to the king's army, as well as to the cities, corporations, great men of the kingdom, &c. All abandoned the unhappy Richard. He abandoned himself: he quitted the few troops he had left, left they should deliver him up to the duke of Lancaster; for they were all foreign mercenaries, ready to sell themselves to the highest bidder. This was the advice of his council: there was no dispute, but about the place of his retreat. The earl of Salisbury, and many others, were defirous of his retiring to Bourdeaux: the earl of Huntingdon, his brother, was for his shutting himfelf up in Conway-castle, on the sea-coast, where he would be secure. " We shall also be secure at Bourdeaux," said the king. " Yes, fire; but that would be to abandon. ". all: it will then be said, that feeling yourself " culpable, you had voluntarily depofed your " crown. Remain in England: this castle will fe- " cure to you the freedom of the sea; you will al- " ways have time to go to Bourdeaux, or elfewhere, if " circumstances should force you to quit the realm." The king yielded to this counsel, and sent the earl of Huntingdon to negociate with the duke of Lancaster. On his arrival before the duke, Huntingdon bent one knee to the ground, and said, " It is " but reasonable, fir, that I should pay you reve- " rence; for your father was a king's son, and my " wife also is your fister."—" Rise, brother-in- " law," said the duke coldly, " you have not al- " ways acted thus." Then taking him by the hand,. he drew him aside, *and they converfed together a long time,*

time, but I knew not what they faid. This alfo fhews the author to have been an eye-witnefs; it is likely he was in the army of the duke of Lancafter, or in the fuite of the earl of Huntingdon, which is much more probable, as he is evidently a partizan of king Richard. The duke retained Huntingdon till the return, as he faid, of the earl of Northumberland, whom he had fent to the king. He thus affured himfelf of an hoftage: he did more; he feemed defirous of retaining him altogether, and of attaching him to his party in fpite of himfelf, for he gave him his order, and caufed Richard's to be taken from him. Thefe are the expreffions in the manufcript; but could it be an order properly fo called? The order of England muft at this period have been that of the garter, inftituted by Edward III. and common both to king Richard and the duke of Lancafter. It feems rather to have been fome badge of party, perhaps the red rofe of Lancafter. Huntingdon was ftruck dumb; *he began to weep, and remained a great while without fpeaking.* The earl of Rutland, fon of the duke of York, faid to him tauntingly, " Dear cou- " fin, don't be angry; if it pleafe God, things will " go well."

Another advantage the duke of Lancafter derived from the arrival of the earl of Huntingdon was, to oblige him to write to the king, that he might place an entire confidence in the earl of Northumberland, who was fent by the duke of Lancafter, and was charged with this letter. When he appeared
before

before the king, with feven attendants, he was afked by him, if he had not met his brother on the road? " Yes, fire," he anfwered, " and here is a letter " he gave me for you." Northumberland de-demanded no other conditions of peace, on the part of the duke of Lancafter, but that the poffeffions of the houfe of Lancafter fhould be reftored, and that he fhould be created lord chief juftice. The king deliberated in private with his friends, and im-mediately imparted to them a fecret he might have difpenfed with. " Whatever agreement or peace," fays he, " he makes with me, if ever I can take " him at an advantage, I fhall no more fcruple to " put him to death, than he did to gain the upper " hand of me." However, the terms offered were fo reafonable, that they could not be rejected. The bifhop of Carlifle only advifed him to take the pre-caution of making Northumberland fwear by the gofpels and the eucharift. He fwore, " and might " be compared," fays our author, " to Judas, or " Ganelon, for he perjured himfelf on the body of " our Lord."

The king appointed Flint-caftle for his inter-view with the duke of Lancafter; and when about to depart, he faid to the earl of Northnmberland, " I rely on your faith; remember your oaths and " the God who has heard them." The earl an-fwered, " My dear lord, if I deceive you, deal " with me as a traitor." He then afked leave to go before, to prepare a fupper for the king and the
                                                    duke

duke, at Flint-caftle, and the falfe traitor faid at his departure; " Make hafte, fir, it is already " near two o'clock."

Richard mounted on horfeback, with twenty-one attendants, and going down a mountain on the road, on foot, and looking into the valley, he faid to the earl of Salifbury, " Do you not fee " below banners and ftreamers?" The earl of Salifbury anfwered, " Certainly, fire, I do; and " my heart forbodes ill :" and the bifhop of Callain (Carlifle) faid, " I fufpect that man has " betrayed you." At the fame time they faw the earl of Northumberland coming to them, with eleven others. " Sire," faid he, " I am come to " meet you." The king afked who the people were he faw below in the valley. " I have feen " none," faid Northumberland. " Look before " you then," faid the earl of Salifbury, " There " they are."—" They are your men," faid the bifhop, " I know your banner."—" Northumber-" land," faid the king, " if I thought you capa-" ble of betraying me, it is not yet perhaps too " late for me to return to Conway."—" You fhall " not return thither," replied the traitor, throwing off the mafk, and feizing the bridle of the king's horfe: " I fhall conduct you to the duke of Lan-" cafter, as I have promifed him; for I do not " break all my promifes." In fact he had placed in ambufcade, at the bottom of the mountain, an hundred fpearmen and two hundred archers, who, at the found of a trumpet, were with him in an inftant.

inftant. " *The God*," faid the king to the earl, *on* " *whom you laid your hand, will reward thee and thy* " *accomplices at the laft day of judgment.*" Then turning to his companions, who were weeping, he faid with a figh, " Ah! O my good and loyal " friends, we are betrayed. But in God's name " take comfort, and remember our Lord, who " was fold and delivered into the hands of his " enemies without having merited it."

The king was fent to Flint-caftle with his companions, " which was furnifhed with a number of " armed men to guard him." He was thus betrayed, and imprifoned on the 21ft of Auguft, 1399.

When he was alone with his friends, he gave himfelf up to the complaints which his fituation infpired. The author of this narrative, who appears to have been prefent, has prefented thefe lamentations. They have a double merit, that of being fometimes affecting by their fimplicity, and of conveying to us feveral anecdotes of the duke of Lancafter.

After many invocations of God, the virgin, and his patron, St. John the Baptift, " Ah !" cries Richard, " deareft lady and fifter ! deareft and " beft beloved companion, Ifabel of France ! never " fhall I fee you more!—Alas! I left you in " the hands of my enemies !—Ah! deareft father " and moft noble king of France ! I commend " myfelf to you, and leave you your daughter : " Would to God fhe were now with you !—Ah!

" deareft

" deareſt father of France, and dear uncle of Berry
" and Burgundy! flower of nobility! never will
" this diſgrace be avenged by you!—Ah! dear
" couſin of Brittany!—Alas! you ſaid truly, at
" your departure; that I ſhould never be ſafe whilſt
" Henry of Lancaſter was alive. Alas! thrice have
" I ſaved his life! for once my dear uncle of Lan-
" caſter, on whom God have mercy! would have
" put him to death for the treaſon and villainy he
" had been guilty of. O God of Paradiſe! all
" night did I ride to preſerve him from death, and
" his father yielded him to my requeſt, telling me
" to do with him as I pleaſed. Oh God! how true
" is the ſaying, that *we have no greater enemy than*
" *the man we ſave from the gallows?* O God! once
" he drew his ſword on me in the chamber of the
" queen (Anne of Luxembourg) on whom God
" have mercy! He was of the council of the duke
" of Glouceſter and the earl of Arundel; he con-
" ſented to my death, that of his father, and all
" my council. Oh my godfather! by St. John
" the Baptiſt, all his offences towards me have I
" pardoned; nor would I believe my uncle, his
" father, who two or three times condemned him
" to death. Alas! I was a fool.—Oh deareſt lady
" and mother, queen of France! I commend my-
" ſelf to you. Alas! I purpoſed to viſit you
" ſhortly, with Iſabel your daughter, my dear lady
" and friend, who has a ſtrong deſire of ſeeing you.
" Oh deareſt brother, noble dauphin of Vienna!
" Alas! too well I perceive that I ſhall never ſee
                                            " you!

" you! Ah brother-in-law, Lewis, duke of Tu-
" renne, and you my fifters of France! were Ifabel,
" my deareft companion, at Paris with you: alas!
" were I certain of her fafety, I fhould die with lefs
" regret. Ah deareft father! take pity on my be-
" loved companion Ifabel, your daughter. Ah
" all you noble lords of France! never did any of
" the noble kings of France experience fuch griev-
" ous treafon as I have from my own kinfmen and
" relations. I moft humbly befeech you that it may
" pleafe you to affift and comfort my deareft father
" and lord, the noble king of France, whenever it
" fhall pleafe him to take vengeance, which I pray
" God to enable him to do fully and fpeedily, as
" fuch an action deferves. Ah my deareft fifter,
" lady, and dear companion, Ifabel of France! if
" I could fee you once more before I die, I fhould
" meet death more readily, and with lefs reluc-
" tance."

This unhappy prince appears to have been at
leaft endowed with fenfibility: he appears alfo perhaps to have been more attached to France than
was prudent for a king of England in thofe times.

The duke of Lancafter, being informed by the
earl of Northumberland of what had paffed, drew
near Flint-caftle with all his army, which confifted
of about eighty thoufand men. Richard obferving
this from the terrace of the caftle, to which he had
gone up to take the air, trembled: tears fell from
his eyes, and he faid to his companions, " My friends,
" in a few moments we fhall be delivered into the
" hands

" hands of our mortal enemies." Lancafter drew
up his army around the caftle, *which made fo great
a noife with trumpets and other inftruments, that it
feemed as if the caftle were falling, and that even the
thunder of God could not be heard.*

During the king's dinner fome curious perfons
of the duke's retinue were every moment entering
into the hall to fee the king, and faid to the king's
attendants and other lords, " Eat heartily and make
" good cheer, for by St. George all your heads will
" foon be cut off." After dinner the king and the
duke had an interview. The king, making an effort to treat the duke with civility, faluted him and
welcomed him on his return. " I am returned
" fooner than you expected, faid the duke, to
" affift you in governing this kingdom, which for
" twenty-two years, that it has been fubject to your
" laws, has not been governed agreeably to the
" wifhes of the people." He then fpoke to all the
lords of the king's retinue, except the earl of Salifbury. We have faid, that when the duke of Lancafter refided in France, Richard fent Salifbury
thither to prevent the duke's marriage with the
daughter of the duke of Berry. Salifbury, being
charged with this commiffion, thought it would be
improper for him to fee the duke of Lancafter at
Paris. Lancafter therefore ordered him to be informed at Flint-caftle, *that as he had not condefcended
to fpeak to him at Paris, neither would he now fpeak
to him.* He made the king mount on horfeback,
and led him in his train to Chefter: he there intrufted

trufted him to the care of the duke of Glouceſter and the earl of Arundel, ſaying, " Here is the " murderer of your father; you muſt be anſwerable for him." To deprive him of his laſt conſolation they ſeparated him from his friends, who embraced him with tears and withdrew, whilſt he, motionleſs with grief, and ſinking under the weight of his miſfortunes, could neither weep nor ſpeak.

The author of this narrative is evidently one of the friends who were torn from him at this cruel moment; for after having related the king's complaints at Flint-caſtle, becauſe he had heard them, he ſays, in this part of his narrative, " of his wail- " ing and complaints no one knew any thing, ex- " cept thoſe who guarded him." On his journey to Litchfield he attempted his eſcape, which cauſed him to be more ſtrictly guarded, *and as a thief or murderer.* He was then led in triumph in the train of the duke of Lancaſter, amidſt the acclamations of the people, who bleſſing Lancaſter and inſulting Richard, demanded of the conqueror the head of this unhappy prince. The duke anſwered, " that " he ſhould be tried by a free parliament."

In this manner they arrived at London, where the perſon of the king could ſcarcely be recognized, ſo much was his countenance bathed with tears. Some pitied him much, others curſed him, ſaying, " Now we are well revenged of the *little* " *baſtard* that has ſo badly governed us."

To underſtand this expreſſion of *little baſtard,* it ſhould be obſerved, that the intrigues of the duke of Lancaſter's father, who, at the death of the Black Prince, would fain have fucceeded him, had raifed fome doubts of the legitimacy of the young Richard. It was reported that he was the fon of a canon of Bourdeaux: it was remarked that his mother's palace was always filled *with young and handfome clerks and canons*, and on thefe grounds they defamed the moft virtuous and refpectable princefs in the world. They even attacked her marriage with the prince of Wales. They faid that the earl of Salifbury, her firft hufband, who had feparated from her without their marriage having been diffolved, was ftill living when fhe efpoufed the prince of Wales. Edward III. put an end to all doubts and fufpicions on this head, by declaring Richard his heir, proclaiming him prince of Wales, and beftowing on him all the honours and eftates of the Black Prince, his fa-ther. But when the nation arofe againft Richard, all thefe old calumnies were revived.

Richard was confined in the tower of London, where none of his friends were admitted to him. Lancafter forced him to receive the duke of York and the earl of Rutland his fon. When he an-nounced them; "*they are my betrayers*," cried Richard; "*fpare me the fight of them.*" Thefe princes entering at that inftant heard this reproach. The earl of Rutland advancing with his hat on his head, gave the king the lye, and threw his hat on the ground in defiance; an action as cowardly then as it would have been rafh before Richard's fall. "*It is too much*," faid the king, "*to be at once a traitor and infolent.*" Lancafter reproached and

threat-

threatened the earl of Rutland, and forbad him to fpeak to the king, whom he wifhed yet to manage, to obtain of him, in appearance a voluntary abdication. " Am I your king, or your prifoner? and why am " I thus guarded?" faid Richard to the duke of Lancafter.—" Sire, you are my king, but the *coun-* " *cil of the realm* orders you to be thus guarded." Richard afked for the queen his wife; " you can- " not fee her," faid Lancafter, " the council has " forbidden it." Richard then claimed the laws of chivalry, and offered alone to combat four of his accufers or oppreffors. Lancafter made no an- fwer to this propofal, only defiring the king to wait the decifion of the parliament. " Well, let me at " leaft appear in this parliament, and let my rea- " fons be heard." Lancafter, without explaining himfelf on this head, contented himfelf with an- fwering, " Sire, you will have juftice."

The manufcript does not fay, as many hiftorians have afferted, that the king, either voluntarily, or by compulfion, figned a deed of abdication.

The parliament affembled the 30th of Septem- ber 1399. Lancafter was Richard's accufer, and the whole affembly condemned him without hear- ing him. The bifhop of Carlifle was the only one that durft fpeak in his favour. " Ah! firs," faid he, " you hear a malefactor, an affaffin in his de- " fence, and you dare condemn your king without " a hearing!" The argument was unanfwerable: the tyrant felt it, and replied by an order to the marfhal of the crown to arreft the bifhop and fend him to prifon, for having infulted the regal ma-

jefty

jefty in his perfon, by defending it in Richard.
This unhappy prince was depofed, and Henry of
Lancafter proclaimed. The judgment given was,
"That Richard of Bourdeaux, ftiled king of England,
is condemned to be confined in a royal prifon; that
he fhould have the beft bread, the beft wine, and
the beft meat that could be procured for filver or
gold; and if any difturbance were made by armed
people coming to his affiftance, he fhould be the
firft put to death."

The laft words of the fentence was the decree of
his death. A confpiracy was formed in his favour
without his knowledge. Inftead of Richard, one
of his chaplains, (the manufcript fays one of his
efquires) called *Maudlin* or *Magdalen*, the refemblance of whofe fhape and figure to that of this
prince was very great, was fhown to the people.
They began by propagating privately a report that
king Richard had efcaped from prifon; and when
they thought the minds of the people difpofed in
his favour, a tournament was appointed at Oxford,
to which it was propofed to invite Henry IV. in
order to take him prifoner, or affaffinate him. The
earl of Rutland, who had by turns flattered and
betrayed the duke of Gloucefter and Richard II.
and who then flattered Henry IV. (Lancafter) to
betray him, was at the head of the confpiracy.
One day, being at dinner with his father the duke
of York, he received a private paper, which he
appeared to hide with care. He was noticed, and
feemed difturbed: the duke of York wifhed to fee
the paper, and fnatched it from his fon by force.

It

It was an account of the confpiracy, and a lift of the confpirators. The duke of York flew into a violent paffion with his fon: " Traitor," faid he to him, " thou knoweft I am pledge for thee to the " parliament, both in my perfon and my fortune: " I fee plainly thou wouldft have my life; but, by " St. John, I had rather thou fhouldft be hanged " than me."

Immediately he mounted on horfeback to haften to difclofe the whole to Henry IV. The earl of Rutland took the precaution to be before him, in order to obtain his pardon. The confpirators knowing that thefe two princes were gone to the king, and thinking they had now but one ftake left, invefted Maudlin with the infignia of royalty. Some of the people believed, or were willing to believe, that he was the king. They found in this chaplain all the graces of Richard, which were fufficient to counter-balance his faults, and whofe fate was unhappy enough to merit pity. The confpirators endeavouring to furprife Henry at Windfor, were themfelves furprifed at Cirencefter, by the mayor of that place, who intercepted them, overcame them, and took their principal leaders prifoners. The earl of Salifbury was flain in the battle. The earl of Rutland, having been unable to join the confpirators, had taken the part of fighting againft them. Who but muft have felt indignation at feeing this traitor carrying on the end of a lance the head of his brother-in-law and accomplice, lord Spencer, and fhamefully prefenting it to Henry, whom he would have treated in the fame manner if the tournament at Oxford had taken place.

The unfortunate Richard, ftrictly guarded in Pomfret, or Pontefract (*Pontus fracti*) caftle, did not long furvive this confpiracy, of which he was ignorant. Some hiftorians fay, that he killed himfelf; others, that he was ftarved to death; but many fay, that he was affaffinated by order of Henry; that he defended himfelf bravely, and fold his life dear. Our manufcript confirms this laft account. A knight, named Peter d'Exton, or Exton, fent by king Henry, arrived at Pomfret-caftle, with feven other affaffins. Richard was at table. Exton called the carver, and gave him orders on the part of Henry, not to tafte the meat ferved at Richard's table, as he had been accuftomed to do; "*For*," faid he, "*he will not eat much more.*" Richard perceiving his carver omit this ceremony, ordered him to perform it. The carver fell on his knees, and alledged what Exton had commanded him on the part of Henry. Richard lofing his patience, ftruck the carver with a knife that was on the table, faying, "Go to the devil, thee and thy "Lancafter." Exton came in at the noife, with his feven men armed. At this fight Richard pufhed down the table, darted into the midft of the eight affaffins, fnatched a battle axe from one of them, laid four of them dead at his feet, to the great ter-

ror

ror of the others; when Exton attacking him from
behind, gave him a ftroke on the head. With this
he fell, ' crying to God for mercy; and Exton gave
him another ftroke on the head. Thus died the
noble king Richard, without having confeffed himfelf, which was much to be be lamented.'

Exton himfelf appeared terrified at his crime.
' He fat down by the fide of the body, and began
to weep, faying, " Alas! what have we done? we
" have put to death him who was our fovereign
" lord for twenty-two years. Now have I loft my
" honour, nor fhall I ever find a country to which I
" can fly from reproach."

Thofe modern hiftorians who have embraced the
opinion of Richard's having been ftarved to death,
have been led to it by a circumftance, which is the
frequent fource of deception, that the body, expofed
in public in St. Paul's church at London, did not
exhibit any marks of violence. But befides that in
fuch cafes it is eafy to difguife appearances, and that
the body, furrounded with guards, is expofed to the
fight only, not the examination of the people, our
manufcript refutes the conclufion that might be
drawn from this circumftance, by afferting that its
only object was to confirm the death of Richard;
for they required nothing more.

Richard was affaffinated on Twelfth-day, in the
year 1400. Various punifhments were inflicted on
fuch of his friends as were taken either in battle or
in flight. Our manufcript enters very minutely
into thefe mournful relations, and it muft be owned

Q 4

the simplicity of the old language seems to lessen
the horror, and render them at the same time more
interesting. Amongst these noble victims of fidelity to Richard, a brave knight, Thomas Blount,
and the earl of Huntingdon, Richard's natural brother, are distinguished.

Sir Thomas Blount, and one Bennet Selly, his
companion, were drawn from Oxford (above three
miles) to the place of execution, ' where they
were hanged ; but the ropes were soon cut, and
these gentlemen were made to talk, and sit on a
bench before a great fire, and the executioner came
with a razor in his hand, and knelt down before Sir
Thomas Blount, whose hands were tied, begging
him to pardon him his death, as he must do his office.   Then Sir Thomas asked him, " Are you the
" person appointed to deliver me from this world ?"
The executioner answered, " Yes," saying, " Sir,
" I pray you pardon me ;" and Sir Thomas kissed
him, and forgave him his death.   The executioner
knelt down, and Sir Thomas Blount (Le Blonc)
made himself ready ; and then the executioner
opened his belly, and cut out his bowels strait from
below the stomach, and tied them with a string, that
the wind of the heart should not escape, and threw
the bowels into the fire.   Then Sir Thomas le
Blonc was sitting before the fire, his belly open, and
saw his bowels burning before him.'   Sir Thomas
D'Arpeghen, king Henry's chamberlain, insulting
Blount, said to him with derision, " Go seek a
" master that can cure you."   Blount only answered

fwered by putting his hands together, faying,
" *Te Deum laudamus*, and bleffed be the hour that
" I was born, and bleffed be this day, for I fhall
" die in the fervice of my fovereign lord, the noble
" king Richard."

Arpeghen wifhed to compel him to reveal the
accomplices of his treafon. " The words traitor
" and treafon," faid he, " belong to thee and the
" infamous Rutland, by whom the flower of Eng-
" lifh chivalry. is this day deftroyed. I fummon
" you both ' before the face of Jefus Chrift, for
" your great treafon againft our fovereign lord the
" noble king Richard." The executioner then
afked him, if he would drink ? " No," faid he,
" you have taken from me the place into which I'
" fhould put it. God be praifed, my bowels are
" in the fire." He afterwards entreated the executioner to deliver him from this world, faying,
" It hurts me much to fee the traitors who are
" prefent." The executioner then knelt down before him, and kiffed him in a very humble manner,
and foon after his head was cut off, and he was
quartered.'

The earl of Huntingdon, the king's brother,
fled into the county of Effex ; but paffing through
a fmall village belonging to the countefs of Hereford, fifter to the late earl of Arundel, he was known
and arrefted. The countefs fent news of it to king
Henry, defiring him to fend her the young earl of
Arundel, her nephew, that he might enjoy the vengeance fhe was going to take on the man to whofe
counfel

counsels she principally attributed the death of her brother; which, it appears, she should rather ' have imputed to the treachery of the earl of Nottingham. The young Arundel haftened thither, and loaded Huntingdon with reproaches. The coun-tefs had affembled her vaffals, to the number of eight thoufand, and delivered to them the earl of Huntingdon in chains, ordering them to cut him in pieces. The unfortunate man entreated for mercy, alledging, that he had never done them any injury; *and all took great pity on him except the countefs* (of Hereford) *and the earl of Arundel.* The coun-tefs flew into a paffion, exclaiming, " Curfe on you " all, villains! you have not the courage to put a " man to death."

An efquire offering himfelf for this purpofe, advanced with his hatchet in his hand; but he was fo touched with the tender complaints of Huntingdon, ' *that he trembled for fear,* and returned to the countefs with tears, faying, " Madam, I would not " put the duke to death for all the gold in the " world."—" Then," faid fhe, " do what thou " haft promifed, or thy own head fhall be cut off." When he heard this, he was fo afraid, that he knew not what to do, and faid, " Sir, I entreat your pardon; forgive me your death." He then lifted his hatchet, and ftruck him fo hard on the fhoulder, that he made him fall with his face to the ground. The noble duke (Huntingdon had been created duke of Exeter by Richard) leaped on his feet, faying, " Alas, man! why do you treat me thus?

" For

" For God's fake, kill me more eafily." He then
gave him eight blows on the fhoulder, for he could
neither hit his neck or his head; the ninth ftroke
was in the neck: and the worthy duke, brother to
the noble king Richard, fpoke yet, faying, " Alas,
" dear friend! have pity on me, and free me from
" my pain." The executioner then cut his throat
with a knife, to feparate his head from his body;
and in this manner was the noble duke put to
death.'

Maudlin alfo was taken, and conducted to London. He afked the mayor, if he fhould be quartered? " No," faid the mayor, " but your head
" will be cut off." Then Maudlin thanked God
that he fhould die in the fervice of his fovereign
lord the noble king Richard.

The bifhop of Carlifle fuffered only about a
year's imprifonment, and the lofs of his bifhopric.
He died rector of Todenham, in the county of
Gloucefter.

Henry IV. remained peaceably in poffeffion of
the throne, and was the firft king of England of the
houfe of Lancafter, afterwards difpoffeffed by the
houfe of York.

HISTORY

Charles VII. and Louis XI.

By AMELGARD, a Prieſt of Liege.

Taken from the Manuſcripts in the King's Library, No. 5962, and No. 5963.

By M. DU THEIL.

WHATEVER be the reſult of the account and extract I here offer to the committee, I regret not the time and trouble they have coſt me. If one of the principal duties of the taſk we have impoſed on ourſelves be, to give ſuch accounts of the manuſcripts we examine as ſhall ſuperſede the neceſſity in thoſe who have recourſe to them, of reading works, which, upon the whole, are but little intereſting, I truſt I have fulfilled my taſk with reſpect to the hiſtory written by Amelgard. I have compared it carefully with the old ſources of information, as the Chronicle of Monſtrelet, the Collection of Godefrey, the Journal of Paris, Rymer's Acts, and even ſome anecdotes obtained from the

Tower

Tower of London, which M. de Breguigny has been fo obliging as to communicate to me; and alfo with the modern hiftorians, Rapin, Thoiras, fathers Orleans, Daniel and Griffet, Meffrs. Bodot de Juilly, Duclos, Villaret and Hume. I have faithfully noted whatever in my author's narrative has appeared different from them, or new. Every unknown circumftance, relative to reigns fo interefting as thofe of Charles VII. and Lewis XI. I thought worth collecting, whilft I was defirous of having it in my power to affirm, that, to whatever accuracy any one may be willing to purfue his enquiries into this epoch of our hiftory, he will find nothing new in Amelgard, after having read my account of his hiftory.

It is remarkable, that not one of the hiftorians above named has cited this work of Amelgard, though it is mentioned in the Library of France, and in the catalogue of the king's library. It would be ftill more aftonifhing, if they totally neglected making themfelves acquainted with it, as in 1729, Don Martenne inferted a part of it, concerning the affairs of Liege, in the fourth volume of his Collectio Ampliffima. The manner in which he announces this work, what he quotes from the beginning of the Life of Charles VII. and the chapters he has publifhed, all, it fhould feem, would have excited in hiftorians, by profeffion, a defire of knowing the whole work. If, contrary to all appearance, they had derived no help from this fource towards perfecting their work, at leaft by fhewing

that

that they had not neglected it, they would have given us a greater reliance on the accuracy of their researches.

Be it as it may, what I shall say with respect to Amelgard himself, of the two copies of his work found in the king's library, its form and diftribution, the literary merit to which it is entitled, the addition to our hiftorical knowledge that may be drawn from it, will appear wholly new, if not interefting.

As to Amelgard himself, it has hitherto been impoffible for me, and will perhaps be always difficult for any one to obtain any confiderable knowledge refpecting him. All the learned men, to whom his work has been known, contenting themfelves with extracting from it what anfwered their purpofes, feem to have agreed in neglecting either to make any enquiries after, or to tranfmit to us, any information relative to the author. Befides the *Collectio Ampliffima*, I find the hiftory of Amelgard quoted in the *Promptuarium facrarium antiquitatum Tricaffinæ diæcefis* [*], noticed in the library of France[†], mentioned in the *Gallia Chrifliana*[‡]; though neither Don Martenne, nor Camuzat, nor Peter le Long, nor M. de Fontette, or, more lately, the Benedictines, add the leaft circumftance refpecting the perfon, whofe authority fome of them borrow, and whofe work others announce. As to Fabricius, and the authors of hiftorical dictionaries,

---

[*] Page 235. [†] Vol. II. Nos. 17268, 17327, 17328.
[‡] Vol. XII. page 514.

as

as well as the bibliographers, whom I had in my
power to confult, not one of them appears to have
known any thing of him. Perhaps I fhould have
received more light from thofe authors who, being
natives of the Low Countries, have written hiftories
of them *ex profeffo*. Thefe, I confefs, I had not
leifure to confult; I had only Aubert le Mire, in
my poffeffion, who gave me no information on this
head.

All that I fhall fay of him here will be confined
then to the little I have been able to collect from
the few paffages of his work, in which the author
fpeaks of himfelf. All that he fays concerning himfelf is, that he was a cotemporary of Charles VII.
and Lewis XI : that he had frequently the honour
of being admitted to the former of thefe princes
and converfing familiarly with him: that he had
cultivated the friendfhip of many perfons of confiderable rank, and worthy of credit, particularly
count Dunois : that, after the expulfion of the
Englifh, he was ordered by Charles VII. to revife
the trial of the Maid of Orleans, and had compofed a book on the examination of that iniquitous
proceeding; and, finally, that in 1482, he lived at
Utrecht.

From the manner in which he expreffes himfelf
in fome places, we may conjecture that he wrote
his hiftory at different times privately, and as the
events took place, at leaft as to part of the reign
of Lewis XI. He tells us precifely the date of his
writing the twenty-fifth chapter of the fecond book:

that

that it was four years and an half after the imprifonment of the bifhop of Verdun, who fhared both
in the good fortune and the difgrace of cardinal
Balue. The thirteenth chapter of the third book
muft evidently have been written before Margaret
of Anjou's return to France.

From thefe few dates it follows, almoft to a de-
monftration, that Amelgard muft have written his
hiftory in the earlier years of the reign of Charles
VII. at lateft, of which he records no other event
or circumftance · than the affembling the ftates of
Tours, which took place fhortly after that prince
came to the throne.   Our hiftorian, at this period,
muft have been advanced in years.   A man who
has always lived as a private individual, as it appears Amelgard did, and who does not appear to
have borne any titles, or poffeffed any dignity, except that of the priefthood, could not, one would
imagine, arrive in his youth to fuch a degree of confequence and perfonal reputation, as we muft fup-
pofe our author had acquired in 1452, or 1453,
when he was charged with the revifal of the procefs
of Joan la Pucelle.   We muft neceffarily admit
him at that time to have arrived at an age of maturity at leaft; of courfe he muft have been in
years in 1484.   If to thefe circumftances we add
his total filence as to all that paffed after this' period, it feems yery probable that he did not long
furvive it.

What I have obferved as to the private manner
in which Amelgard appears to have· lived, deter-

mines nothing refpecting the rank in which he was born. But, from the confideration which he enjoyed during his life, we muft either conclude that he was poffeffed of a high degree of moderation, if he neglected the purfuit of dignities, to which both his rank and his abilities entitled him; or that he muft have poffeffed fuperior merit, if prevented by his birth from occupying places of honour: he. was equally admitted and efteemed in the fociety, and employed in the affairs of kings and princes.

The view of the author in compofing this work, the freedom with which he fpeaks his fentiments of the princes he mentions; the ftile in which he writes; the knowledge and cultivation of mind which his manner indicates; all confpire to corroborate the latter opinion.

In a fhort preface, in which he boafts of the utility of hiftory, and condemns the falfehoods that perfonal intereft fometimes fuggefts to hiftorians, he declares that he will write only what he has feen himfelf, or learned from witneffes moft worthy of credit, and with the fole defign of rendering his labours ufeful to pofterity. He expreffes himfelf with freedom and boldnefs when he mentions circumftances that reflect on Charles VII. whilft at the fame time he pays the moft fincere homage to his great qualities. He fpares not the attrocious vices of Louis XI. without paffing over in filence the lefs blameable parts of his conduct, or the talents he difplayed. If we go through his work we fhall acknowledge his impartiality, except that he feems

more

more favourable to the duke of Burgundy, Philip
the Good, than to Charles VII. fuppofing him
more fincere than the king, in forgetting their mutual quarrels, and defiring to keep the treaty of
Arras. He feems not to reflect, that, admitting
the difpofition he afcribes to thefe two princes to
be ftrictly true, Charles was excufable in feeling
the weight of the conditions, which neceffity alone
could have induced him to accept from a rebellious
vaffal, and a relation more zealous for his own
power, than the intereft of his family and king.
This tint of partiality to Philip, and a greater in-
dulgence for the French than the Englifh, both
perhaps excufable in a countryman of the former,
are, in my opinion, the only inftances of the kind
that merit blame.

A proper attention to the order of time, which
he too frequently confounds, is indeed too much
neglected by him. We could alfo wifh for more
information in the feveral events that occurred in
provinces at a little diftance from thofe in which
he appears to have paffed his life, and which are
only Flanders, Picardy, and Normandy; a more
extenfive knowledge of what paffed out of France;
fewer omiffions of interefting facts, which it is aftonifhing to find not even mentioned by him! From
thefe defects his work cannot at prefent fupply the
place of our modern hiftorians, nor in general be
of any great utility.

Yet the reader would not find it tirefome.
From the frequent quotations to be met with in

the courfe of it, and which are almoft always aptly cited, it appears that he was well read in the beft Latin authors, both in poetry and profe, Virgil, Lucretius, Lucan, Seneca, Cicero, Salluft, and Livy. In imitation of the latter, he fometimes puts fpeeches into the mouths of his perfonages. His ftile is clear, elevated and precife, though the La-tinity is not always pure; and in many places it is far from unpleafing, particularly in the chapter, in which, after having mentioned the conclufion of the truce in 1444, he ftops to delineate the plea-fures and enjoyments of peace, fo defirable to France, long and cruelly torn by foreign and civil wars. Amelgard was not ignorant of philofophy, though piety, a duty fuitable to his character; and a more common virtue in his age than in ours, is obferveable in many paffages of his book. He fre-quently, it is true, relates thofe popular traditions, that devoutly point out the finger of God in events, over which providence undoubtedly prefides, but which has never been proved, nor is it probable that it has made an obvious, predicted, or forefeen confequence of prior occurrences. He recites thofe teftimonies which affure us that the new and un-expected calamities, to which human nature is fo liable, are the neceffary chaftifements, or miracu-lous annunciation of preceding crimes, frequently exaggerated at leaft, and fometimes fictitious. But in recording thefe reports and notions, eafily cre-dited by an unenlightened people as our anceftors were, he exhibits little perfonal credulity, and we

may

may perceive that he did not embrace thefe groundlefs perfuafions. He even almoft always invites the
reader to explain events by natural caufes, without
attempting to fathom the defigns and ways of divine wifdom; and may be confidered rather as a
Chriftian philofopher, than a fuperftitious devotee.'

I leave it to the reader to confirm, or rectify, the
judgment I have ventured to give of the work by
the extract that will follow; but before I give it, it
is proper to defcribe the appearance of the two
copies I have examined.

The copy, numbered 5962, is in folio, covered
with red Morocco, with the arms of Colbert. It
contains, befides a table of the contents of all the
chapters, 1054 pages, very neatly written, correctly
fpelt, but very difficult to read, refembling what is
called *écriture de chicane*, the precife date of which
I have thought it unneceffary to endeavour to determine; but which I believe to have been about
the middle of the fixteenth century. At the head
of the index to the chapters, there is written in a
different hand, *fomi comitis de Lalaing*, which is repeated at the third leaf of the hiftory itfelf. Short
notes in Latin, written fince the manufcript, of
little importance, chiefly referring only to the chronicle of Monftrelet, are fometimes found in the
margin.

The copy marked 5963, alfo in folio, is covered
with calf. It contains 556 pages; the writing is
much more modern, lefs neat, more eafy to read;
but clofer, lefs regular, and lefs accurately fpelt

than

than the other copy. The four leaves, or eight pages, that conclude the hiftory of Charles VII, are wanting, and the laft leaf of the life of Louis XI. is worm-eaten. Befides thefe defects, the great number of faults, of words changed, or entirely omitted, that disfigure almoft every page, make this copy almoft as tirefome to read as the other, and compel us to a kind of collation that renders the labour tedious. In the latter copy, at the head of the firft chapter of the hiftory of Louis XI, the title is written in very bad characters, and fol- lowed by thefe words, *ex bibliotheca viri clariffimi Johannis Baptiftæ Haultin regii in caftelleto Parifienfi confilianii.*

The form or divifion of the work is the fame in both copies. The part concerning the life of Charles VII. (the only one from which I purpofe to give an extract at prefent) is divided into five books.

The firft book, containing fixteen chapters, ex- clufive of the preface, treats on what paffed in France, from the birth of Charles to his acceffion to the throne. Thus the hiftory of the reign of that prince occupies, in fact, but four books; the firft divided into twenty-one, the next into twenty, and the two laft into twenty-fix chapters each. The twenty-fifth and twenty-fixth chapters of the laft book are wanting in the copy marked 5963.

It would be ufelefs to tranfcribe here the index to all the chapters of each book; I fhall therefore only

only extract what has appeared to me either new, or worthy of remark, in the course of the work.

I shall follow the author's order, and shall note in the margin the numbers of the chapters from which the remarks or extracts are taken, passing over none unnoticed but those in which nothing is to be found that is not equally well, or, as it frequently happens, much better related elsewhere.

CHAP. I.   The author begins with a general
Folio 2,   picture of the events of the reign of
Verso.   Charles VII.

CHAP. II.   He then explains the origin of the
Folio 2,   quarrels between the dukes of Bur-
Verso.   gundy and Orleans: affigning as the
              principal cause of their enmity, the
affront the duke of Orleans had given to the wife of John the Bold, before he was duke of Burgundy. He tells us, as a certain fact, that had been related to him by people well informed on the subject, that the duke of Orleans had attempted to violate that princess, on some festival, in the king's palace*.

R 4   He

* *Cum enim haberet dux Burgundionum generosissimam dominam in conjugem, filiam unius ducum Bavaria, decore, & elegantia formæ speciosissimam, quæ & ipsa, ut pleræq. fæminæ nobiles, alti & magni animi erat; contigit quâdam vice, dum in palatio regali, choris & lasciviis, nocturnis jam horis, plures tam viri quam fæminæ procerum ac nobilium, ex more se recrearent, ut Aurelianiensium dux, qui, ut satis formosus hinc habebatur, ad omnem ferme speciosam mulierem,*

CHAP. III.   He next gives an account of the
Folio 2,   perfeverance and addrefs that John,
Verfo.   afterwards duke of Burgundy, dif-
. played in the preparation and execution of a project to deftroy his enemy; a project,
which, according to him, John formed at an early
period, but which he was advifed to delay till he
had made his rival hated by the people and the
great men of the realm, which he effected more
eafily with the people, than with the nobility and
head officers of the army.

CHAP. IV.   Then follows the beginning of the
Folio 4,   bloody war between the   and
Verfo.   Burgundians. From this period he
ftiles the count Armagnac conftable,
though it was many years after that this nobleman
was advanced to that dignity.

The battle of St. Cloud is defcribed by Amelgard much more minutely than by M. de Villaret,
or even Monftrelet.

mulierem, velut equus aliquis emiffarius adbinniebat, in quadam
abdito palatii loco ipfius dominae veftigiis infidiatus, &, ut fua
aeftimatione reputabat, loci ac temporis opportunitatem nactus, eam
de ftupre feu adulterio follicitavit. Cui fceleri magno animo refif-
tenti, vim etiam inferre attentare praefumpfit. Quam injuriam
aegre nimis & anxiae ferens, ut generofa atque magnanima domina,
optimo & ardenti animo viro fuo conjuncta, vi repulfa, & nefando
ipfius adulteri conamine depulfo, fe viro fuo protinus querelam fac-
turam de tanta injuria comminata eft; quod & facere non
obraifit.

At

At this period he tells us count d'Aumale was expelled from Rouen. This is a fact I do not find mentioned in our authors, unless it is the same that M. Villaret dates in 1418.

CHAP. V.   In relating the taking of Soiffons, which, according to him, happened in 1414, on the feftival of Saints Crifpin and Crifpianus, he adds that the inhabitants had too juftly merited, by their diffolute manners, the chaftifement they experienced; and that, according to vulgar tradition, the facking of the city had been foretold. Forty years before, a child, led with his playfellows, by a fchoolmafter, to the edge of the river, found a plate of metal, on which was written in ancient Roman charaters, *væ tibi Sueffio, peribis ut Sodoma.* The horrors to which the city was expofed in this inftance are more fully defcribed by Amelgard than any other writer.

CHAP. VII.   In like manner he fays that the
Fol. 6,   taking of Harfleur may be confidered
Verfo.   as an effect of divine juftice, which
decreed that the city from which fo great a number of pirates had for a long time iffued fhould become in its turn the pray of the enemy, according, fays he, to the faying of Ifaiah: *væ! qui prædaris, nonne & ipfe prædaberis, & qui fpernis nonne & ipfe fperneris! cum confummaveris deprædationem, deprædaberis.*

He

CHAP. VIII.   He afferts that at the battle of
Folio vii.   Azincourt, the French army was
Verfo.   four times as numerous as that of
              the Englifh. He relates, but, without any confirmation, that Henry, before he refolved on giving battle, had offered the reftitution of Calais and a large fum of money; and he fays, that when the action was juft about to begin, Henry harrangued his army in the following words:

  " Brave and dear companions, the hour is
" come that you muft fight, not for glory and
" renown, but for life. The arrogance and cruelty
" of the French are well known. It is certain, that
" if through fear and cowardice you fuffer your-
" felves to be conquered, they will not fpare a man
" of you, but will flay you like fo many fheep.
" This will not be my fate, nor that of the princes
" of my blood; for the enemy will be more careful
" to preferve us, from the hopes of obtaining a
" large ranfom, than they will be eager to deftroy
" us. But you have no refource but in your cou-
" rage; nor can you flatter yourfelves that the
" thirft of gain will induce a nation that bears you
" the ftrongeft and moft inveterate hatred, to fpare
" your lives. If then you think life preferable to
" death, remember, like heroes, the blood from
" which ye fprung, the glory and fame that the
" Englifh have acquired in war, and fight like
" brave and valient men, for the prefervation of
" your lives."

He

CHAP. IX.   He dates this battle on the feftival
Folio 7,   of Crifpin and Crifpianus, not omit-
Verfo.   ting that in this circumftance we may
obferve the finger of God thus punifh-
ing the acts of violence committed on the fame
day in the preceding year at the facking of Soiffons, in the monaftery dedicated to thefe two faints.
Let us add, however, to the praife of our author,
and in confirmation of the fentence we have paffed
above, that he leaves the reader at liberty to adopt
or reject this reflection. Thefe are his words :
" In this refpect every one may think as he
pleafes ; contenting myfelf with giving a true relation of events, I leave to bolder men than myfelf
to endeavour to penetrate into the fecrets of divine
providence."

CHAP. XI.   Speaking of the fecond invafion of
Folio 8,   the king of England in Normandy,
Verfo.   Amelgard reprefents the inhabitants of
that province in a condition which we
cannot eafily conceive to have been poffible. According to him, the people of this country, rendered
effeminate by flavery and a long peace, were in a
ftate of extreme fimplicity. The greater part believed the Englifh not to be a nation, but a kind of
wild beafts, who fell upon men to de-
CHAP. XIII. vour them. This affertion he repeats
Folio 9,   further on, adding, that this circum-
Verfo.   ftance was aftonifhing, as the inhabitants of Normandy were only feparated

parated from the Englifh by a narrow arm of the fea.

CHAP. XIV.   He fays, that after the treaty of
Folio 10,   Troyes, whilft Paris remained in the
Verfo.   hands of the Englifh, all the fcholars
of the univerfity that took any de-
gree were obliged to fwear to obferve that treaty.

CHAP. XVI.   Amelgard pretends that Henry V,
Folio 10,   when he learned the death of his
Verfo.   brother, the duke of Clarence, at
Beaugé, faid, that he would have condemned the prince to death, if he had furvived the
battle, as a punifhment for his rafhnefs, and for
having fought the enemy contrary to his orders.

The death of Henry he relates nearly in the fame
manner as Monftrelet; adding, that the people
confidered his death, occafioned by the difeafe vul-
garly called *Saint Fiacre's*, as a punifhment of the
order, or at leaft permiffion, which that prince gave
his army, in cold blood, to plunder the oratory and
poffeffions of St. Fiacre, near Meaux, in an expedition of which I find no trace in any of our hiftorians, not even in Dupleffis.

BOOK II.   Amelgard's narrative is rapid. The
CHAP. III.   only event of the two firft years of
Folio 13,   the reign of Charles VII. that he
Verfo.   relates circumftantially, is the battle
of

of Verneuil, and his account differs in many refpects from that given by other hiftorians. According to him, the Italians, whom others ac-
cufe of having fled firft, and thrown the French
line into diforder, by falling back upon it, performed, on the ·contrary, prodigies of valour.
They not only pierced the line of infantry, in the
van of the Englifh army, but they penetrated
through the midft of the remainder of the enemy,
who would have loft the battle, if they had not
opened to give a free paffage to this determined
troop. " The Italians," continues our author,
" perfuaded that the French were following them,
pufhed on to the baggage of the Englifh, the
greateft part of which they plundered." The
Journal of Paris* agrees with Amelgard in this
fact, but relates it in a manner by no means honourable to thefe foreigners.

Amelgard does not determine the hiftorical
doubt, refpecting whom we are to cenfure for the
imprudence that brought on fo ill-timed a battle,
the confequences of which were for a long time fatal
to France. He appears inclined to throw the blame
on the Scots : at leaft he afcribes to their pride and
arrogance the cruelty of that day's fight. According to him, the duke of Bedford, juft before the
action, fent to their chiefs to know on what terms
they wifhed to engage; they, full of arrogance,
confiding in the ftrength and number of their

* *Journal de Paris,* 1424, pages 99 and 101.

troops, anfwered, if they were conquerors, they intended to give no quarters to the Englifh, and expected no mercy if they were conquered. This circumftance is not mentioned in any hiftorian that I have ever read, except that the Journal of Paris* feems to attribute thefe fentiments to all the French army in general. Amelgard gives

Chap. XIV. this fact for a truth fo undoubted, that
Folio 13, he allots a whole chapter, not a long
Verfo. one indeed, to inform us, that this flaughter and deftruction of the Scottifh auxiliaries was a compenfation, and even an ample one, for the misfortunes of that day. This he affures us he often heard from the wifeft minifters, with whom he had opportunities of converfing. " Such," faid they, " were the audacity and
" prefumption to which thefe ftrangers had arrived,
" that, defpifing and confidering as nothing the
" troops of France, exhaufted by fo many foreign
" and civil wars, they purpofed, had they been
" conquerors at Verneuil, to put to death all the
" nobles of Anjou, Touraine, Berry, and the
" neighbouring provinces, and to appropriate to
" themfelves, as fpoil, their wives, property, and
" eftates."

Book III.   The fixth chapter of the third
Chap. VI.   book is entirely taken up in painting
Folio 16.   the calamities that laid France defolate, exhibiting a moft affecting pic-

* Page 101.

ture

ture of the acts of violence and rapine committed
by robbers. The reader would be tempted to fup-
pofe that the author is fometimes guilty of exaggeration when he fays, that " in one year not lefs than
ten thoufand were taken and condemned to death by
the courts of juftice in the province of Normandy
alone." Yet we can fcarcely avoid crediting him,
when he adds, that " this might eafily be verified,
both by the public regifters and the account of
fums paid for informations or taking of malefactors,
whofe heads had a price fet on them."

CHAP. VII.   In his account of the day of Her-
Fol. 18.   rings, Amelgard agrees with other
Verfo.   hiftorians in almoft every circum-
        ftance. In the fuperiority in num-
bers of the French army, however, he agrees only
with the Journal of Paris, which makes it amount
to feven thoufand men, whilft the Englifh was only
two thoufand.

CHAP. X.   His account of *La Pucelle* is con-
Fol. 19.   cife. I have only remarked that he
Verfo.   fays, on her arrival at Tours, fhe was
        there three months (Monftrelet fays
two months) before the king could refolve on giving her an audience. He alfo reports, affuring us,
that he heard it repeated by the count De Dunois,
that Charles VII. confeffed that this extraordinary
maid, as a proof of her miffion, had told him things
concerning himfelf, which had been fo fecret that
                                            fhe

she could have only known them from himself, or
by divine revelation.

CHAP. XIII.   Mentioning the reftoration of
Fol. 20.   Troyes, we find a paffage that ferves
Verfo.   to explain the kind of prediction, for
which La Purelle at that time had the
credit: that three days would not elapfe before the
king would be received into the city.. Amelgard
takes no notice of this prediction, faying only, *ag-
greffus itaque Trecas Companiæ urbem, concilio atque
operâ probatiffimi atque fapientiffimi viri, magiftri Jo-
bannis Acuti, qui illius urbis epifcopalem cathedram
tenebat, & ecclefiaftica.ftrenuè & nobiliter adminiftrabat,
in eâ urbe cum pace & lætitiâ receptus eft.*

Amelgard mentions a remarkable circumftance
refpecting the king's coronation. He fuppofes this
coronation to have taken place at St. Dennis; and
not through miftake, for he twice diftinguifhes the
confecration at Rheims from the coronation of St.
Dennis *.

But,

* Folio 20.   *Carolus, Francorum rex, qui nondum inunctus*
Verfo.   *more Chriftianiffimorem Francorum regum fuerat, nec
regio diademate infignitus feu coronatus, eo quod
Remorum civitas in quá reges* confecrari, *& Parifiorum urbi &.
villa feu oppidum S. Dionyfii in quo* coronari eos affuetum erat,
fub Anglorum poteftate adhunc tenerentur.* · · · · ·

Fol. 21.   And farther on : *fuitque Remis cum magno tri-.
umpho & ingenti Francorum alacritate oleo fancto* inunctus & facratus, *comitante femper Johanná Puellá, in virtli vefte &
armis, regium exercitum cum fuis antidictis militaribus fignis.*
Volens

But, independent of the abfolute filence of all other hiftorians, his narration being fometimes confufed and full of anaChronifms, and particularly in this place, is fufficient to prevent our giving credit to a faĉt of this kind. For inftance, he places a retreat of Charles VII. and a march of the duke of Bedford toward Senlis, then in the poffeffion of the Englifh; after the unfortunate affault of Paris: two faĉts not eafily to be reconciled with the fequel of the hiftory.

His reflections concerning La Pucelle are pious, but judicious. He is evidently inclined to believe that the divine power influenced thofe events in which fhe was concerned, and that there was fomething fupernatural in that hiftorical phenomenon. But, faithful to the laws of impartiality, he leaves his readers at liberty to think as their information, judgment and inclination, may lead them. *Talibus igitur de Johannâ Puellâ recenfitis, de cujus miffione & apparitionibus & revelationibus per eam affertis, nulli pro fuo captu & arbitrio quod voluerit fic vel aliter fentiendi adimimus facultatem.* It is here he adds, that, after the expulfion of the Englifh, being ordered by the king to revife the trial of this unfortunate

---

Volens autem rex, & alias regni urbes, & loca provinciafque quæ adhunc fub boftium erant poteftate, perluftrare, & præfertim regiam illam fuam infigniffimam Pariforum civitatem, atque S. Dionyfium, ubi diadema fceptrumque regale fufcepturus erat, regnique folium confcenfurus, S. Dionyfium cum fuo exercitu petiit; quo loco, cum tanta militiæ atque potentiæ ad refiftendum inefficax effet, etiam in pace receptus eft, atque inibi, ut regibus novis moris eft, coronatus.

heroine, he compofed a book, containing an examination of all the machinations that had been employed againft her.

Book III.   The firft chapters of the third book
Chap. I. II. are taken up in defcribing the deplo-
III. IV. V.   rable ftate of Normandy at that period,
              and relating more or lefs circum-
ftantially fome of the actions of that war, that took place, when the inhabitants of that province, rifing of their own accord, would have eafily driven out the Englifh, if they had received the leaft fuccour from Charles VII.   Amelgard, in this inftance, does not flatter that prince.   He openly and boldly reproaches him with having betrayed, as it were, thofe unhappy people, whofe natural inclination for their lawful fovereign rendered them the victims of the enemy : nor does he fcruple to attribute to the king's love of pleafure and quiet, his omitting to avail himfelf of the exertions of his unfortunate fubjects, who deferved a better fate.   *Illi enim fimpliciffimi agrorum cultores, juftiffimam cum pietate vitam agentes, zelo ferventiffimo ac naturali quodam amore, quibus ad Francorum regnum & regem, tamquam vetus & naturale imperium, erant affecti, patriam pro magna parte de Anglorum manu recuperaverunt ; & fub regis fui revocarant dictionem. Ipfe vero, conviviis & lafciviis fuas exfaturans libidines ; & luxu atque inerti otio torpens, nullam providentiam adhibebat, ad illos fibi fideliffimos, fuique honoris & fublimationis zelantiffimos amatores, fuendos atque defenfandos. Sed potuis,*

potuis, ab illis immaniffimis hoftibus fuis, tanquam a cruentiffimis beftiis, eos jugulari paffim & difcerpi fime-bat, & quodam modo faciebat.

Thefe laft words he explains, by faying, that the king's partizans were guilty of no lefs cruelties and robberies, than the Englifh troops. He adds, that Charles VIIth's foldiers faw with regret the cities and towns of Normandy return voluntarily to the king, as it deprived them of the hopes they had entertained of enriching themfelves at the taking and pillaging of thefe places, if they had been compelled by force of arms to fubmit. *Dolebantque quod tot oppida & caftella patriæ ab Anglorum poteftate eruiffant, quafi minor prædas agendi, ad quas folummodo inhiebant, facultas per hoc eis relinqueretur.*

CHAP. IX.   The infurrection of Normandy, the devaftation of the country of Caux, the defeat, the wounding and death of the earl of Arundel at Gerberoy, are all defcribed by Amelgard more carefully and circumftantially, than by any of our hiftorians; as is alfo the ineffectual fiege of Calais by the duke of Burgundy.

CHAP. XI.   There are alfo fome new particulars refpecting the fiege of Harfleur by the Englifh, and the vain attempt of Count de Dunois, to fuccour that city.

CHAP. XV.   One of the events of that war, which Folio 40.   he takes moft pains to relate, is the

fiege of Pontoife in 1451. He mentions particularly circumftances that I do not find in any other
hiftorian, refpecting Talbot's attempt on Poiffi,
where Charles VII. retired after the Englifh had
paffed the Oife. According to him the king was
within lefs than an hour of being taken. He was
in bed when he heard that the Englifh were at the
gates of the city. He had fcarce time to efcape
out of it, and, to ufe the expreffion of our hiftorian, " his fheets were not cold," *adhuc cubilis fui
linteamenta calentia invenerunt*, when Talbot entered
the chamber of the convent of Poiffi, from whence
the king had juft retired to Conflans. He does not
conceal the cruelties that were committed at the
taking of Pontoife. To fhow to what a point the
troops were incenfed againft their enemies, he relates, that an Englifhman, who, to efcape death, had
taken refuge under the belly of the king's horfe,
could not even there find the protection he fought;
but, in fpite of the entreaties, orders, and even
menaces of the king, this wretch was torn in pieces
with fuch fury, that the horfe itfelf was near falling a victim. This exceffive animofity, which,
he fays, he had from the king's mouth, Amelgard
in fome meafure excufes. The French were irritated by Talbot's having inhumanly maffacred,
with his own hand, by cutting him to pieces with a
hatchet, a French prifoner, whom he caufed to be
brought before him, after one of the actions that
took place on attempting to fupply the befieged
with provifions.

CHAP.

Chap. XVII. I ought not to omit, that between the taking of Pontoife and the ſiege of Dieppe by Talbot, then earl of Shaftſbury, Amelgard places an expedition of the duke of Somerſet, of which I find no trace in our hiſtorians, except a ſlight mention of it * in Daniel and Rapin Thoiras. All he ſays here on the project of the duke is preſumption, his conduct in that expedition, the unſuccefsfulneſs of his enterpriſes, his returning with diſgrace to England, which was ſoon followed by his death, is new; nor does it agree with the ſequel of the account given by the Engliſh hiſtorians. It is not my object to reconcile Amelgard's relation with theirs. I ſhall content myſelf with adding, that this writer gives to the duke of Somerſet a ſaying, of which, ſince the ancients, many ſtateſmen have had the credit. The general officers of his army aſking him one day his plan for the campaign, " if I

Plutarch, Ηερί " thought," replied he with a grave αδολισχίας. p. and thoughtful air, " that my ſhirt 506, 33, de " knew my ſecret, I would burn it Metello. " this inſtant.

Chap. XIX. There is alſo ſomething worthy to be remarked in what he ſays on the marriage of Henry VI. with Margaret of Anjou.

According to him, the chancellor, who was one of the principals in negociating the treaty, by

* Dan. vol. VII. page 201. Rap. Th. book XII. p. 102.

　　　　which

which the truce between the two kingdoms, and
the marriage of the king were concluded, was at
this time bifhop of Chicheſter. On their arrival at
Tours, (he adds) the Engliſh plenipotentiaries ſaid
that Henry would have ardently wiſhed to obtain in
marriage one of the daughters of the king, but that
he was reſtrained by an infurmountable fear. The
marriages of the daughters of kings of France with
Engliſh princes had always been ſo unhappy, that
even in France it was dreaded as ominous. In reality,
theſe alliances had been the ſource of many calamities to that kingdom, as they had ſerved as foundations and pretexts to rights or pretenfions, which
England had ſo long endeavoured to ſupport by
force of arms. Defirous, therefore, of ſubmitting
to the will of heaven, that ſeemed to reprove ſuch
unions, and not to renounce his alliance with ſo
illuſtrious an houſe, their maſter contented himſelf
with demanding a niece of the king, the princeſs
Margaret, daughter of René d'Anjou, king of
Sicily, Charles VIIth's brother-in-law.

On occaſion of this marriage, Amelgard makes
ſome philoſophical reflections on the ſad deſtiny of
that princeſs, whoſe birth promiſed her more happineſs. This is one of the places where his frequent and well-adapted quotations from Latin
authors, particularly of verſes and paſſages from
the two Senecas, atteſt him to have poſſeſſed much
learning, and a confiderable degree of taſte for the
age in which he wrote,

Book

Book IV,   I muſt give the ſame opinion of the
Chap. I,   firſt chapter of the fourth book, which
I have already mentioned. It is wholly
taken up in deſcribing the joy cauſed through
all France by the concluſion of this truce, and the
rejoicings of the people, The ſtile of Amelgard
appears here to be animated, flowery and elegant.
This chapter is full of imitations of Virgil.

Nothing particular reſpecting the eſtabliſhment
of the companies is to be met with in Amelgard,
except what is related in the chronicle, page 427,
publiſhed by Godefroy, which is no where elſe to
be found. The chronicle ſays, " at the beginning of their eſtabliſhment, an ordinance was made
for the cities of the kingdom to furniſh them (the
companies) with lodging and diet, and a certain
quantity of proviſion was allotted to each, both for
themſelves and their horſes, to be delivered to them
by the people." But this ordinance has ſince been
changed, it being ordered, that each man at arms,
properly equipped, ſhould be paid thirty livers a
month (for himſelf, his page and footman, two
archers and a tent-maker) which was to be paid
quarterly.

Amelgard ſays, *Porro, cum initio quo hujuſmodi
ordo & numeri militum ſtatuti ſunt, tanta eſſet exigui-
tas, pauperies atque inopia populorum, quod fiſcalia &
tributa regia in nibilum prope in quamplurimis Gallia-
rum provinciis defluxiſſent, neceſſarium fuit in illis ex-
ordiis, magnâ ex parte ſtipendia militibus, non in
numeratâ pecuniâ, ſed in quantitate certæ annonæ &*

victualium

victualium necessariorum tam pro personis quam equis, taxari. Ita, quod una parochia, vel plures, si valde tenues, uni lanceæ providerent de annonâ taxatâ, alia alii, vel pluribus secundum multitudinem facultatem que parochiarum. Pedentim vero, cum inchoarent paro-chiæ in fortunas exerefcere pinguiores, ex regiis vectiga-libus quæ pro folutine hujufmodi, lanciarum conftituta funt ftipendia folvi militibus conftitutum fuit, & annonæ illæ militares in pecuniariam quantitatem mutatæ funt, atque quolibet menfe pro lanceâ cum duobus fagitariis viginti fcuta ami taxata,

This quotation I thought not superfluous, as what relates to the eftablifhment of a remarkable epocha in our hiftory, is not at prefent clearly known, as the decrees or ordinances, by which they were inftituted, no longer exift. This account of Amelgard does not inform us whether this arrangement received its final fanction at Nanci or Chalons; a point on which hiftorians by no means agree.

CHAP. IV.   What Amelgard fays of the free-
Folio 48.   archers agrees with what is related by
          other hiftorians, except one particularity which I find in him, that one archer was raifed for every fifty hearths. *Ita quod per omnes civitates oppidaque atque rura ex quibufque quinquaginta domibus unus vir deligeretur.* I know that the ordinance by which this fecond ftanding body of troops was eftablifhed, exifts; but as it is not yet publifhed, I

have

have not been able to afcertain whether Amelgard
be in the right on this article.

CHAP. V.   Immediately after we meet with
and VI.   a kind of diſſertation, or rather decla-
Folio 49.   matory *diatribe*, on the inconveni-
              encies that aroſe from the eſtabliſh-
ment of thoſe two bodies. Probably the author,
viewing the acts of violence, tyranny, and exaction,
that were exerciſed in the reign of Louis XI. perhaps too, fearing that the example given in France
might ſoon be followed in the ſtates of the duke of
Burgundy, in whoſe welfare he was much more in-
tereſted, ſaw that whilſt this eſtabliſhment contributed to ſtrengthen the prince againſt the enterpriſes of foreign enemies, it had at the ſame time
furniſhed him with the means of enſlaving his ſubjects, with a pretext too plauſible, and unfortunately always ſubſiſting, of impoſing arbitrary tri-
butes, and the force neceſſary to levy contributions. Probably too, the admirable order in which
Charles VII. had put and kept the ſeveral parts of
adminiſtration, during the latter part of his reign,
had not long ſubſiſted under his ſucceſſor; and the
ſoldiery, who had been narrowly watched whilſt the
glorious and beneficent reſtorer of the French mo-
narchy lived, leſs reſtrained and more favoured by a
tyrant, who was obliged to keep well with them to
maintain his deſpotiſm, ſoon indulged themſelves in
exceſſes and oppreſſions, of which the unarmed
multitude were daily the victims.

                                        The

The picture Amelgard has given us of the wrongs and injuries which the inhabitants of the country, of the villages, or even of the cities, that were conftrained to receive and lodge thefe dangerous guefts had to fuffer from them, can fcarcely be fufpected of falfehood, or indeed of much exaggeration. We may eafily believe too, that Louis XI. naturally greedy, covetous, and cruel, had often fet forth the neceffity of fupporting an eftablifhment that appeared in the higheft degree to have contributed to his father's glory, to authorife his increafing the taxes, or arbitrarily laying on new duties. But though we may agree with our hiftorian on the facility which this foldiery, always fubfifting and depending entirely on the prince, gave our kings the means of exercifing a more arbitrary and defpotic authority than their predeceffors had enjoyed; yet it is not eafy to admit all the reafonings by which he endeavours to prove, firft, that at all times they might have been difpenfed with; fecondly, that at the time when he wrote (which I have already faid muft have been about the beginning of the reign of Charles VIII.) there was no longer any reafon for preferving it, and that the circumftances, which at the beginning had feemed to render it ufeful (namely, the neceffity of driving out of the heart of the kingdom, or at leaft of every moment repelling a powerful and dangerous enemy), no longer exifting, in future there could be only inconveniencies and no good to be

expected

expected from it. This paſſage, however, does honour to the ſenſibility, prudence, and ſagacity, of the hiſtorian.

Theſe two chapters are well written, and preſent reflections and political views, which, though not equally juſt, give not the leſs favourable idea of the heart and intentions of the hiſtorian, and are at the ſame time intereſting to the reader. The different quotations of the beſt Latin authors, and the compariſon of the ſituation and government of ſeveral ancient ſtates with thoſe of France, are a freſh proof of the erudition I have above aſcribed to him.

Chap. VII.   His relation of the expedition of
Folio 52,   the dauphin againſt the Swifs, ſhort
Verſo.   as it is, offers us particulars not to
    be paſſed over unnoticed, becauſe of the obſcurity in which this fact is involved from the diſagreements in the accounts given by hiſtorians; and alſo becauſe in one circumſtance he contradicts them.   Moſt writers aſſure us, that the garriſon of Baſle made a ſally, during the action that took place in the environs of that city.   Amelgard ſays directly the contrary: he poſitively affirms that the inhabitants remained ſimple ſpectators of the maſſacre of the Swifs, borne down by an army too ſuperior to them in number, for all their courage to reſiſt. Yet it was partly to defend that city, againſt the deſign they ſuppoſed the dauphin had of attacking it, that they had come under its walls.   Ac-
    ccording

cording to our author, the people would have gone
out to affift the Swifs, but were withheld by their
more prudent chiefs, who forefaw the danger to
which they would be expofed : " A fage refleftion,"
adds he, " and which I cannot but think falutary,
as an unarmed multitude on foot, however numerous, marching againft troops ftrong in cavalry, well
armed and difciplined, would have ferved only to
increafe the carnage, like a herd running blindly to
the flaughter."

The reft of this narrative is by no means dero-
gatory to the glory of the Swifs, and agrees with
their account, which makes their number amount
only to two thoufand men.

CHAP. IX.   All that Amelgard fays of the dif-
Folio 54.   ferent negociations that took place
             during the years 1445, 46, 47, 48,
and preceded the retaking of Mans, which the
Englifh had promifed to evacuate on their firft ac-
ceding to the truce at Tours, in 1444, is exaft,
though not very circumftantial. He even mentions a voyage of the Count de Dunois to England,
which certainly took place, as is proved by the afts
inferted in Rymer's Colleftion, though not mentioned by Daniel or Villaret, perhaps becaufe none
of our original hiftorians fay any thing of it.

CHAP. X.   After this he briefly relates the trou-
Folio 55,   bles of England, and the death of the
Verfo.   duke of Gloucefter. He does juftice
                                                    to

to the great qualities of that prince, and reprefents him as a man of much learning and erudition. We meet with one particularity here which
feems to me to be worth mentioning. Our author
relates that the bifhop of Chichefter, Adam de
Moleyne, the lord chancellor, who had been fo
frequently employed in the different negociations
begun, interrupted, and refumed, during the truce;
at his final return to England, difputing with the
crew of the fhip that had carried him, about the
price agreed on for his paffage, they arofe and cut
off his head. I am not furprized to find no mention of this particular circumftance, either in Rapin
Thorias, or Hume, though the perfon it concerns
makes a confiderable figure in hiftory, his conduct,
as well as the treaties of which he was the nego-
ciator, or rather arbiter, having greatly contributed
to the important revolutions which at this period
ruined England and reftored France: in Monftrelet * only is there any thing to be met with, which
feems to have a reference to this event. " At
this time, and in the faid year (1449), about the
end of Lent, a great commotion of the people of
London was excited, at the head of which was the
mayor of that city, who, inftigated by the unrea-
fonable will of the enemy, inhumanly murdered
the bifhop of *Cloxetre*, chancellor to the king of
England, who was a plain good man of great learning." But, befides that Adam de Moleyne was
bifhop of Chichefter, not of Gloucefter, if he was

* Vol. III. fol. vii. anno 1449.

killed,

killed, as Amelgard relates, his death muſt be placed between the end of December 1449, and the early months of 1450; for I find in Rymer, a letter of king Henry VI, dated the

VOL. V.   9th of December 1449, by which, in
Part 2,   conſideration of the great age and long
Page 20.   and important ſervices of that prelate, he diſpenſes with all the duties of his office, and gives him permiſſion to leave the kingdom, and return to it whenever he ſhould pleaſe, with liberty to take with him, or cauſe to be carried by whom he pleaſed, to the value of five hundred marks. And farther on, in the ſame

Page 25.   collection, we meet with another letter of the ſame prince, dated the 30th of May 1450, granting Renaud, biſhop of Aſpaw, lately appointed by the pope (theſe are the terms of the letter) to the biſhopric of Chicheſter, replevy of the regales of the latter, as having the oath of allegiance, reſpecting whatever the pope's bulls might contain contrary to the rights of the king.

Orleans, it is true, ſays that the death

LIB. VI.   of the biſhop of Chicheſter was an ef-
Page 97.   fect of the intrigues of the York party, and that he was aſſaſſinated at Portſmouth by a band of fiſhermen: but as he places this fact in 1453, it is evident that he has taken no pains to acquire accurate information. The examining into theſe circumſtances has ſerved more and more to convince me, of what has already been remarked by ſeveral, that the chronicle of

Mon-

Monftrelet has been copied in feveral places, word for word, from that of John Chartier; this latter, however, fays nothing of the death of the bifhop of Chichefter.

CHAP. XI.　　Amelgard appears more exact than
Folio 55,　　other hiftorians in his account of the
Verfo.　　　nomination of the duke of Somerfet
　　　　　　　to the command in Normandy. He fays that this poft was long contefted between this nobleman and the duke of York. Each had many partizans in the council and in the parliament of England, and firft one carried it, and then the other: the authors words are, *unde evenit ut, per fautores partum in Anglicano confilio, uni hodie provincia regenda, alteri vero in craftino committi alternardo, decreta obftineretur.* One day a commiffion was publifhed at Rouen, giving the government to the duke of York; and the day after another, reftoring it to Somerfet, with whom it finally remained. He would have been capable of rendering great fervice to his king and country in this poft, if avarice had not ftifled the good qualities he poffeffed.

CHAP. XII.　　The taking of Fougeres, which
Folio 56,　　ferved as a reafon or pretext for
Verfo.　　　breaking the truce is very circumftantially related.

The

CHAP. XIV. The exact and natural picture
Folio 58, Amelgard gives of the different emo-
Verso. tions with which the duke of Somer-
set was agitated, when he learnt at
Rouen, where he then was, the surprise of Pont de
l'Arche, is very interesting. None of the other
historians enters into this minutely. He says,
on this occasion, that the bishops of Bayeux, Aur-
anches, and Lisieux, were that day
Monstrelet, (according to Monstrelet the 16th of
Vol. iv. May, 1449), present at Rouen, be-
Folio 8. cause they had been enjoined to be
there the day before to hold a coun-
cil. This, perhaps, would deserve attention, and
furnish matter to some researches that might not
be uninteresting, but which are foreign to the object
of this extract.

CHAP. XVI. At the taking of Pont-audemer,
Folio 60, what historians call newly-invented
Verso. fusees, Amelgard only says was a
common arrow set on fire, which,
shot by an archer, fell on thatched roofs, where the
fire catching was communicated to other houses.

CHAP. XVII. Our historian, like others, speak-
Folio 60, ing of the surrender of Lisieux, gives
Verso. the honour of it to the wisdom and
prudence of the bishop, Thomas
Bazin. Without wishing to diminish the reputa-
tion

tion of that prelate, I cannot but obferve that Amelgard might have added, that this negociation-was
not ufelefs to the increafing the epifcopal rights:

Vol. XI.
Col. 795.

of this we may be convinced by
reading the article in *Gallia Chrif-
tiana* concerning this bifhopric.

Chap. XVIII.
Folio 62.
Verfo.

The figure which Thomas Bazin makes in hiftory, during the
reign of Louis XI. renders it worth
noticing, that Amelgard afcribes
to him alfo, the plan of operations followed by the
generals of Charles VII. at the beginning of the
invafion of Normandy. According to him, the
counts of Dunois and St. Paul, Gaucourt, Pothon
de Xainctrailles, Brefé, Torcy, &c. were obliged
to yield to the interefted counfels the bifhop gave
them, for the direction of their marches and enterprifes.

Chapters
XIX. XX.
XXI. XXII.
XXIII. XXIV.
XXV. XXVI.

In all that concerns the retaking of Normandy I have remarked but two things: one relative to the date of the furrender
of Rouen, which Amelgard fixes
on the 27th or 28th of October
1449; the other concerning the artillery that ferved
at the fiege of Caen: what he fays of this appears
exaggerated. He pretends that, amongft others,
there were twenty-four bombards or padereroes,
of fo great a bore that a man might fit within it,

with his head upright; and that a fhot was fired
from one of thefe pieces with fuch force that, having
overturned a tower, and beaten down many houfes,
it afterwards went through feveral walls.

Booк V.   The abridged relation Amelgard
Chap. III. gives of the troubles in England, at
Fol. 74.   the return of the dukes of York and
Recto.   Somerfet, by no means agrees with
           that of other hiftorians. If we may
believe him, Somerfet did not fall in the battle of
St. Albany, as almoft all writers fay, but was knocked
on the head in an inn, where he had a kind of
interview with the duke of York. The king was
wounded with an arrow on this occafion : the duke
of York brought him to London, and remained
there fome time mafter. Shortly after, obliged to
quit that city, he raifed an army, but was in a ftill
fhorter time under the neceffity of feeking a reconciliation with the king. He obtained his pardon,
but was obliged to enter London in an ignomini-
ous manner, going before the king, with his head
bare, between two prelates, or peers of the realm.
All thefe relations are far from exact, are confufed,
given in an irregular order of time, and not well
authenticated. It is not my bufinefs to fet them
right, or put them in proper order ; but I thought
it right to point them out, as a proof of what I
have faid, that Amelgard does not appear to have
taken much pains to inftruct himfelf thoroughly
in what paffed in foreign countries, and that his narrative

rative is only exact, and to be depended on, with
respect to the affairs of Normandy, or the neighbouring provinces.

CHAP. IV.   The fourth chapter of the fifth
Fol. 75.   book is perhaps one of the moft inte-
Verfo.   refting of this hiftory, as it throws great
light on the revolution that happened
in Aquitaine; the caufe of which neither ancient
nor modern hiftorians have well explained.   Monftrelet alone feems to have had an idea
Monftrelet,   of the caufe to which our author attri-
page 55   butes this infurrection.   " And it was
anno 1453.   generally reported, that the inhabitants
of the country of Bordelois furrendered
voluntarily to the Englifh, on account of the great
difpleafure they took in the king's having laid
great taxes and fubfidies on the country after his
conqueft; fo that the fervants of the king treated
them much more rigoroufly than the Englifh had
done." In the hiftories of John Chartier and
Matthew de Coney, who have been followed by
P. Daniel and M. de Villaret, we find no fufficient
reafon for this fudden and unexpected rebellion.
Let us hear Amelgard : he will explain it.   Perhaps this quotation, more extenfive than all we have
hitherto inferted, will not be difpleafing; perhaps
too it will not be ufelefs to the perfect knowledge
of the ftate of the interior adminiftration of the
finances and commerce of France and England at
this period.

T 2   " After

" After Acquitaine had voluntarily returned to
its allegiance to France, in 1450, (Amelgard is
miſtaken, the capitulation of Bourdeaux, and the
entire reduction of Acquitaine, did not take place
till 1451; but we have already obſerved, that this
writer's chronology is not exact) the people were
at firſt treated with ſufficient mildneſs and humā-
nity. For one year they were exempted, as they
had been promiſed, from taxes, impoſts, and other
exactions, that had unhappily for many years op-
preſſed the reſt of the kingdom. But the tyrannical plunderers of the other parts of France, en-
vious of the liberty and happineſs of theſe new ſubjects, ſoon endeavoured to reduce them alſo under
the yoke. They began to levy taxes and cuſtoms
on them; the laying on of which they gloſſed over
with the moſt plauſible pretext. They aſſerted,
that it was neither for their own private emolument,
nor that of the public treaſury; but ſolely for the
benefit of the province, that the king authorized
them to exact theſe duties. The money raiſed by
them, they ſaid, was only for the payment of the
troops garriſoned there, in order to be ready to
repreſs the enterpriſes of the inveterate enemies of
France. Charles had no other end but to maintain the repoſe of Acquitaine, both in time of war
and peace. It ought not to conſider this as a heavy
or vexatious burthen, ſince the money paid, would
remain in its own diſtrict, and, being expended by
the troops amongſt thoſe by whom it was contributed, would return to the purſes from whence it
                                                    had

had iſſued. The king had juſt reaſon to fear the ill intentions, treachery, and machinations of an enemy who had ſo long held Acquitaine under its dominion. The Engliſh, deprived of the advantages that accrued to them from the poſſeſſion and habitation of ſo fine a country, would certainly attempt every method, both of ſecret intrigues and open force, to recover the dominion they had loft. From Acquitaine they obtained the wines England wanted. In Acquitaine they found a ſure vent for the cloaths and merchandizes with which their kingdom abounded, with a facility of conveying them into Spain and the other neighbouring countries, to the great advantage of their nation, rather than of the Bordelois and inhabitants of the province. Conſequently, enterpriſes were to be feared on their part, the conſequences of which a wiſe prince ought to prevent, though they ſhould be mad enough to riſk the danger."

" By theſe pretexts and diſcourſes (common to financiers, when they would ſtifle the complaints and murmurs of the provinces of France, whoſe ſubſtance they confume) they ſought to make the Bordelois and Gaſcons ſubmit to the burthen of their impoſitions; but the people always reſiſted them. They ſent to the king a ſolemn deputation to requeſt that they might be permitted to enjoy the liberties, immunities and repoſe, that had been promiſed them on the ſubmiſſion of the province. The conceſſions that had been made them, ſealed with the royal ſignet, ought to be reſpected by

T 3   the

the king, as the oath of fidelity which they had taken, was refpected by them. They afferted, that they were capable of protecting themfelves againft the enterprifes of the Englifh, much better than any garrifon that could be ftationed in the country. This was their fituation under the Englifh: they had always been free from the inconvenience of garrifons, impofts and taxes, though their enemy was then much nearer them; nor were the places in their poffeffion feparated from them by a wide fea. At prefent, inftead of enemies, they had the friends and allies of their king around them, whilft the ocean ferved as a barrier againft the Englifh. They could not therefore fear being able to defend themfelves alone againft thofe iflanders. It would be ill providing for their real advantage, if they were to be fubjected to a prefent and perpetual flavery, (more fatal than the worft they had to fear from an enemy) from a groundlefs apprehenfion of uncertain and improbable evils. They had no need of thefe remedies, worfe than all the ills that could poffibly happen to them."

" Thefe remonftrances, by which the Acquitaines endeavoured to defend themfelves to the king, were fcarcely liftened to. Charles, prejudiced by his officers of finance, as well as by his generals and captains, paid little attention to them; and anfwered, that they muft fubmit to pay the impofts for the fupport of the troops neceffary to the fecurity of the province."

" This

" This deputation," continues Amelgard, " found the king at Bourges. At their return they had only to give an account of the refusal they had met with. The province was enraged at it; and inftantly concluded that it was refolved to fubject it to the fame flavery as the provinces of France, where the blood-fuckers of the ftate boldly advanced, as a fundamental maxim of government, that the king had a right to tax all his fubjects, how and when he pleafed. This is to eftablish the principle, that in France no one has any thing he can call his own, and that the king may take every man's all at his pleafure; the true condition of flaves, whofe poffeffions, though the produce of their own induftry, and which their mafters permit them to have, belong to him in reality, as much as their perfons, and may be taken from them at his will. In this fituation the people of Acquitaine, particularly the inhabitants of Bourdeaux, affrighted, and inftigated befides by a part of the nobility, were fecretly employed in feeking the means of recovering their ancient liberty; and as they had ftill many connexions of friendfhip and intereft with feveral Englifh lords, they entered into treaty with them, &c."

CHAP. V. As to the relation of the actions that
Fol. 76. took place after the open revolt of the
Verfo. province, and the account of its frefh
reduction under the power of the king,
our author fays nothing but what is to be found
elfewhere.

Chap. VI. elfewhere. I have only remarked, that
Fol. 77. in making the eulogium of the cele-
Verfo. brated grand mafter of the artillery,
John Burean, he fays pofitively, that
John had been many years in the fervice of the
Englifh, which fcarcely agrees with what P. Griffet
fays, in a differtation, annexed to the feventh vo-
lume of the new edition of P. Daniel,
Page 363. and where is collected nearly all that
has hitherto been known of the two
brothers who have made the name of Burean fo
famous,

I obferve alfo that Amelgard, in
Chap. VII. relating the action in which the fa-
Fol. 78. mous Talbot fell, is lefs favourable
Verfo. to that general than moft other hiftorians. He places in a ftronger light
the unpardonable imprudence with which that old
warrior (he was then above eighty) perfifted in attacking the French intrenchments without fufficient forces, on the fole perfuafion that they would
yield to the terror of his name. He makes him
alfo die lefs glorioufly than is elfewhere reported.
According to him, Talbot being wounded, intreated
they would fpare his life, offering large fums for
his ranfom ; but the archers who had overtaken
him, would not liften to him, and pierced him with
wounds, in revenge, adds Amelgard, for the cruelties he had fo often exercifed againft their country-
men. And it was right, continues he, that the
man who had always fhown himfelf fo inhuman, fo

thirfty

thirſty after blood, ſhould at laſt receive a juſt re-
compence for the manner in which he had lived.

CHAP. XI.   I cannot avoid remarking, that
Page 84.   Amelgard, in ſpeaking of the diſeaſes
   that reigned in Flanders after the
taking of Ghent, towards 1453, 1454, mentions
what was in his time called *peſtis inguinaria.*

CHAP. VIII.   Amelgard appears, in all that con-
IX. X. XI.   cerns the war that broke out between
   the duke of Burgundy and the peo-
ple of Ghent, more inclined to juſtify the motives
of the duke than thoſe of the unhappy citizens.
It is well known that the firſt occaſion of the rebellion of the Flemings was the impoſition of the
gabelle, which appeared to theſe people in general
an inſupportable burden, and to the inhabitants of
Ghent, in particular, a violation of their privileges.
Our author inclines to believe, that it was the pride
of the latter alone by which they were induced to
revolt from their ſovereign, and that the new impoſt did not in the leaſt contribute to it. This
opinion he founds on two reaſons: the firſt, that
the duke remaining conqueror, and capable of ex-
terminating, if he had pleaſed, all the inhabitants
of Ghent that were left, we no where find him per-
ſiſt in his intention of eſtabliſhing this impoſt : the
ſecond, that if the real and common intereſt of
their country had alone animated theſe proud citizens, they certainly would not have been deſerted,
as they entirely were, by all the Flemings. If he
tells

tells us nothing new with refpeft to the events of this war, which was cruel and deplorable, for that country he at leaft relates them with energy; and notwithftanding his partiality for the duke of Burgundy, he commends Charles VII. for not affifting fubjects in rebellion againft their legal mafter, otherwife than by his mediation.

CHAP. XII.   All that Amelgard fays of the
Folio 84,   conduct of the dauphin Louis in
Verfo.   Dauphiny, and of the fubjeets of
              difcontent he gave the king his father, perfectly correfponds with what is found in the remarks of P. Griffet, and abfolutely contradicts the manner in which M. Duclos reprefents thefe circumftances.

CHAP. XV.   We not only learn nothing new of
Folio 87,   the retreat of the dauphin into Bur-
Verfo.   gundy, the reception he met with
             from duke Philip, the propofal which the latter had made fome time before to Charles VII. refpecting a crufade againft the Turks, and the negociation of the marriage of Ladiflas, king of Hungary, with a daughter of the king; but we alfo perceive, ftill more ftrongly than any where elfe, how heartily the author was a partizan of the duke of Burgundy.   He omits nothing that tends to difcover a difpofition in the king to difquiet the duke, or weaken his power, and at the fame time does not fail to difplay the good faith and fincerity

with

with which he fuppofes the latter became and remained reconciled to the king of France.

CHAP. XVI.   In the fame fpirit, he believes that
Folio 89,   Charles fupported Henry VI. againft
Recto.   the duke of York, merely to injure
              the duke of Burgundy; as if the
ties of kindred that bound him to a rightful, unfortunate, and weak king, were infufficient to induce a prince, as generous as Charles VII. to fupport him againft unjuft pretenfions.

CHAP. XXI.   For the fame reafon, undoubtedly,
Folio 94,   when he relates the death of Charles,
Verfo.   he appears more fenfible of the advantage the duke of Burgundy would
derive from the melancholy event, than of the irreparable lofs France would fuffer. He does not conceal that his death was fufpected to have been occafioned by poifon; but he fays nothing of the abftinence to which it is pretended Charles condemned himfelf. If M. de Villaret had been acquainted with the work of Amelgard, he would not have afferted that no contemporary hiftorian mentions the indecent joy that Louis XI. is reproached with having fhewn on hearing the death of his father. Our author thus expreffes himfelf:

" The fufpicion of poifon was fo much the more credited, as the dauphin not only fhewed no figns of grief at his father's death, but made prefents,

and

and even confiderable ones, to the perfon who
brought him the firft news of it, as if he had heard
of the moft agreeable event. He fat off immediately for Avefne-le-Comte, where he caufed no
other obfequies to be celebrated for his father than
a few maffes one morning, without any folemnity;
and the fame day, at noon, he appeared in a fhort
coat of white and purple, his head covered with a
hat of the fame colour. In this drefs he hunted
in the afternoon, with his courtiers dreffed like himfelf. One of his firft cares was to fet at liberty his
father's phyfician, Adam Fumée, who Charles VII.
had caufed to be imprifoned in the caftle of Bourges the moment he feared being poifoned; and not
content with fetting him at liberty, he treated him
with much honour. He did the fame to a furgeon,
who, even before the king expired, feeing himfelf
fufpected, had fled to Valenciennes. Finally, when
at his return into the kingdom, many of the officers and other perfons of his court came to meet
him, cloathed in mourning, out of refpect and love
for the late king, he forbade their appearing before
him, till they had taken other dreffes, and quitted
thofe marks of forrow and regret."

CHAP. XXII.   The laft chapters are employed
XXIII. XXIV.   in tracing the portrait, character,
XXV. XXVI.   and general conduct, both in the
Folio 94.   higher departments of admini-
                        ftration, and in particular af-
fairs of Charles VII.

                                    Amelgard

Amelgard is by no means favourable to Agnes Sorel, whofe fidelity he praifes no more than that of the king in their mutual amours : *nec eam quippe folam, nec ipfa eum folum.* He called the place where he died Adefville, adding (what I find no where elfe) that Charles gave the eftate of Anneville to the abbey of Jumièges, to found an obituary in commemoration of Agnes Sorel.

One of thefe chapters is dedicated to the Hiftory of Jacques Cœur. What Amelgard fays of him agrees with all that has hitherto been afcertained refpecting this celebrated perfon, namely, his imprifonment; trial, condemnation, releafe, or flight; his new detention or retreat, whether forced or voluntary, at Beaucaire; and his efcape, favoured, or rather procured, by one of his affociates. Our hiftorian's account ftrengthens the more than probable conjecture of M. Bonamy, on the manner in which Jacques Cœur finifhed his days, not in Cyprus, but Chio. " After his efcape from Beaucaire," fays Amelgard, " Jacques Cœur obtained of pope Nicholas V. (it ought rather to be Calixtus III.) the command of fome gallies which that pontiff had armed againft the infidels. In this naval war, during which he died, leaving a great reputation, he diftinguifhed himfelf for fome time."

In another chapter, Amelgard does juftice to the zeal, always moderate and circumfpect, towards the Romifh church and its chief, with which
Charles

Charles VII. defended the liberties of the Gallic
church.   He boafts the wifdom and advantages of
the *pragmatic fančtion*.   He alfo honours Charles
for having refpeɗed the goods and poffeffions of
the clergy and churches of his realm, even in the
midſt of the moſt preffing neceffities.

In fine, he does homage to the mildnefs of that
prince, his clemency and regard for his fubjeɗs;
but he does not diffemble that his weaknefs and an
irrefiſtible inclination for pleafure, leading him into
expences, often exceffive, were the caufes, that,
under a king, otherwife fo great, wife and good, the
people were over-burthened with taxes, and more
ill-treated by the financiers, than they might or
ought to have been.

A N

ACCOUNT

O F A

SWEDISH MANUSCRIPT.

No. 10204,

ENTITLED

*Cronicum regum Sueciæ fcriptum ab Olao Petri, fratre
Laurentii Trici, primi poft reformationem archi-
epifcopi, qui vixit circa annum* 1520.

By M. DE KERALIO.

THIS manufcript, in folio, on paper, is of the
feventeenth century. The author has begun
his chronicle at the reign of Eric I. and has finifhed
it with that of Chriftian II. He fpeaks in the
preface of this work of the obfcurity, partiality,
uncertainty, and fabulous narrations, with which the
ancient chronicles of the north are filled; but in
his own obfervations on the antiquities of Sweden,
he fhews but little criticifm or knowledge. His
work is very defective in the early times, but more
exact in the middle age; and the author there particularly diftinguifhes himfelf by a great regard for
truth. He blames the Swedifh and Danifh writers
for having praifed, in their anceftors, the fpirit of
conqueft,

conqueſt. " If we would judge equitably," ſays
he, " of their expeditions, we ſhall find little glory
" in invading a country, the inhabitants of which
" have not done us any injury, to plunder, kill
" them, burn and deſtroy the effeƈts of thoſe who
" only wiſh to live in peaee. 'It would have been
" more honourable for our anceſtors to have been
" always peaceable, mild, humane, and contented
" with what Providence had given them, without
" invading and plundering the properties of others.
" Let the courage of the Goths be vaunted as
" much as we pleaſe, thoſe who were the viƈtims
" did not conſider it in the ſame view; they found
" in them only a ſwarm of murderers and tyrants,
" who took cities and provinces to which they had
" no right, and deprived millions of men of their
" fortunes and lives. Such were the effeƈts of that
" courage ſo much extolled." Olaf Petri manifeſts the ſame ſentiments in his whole work, and
always gives pacific princes the greateſt eulogia.
It was uncommon to think thus, and manifeſts great
courage to ſpeak in ſuch ſtrains, in an age, among
a nation, and under a king, who aſſigned the firſt
rank to military glory. It was perhaps this generous freedom which cauſed our author to fall under
the diſgrace of Guſtavus I.

Olaf Petri allows the uncertainty which reigns
in the Chronology of Sweden, before the eſtabliſhment of Chriſtianity in that kingdom; and according to the example of moſt of the chronicles of
his age, begins his work only with the birth of

Jeſus

Jefus Chrift, confeffing, that what concerned the firft kings he treats of, is dubious; that there has been perhaps either a greater or fmaller number than thofe he mentions. He particularly follows the hiftory of Eric Olaï: thefe two authors have chofen unfaithful guides, and abandoned the fafeft, which are the annals of the Icelander Are-Frodé, born in 1068, and the regifter of Upfal. Thofe two genealogical tables of the kings of Sweden, agree perfectly together, and it is probable that they contain only the princes who have been fovereigns. The chronicles of the fifteenth century have inferted feveral names of petty tributary kings, called *Fylkis Konungar*, and by this involved the hiftory and chronology in the greateft confufion.

The firft king the chronicle of Olaf Petri makes mention of, under the name of *Eric*, is not found in the two genealogical tables we have fpoken of, any more than his fucceffors Haldan, Goderik, Filmer, and probably Riorder, grand-child of Oden; but he makes him reign above one hundred years after the birth of Jefus Chrift; and according to the chronology adopted by M. Lagerbring, Riorder reigned about one hundred years before that epocha. His fon Inghe fucceeded him, and was the head of the houfe of the Inglingarians.

INGLINGARIAN RACE.

This prince is notorioufly the fame, whom Inghe of the Regifter of Upfal, and the Ingve of Are-Frode mention. It is he that fixed the refidence of the princes at Upfal, and built the famous temple, where all the people reforted to worfhip the gods of the country. Olaf Petri gave him for fons Nearque and Frode, who fucceeded him, he fays, and governed with fo much wifdom, that they were honoured by the people like gods. Nearque having died, Frode reigned alone, and maintained his kingdom in peace, as it is, adds our author, the duty of kings to do. The Swedifh chronicles attribute to this prince, what the Danifh relate of the king of the fame name, who was then reigning in Denmark; namely, that he ordained fuch fevere punifhments on violence and injuftice, that none of his fubjects, of what rank foever, durft offend againft the laws. When they hailed the happinefs of a man, they wifhed him *the peace of Frode.* The genealogical tables above cited, not making any mention of this prince, it is probable, that the Swedifh chronicles have not reckoned him among the kings of Sweden, but out of envy or vanity.

Olaf gives him for fucceffor, Urban; and to him, Oftan. He reports, that Nore, the brother of the latter, reigned in Norway; and that his fubjects having flain him, Oftan gave them a dog for fovereign, ordering, that whofoever would not render him the honours and the fervices due to his prince, fhould lofe his head.

Here our chronicler places Fioln, or Sioln, and refumes his fucceffion of kings, interrupted by the ill-placed infertion of Urban and Oftan. Agreeable to the moft credible authors, this Fioln, fon

of

of Ingve, mounted the throne after his father. He lived in peace with his neighbours. It was not yet thought on, fays Lagerbring, that, to maintain the profperity of the kingdom, it' was indifpenfible to perfevere in perpetual hoftilities with Denmark. The wife Frode was then on the throne; a clofe friendfhip fubfifted always between thefe two peaceful princes. The Danifh monarch having paid a vifit to that of Sweden, the latter withdrawing from the repaft, where, according to the manners of thofe times they drank to excefs, he ftrayed during the night, and drowned himfelf in a tub of mead.

Swerker, or Swedgker, his fon, reigned (A. C. 1) after him. The Edda and the Iceland hiftories refer the reign of Frode, king of Denmark, to this epocha. Thus Swerker, or his father, was on the throne when Jefus Chrift was born. Yet, following the fucceffion of reigning princes, and the chronology adapted by Olaf Petri, Swerker would be pofterior about three hundred years to the birth of Jefus Chrift.

Vanlander, his fon was a warlike prince; but his expeditions are not known. He had a fon named Wifbour, who fucceeded him; the latter was burnt in his houfe with his whole attendance, by his two fons. Olaf Petri, following here Eric Olaï, who has confulted the ruined chronicles only, fays, that they were induced to this action by the defire of reigning; but they were urged by another motive, which palliates a little the atrocioufnefs of their crime. Wifbour had repudiated their mother, and

U 2   refufed

refufed to pay her dowry, which was an injuftice and a violation of the law. They did not reign after their father; it was Domalder, born of a fecond marriage, who aftended the throne. All Sweden was diftreffed in his reign by a fcarcity: the people offered to the gods in the firft year the ordinary facrifices, but in the fecond, human victims; but feeing that the fcourge could not be averted, they judged the fovereign to be the caufe, and Domalder was facrificed. Our chronicle feems to believe, that this prince had, with his brother, ftained his hand in the murder of their father; but he had not the fame reafons, and the rhyming chronicle, which this author copies, generally is filent about it.

After the death of Domalder his fon Domar afcended the throne; his reign was long and peaceful.

Olaf Petri gives him for fucceffor, a fon named *Attil*, who is not in the genealogical tables of Upfal and of Are-Frodé; he attributes to him the conqueft of Denmark, and the eftablifhment of a dog, called *Racka*, for the fovereign of that kingdom, with feveral circumftances of which the Danifh annals make no mention, any more than of the dog Racka.

According to our chronicle, Dingner, fon of Attil, reigned in Sweden after his father. This Dingner is without doubt the Dugwé, fon of Domar, whom the above-cited tables give him for fucceffor. He was the firft of the Inglingarian family who affumed the title of king. The princes of the former family, called

called *Forniotherian;* had borne it, but fince Oden inclufive; the fovereigns of Upfal had taken only the title of drott or lord.

Dagher, fon of Dugwe, having fucceeded his father, (anno domini 200) was defirous to obtain from the Danes the tribute they paid to his anceftors, and was killed on his return from an expedition he had made into their country.

Our chronicler ftill fubverts the order of the generations and fuccéffions; giving as fons to Dagher, Alric and Eric; thefe two princes were born of Agne, fon and fucceffor of Dagher. Agne fubdued Finland, where Frofté then held the fceptre: the latter had a daughter named *Schalf;* the conquering prince fell in love with her and efpoufed her: this union, which was an error in politics; coft him his life. The queen furprized the king, who was attending a great feaft, in drunkennefs, hung him on a tree, and difappeared with her attendants.

His two fons, Alric and Eric, reigned together after their father. The hiftory of Sweden here makes mention, for the firft time, of the *filkis-konungar,* or tributary kings, though it be a fact, that before that time, feveral lords had taken the title of kings; particularly thofe who defcended from the royal houfe of Upfal, that is, from the Forniotherian family: Sturlefon fays that Alric and Eric were rich men, great warriors, and induftrious. They had at their court twelve valiant men, who were the fupport of the throne; to them was added a famous warrior of that time, called Starkader, who in the fame time was fkald or poet. The other worthies of that court took umbrage, and beftowed on him contempt and injuries; but Starkader repelled them only by fhewing to the enemies of his fovereign, a courage fuperior to that of his rivals.

The favourite diverfion of Alric and Eric was exercife on horfeback, and the ability in the art of riding, was for them a fubject of rivalfhip. They one day went from thofe who accompanied them; the latter miffing them, went in queft of them a long time; at laft they perceived their horfes ftraying in the country, and looking about them, they difcovered the two princes on the ground near each other, their faces covered with blood, and in their hands the bridle of their horfes: they prefumed that they had quarrelled, and being unarmed, they fought each other with thofe bridles.

Alric died and his brother reigned alone. He had only one daughter, named *Thorborg*, who, difdaining the ordinary feminine occupations, confecrated herfelf from her earlieft years to all the exercifes of war. When her father had fettled an eftate on her, fhe took man's habits, the cuirafs, helmet and fword, changed her name from that of Thorborg, and took the title of king. She fixed her refidence at Oulleroker, (Ulleraker) and received with diftinction all warlike people that came to her court, as long as they had no intentions of marriage.

A warrior famed for his valour reigned in the Weftern Gothland; his name was *Rolf*. The fovereign power he was vefted with did not belong to him by right of nature, but Kiettil, his elder brother, had the generofity to yield it to 'him, as he knew himfelf inferior to Rolf in the requifite qualities for a good governor. Kiettil knowing of no wife that might fuit his brother better than the princefs of Sweden, advifed him to afk her in marriage. Rolf having at firft obtained the confent of king Eric, went to prefent himfelf to Thorborg, covered with one arm, and fword in hand; the demand was as ftoutly rejeded as it was made. Thorborg anfwered that it had never been her intention to turn a drudging woman or a maid to any one; and fhe having taken up her weapons, and armed her people, forced this pretender to make his retreat. Judging however that a warrior like Rolf, would not be frightened from his enterprize, fhe haftened to encompafs her houfe with an intrenchment. Eric gave permiffion to this prince to effed his projed at any rate; he returned therefore at the head of a numerous troop, and after repeated fruitlefs attacks, leaped over the entrenchment. Surprized to find nobody therein, and to fee only tables covered with all kinds of difhes, he was foon aware that a fecret paffage had favoured the flight of the princefs, and that thofe difhes were left there only as a temptation in their way, on the purfuit. Every corner was fearched out; they difcovered the entrance of a fubterraneous paffage, they traced it, and, at the other extrem ty, they faw Thorborg and her troop in order of battle. The

U 4   combat

combat was hot, and for fome time uncertain; victory at laft declared for the prince, and Thorborg became his prifoner. She was treated with the greateft refpeft, and repaired to Upfal, to her father, where fhe quitted her man's drefs, and married her conqueror.

Eric left two fons, Alf and Ingve, who reigned together; Olaf Petri calls the latter Ingheller; Alf was of a fretful temper, flow, melancholic, infenfible to military glory; Ingve on the contrary was fprightly, chearful, affable and courageous, loving arms, and ambitious of glory and combats; thefe qualities pleafed Bera, wife of Alf. When her brother-in-law was returning from his expeditions, fhe loved to entertain herfelf with him 'till late in the night, whilft her hufband, who was fond of reft, went to fleep at an early hour in the evening; he frequently told her that he was diffatisfied at waiting for her fo late in the night, and the princefs imprudently replied, that fhe fhould be much happier to be the wife of Ingve than of Alf. The prince, irritated, one night ran into the room where Bera and Ingve were converfing together, and run his brother through before the perfons prefent could perceive it. Ingve feeling himfelf wounded, drew his fword, gave Alf a mortal wound, and fell dead near him.

This event, and fome others of the fame reign, give a fpecimen of the manners of thofe times. There was then, at the court of Sweden, a celebrated warrior named Hialmar, in an expedition

he

he undertook with fifty veffels each, and an hundred men on board, he landed with his whole troop, and was met by Orwar Odd, a famous pirate, who having with his people, flipped into an adjacent wood, could furprize and defeat him with facility. But fuch eafy victories were then exploded; he put off the battle to the next day, and prefented himfelf in combat to the Swedifh warrior, who afked him who he was, and what was his intention. It was anfwered, that Orwar Odd was defirous to learn which of them was the better man; Hialmar accepted the propofal, and as his troop was the moft numerous, he difmiffed the excefs, and rendered it equal to that of his adverfary, as was the cuftom at this time by fea and land: the fight lafted the whole day without any advantage on either fide; towards the evening the chiefs held out their fhields, and the troops ceafed to fight. The trial was recommenced on the morrow with the fame fuccefs. The third day, the two parties being upon the point of giving a new proof of their ftrength, the two chieftains, fatisfied with the valour they had fhewn, mutually fwore an eternal friendfhip, and became companions in arms. But Hialmar ftipulated the conditions that none of them fhould ever eat raw flefh, nor drink blood, nor plunder the merchants or peafants, except in extreme neceffity, and that they would oblige no woman to accompany them.

After feveral expeditions into Zeland, Ireland, and in feveral other countries, the two brothers in arms went to the court of Upfal, and there
fixed

fixed their ordinary refidence. There was then a famous warrior, named *Arngrim*, who inhabited Bolmſeu (Bolmſo); he had twelve ſons, among whom Angantyr was renowned for his extraordinary courage; the third of theſe children, Hiorwarder, vowed to eſpouſe Ingheborg, daughter of the king of Sweden, or never to marry. The twelve brethren went to Upſal the following ſpring, and propoſed that alliance. Hialmar loved the princeſs, but he did not dare to open himſelf, becauſe it ſeemed that Ingve was not diſpoſed to grant her to any one but a ſovereign: when he heard of the propoſal of the ſons of Arngrim, he declared his pretenſions, and begged to be preferred to a foreign warrior, who was known only by violences and robberies. The prince having referred the choice to his daughter, ſhe preferred Hialmar. Immediately Hiorwarder, in compliance with the cuſtom of the worthies of thoſe times, challenged Hialmar to a duel at Samſeu (Samſon); Hialmar joyfully received the propoſal, and the day of combat was fixed. Unuſed to count the number of his adverſaries, he repaired to the field of battle, accompanied only by his brother in arms, to fight the twelve ſons of Arngrim: the fame of Augantur was ſo great, that he was looked upon as more formidable than his eleven brethren. Orwar was glad to bring ſuch an antagoniſt to the teſt; but Hialmar judged that it would be ſhameful for him to permit his friend to be expoſed to ſuch danger, and took to himſelf the honour of fighting this all-

potent

potent warrior: thus Orwar withftood the eleven
other brethren, and killed them all in fucceffion.
The other battle was longer and more ferious:
Angantur fell at laft, but Hialmar died of his
wounds; in expiring he delivered his ring to his
brother in arms, and recommended him to carry it
to Ingheborg with his laft farewell: the princefs
received it, and died with grief.

Olaf, always keeping to the Danifh chronicles,
reports, that Iorunder was fon and fucceffor of
Ingve; that he had three fons, named Olaf, Inghé,
and Ingheller, who made war on Harald Hildetand,
king of Denmark, and were vanquifhed. According to him, the firft two perifhed; Ingheller was
obliged to make his peace, and efpoufed the fifter
of Harald, by whom he had two fons, one named
Hokenn Ring; who, with the protection of his
father-in-law, inherited the throne. The fame
author adds what is related in the Swedifh chronicles; according to thefe chronicles, Hokenn
Ring, fon of Iorunder, wifhing to avenge the death
of his father, took up arms againft Harald Hildetand, and gave him a great defeat, in which the
king of Denmark was flain with a club, by the conductor of the chariot, on which he was mounted.
The Swedes loft twelve thoufand men, and the
Danes thirty thoufand. The latter, frightened by
fuch a confiderable lofs, fubmitted to Hokenn;
they afked of him for their fovereign, a young maid
named Heta, and the king of Sweden granted them
this demand. However he kept the poffeffion of

Scania

Scania for himself, and entrusted with its government a Norwegian, one of his relations, named Olo. The Danes, little satisfied with the administration of Heta, took this Olo for their king.

These facts, destitute of connection, truth, or coherence, deserve less credit than the plain and consistent recital of the Iceland authors. They report, that after the death of Olaf and Ingve, Houghleik, son of Olaf mounted the throne of Upsal: Eric and Iorunder, sons of Olaf, being minors, had no share in the government. Houghleik loved peace, rest, and pleasures: he drew together and maintained a great number of musicians and instrument players about him. In an age when military exploits were the only occupation which was looked upon as worthy of a king, this method of living must appear but slothful and effeminate. The famous and old warrior Starkader could not prevail on himself to remain in this inaction; he joined with a known pirate, named Hake, whom, according to all appearance, he persuaded to attack Houghleik by surprize. This prince, wholly employed in feasts and pleasures, took no precaution for his safety; he learned, unexpectedly, that an army of strangers was almost at the gates of Upsal. Immediately he assembles some troops in haste, marches towards the enemy, and came up with him near Furiswal; but his army, little disciplined, could not long face the enemy. Two brethren, named Swipdagher and Gheigadar, did prodigies of valour. Hake was obliged to oppose to each

of

of them fix of his braveft warriors; but the ftrug-
gles of thefe two valiant combatants were of little
ufe; they fell into the hands of the enemy. The
Swedes terrified, took flight, Houghleik and his
two fons were killed, and Hake took poffeffion of
the throne of Sweden,

Eric and Iorunder, the two fons of Ingve, attempted to wreft from the ufurper the inheritance of their father, after fome expeditions which
they undertook to exercife themfelves, they entered
Sweden at the head of an army, which progref-
fively increafed, as it was known to be conducted
by the two princes, Hake marched againft them
with forces very unequal, yet he proved victorious,
killed the prince Eric, and drove Iorunder from
the field of battle; but the conquering king, mortally
wounded, faw that his end was drawing near. To
clofe it in a manner that might render his memory
immortal, he ordered a veffel to be filled with dead
carcaffes, arms and wood; he caufed fire to be put
to it, and the fails hoifted; and thus on this float-
ing pile, he went to perifh in the middle of the
fea.

The death of the ufurper left the legitimate heir
in undifturbed poffeffion of the kingdom. Iorunder loved war: he turned his arms againft Denmark, and facked feveral diftricts of Jutland. But
a Norwegian, named Gallangher, overtook him
with a formidable fleet, in order to avenge the death
of his brother, whom Iorunder had worfted, and
ordered to be hanged. Seconded by all the inhabitants

bitants of the coafts, which the Swediſh prince had depredated, he attacked him with fuperior forces, defeated his fleet entirely, made him prifoner, and condemned him to perifh on the gallows, as he had done his brother.

Our chronicle here paffes over in filence the reign of Ane, or Aune, who has been rendered fo famed for his fuperftition, imbecility, and pufillanimous attachment to life. Haldan, king of Denmark, drove him from the dominion of Upfal; and this fugitive prince lived in the Weftern Gothia during fifteen years. After the death of the Danifh prince he re-entered his dominion; but Ale, nephew of Haldan, conftrained him agian to retire into Weftern Gothia. A warrior, named Starkader, having killed Ale, the old king of Upfal, left his retirement; he was then turned of one hundred years, and his attachment for life had not yet been diminifhed. He interrogated Oden on the means of obtaining a long life; and he anfwered, that the king would live as long as he would facrifice every tenth year one of his fons: it is faid, that he immolated nine. He became fo old and feeble, that they were obliged to feed him like a child. However, he ftill wifhed to live, and he was going to facrifice his tenth fon; but his fubjects oppofed it, and Aune died.

Eignil, his tenth fon, fucceeded him, anno J. C. 400. Although he loved peace, like his father, his reign was not undifturbed. One Tounné, who, from fervant of the late king, had attained the employment of treafurer, had diverted a part
of

of the treafure at the death of the prince. When Eighil was upon the throne, Tounné had been reduced to his former condition ; and diffatisfied with this reverfe of fortune, affociated with fome men of the fame character, and turned a leader of robbers. The king was willing to reprefs his robberies ; but, either through contempt for fuch an enemy, or Incapacity in war, he was furprifed and put to flight. Tounné ravaged his ftates, and had the advantage in feven combats. He was worfted at the ninth. Eighil difcomfited him with the fuccours he obtained from Frode Froekne, king of Zeland, and reigned afterwards in peace. Hunting was his favourite diverfion, and proved the caufe of his ruin ; he was killed by an ox, who having efcaped the facrifice, had retired to the forefts.

His fon Ottar fucceeded him. Olaf Petri calls him Ottar, or Gothar, and fays, that Siward was then reigning in Denmark. The latter, fays he, had feveral daughters, whom their beauty had rendered famous. Ottar fent to afk one ; but the perfon he fent for the reception of the princefs, was affaffinated in Hallandia. The king of Upfal did not doubt but that it was by order of Siward; he made fail with all his forces towards Denmark, twice overcame the Danifh king, and ftripped him of Scania and Hallandia.

The Iceland authors fay, that Frode was ftill reigning in Denmark when Ottar mounted the throne. According to them, Frode fent to afk of the king of Upfal the fubfidies his father was engaged

gaged

gaged to pay him, when he had required his affiſt-
ance againſt Tounné. Ottar having anſwered, that
he had never paid any tribute, and would not pay
any; Frode came over to lay Sweden waſte, and
carried off with him conſiderable plunder. Ottar
making repriſals, went to carry fire and ſword into
the Daniſh provinces; but having inconſiderately
advanced, he was ſurrounded and ſlain with almoſt
his whole army. The conquerors left his body to
the wild beaſts, and ſent to Sweden a crow, whoſe
name was then deemed an injurious appellation;
adding, that the king Ottar had no more valour
than that bird. This prince was afterwards ſurnamed Wendilkroka, a name which our chronicle
aſcribes to his father Eighil.

Adil, or Attil, ſon and ſucceſſor of Ottar, diſtinguiſhed himſelf in military atchievements, in which
he employed courage and ſtrength, with an art and
judgment uncommon at that time. He carried
off from the coaſts of Germany a young maid,
called Urſa, who was tending her flocks. She was
an extraordinary beauty. Adil conjecturing that
ſhe could not be born with ſo much beauty, in an
obſcure rank, did not heſitate to take her for his
wife.

Helghe, king of Ledro, having made a deſcent
on Sweden, compelled Adil to take a precipitate
flight, and carried away the queen Urſa. The
charms of his captive had the ſame power upon
him as upon Adil, and ſnatched her from the throne
a ſecond

a fecond time. This marriage difcovered her origin: in one of his expeditions in Germany, Helghe had done violence to a princefs named Alof, who became mother of the beauteous Urfa. Senfible of the affront fhe had received, and not able to bear the fight of a child, which conftantly upbraided her with fhame, fhe had fent her away among thofe who kept her flocks. When fhe heard that Helghe had married her, fhe acquainted him that he was her father. The prince heard it with forrow, and fent her to king Adil, who received her with joy, although fhe had given a fon to her fecond hufband. This fon became king of Denmark, under the name of Rolf Kraké.

To difpel his chagrin, Helghe recommenced his expeditions, but having been furprifed and furrounded by Adil, he perifhed in the fight.

Urfa, difconfolate with the death of her father, never pardoned her hufband, and fecretly made ufe of all the means fhe could think the moft efficacious, to reduce his military forces. Adil had about his perfon twelve warriors, who formed his principal fecurity. The queen did not omit any artifices to prevail upon him to remove them; but the king, though devoted to Urfa, had the prudence not to difgrace perfons who had merited his attention, becaufe they did not pleafe the queen. The little fuccefs fhe obtained, did not hinder her from purfuing her projeƈt, by fowing jealoufies, and keeping up mifunderftanding among the warriors of Adil, and another warrior, named Swipdagher, arrived a little time before at the court of Sweden. She fucceeded in deftroying a part of them, arming them againft one another, and removing the reft. In the fame time fhe kept up a clandeftine correfpondence with her fon Rolf Kraké. He made a journey to the court of Upfal, undoubtedly to confult with the queen; but a fatal accident prevented the execution of their defigns. Adil, in a folemn facrifice, making the round of a temple, fell with his horfe, and dafhed his head againft a ftone.

Fiften, or Often, fon of Adil and of Aulruna, a Norwegian princefs, of the family of Forniother, (Anno Domini 500) inherited the throne, but not the qualities of his father. The Danifh and Nor-wegian pirates devafted Sweden without this lazy king taking a fingle ftep for the defence of his fubjects. He paid the punifhment for his cow-ardice. Olaf Petri fays, that his friend burned him with his whole train, but that it is not known in what manner. Agreeable to the Iceland authors, a pirate named Seulve, furprized Eiften during night, fet fire to the houfe, burnt him and all his people, and compelled the Swedes to take *him* for their king.

Seulve was of Niardeu, in Norway, and de-fcended in a ftrait line from Garder, fon of Noré. He had fubdued Jutland, and bore the furname of Juthe. Whilft he reigned in Sweden, he made an expedition into Norway, to revenge the death of his nephew, whom Afmund, father-in-law of Half, had caufed to be affaffinated. At his return, the Swedes

punifhed

puniſhed him for his uſurpation, dethroned him, and took away his life. It was about the ſame time that Rolf Kraké was aſſaſſinated with all his war- riors, by the king Hiorward, his brother-in-law.

After the death of Seulve, Ingwar, or Inghemar, reigned without oppoſition. Then the Daniſh and Eſthonian pirates infeſted all the coaſts of Swe- den. The new king concluded a peace with the former, the better to reſiſt the others, and to remove the war from his country, he carried it into their's. He was killed in a fight near a place called Adal- ſulſl.

His ſon Anund, attending leſs to his own incli- nation than to the ſpirit of the times, which at- tached honour to revenge, paſſed into Eſthonia with an army, defeated thoſe who oppoſed him, ravaged their country, and returned to his kingdom rich with booty.

This firſt ſucceſs did not induce him to attempt other expeditions. Guided by an enlightened un- derſtanding ſuperior to his age, he formed the pro- ject of enriching his nation by other ſyſtems than that of war. The foreſts were levelled, the land cultivated, the deſerts inhabited, the ways between the provinces opened, a nation of ſoldiers turned cultivators, and he ſaw a plenty reign in his coun- try unknown before. Thoſe happy eſtabliſhments procured him the name of Braut Anund, or Brant Anund, that is, the Conſtructor of the Ways, or the Burner of Foreſts. The national preju-

dices

dices which always refift the moft falutary infti-
tutions, were confounded by the wifdom, prudence,
mildnefs, and affability of this great king. An
unfortunate accident terminated his pacific and
glorious reign: on a journey he undertook to
vifit his kingdom, and to fee with his own eyes the
happy effects of his wifdom, a fnow-drift rolling
from the mountains, buried him with a part of his
attendants.

The rhymed Swedifh Chronicle that we are giving an account of, and the hiftorians that have
adopted it, afcribe the death of Anund to his brother Sigward, " who, jealous of his glory, and of
his power, killed him," fay they, " in Nericia,
near Heuga Hed." But there exifts no proof of
this event ftrong enough to be admitted in hiftory.

This Anund and Sigward have perhaps been of
the   nber of thofe petty kings fo often ridiculoufly
introduced in the hiftory of the kings of Upfal.
Such are Freu (Fröö), Herold, and Bieurn, whom
the Danifh Chronicles, and after them, Eric Olaï,
Olaf Petri, and Puffendorf, place after Braut
Anund.

This prince left the kingdom in a flourifhing
ftate (Anno Domini 600) to his fon Inghiald,
named Ingheller by Olaf Petri. His education
had been entrufted to Swibdagher, petty king of
Tiuandaland; and Sturlefon relates, that he, remarking in his pupil fome want of courage, made
him eat the heart of a wolf. It might be that a
Swede of that time was fo fuperftitious; but it is
also

alfo poffible that it might be the fiction of a
bard, forged after the cruelties this prince was
guilty of. When he afcended the throne, feveral
petty princes governed particular diftricts, and
though inferior to the king of Upfal, his authority
was circumfcribed by them. Inghiald ordered a
great feaft to be prepared for his inauguration, and
invited the principal of thofe petty kings, with all
their fons. Towards the end of the repaft, when
he faw them overcome with drunkennefs, he left
the banquetting room, furrounded it with foldiers,
and ordered it to be fet on fire. Thofe who attempted to efcape were affaffinated, the reft perifhed in the flames. Inghiald went without lofs of
time to take poffeffion of their kingdoms, and thus
made himfelf mafter of all Sweden, except Sudermania, where Granmar was king, and Oftrogothia, where Heugné reigned.

· Thefe two princes contracted an alliance with the
pirate Hiorward Oulfing, and made war on the
tyrant. The troops he had levied in his new poffeffions, abandoned him during the combat. He
received feveral wounds, and was put to flight ; but
the war was not ended by this defeat ; hoftilities
continued without any decifive advantage on either
fide, and both parties determining to make peace,
fwore to preferve it during their whole lives. Granmar and Hiorward relying on the faith of oaths, took
no precautions for their refpective fafety. But the
cruel Inghiald watched the reft of his prey ; he
marched fecretly to the place of their refidence,

furrounded it during the night, fet fire to it in every quarter, burned them, and took immediate poffef- fion of Sudermania.

Twelve kings had perifhed by the perfidiouf- nefs of Inghiald; all Sweden, except Oftrogothia, obeyed him. Heuegne alone had efcaped the ambi- tion of this monfter; while he was increafing his power by crimes, Afa, a worthy daughter of fuch a father, fowed difcord between her hufband Gou- drauder, king of Scania, and his brother Haldan, prince of the royal houfe of Denmark. Goudrau- der, inftigated by this fury, killed his brother, and was affaffinated by order of his wife: but with a cruelty and perfidioufnefs equal to her father, fhe had not the fame forefight. Inghiald was fure al- ways to deftroy the fons with the father. Haldan perifhed under the hand of his fifter-in-law; but Iwar, fon of Haldan, breathed vengeance: he re- turned from an expedition, and Afa hardly found time to take refuge with her father.

Iwar fet fail, landed in Sweden, marched ftrait to the place where Inghiald was, and this king, de- tefted, received no advice of the enemy's arrival; he knew it only by the fight of his army. He had no time to affemble his troops, and if he had, he could put no reliance in them. It only remained to fly, but where could he find an afylum? He took another way to fecure himfelf from the vengeance of Iwar; he ordered a great feaft, fat himfelf at table with his daughter and the principal men of his court; and towards the end of the repaft, when

all

all the guefts were drunk, the houfe was fet on fire by his order.

Thus perifhed Inhiald the Cruel, as he had caufed feveral other kings to perifh. " He was," fays Olaf Petri, " a lion in time of peace, and a lamb in war. The only fervice he rendered his nation was that of affembling in a fingle code the ancient laws of Upland. Wigher Spa, or the Learned, was charged with compofing this collection, which ferved for a ftanding rule in the tribunals, and for a bafis to the pofterior code compiled in 1296."

Inghiald left a minor fon, named Olaf, whofe education his mother had entrufted with Boyl, lord of Weftrogotha. The young Olaf hearing of his father's death, affembled fome troops, and marched as far as Nericia; but either for his youth and incapacity for the adminiftration of the kingdom, or becaufe the averfion of the people to his father extended even to him, he was conftrained to retire into the deferts of Vermeland. He cultivated a part of it, formed a kind of little kingdom about him, and never attempted to recover the throne of Upfal, at the price of the blood of his fubjects; an admirable conduct, efpecially in a time when this wifdom and humanity was ftigmatized with weaknefs! They gave him, out of contempt, the furname of Trætilia, that is, Cutter of Trees. His virtue was crowned by a long and peaceful life. The moft part of the hiftorians rank him among the kings of Upfal; but neither he, or any of his defcendants ever re-afcended the throne. Iwar

X 4 took

took poſſeſſion of it without oppoſition, and became the head of a new family.

IWARIAN RACE.

Olaf Petria ſeems to doubt whether Iwar ever reigned in Sweden. Some other hiſtorians, and among them M. Holberg, author of a Hiſtory of Denmark, have denied, as I may ſay, his exiſtence, aſſerting, that his name was not to be found either in the Swediſh or the Daniſh chronicles. They are miſtaken; the little rhymed chronicle makes mention of him, as alſo the Catalogue of the Kings of Sweden, publiſhed by Benzelius.—*Monument. Hiſtor. Vet. P.* 68.

According to the Iceland annals, this ambitious prince conquered Eſthonia, Courland, and a part of Germany and England. His continual expeditions were the reaſon that he was ſurnamed Widfadne, Widfarne, or Widfarin; that is, who takes diſtant courſes. Artifice and crimes rendered him maſter of Zeland. Helke and Reurik reigned there. Iwar gave his daughter Auda to Reurik in marriage; he then accuſed her of a criminal commerce with his brother-in-law Helghe, engaged this too credulous prince to kill his brother, and cauſed him to be aſſaſſinated, under pretence of avenging the death of his ſon-in-law. Auda, frightened, flew to Ruſſia with her ſon Herald Hildetan, whom ſhe had by Reurik. Iwar purſued her; but irritated againſt his ancient go-

vernor

vernor Horder, who reproached him for his crimes, he challenged him, went out with him, and was never heard of afterwards.

It was during his reign that Olaf Tretelia terminated his long and peaceable life. Olaf Petri claffes him with the Swedifh kings, and paffes over the circumftances of his death. Eric, Olaï fays, after having governed Sweden a long time and in peace, died at Upfal, and was interred with becoming honours. (*Hiftory of Sweden, p. 20.*) This recital is without truth, and filled with contradictions; he fuppofes that a politic, artful, cruel, and conquering prince has fubdued Sweden, and has generoufly reftored it to the lawful heir, or that the pacific Olaf has expelled the ufurper, an event no chronicle nor any hiftorian fpeaks of. He does not fay at what time Olaf has regained the throne of Upfal. In the Iceland annals, on the contrary, all tranfactions are connected, fpring naturally the one out of the other, and agree with the characters of individuals and general manners. A great number of Swedes detefting, and relinquifhing Iwar, retired to Vermeland, to Olaf Tretelia. This defection feemed to have weakened his forces, and to augment thofe of the legitimate prince; but his fmall province, too circumfcribed and unfertile, was not in a capacity of maintaining fo many inhabitants: a famine was the confequence. The fuperftitious people, ufed to believe that the heaven, to avert heavy fcourges, required great victims, affembled round the dwelling of Olaf, and burned him there,

in

in honour of Oden, to obtain from that god plentiful crops.

After the death of Iwar, his grandfon Harald
Hildetan governed the Weftern Gothia, Denmark,
and a part of England, which Iwar had made himfelf mafter of. Our chronicle does not fpeak of
this prince, any more than of the fucceeding kings,
'till Eric Segerfel.   •

SIGOURIAN RACE.

The death of Harald, (A. D. 700.) having left
Sigour mafter of Sweden and Denmark, placed on
the throne a new family. Sigour eftablifhed in his
ftates, tributary kings, and *jarles*, or governors. After
fome expeditions into Germany and Finland, he
died and left Denmark to his fon Ragnar Lod-
brock. Eiftên Beli, fon of Harald, was tributary
king of Upfal; he became fovereign, and lived always with Ragnar in the greateft concord. The
Iceland annals characterife him as the rich, powerful, and learned king. His courage awed his enemies, he did not attack the poffeffions of others;
he was a lover of poetry, and maintained at his
court a great number of fcalds. Iwar Bieurn,
(Biòrn) and Hwitfœrk, fon of Ragnar, having attempted to ravage the coafts of Sweden, to avenge
the death of his brothers Eric and Agnar, who
perifhed in a fimilar expedition, Eiften marched
againft them and was killed in the combat.

Ragnar fucceeded him in default of male heirs.
His whole life was a feries of military expeditions;
he

he conquered a part of Norway, and then paffed to Scotland; but after he had landed, a ftorm deftroyed his veffels; the Scots maffacred his troops, and he perifhedwith them.

His fons divided among themfelves his ftates. Bieurn Jœrnfider, or Ironfide, had Sweden and the two Gothias. Eric his fon fucceeded him, and left the throne a fhort time after to Refil his brother. His fon Eric reigned afterwards, and after him, his two fons, Emund and Bieurn Po Hoga (Biòrn Pà Hàga). It is to his reign that the firft preachings of the gofpel in Sweden, by St. Anfgarius, (Anno Domini 832) are related to happen. Olaf Petri coincides in this point with the firft writers of the north; but he is miftaken, when he fays that Thora, mother of Bieurn, was daughter of a king of Sweden. Her father, named Heraud, governed Eaftern Gothia, with the title of *jarle*, or tributary king: he was defcended of Oden, and had rendered himfelf famous by his piracies.

Our chronicle is alfo miftaken in the date of the arrival of St. Anfgarius, which he places in the year 845 of the Chriftian æra. Anfgarius went at firft to Denmark, and preached the Chriftian faith during two years. He was recalled and fent to Sweden by Louis-le-Debonnaire, from whom Bieurn had folicited fome ecclefiaftics to inftruct his fubjects. He exercifed his miniftry with fome fuccefs during eighteen months, and, when he returned, the emperor inftituted him archbifhop of Hamburgh, by a diploma which is ftill preferved,

and

and which is dated the ides of May, XXIft year of his reign, indiction XII. that is the 15th of May 834. We may then place the return of Anfgarius towards the end of the year 833; and reckoning ftill two years for his ftay and travel, he will arrive in Sweden towards the end of 831, or at the beginning of 832.

Mr. Lagherbriug calls in queftion the authenticity of the diploma, the date of which we have juft fpoken of, and that of the confirmation of this diploma by the Pope Gregory IV. becaufe Iceland difcovered in 861, by Naddodr, a Norwegian pirate, and Greenland in 982, by an Icelander, Eric Raudé, are fpecified among thofe countries comprifed in the miffion of the archbifhop of Hamburg. It would not be altogether improbable, that under the reign of Louis-le-Debonnaire, fome knowledge might have been had of thofe countries by way of England or Ireland, and efpecially of Iceland fince the firft colony that settled there in 874, under the conduct of Ingolfr, found the inhabitants Chriftians, whom the Norwegians called *papas*, or papifts, and who by books, ftaffs, (or bifhops crofiers) and bells, were known to be Irifh. But it has not at firft been called by the name of Iceland, that was given to it but by Floke, the Swede, who fought, and found it from the defcriptions of another Swede, named Gardar, who had difcovered it in 864. He named it *Gardarfholmour*, or *Ifle of Gardar*. Naddodr, who difcovered it in 861, gave it the name of *Snieuland*, (Snioland) or *ccuntry cf fnow*,

It

It is then proved, that the names of Iceland and of Greenland cannot be fo old as the years 834 and 835; nor do we find them either in the diploma of Louis-le-Debonnaire, or in the brief of Gregory IV. publifhed by Phil. Cæfar and by Mabillon; we only fee them in the manufcripts of Bremen, publifhed by Speghel, and in German, Swedifh, and Danifh hiftorians, who have followed this author. It is an interpolation of fome German monks, who ftrove to include, in the miffion of St. Anfgarius, all the countries difcovered in the north fince his preaching; but this pious fraud cannot invalidate either the authenticity of the diploma, or that of the brief that confirms it.

Anfgarius was a monk of Corbie, and not bifhop of Bremen, as Olaf Petri fays; he was not fo for a long time after. Charged with the converfion of all the nations of the north, he fent to Sweden a relation of Ebbon, named Gaulbert, who, receiving the epifcopacy, had taken the name of Sigmon. He was well received by the king and the people; but the foundations of every new religion are ftained with blood. Some Swedes, attached to the ancient worfhip, killed Nitard, the nephew of Simon, and ignominioufly drove away that prelate, as alfo all the priefts who accompanied him.

Seven years after this difafter, (towards the year 855) Anfgarius fent to Sweden an hermit named Ardyard; he went himfelf afterwards, and obtained of Olaf, king of Bieurken (Biòrkò), permiffion to

build

build churches, to eftablifh priefts, to preach, and to baptize. But notwithftanding the prefents he made to the principal men of the kingdom; notwithftanding his zeal, his cares, and thofe of his fucceffors, the light of the gofpel was not extended all over Sweden, and almoft the whole people returned to idolatry, or perfifted in it. Our chronicle agrees in this point, and makes no mention of the miracles related by other authors, and even by more recent hiftorians.

About the year 845, and before the fecond journey of Anfgarius into Sweden, Norman pirates, that is, Norwegians, Danes, and Swedes, facked Hamburgh and feveral other cities of Germany. Anfgarius, reduced to indigence, was received by Lauderic, bifhop of Bremen, whom he fucceeded in that bifhopric.

Our chronicle always confounds the dates; and intruding particular or tributary kings among thofe of Upfal, or Sweden, he places after Bieurn, Ingwar, Olaf, Trætelia, his fon Ingve, and Wæderhat: it was Eric, fon of Edmund, and nephew of Bieurn, who fucceeded him.

This ambitious prince turned his arms againft the petty independent kings, who inhabited the north of Sweden, united Vermeland to the other poffeffions of the crown, fubdued Finland, Efthonia, Courland, and was always in a ftate of warfare with Harald Horfagher, who had made himfelf mafter of Norway. The death of Eric Edmundfon is the firft event of which the hiftory of Sweden

transmits

tranſmits a date. He died ten years after Harald
had ſubdued Norway; that is, in 883.

His ſon Bieurn ſucceeded him, maintained the
kingdom in the ſtate he had received it, reigned
fifty years, and left the throne (in 933) to Eric and
Olaf. The latter lived but a ſhort time, and Eric
reigned alone : it is with him that Olaf Petri re-
ſumes the line of the kings of Sweden. Repeated
ſuccefsful wars procured him the ſurname of Se-
gerſel, that is, victorious. Olaf Petri has not
mentioned, or rather has ſpoken with great incor-
rectneſs of ſome tranſactions that paſſed during, or
ſoon after, the reign of Eric, and which deſerve to
be remarked; the one is, the firſt demarcation of
the limits between Sweden and Denmark; the
others are relative to queen Sigrid, and ſerve to
make known the manners of thoſe times. Sigrid
was daughter of Skoglar Toſte, a wealthy nobleman and famous pirate: her wit and beauty had
rendered her celebrated. Eric took her in marriage, but the oppoſition in their characters obliged
them to ſeparate. Sigrid withdrew into Gothia,
where ſhe had extenſive poſſeſſions.

After the death of her huſband, ſeveral princes
courted her. Harald Greunched, (Grönſke) tributary king of Norway, went to aſk her hand, and
found her with a Ruſſian prince, named Wiſawal-
dour, who was come with the ſame intention; Sigrid received them with attention, and lodged them
in an ancient houſe, ſeparated from her's. When
ſhe thought that they and their attendance were
aſleep,

afleep, fhe armed her people, and fet fire to the houfe. The two princes were burnt with almoft their whole retinue : thofe who efcaped the flames, were maffacred. To juftify this action, fhe faid, that fhe wanted to frighten petty kings from pretending to her bed; and this pride was the caufe of her being afterwards named *Horroda*, that is, the Proud. We fhould imagine, that this attrocious crime would have deterred all future pretenders; but at that time the lofs of life was little regarded, and a violent death was fought after as a happy and honourable end. The barbarity of Sigrid did not in the leaft ftain her reputation. A fhort time after, Olaf Trugwafon, king of Norway, afked her hand, and obtained it; but he ftipulated, that fhe fhould embrace Chriftianity : on her refufal, he ftruck her with his glove, fwearing, that he would never live with a heathen bitch (*en kednifh hund.*) The haughty Sigrid withdrew, burfting with projects of vengeance, and efpoufed Swen Tioufscheg (Tuiffkiag,) king of Denmark.

Eric Segerfell died toward the year 990. This prince is in all likelihood the fame as Eric Woederhat, put by Eric Olaï and Olaf Petri in the number of the kings of Sweden. The rhyming Swedifh chronicle makes mention of Eric Woederhat indeed, but it afcribes the fuccefs which Eric Segerfell had againft the Danifh king Swen Tioufscheg: thefe two furnames given to the fame prince, may poffibly have led the hiftorians into miftake.

Olaf

Olaf Petri obferves, that at this epocha the Swedes had five or fix times fubjugated Denmark; that Denmark had conquered Sweden five or fix times; and that neither of them could have been able to fhew what they had gained by it. " If one of " them," fays he, " has had fome advantage over " the other, he has paid double for it in dead and " wounded. To fpare our enemies, when there is " a poffibility of doing it, is always more ufeful " than to expofe ones friends : it is a detrimental " commerce to purchafe the death of an enemy by " the death of a friend; and the grief and prejudice " fuftained in the lofs of a friend, is often greater " than the joy and profit we have from the death " of three thoufand enemies flain."

Olof Stheut Konung (Skiöt Konung) had fuc-ceeded to his father Segerfall. Olaf Petri places one Stenkil before him, whom feveral hiftorians take for the brother of Olaf Scheut Konung; it is certain that this Stenkil did not reign; all we know is, that he embraced Chriftiany. Our chronicle makes mention, under his pretended reign, of facts pofterior to that epocha, which we fhall transfer to their place.

Before Olof Scheut Konung, they had in Swe-den a fpecie of little value, ftamped only on one fide, chiefly defigned for the payment of falaries. Each little canton had its place of commerce, called Keuping. The goods and merchandizes were ex-changed, or paid in money, counted by *marc*, *eure*, *eurtoug* and *penning*. The marc was of fixteen lod,

VOL. II.   Y   or

or half-ounces; the eure was the eighth part of a lod; the eurtong the third part of a eure; and the penning the eighth part of the eurtong. Olof Sheut Konung employed Englifh workmen, and coined money at Sigtoune: then, a marc of filver weight and a marc of filver fpecie, were of the fame value. There were in the whole kingdom but three commercial towns, Bieurkeu, Sigtoune and Scara.

Anund Jacob having fucceeded his father, he acted little in the wars which were carrying on between the kings of Denmark and Norway. His court was the afylum of all princes, who in the revolutions of thofe two kingdoms, loft their fupreme power; he received and treated them in a manner fuitable to their rank, without interfering in the re-acquifition of what fortune, and their own faults, had wrefted from them. This wife politician infpired no fear in his neighbours; his reign was peaceable. He favoured the propagation of Chriftianity, but without any violence. Olaf Petri, and feveral other chronicles, have reported, that he has been furnamed Kolbrenna, or Coal-burner, becaufe he had ordered to be burnt in part, or the whole of the houfe of him that did any damage to his neighbour, in proportion to the eftimation of that damage. This law is fo abfurd, that we may doubt its exiftence. There was no written law as yet; it was then eafy to mifconftrue fome degree of Anund, to explain a furname given for fome unknown event, or perhaps to an unknown

known Anund, who might have been taken for the king of this name.

Olaf Petri fays, that the king was then the book of the law, (lagboken) and that all that carried the appearance of juftice to him, became the law. Thefe exaggerated expreffions are far from truth: the kings of Sweden have never enjoyed this unbounded authority: from time immemorial, the Swedes had their particular judges, who adminiftered juftice agreeable to the cuftoms ratified by the people, and confirmed in the national affemblies. There exifted at Upfal a fuperior tribunal, compofed of twelve judges: Oden introduced, or perhaps preferved this form, and it has fubfifted long after him. The king pronounced judgments without appeal; but it was in conformity with the cuftoms, and the lagmen, or judges, the herfes, the jarles, pronounced alfo without appeal. The power and authority of the kings received increafe from reign to reign; yet when they faw that a written law would prove ufeful, far from erecting themfelves fupreme legiflators, they ordered the cuftoms followed in different provinces to be digefted into a general law, to which the people and the king gave fanction; that of the lagmen, joined to the confent of the people, was fufficient. (Sturles, tom. I. p. 478.)

Olaf Petri relates the formalities which were obferved in a duel; he fays, that when a caufe could not be decided by the evidence of witneffes, it was to be fettled by a combat between the two parties, and he who proved fuccefsful gained the

caufe.

caufe. It is likely that this cuſtom prevailed in thoſe epochas when there exiſted neither laws nor judges. The king Frode eſtabliſhed this in Denmark as law; but there is no proof of its ever having been legally enacted in Sweden; however, individual combats have always been in uſe to avenge private injuries. Our chronicle relates the text of the ancient law concerning combats. We ſhall here tranſlate it: " When a man provokes another, " ſaying to him, *Thou art not a man in the heart,* " and that the other anſwers, *I am as well as thou,* " they muſt both repair to a place, formed by " three ways. If he who has given the challenge " comes, and he who has received and accepted " it comes not, the latter muſt be reputed what " the other had called him, and incapacitated " to take any oath, or bear any teſtimony for man " or woman. But when he who has received the " challenge appears at the rendezvous, and he " who has given it does not appear, the other is " to call him with a loud voice, *threefold coward,* " and make a mark on the ground. Then the ab- " ſent is reputed a man deſtitute of honour, who " has ſaid what he has not done. If they both " come, they are to fight with their arms. If he " who has received the challenge is killed, the " other is obliged to pay half the fine fixed for " the murder of a man. (See Extracts of the " Laws of Sweden;) but if the aggreſſor loſes his " life, his words have been vain, his tongue is the

" homi-

" homicide; his antagonift is not kept to the
" fine."

Olaf afterwards fpeaks of the judgment of God,
by the trial of red-hot irons. We find it ordered
in the ancient laws for doubtful caufes; but it is
probable the priefts have introduced it into Sweden:
we fee no trace of it in the hiftory of anterior
times.

Anund died anno 1051. Emund, his elder brother, afcended the throne after him; his reign was
of fhort duration, and little is known of him. In
an ancient genealogy of the kings of Sweden, we
read, that he was compliant, but not to be depended
on, when he had an objeft in view; and that he
was furnamed Slemmæ, that is, Slippery. Olaf
Petri repeats what Adam of Bremen has faid of
this prince: he accufes him of want of fenfe and
judgment; but to prove this reproach to be
grounded, he attributes to him tranfaftions which
did not happen under his reign. Of this kind is
the demarcation of the limits, which feparated
Scania from Sweden, and annexed it to Denmark;
for which the fovereigns of thofe two kingdoms had
made fuch frequent wars: this demarcation was
made under Eric Segerfâl, about a century before
Emund. Such is alfo a defeat of the Swedes near
Stonga-pelle-bro in Scania, by Knout, or Canute,
king of Denmark. If it is true that this prince, who
died in 1042, beat a Swedifh army in this place, it
could not have been commanded by king Emund,
who did not reign until nine years afterwards.

The Stenkil we have juft fpoken of, is that which Olaf Petri puts in the fucceffion of the kings after Eric Segerfal. He fays, that then two *good men* were fent to Sweden, the one named Adelward, the other Stephen ; and that when Adelward was ce-lebrating the mafs at Sigtoune, there was fuch a num-ber of affiftants, that the offerings were *fixty marcs of filver clear.* It is true Stenkil mounted the throne, but it was not at the time when he protected Adelward. The latter preached for fome time in Upland, and died there. Adam of Bremen afcribes to him great zeal, and many miracles; among others, that of having given to the barba-rians, at his pleafure, rain and funfhine. However, St. Bryniolphe, (who died in 1317) the author of a rhyming chronicle of the bifhops of Scara *(Er. Benzel. Monum. Ecclef. Sweogoth,)* doth not make his eulogium. "Harvad the elder came to Sweden; he fpent his time as agreeably as he could; nothing can be faid of what he has performed. Death came to terminate his days, and he died as many others had done before him." Olaf Petri fays, that Adelward, abandoning himfelf to a facred fury, broke the idols, and put to the flames the helghe-lundar, or facred woods ; that Stenkil having unfuc-cefsfully warned him of the danger he was bringing on himfelf, the holy prelate was maffacred, and the king fhared the fame fate, though he had re-nounced Chriftianity to preferve his life. He adds, that Stephen went to preach in Helfingland, and that it is thought he was killed there. Our chro-nicle

nicle confounds here the facts, times, and perfons. The legends name two Adelwards; the elder we have juft fpoken of, and the younger, who came to Sweden after the death of Emund, under the reign of his fucceffor. It is the younger who fuffered himfelf to be hurried by an inconfiderate zeal, which the king blamed, but which did not coft him his life. He was whipped at Sigtoune, and expelled the town. It was alfo the fame Adelward (and not the elder, as Olaf Petri fays), who received at his mafs fixty marcs of money.

Emund having left no male iffue, the people elected for king (anno domini 1053) Stenkil, fon of jarle Ragwald and Aftrid, daughter of Malfin of Halogaland. Ragwald was a grandchild of Skoglar Tofte, father-in-law of Eric Segerfal. The maternal defcent of Stenkil was not lefs illuftrious: Nial, her maternal grandfather, defcended in direct line from Harald Horfagher, by his daughter Ingheborg, whofe fifter Alof Arbot, was a relation of Rolf or Rollon, firft duke of Normandy. Thus Stenkil was allied to the Sigurian family, fprung from the Inglingarian, a kindred to the kings of Ruffia and to that of Norway, Harald Hordrode (Hardrade). He mounted the throne about the year 1053, and gave his name to a new family.

STENKILIAN RACE.

Stenkil loved peace, and protected the Chriftian religion. During his reign Harald king of Nor-

way made fome excurfions into Sweden, with a view
to take revenge of the jarle Hokan (Hakan), who
had there taken refuge, and whom he accufed with
having let Swen Oulfson, the king of Denmark,
efcape in a combat. Olaf Petri is miftaken in
faying, that Stenkil made war on a Danifh prince,
whofe name is not known. He efpoufed the daughter of Anund Jacob, and had two fons by her,
Inghe and Halftan. After a reign of thirteen
years he died, in 1066,

The election of a new king occafioned a civil
war, in which a great part of the nobility perifhed.
Two Erics difputed the throne, and killed each
other in a fingle combat, or perifhed in a battle
(*Adam. Brem.* I. *IV. c.* 13). The two fons of Stenkil were afterwards elected, then depofed; and the
people, with almoft unanimous voice, placed Hokan Reude on the throne. This Hokan was born
in the Weftern Gothia : he reigned thirteen years.
The hiftorians differ as to the place he is to occupy
in the fucceffion of the kings of Sweden. The
little rhyming chronicle (which is annexed to the
laws of Weftern Gothia), Eric Olaï, Joannes
Magnus, and Olaf Petri, place him before Stenkil;
but the author of the Herwarar Saga, and Sturlefon,
who are more ancient than thofe I have juft named,
fet him immediately after that king; and their fen-
timent is confirmed by the ancient fcholiaft of
Adam of Bremen and of Landfetgatal. Hokan
died about the year 1079. There was before
this king a general perfecution of the Chriftians;
and

and without the interference of Eghino, bishop of Scania, Christianity would have been extinguished in Sweden.

After the death of Hokan, Inghe, or Inghemund, son of Stenkil, mounted the throne. He had embraced Christianity, and as the most part of the Swedes were still attached to the religion of their fathers, they wished to compel the king to sacrifice to the idols. Inghe, irritated, caused all the temples of Upsal to be set on fire, and ordered his subjects to receive baptism. The latter, in a general diet, gave him his option, either to follow the ancient worship, or to quit the throne. He persisted in his faith, and was driven out by the people with stones. His brother-in-law, named Swen, offered to sacrifice to the idols, if the nation was willing to accept him for their king. He was immediately elected, and Inghe constrained to withdraw into Western Gothia. But his vengeance was quick: he surprised Swen in his dwelling, set fire to it, and burnt it. He afterwards reigned over Sweden with his brother Halftan. The latter died very soon, and was bewailed by all the people, whose affection he had merited by his virtues. Misfortune had instructed Inghe; he distinguished himself by a constant wisdom, and by a great respect for the laws of his country (*Catal. Reg. Suec. Benzel. monum. ecclef. p. 70*). He courageously repelled the hostilities of Magnus, king of Norway, but he never attacked any of his neighbours. Olaf Petri, and the other modern chroniclers say, that

he

he had a war to fuftain againft the king of Denmark ; yet neither has Saxo, nor the ancient chronicle of Upfal, made any mention of it. Inghe
died about the year 1112 : he had threee wives;
the one named Meu (Mò), and fifter of Swen;
the fecond Ragnilde, and the third Helena. It is
not known whether the firft brought him any children ; by the fecond he had Chriftina, who married the Ruffian prince Harald, fon of Jaroflaw;
and of Inghered, daughter of Olaf Scheut Konung
(*Henr. Ernft. vet. Chronic. Ecclef. Laudun, c. 6*).
He had by the third, a fon, named Ragwald, and
two daughters, viz. Marguerita, who was married to Magnus Barfot, of Norway, afterwards to
Nils Swanfon, king of Denmark ; and Catherine,
who efpoufed Bieurn Haraldfon Jærnfida, or Ironfide. The hiftory of Sweden making mention only
of the birth of Ragwald ; it feems likely that he
died before his father.

The fucceffors of Inghe were Philip and Inghe II.
fon of Halftan. The former was an ·equitable
prince; he reigned only fix years, and died in the
year 1118. Inghe II. was a friend to peace, perhaps out of indolence. Under his reign the inhabitants of Iempteland fubmitted themfelves fpon-
taneoufly to Eiften, king of Norway, an affable and
generous prince. His brother Sigourd, who fuc-
ceededhim, ravaged the province of Smoland, and
Inghe did not take one ftep for its defence. Olaf
Petri fays, that this prince efpoufed Ragnilde, who

was

was afterwards beatified. This is an error: the epitaph of St. Ragnilde, related by Benzel in his notes on Waftow, imports, that fhe married king Inghe, who was expelled his kingdom: this circumftance can only be applied to Inghe I.

Inghe II. died at Wreta about the year 1130. He was fufpefted to have been poifoned, and feveral modern hiftorians have afcribed this crime to Magnus, prince of Denmark, grandfon of Inghe I. becaufe, feeing fay they, the king of Sweden without male iffue, he had pretenfions to the crown. But the ancient hiftorians have not imputed this crime to prince Magnus, though they have afperfed him with many others; and this poifoning may even be made a queftion, becaufe, in thofe illiterate times, it was eafy to miftake the figns of poifon; this kind of crime was, it may be faid, unknown in Sweden, and there are no precedents of it to be found in the hiftory of that kingdom.

The neareft relations to Inghe were the princes of Denmark. The inhabitants of the Weftern Gothia, devoted to the houfe of Stenkil, elefted for their king Magnus Nilfon, grandfon of Inghe I. by his daughter Margarita, furnamed *Fridkoulla.* The Uplanders, to whom the firft fuffrage belonged, according to the law, had no regard for this eleftion, and nominated Ragwald Kanapheuvdé (Knaphòzde). The latter, fiery and enterprifing, had no doubt but his prefence would overawe the partizans of the prince of Denmark; he went to

Weftrogothia

Weftrogothia and was killed. Olaf Petri fays that he has been cenfured with violating the law of the country, in making the tour of the kingdom pre-fcribed to the new king, without taking hoftages in each diftrict; however this is but a conjecture of the modern chronicles. We read, in an ancient catalogue of the kings of Sweden, that Ragwald prefented himfelf to the people then affembled at Carleby, without having given the previous notice of it, as it was prefcribed by the law, and that the Weftrogoths, incenfed at this kind of contempt, killed him. (*Eric. Benzel. mon. ecclef. p.* 70.)

After a fhort interrregnum, the inhabitants of the Eaftern Gothia elected for king Swarker Kolfon. It was towards the year 1134, in which the battle of Fotewick was fought, where prince Magnus loft his life.

Swerker was a pacific prince, he did not even take up arms to protect his country againft Swen Ericfon, king of Denmark; he left this care to the peafants, who themfelves deftroyed the enemy's army.

At the beginning of his reign he feduced Oulf-hild, wife of the Danifh king, Nils Swenfon, and efpoufed her whilft her hufband was ftill alive. When death had bereft him of her, he efpoufed Richiffa, widow of Magnus, fon of Nils, and the priefts were filent on thefe two illicit alliances, becaufe he had allotted them donations and founded monafteries.

Swer-

Swerker had by his firſt wife, prince Charles, who was afterwards king of Sweden: it is thought that the ſecond was the mother of his other ſons, John, Kol, Buriſſef, and Sounofik, and that he had alſo the princeſs Sophia, who married Waldemar I. king of Denmark. After a reign of twenty years, he was aſſaſſinated by his maſter of the horſe or chamberlain, towards the end of 1154, or at the beginning of 1155. Until the reign of this prince no monks had been ſeen in Sweden. He founded, in 1144, the monaſtry of Alwaſtra and ſeveral others, whither St. Bernard ſent ſome religious of his order.

Eric Jedwardſon ſucceeded him. Some relate, ſays Olaf Petri, that he was the grandſon of a rich peaſant; others that he was of the royal blood: be it as it may, adds the ſame author, Eric was noble, ſince he was virtuous. It appears, by the ancient chronicles, that this prince was elected ſome years before the death of Swerker. His firſt care, when he was king, was to viſit his kingdom, to diſtribute juſtice to all his ſubjects, to ſettle diſputes in a friendly way, to grant his protection to the feeble and unfortunate, and to ſet juſt limits to the power of the rich and noble. This wiſdom acquired him the affection, gratitude, and veneration of his people. The only injuſtice he can be charged with, was committed by his exceſs of zeal for the propagation of the faith: with arms in hand, he undertook the converſion of the Finlanders. After having won a battle over them, he eſtabliſhed prieſts in their country; he built churches, and left there

the

the bifhop Hewcy, who a fhort time after, (anno domini 1160,) was affaffinated: Eric experienced the fame fate the enfuing year. He was attending mafs at Oftra-aros when it was reported to him that prince Magnus Henrikfon was advancing at the head of a fmall armed troop, with a refolution to take away his life. He would not quit the church before mafs was celebrated; when it was over, he marched againft his enemies, with the few perfons who accompanied him; he attacked them, and was killed. Some authors have related, after popular rumours, or after their own conjectures, that Charles, fon of the king Swerker, and Henry Swenfon, were accomplices in the crime of Magnus, but Henry had been dead fix-and-twenty years; he fell in the battle of Fotwig in 1134; and Charles, who had pretenfions to the throne, who had even, according to fome authors, been elected king by the Goths in 1152, would not have been inftrumental to the ambition of a foreign prince.

Olaf Petri and moft part of the modern hiftorians have written that Eric efpoufed Chriftina, daughter of king Inghe, and of Ragnilde; but in the Icelandifh annals it is reported, that it was Chriftina, grand daughter of the king Inghe Stenkilfon, by his daughter Catherine, married to Bieurn Jæmfida.

Eric had by Chriftina, Knout or Canute, who reigned afterwards; Philip, Margarita, and Catherine. He was honoured as a faint in all the North; Pope Alexander IV. gave him that title in 1255,

and

and in a bull of Clement IV. in 1266, it is mentioned that his feaft was celebrated with much folemnity.

As foon as Magnus had committed this crime, his party proclaimed him king; but other fuffrages were ftill requifite, and the people were forrowful and offended, thought only of revenging the death of a prince they admired. Some inhabitants of Helfingland took up arms; their example was followed in other provinces: Charles, fon of Swerker, joined to them, and Magnus, attacked at a little diftance from Upfal, was killed with all his men.

Charles reigned peaceably. He obtained from Pope Alexander III. the erection of Upfal from a bifhopric into an archbifhopric, and a monk, named Stephen, firft occupied this fee. He went to vifit the Pope, who was then in France, and was confecrated at Sens, in his prefence, by Efkil, archbifhop of Lunden, who had accompanied him. This new eftablifhment was a great political miftake; it deprived the kings of Sweden of a portion of their authority, and that of the pope was encreafed. Alexander III. declared that the archbifhop of Upfal fhould be fubmiffive only to the pope; he prohibited all ecclefiaftics from appearing before civil magiftrates; exacted that all the faithful fhould pay a tenth of their goods to the clergy, alledging, that both the old and new law demanded it; that God deigned to accept this offering, not for him, but for the benefit of thofe who made it, becaufe he rewarded them by an abundance of terreftrial

reftrial and celeftial goods, the want whereof was an effect of the anger of God againft thofe, who not paying the tythes exact, defrauded himfelf in the perfon of his minifters.

Knout, fon of Eric, had well-grounded pretenfions to the throne of Sweden, and thought, perhaps, that king Charles had joined in the affaffination of his father; he exerted fome unavailing efforts to recover his rights, and retired to Norway, where he remained undifcovered during three years. It was in 1168, or according to other chronicles in 1167, that he left his retreat, came fecretly to Sweden, overtook Charles near Wifingfeu (Wifingſö), affaffinated him, and took poffeffion of the throne; but it was contefted with him by three princes of the Swerkerian family. He overcame them, and reigned peaceably to his death, which happened in 1199: from this epocha to the year 1520, at which Olaf Petri ends his chronicle, this author obferves the chronology with more exactnefs than he did in preceding times. He relates, with precifion and fidelity, the tranfactions he fpeaks of; but as all modern hiftorians relate them likewife, and more circumftantially, we refer our readers to them.

ACCOUNT

.OF THE

CRIMINAL PROCESS

AGAINST

ROBERT OF ARTOIS,

COUNT DE BEAUMONT, PEER OF FRANCE.

Among the Manufcripts of Brienne.

From the Manufcripts in the King's Library, No. 178.

By M. DEL AVERDY.

FIRST PART.

THE manufcrips of Brienne, which are in the king's library, contain eighteen volumes of criminal proceffes, carried on in France againft dif-ferent perfons, from No. 178 to 195 incluſive. Thefe are manufcripts of which we fhall undertake to give an account of fucceffively.

The firft is that of the procefs againft Robert of Artois. The volume is bound in red Turkey leather, with the arms of Brienne, and on the back is written, *Criminal fuit againſt Robert of Artois.* It contains five hundred and fixty-one leaves, which m\akes eleven hundred and twenty-two pages.

The copy is of the laft century; but it is authentic, and we read on the firft leaf, *marked by us, counfellor of the king in his court of parliament, commiffary in this part, according to our procés-verbal of the 15th of January*, 1652. Below are the original fignatures of M. Pithou and M. Petau.

Folio 3, prefents the genealogy of Robert of Artois in the following fucceffion: Louis VIII. king of France, is the ftock of this branch of the royal family.

His fon, was Robert of France, firft of this name, count of Artois.

He had for fon Robert II. count of Artois, killed at the battle of Courterai.

He had efpoufed Amicia of Courtenay, by whom he had a fon and daughter.

Philip of Artois, his fon, efpoufed Blanch of Britanny, by whom he had Robert of Artois; but having died befort Robert II. his father, the county of Artois, which was not a male-fief, was recovered by Mahaut, or Matilda, of Artois, married to Otho, count of Burgundy. She grounded her title on the right of reprefentation, not being then admitted in Artois, even in a direct line; which excluded Robert of Artois, her father having preceded his grandfather.

Joanna, daughter of Mahaut and Otho, and coufin to Robert of Artois, efpoufed Philip-le-Long, and was countefs of Artois, by her mother's fide, and countefs of Burgundy, on her father's.

Joanna

Joanna of France, their daughter, was married to Eudes, duke of Burgundy; and it is between her and Robert of Artois that this suit was terminated.

As for Robert of Artois, he espoused Joanna of Valois, sister of Philip of Valois, who mounted the throne of France; he had the county-peerdom of Beaumont.

The difcontent of Robert of Artois, count de Beaumont, at his not being able to procure the property of the county of Artois, proved the fource of a great number of misfortunes and fuits, which took place under Philip of Valois, and of the bloody wars with England, which defolated France.

The pretenfion of Robert of Artois, though defencible in common right, was however contrary to a cuftom, which it became neceffary afterwards to abolifh, and confequently it had not any real foundation. The reprefentation in direct line not being adopted in Artois, and this county happening to fall in portion to females, Robert could have only a particular title, which would have been a derogation from the general law.

Inftead of enjoying this particular title, the treaty of marriage of Philip, father of Robert, with Blanch of Britanny, confirmed by the letters of the king, of the year 1280, and related fol. 239 of the manufcript, argued againft him; fince that act, forefeeing the cafe that Philip might die before his father, in leaving an offspring *begotten and born in the faid marriage*, only the property of a particular land,

and the goods coming from the ſtock of the mother of Philip was intailed·on this offspring. So
we find that the arrets and acts had aſſured to Mahaut, after the death of her father Robert II. the
property of the county of Artois, and ſhe had enjoyed the poſſeſſion of it, as had alſo her iſſue, notwithſtanding the claims of Robert.   The acts in her
favour were dated in the years 1309 and 1318:
they are found copied at large in the manuſcript,
fol. 244 and 265.

It was then the efforts of Robert of Artois, and
of Joanna of Valois his ſpouſe, to reverſe theſe
judgments that have given room to the proceedings in queſtion. We ſhall examine them, obſerv-
ing the cuſtoms of thoſe times, and comparing them
with thoſe which are now actually followed in the
kingdom.

But before we enter on theſe details, it behoves
us to recollect how the hiſtorians have related this
affair, which has been attended with ſuch ſerious
conſequences.   In general they report it in an uni-
form manner.

According to them, Robert of Artois, after the
death of Lewis-le-Hutin, took advantage of an
inſurrection of the nobility of Artois againſt the
counteſs, to try to reduce this county.   Philip-le-
Long, then regent of the kingdom,. wiſhed to put
an end to thoſe troubles, but he was not obeyed,
and Robert made himſelf maſter of Arras and
St. Omer.

Philip

Philip then marched againſt him at the head of an army. Robert was forced to conſent, to abide the courſe of juſtice, and repair to Paris, where the property of the countefs of Artois was once more confirmed to her.

Robert ſaw himſelf defeated in his hopes; but inceſſantly foſtering an ardent defire to recover that county, he waited for favourable circumſtances. He thought he had found them at the acceſſion of Philip of Valois to the throne; being brother-in-law to this prince, he rendered him the greateſt fervices, and contributed more than any other, by his vindication of the Salic law, to exclude the king of England, and to elevate Philip of Valois to the throne. He was cheriſhed; he had the greateſt influence on his mind, and his wife experienced, on the part of her huſband, a tender friend-ſhip: with ſuch great advantages, he thought he might do any thing. He wiſhed to revive the af-fair, and to bring it to a deciſion; and did not doubt of ſuccefs, if he could be admitted to bring the quef-tion to a new inveſtigation.

To attain this point, ſay the hiſtorians, he cauſed a lady of the name of Divion, a native of Bethune, whom they deſcribe as a perſon ſkilful in forging of writings, and whom ſome of them call a forcerefs, to counterfeit deeds; and among others, a treaty of marriage of Philip of Artois his father, ſtrengthened with the ſeals of the peers of France, a confirma-tory letter of this treaty, ſealed with the king's great ſeal, as alſo a letter of Matilda's acquieſcence, ſealed

with

with her feal, which confirmed to Philip the county
of Artois, his father referving only an ufufruĉtuary
right; and they add, that he brought evidences in
fuppor of thefe aĉts.

He then went to fee the king, expofed to him
the means by which, as it were miraculoufly, he
had been brought to the difcovery of thofe long for-
gotton titles, and obtained a revifion of the fuit.
His opponent pretended, that his titles were falfe.
The demoifelle Divion being brought to Paris,
confeffed it in the king's prefence, faying, that fhe
had made thofe titles; that fhe had applied the
neceffary feals; and that fhe had procured them by
taking them off the aĉts to which they were attached.
She was burnt, they fay, as a forcerefs, and guilty
of forgery, and Robert was for ever excluded from
the county of Artois.

Equally enraged at the difappointment as afhamed
of his crime, he at firft took refuge in Brabant,
and afterwards with the king of England; he never ceafed intriguing againft the king of France,
and excited divifions which proved the fource of a
long and cruel war.

Philip incenfed, with reafon, at the conduĉt of his
brother-in-law, publifhed in 1336, a letter patent,
which declared him an enemy to the ftate, guilty
of high treafon, and interdiĉted all his vaffals from
receiving him in the kingdom ; *or any out of the kingdom*, (terms which explicitly glance at the king of
England) to fuffer him in their lands.

Robert

Robert of Artois, during a truce, took advantage of the troubles of Britanny to attack Philip of Valois, perfuading the king of England to take the part of the countefs of Montfort againft Charles of Blois. He went with the countefs of Montfort to lay fiege to Vannes, and rendered himfelf mafter of it; but not long after was furprized there, dangeroufly wounded, obliged to take refuge at Hennebond, and to pafs over to England, where he died in 1343, of the confequences of his wound, which had been exafperated by the fatigues of a fea voyage.

Such is nearly the manner in which matters are related by the hiftorians. A clofe inveftigation of the different proceedings we now give the relation of, will throw light on feveral articles of this recital, and prefent fome details, relative to interefting objects.

The titles by which Robert of Artois pretended to receive the fuit of the county of Artois, are related fol. 128 et feq in the manufcript.

The firft is a confirmatory letter of Philip-le-Bel, of the treaty of marriage between Philip of Artois and Blanch of Britanny, by which Robert II. count of Artois, gives to his fon, and his heirs, in favour of this alliance, the county of Artois; referving however the enjoyment of it, and the liberty to difpofe of fome lands. The fecond is another act in which Robert count of Artois, after the death of his fon, acknowledges the validity of this claufe of the matrimonial contract, in prefence of witneffes, who

fealed

fealed this act with their refpective feals. The third is another act of the fame prince, which announces, that his daughter Mahaut confented to this claufe of the marriage contract of Philip her brother; and the fourth is a declaration of the countefs Mahaut, who acknowledged, before her death, the truth of the facts afcertained in the three preceding acts. Robert did not then produce the falfe will of the bifhop of Arras, which he had likewife caufed to be drawn.

Armed with thefe titles, Robert of Artois, without weighing the difficulty he had to encounter to perfuade his judges, that fo important a claufe in a matrimonial contract, tranfacted under the eyes of the king and the grandees of the kingdom, had been unknown or obliterated in the courfe of thofe proceedings, which the demand of the countefs of Artois, his aunt, had given room for; without being intimidated by the reiterated fentences that had been pronounced in the intermediate time, nor confidering the falfity of the acts on which he was grounding his hopes; thinking himfelf irrefiftible, he prefented a petition to the king.

This petition, which will be repeated at large afterwards, is only mentioned in the letter of 1329, in an obfcure manner as to the fact; they content themfelves with making this prince fay, that, *after feveral good, juft, and loyal caufes, newly come to his knowledge, which had been concealed from him to that time, he afks* " permiffion to fay, propofe and prove, as he ought, the rights he has on the faid county....

not-

notwithftanding all arbitrations, arrets, fentehces, ordinances, pronounciations, compofitions, tranfactions, treaties, agreements, confirmations, or other
things."

We here fee the principle adopted, of cafes where
letters of civil petition may be obtained, or letters
of revifion againft arrets and treaties may be taken;
and that it was already the cuftom in the kingdom
to recur in fuch cafes to the authority of the fovereign.

Philip de Valois thought it incumbent to conduct himfelf in this demand with wifdom, circum-
fpection, and a fpirit of juftice. He endeavoured
to make himfelf acquainted with the truth, before
he fhould grant or refufe what his brother-in-law
was afking of him; and to verify the facts, iffued at
firft letters.

By thefe letters of the 7th of June, 1329, he
addreffed a commiffion:

1. To M. Thibaut, of Navarre.

2. To M. Adrian, of Florence.

3. To Bouchard, of Montmorency.

4. To Pierre de Roie.

5. To Pierre de Cuignieres.

6. To Jean de Chartelet.

7. To Pierre of Villebrune, his counfellors. He
fays therein, that he was given to underftand,
that by a treaty of marriage of his coufin Philip of
Artois, and of Blanch of Britanny, his wife, made
by his coufin Robert, then count of Artois; it was
agreed, that " the county of Artois, after the de-
" ceafe

" ceafe of the faid duke, fhould fall to Philip,
" and after him to his heirs of a legitimate marriage;
" but if the faid Philip fhould die before his father,
" or after him, that there had been two fets of let-
" ters made, confirmed by Philip le Bel, then king
" of France, and fealed with green wax, and filk
" ftrings, one of which remained with the faid
" count; the other was put in the archieve of the
" king's palace at Paris, and was entered in the
" regifters."

That thefe letters have been purloined, fince the
deceafe of the faid count, by his coufin Mahaut of
Artois, or by others in her intereft, or at her infti-
gation; and the faid regifters have been defaced,
in order to defraud and take away from his moft-
beloved brother Robert of Artois, count of Beaumont, fon of the faid Philip and Blanch, the faid
county, to whom it was belonging, according to the
above agreement and treaty; and that in confequence of this deprivation, arrets had been given
or pronounced in parliament in the time of his
predeceffors, formerly kings, by which the faid
county has been awarded to the faid Mahaut, which
would never have been iffued, if the faid letters
had not been fecreted.

This fuggeftion is notorioufly the fame which
Robert of Artois made to the king. He charged
the countefs Mahaut with a criminal deprivation,
as alfo all thofe who have acted by her orders, and
folicited them to be brought to condign punifhment.

In

In confequence of thefe facts, the king, defirous to know the truth, and to do his brother fuch juftice as he might be entitled to, committed it to the above perfons, and ordered them, that the faid things, and all others that may refpect them, or depend on them : " You all together, feven, or fix, or four, or " three of you, fhall underftand and inform your- " felves of, by all ways and means by which truth " may be known ; and that you fhall relate and fend " the report you may make under your feal." The king alfo gives full power to call and order be- fore you, to arreft and hold, if neceffary, the perfons by which you may think that the truth of the faid things may appear, and to put them in our guard and power.

At laft the king empowers them to depute one or more perfons, as they fhall think moft proper, to act in their ftead.

It does not appear that thofe letters which gave fuch ample powers have been regiftered. The commiffaries proceeded to their enquiries without lofs of time. Thibaut of Navarre, archdeacon of Bourges ; Adrian of Florence, treafurer of Rheims ; Pierre de Cuignières, knight ; and Pierre de Ville- brunne, began their *procés verbal* at Amiens the 9th of June 1329, where they firft caufed to be inferted, word by word, the letters which conftituted their powers.

In this *procés verbal*, it is faid, that by virtue of thofe letters and commiffion, the faid 9th of June, in the faid city of Amiens, they have fummoned
the

the firſt witneſs preſent (it is ſaid), and called to that, and all things above written : M. Giraut d'Abuzat, and M. Pierre Ceſſon, notaries of the the ſaid lord our king, to put in writing the evidences of thoſe they had to hear and examine.

Theſe latter words contain an eſtabliſhment of a ſecretary to the commiſſion; and probably it was not the cuſtom then, as it is now, to take their oaths for the particular affair they were charged with, when they are eſtabliſhed griffiers, or ſecretaries, conſidering the original oath they had taken as notaries, or royal officers as ſufficient.

Theſe commiſſaries took two informations, the one after the other, in the courſe of the month of June. Theſe are the obſervations that have been made as to their form.

1. The witneſſes were obliged to take their oath on the holy goſpel, " who in our preſence ſwore upon the holy goſpel, by him or her corporally touched, to ſay the truth on what ſhould be aſked him or her, of the things concerning our commiſſion above written."

2. This form of oath is the ſame for all perſons, as well eccleſiaſtical as ſecular; whereas now it is not the cuſtom to take the oath on the goſpel, but to raiſe the hand, and to promiſe God to ſpeak truth; and that the eccleſiaſtics, inſtead of raiſing the hand, lay it on their breaſt.

3. There is no mention, either about the age, quality, or abode of the witneſſes; neither if they are relations, allied, or ſervants to the concerned

parties;

parties; circumftances fo reafonably required at this time, in order to appreciate, fufpect, or admit the veracity of a witnefs.

4. The depofitions were then made, not only by way of declaration, but alfo by way of interrogation on the part of the commiffary, an abufe which has fince been feverely profcribed, feeing the evident danger it cannot fail creating in prejudice of truth, on a great many occafions.

5. If the information proves that the commiffaries feeked it honeftly, it tells us at the fame time, that they then took means which would not be admitted at this time, fince (folio 48, verfo,) they order the twelfth witnefs to appear, and read to him a part of the depofition of the fecond witnefs, to interrogate him anew on various facts; and further, that the witneffes were permitted to return of themfelves to add to their depofition (folio 40, verfo). The witnefs who fo returns, fays, *that he had minded and recollected by his oath, that*, &c. which oath they do not caufe him to renew according to the prefent cuftom, which confifts in taking it at every time the judge is fpoken to. This form of admitting a witnefs to return thus to his depofition, has probably been the origin of what is called the *recollement* (re-examination) in affairs of high criminality, when all the witneffes are recalled anew, to add, retrench, or correct in their depofitions, what at firft might have efcaped them.

6. In the whole fuit we find no trace of confronting witneffes, that is, of the act by which the witnefs

is

is brought face to face with the accufed, to declare whether it is of him he has fpoken in his depofition, and that the latter may anfwer to the depofed facts, and the other fupport or explain them.

The firft information begun the 9th of June, 1329, and contains twenty-eight depofitions; the fecond, which began on the 20th of the fame month, includes thirty-one.

Philip of Valois and the commiffaries could not fufpect that a crowd of witneffes had been prepared to make falfe depofitions, yet this has been the cafe. It is ufelefs to enter on a detail of thefe different depofitions; it fuffices to prefent, in abridgment, what might have enfued from them, if their fallacy had not been detected afterwards.

It might have then been faid, that thofe titles had been committed as a depofit to Thie-roy, bifhop of Arras, to conceal them; that the demoifelle of Bethune difcovered them to be in his hands; and that the latter bound her to fe-crecy; that before his death he charged this lady, upon her confcience, to return them if he fhould recover of his illnefs, which was mortal; that fhe concealed them in a room, at a place fhe named to which the commiffaries went, without finding any thing; that the countefs Matilda made ufe of all imaginable means to get them in her poffeffion, fuch as violences, threats, &c. that in all likelihood fhe fucceeded, fince it is by a fortunate chance that they have returned to the count of Beaumont.— Such is the idea of the fiction they had prepared,

and

and which was proved by the depofition of the witneffes.

When Philip of Valois had taken cognizance of
thefe informations, he granted the demand of Robert
of Artois, by letters of Thurfday after Chriftmas,
1329; " Heard the faid petition," it is faid, (it is
the fame that has been mentioned before), " and
" made a dutiful information on the things con-
" tained in that petition ; and thereupon, with our
" great council, with deliberation, we in council
" have granted to the faid count (of Beaumont) to
" be heard on the things contained in the faid fup-
" plication, to fpeak and propofe in the beft manner
" againft the queen Joanna of Burgundy, daughter
" of Mahaut, formerly countefs of Artois."

- It is thus that the civil fuit for the county of
Artois was opened; but on the view of the titles
then produced, they all exclaimed againft their fallacy; it feems that every body was convinced of
it; and in fact the report of the true contract of
marriage, which we have before extracted, was alone
fufficient to difpel all doubts.   We fhall foon give
the account of the civil proceeding.

Juftly irritated at fuch a furprize, and ftill more
at the intrigues practifed to bring together fo many
corrupted witneffes, Philip of Valois ordered the
demoifelle Divion to be arrefted, as alfo other
fufpected witneffes.   An information of perjury
was brought againft them, but in a form which bears
no refemblance to ours, as may be feen in the courfe
of this account.

One

One of the witneſſes to purchaſe his pardon, avowed the whole intrigue, and confeſſed all the forgeries that had been committed ; on which the demoiſelle Divion was ſtopped and ſent to Paris. She confeſſed the truth, that it was M. de Beaumont (Robert Artois) and Madame de Beaumont (Joanna de Valois), who had engaged her to make, and cauſe to be made thoſe falſe acts ; that they had acquainted her with the names of the perſons, whoſe ſeals were neceſ-ſary to be procured ; that ſhe had got them by means of money which they had ſupplied, by pur-chaſing the letters to which the neceſſary ſeals were affixed ; and that after many experiments they had ſucceeded, in applying them to thoſe falſe titles. She declared thoſe ſhe had written by their orders, ſhe repeated thoſe declarations ſeveral times, firſt, before the king, and a ſecond time, Auguſt 4, 1331, before the provoſt of Paris. She added, that Madame de Beaumont had ſaid, that M. de Beaumont would have her burnt, if ſhe did not complete the work.

Laſtly, ſhe perſiſted in her declaration of the 6th of October, 1331, before ſhe was tortured ; when, among other things, ſhe ſaid, that Monſ. and Madame de Beaumont would have put her to death very unjuſtly ; that ſhe could not refuſe M. de Beaumont any thing, he was ſo powerful ; that he threatened to drown her if ſhe did not procure the letters ; and had aſſured her it was his right, that there was no ſin in it, and that no one would die for it ; and ſaid ſhe would rather have died a thouſand times, and loſe all ſhe had.

The

The other perfons who had knowledge of thefe facts, or who had concurred in them, were examined, and depofitions made in the fame form as thofe mentioned above, or elfe by forms of confeffion and declaration, fome made before the provoft of Paris, others under fignature, and fent fealed : all thefe appar every extraordinary forms in our days; and nothing was more clearly proved than the fallacy of the titles.

The demoifelle Divion was fentenced to be burnt alive, and was executed on the 6th of October, 1331. There is not one word in this firft fuit that has the remoteft tendency to witchcraft, whatever the hiftorians fay. Thus the forgery committed on the feal of the king, on that of the Chatelet, and the three baillages, as alfo thofe of different perfons, was punifhed by fire; and it will be feen, that the chambermaid of the demoifelle Divion, who had affixed to the falfe acts the feal of Philip-le-Bel, was condemned to the fame punifhment; divers punifhments alfo were pronounced againft the falfe witneffes by an arret, on review of the fuit, of which we fhall give an account in the fequel.

As to the falfe titles, and the two informations, pronounced and judged falfe, their doom was already fixed by an arret of the 23d of March, 1330, reported, fol. 265, which we fhall foon fpeak of, in the relation of the civil fuit. They were cancelled, and all the acts and proceedings have afterwards been depofited in the treafury of the Saint-Chapel at Paris. The copies of the falfe acts and falfe informations, inferted in this manufcript, are alfo cancelled by a vertical ftroke the length of the whole page, as it is announced in a kind of adver- tifement without title, in the front of the manufcript, where they are called *the falfe informations procured to be made by Robert of Artois*; which, by arret of parliament, have been declared falfe, and cancelled as fuch; and he adds, that on account of that, they were cancelled *à la penne* (with the pen) in this ma- nufcript, at the chapel of Paris.

The fame advertifement has alfo, as it is called, the " ordonnance of this book, which contains the " juft and loyal procefs made by the king in his " noble court duly attended, at the motion of his " attorney, and of the noble office of the faid " court."

Then comes an index of matters, which refers each article to a folio of the book, but they have neglected to number the pages.

The fame advertifement fays alfo, " that the " great loyalty and juftice of the faid fuit may ap- " pear the more clearly, it behoves to fhew the fal- " fities procured by the faid Robert, in his attempt " to obtain the county of Artois; and after that, " how the faid falfities have been detected; and " laftly, how the king has done good and loyal " juftice, as a moft equitable, moft upright, and " moft loyal prince, who has had in his eyes chiefly " God, juftice and loyalty, to which he is bound " by the dignity he has and holds from God alone."

All

All we have related takes up two hundred and
fixty-four leaves of the manufcripts; after which
the fuit of Robert of Artois begins. But before
I give an account of it, I thought proper here to
report fome details relative to the civil fuit, concerning the property in the county of Artois.

We have feen that the caufe had already been
decided feveral times, in favour of the countefs
Matilda, and that Robert and his defenders had
acquiefced; which had obliged him to recur to the
king for obtaining permiffion to refume the fuit, in
defiance of thofe arrets and acquiefcences.

Robert of Artois had in confequence fummoned
the countefs of Artois to parliament: fhe made
her appearance at the court, and thefe are the facts
refulting from an arret of the 23d of March, 1330.
They there recite the prefentation of the falfe titles ;
the fufpicion of forgery which the opponent of
Robert of Artois objected againft their validity, and
againft the feals that had been fixed on them; the examination that had been taken ; the friendly exhor-
tations the king had ufed to Robert his brother-
in-law, not to perfift any longer in the ufe of thofe
acts; the reprefentations he had made to him of
the danger he would expofe himfelf to, if he fhould
perfevere in ufing them; as alfo the objections
refulting, as well from the intelligence which feveral prelates and barons had acquired feveral times
of it, as by the avowal of the demoifelle Divion: that
thofe titles were compromifed, and that the feals

A a 2   had

had been fraudulently put on them: thefe are all facts communicated by the king to his brother-in-law, who would never confefs the truth, notwith-ftanding the moft glaring proofs that appeared againft him.

Robert of Artois, not fubmiting himfelf to fo many efforts of the king, was fummoned before parliament on a fixed day, that the court might be fufficiently attended with peers, whofe prefence was indifpenfible, confidering that there were certain complaints of forgery againft Robert of Artois, who was prefent. He had produced titles, fufpected at leaft to be falfe, and on which they ought to deter-mine. The attorney-general moved the forgeries refpecting the feals, and how the acts had been made, as alfo the confeffion of the demoifelle Divion, and others; and concluded, that *the faid Robert fhall anfwer to the faid letters, or no; and that he fhall give a precife anfwer.*

" The faid Robert alledged feveral reafons, that
" he might not be conftrained to anfwer to that;
" faying he trufted the faid feals were good, and if
" he had known them to be falfe, it was not his
" intention to make any farther ufe of them; that
" this was a fufficient apology; and that he was
" not bound to do any more, and begged therefore
" that he might be dealt with according to juftice.
" But our attorney propofing, that he fhould anfwer
" precifely as it was fixed above, he requefted that
" juftice might be done to him in this refpect."

So

· So even at this time, in a civil fuit, before a title. was attacked as falfe, they obliged (as they do now) him who produced it to declare, whether he meant to make, or not to make, any ufe of it; which does not impede the public minifter from profecuting in chief both the authors and accomplices of the fraud, as it was obferved then, and is ftill practifed at the prefent time.

The parties being heard, and the court fufficiently attended by peers, in prefence of the king, they ordered, that Robert fhould give a precife an-' fwer, whether he was willing to continue to make ufe of the faid letters, or no; *which arret pronounced, it was required by our faid attorney, that the faid Robert fhould anfwer.* Then Robert having deliberated with his counfel, faid, that he would not make ufe of them.

The attorney-general having concluded on this anfwer, the court being fufficiently attended with peers, declared, in prefence of Robert of Artois, that the faid letters were falfe, and as fuch fhould be cancelled and torn; and it is fubjoined, "which arrets having been thus pronounced, the faid letters were cancelled and torn as falfe, in the prefence of the king and the count of Artois."

At length, by a letter of Philip de Valois, prefented in parliament the 18th of February, 1331, the letters which had authorized Robert of Artois to proteft againft the preceding arrets and treaties were *annulled, recalled, and annihilated,* at the requeft of the duke and duchefs of Burgundy.— Thus, if the peers were convoked for this affair,

A a 3 and

and if the arrets bear thefe words, *the court fufficiently attended with peers*, which implies the neceffity of convoking them, it was on account of the crime of forgery; for in a civil and ordinary caufe, concerning a freedom, it was then no more neceffary than it is at prefent to affemble them.

The affair in queftion of the county of Artois, furnifhes an undeniable and interefting proof of this.

An arret of the year 1317 announces, that Robert of Artois had then fummoned the countefs Matilda before parliament, to reclaim the county of Artois. The king repaired to parliament with his prelates, his barons, and his counfellors, without having convoked the peers of France. The countefs Matilda attended the fummons, to anfwer to the petition of Robert of Artois. He, previous to his plea, requefted the king to command the affiftance of the peers. *Cum*, faid he, *ad cognofcendum & judicandum caufas Paris Franciæ, curia parlamenti, debeat effe paribus Franciæ munita, requifivit quod nos, ad cognofcendum de dictâ caufâ, & ad eam decidendam, curiam noftram haberemus paribus Franciæ fufficiter munitam.*

After this requifition, the demand and the fummons of Robert of Artois were read; and then *per arreftum noftræ curiæ dictum fuit quod abfque vocatione parium Franciæ, quantum at prefens curia parliamenti • • • • • fufficienter erat munita.* Thus it was judged that the convocation of the peers was not indifpenfible

penfible for the prefent, confidering the nature of this affair, which had as yet been merely viewed in a civil light.

It is true that it is added in this arret, as an indication of the fact, the king efpecially being prefent with his prelates, his barons and his counfellors : *maxime nobis itidem affiftentibus cum prælatis, baronibus & noftris confiliariis*, whence the author of a note in the manufcript, at the head of the arret, has injudicioufly inferred, that the king may profecute a peer of France, without the affiftance of the other peers. This claufe of the arret prefents only a greater folemnity for the arret to interfere ; a mark of refpect for the king's prefence. It by no means infinuates that his prefence can fupply the convocation of the peers of France, while the fame arret acknowledges, on the contrary, the indifpenfible neceffity of their meeting in caufes, where by right they ought to affift.

Verum tamen, fi dictus Robertus fuam faciat petitionem contra comitiffam prædictam, factû dictâ petitione, tam fuper eam quam fuper ea quæ a dictis partibus requirentur ac fuper ea, fi fint aliqua quæ curiæ noftræ oficio facienda fuerint, tam et maxime fuper paribus Franciæ · · · · · in dictâ caufâ, vel alius quibufcunque, curia noftra faciat id quod rationabilitur fuerit faciendum.

After this fentence, Robert of Artois requefted time to confult; but the countefs Matilda urged, that having been fummoned, and her adverfary refufing to proceed, fhe might recede from the fummons, *petivit licentiam recedendi.*

Then

Then Robert of Artois, perfifting in that fyftem, which had been explicitly profcribed by the arret, anfwered, that he meant not to ftart his claims until the court of parliament would be attended with peers: *quoufque curia parliamenti Parifiis, paribus Franciæ fufficienter effet munita.*

The countefs Matilda infifted upon her being difmiffed; and notwithftanding the abfence of the peers, fhe prevailed by the arret that was rendered the fame day: *per arreftum noftræ curiæ data fuit eidem comitiffæ contra dictum Robertum licentia recedendi.*

We cannot find a queftion more folemnly decided; and it is a rule which remains ftill at this day.

The criminal procefs againft Robert of Artois, for forgery, and againft the authors of the forgery, the falfe witneffes, fuborners and fuborned, will be the fubject of the reft of this account.

SECOND PART

Of the Account of the Procefs of Robert of Artois.

WHEN Robert of Artois had been forced to difclaim the record he produced for reclaiming the county of Artois, and when the fame records had been adjudged falfe, and been annulled in his prefence, before the king and the court of peers, the authors of the forgery were already known; and notwithftanding the civil and criminal

nal proceedings were complicated, almoft confounded together, no doubt could fubfift any longer
on this fubject. The demoifelle Divion and her
chamber maid, principal and immediate authors of
the fact, had confeffed it; thofe who had co-operated
in it, or who had any knowledge of it, declared it;
and one among them, in the hope of obtaining
his pardon, which he effectually gained, had unveiled the whole. In fine, the avowals, the depofitions of the witneffes, the difavowal of the falfe
witneffes, were in the procefs.

Philip would then have acted according to the
common rules of juftice, if he had committed Robert of Artois prifoner, and ordered his procefs.
He had already unfuccefsfully employed, before
the fentence paffed on his evidences, all the moft
engaging means to perfuade Robert not to prefent, to a court of juftice, the falfe records which
were the bafis and proof of his claim; in vain had
he read lectures to him, of the declaration of the forgeries, the retraction of the falfe witneffes, and the
depofition of witneffes; in vain had he attempted
to diffuade him by the princes of his blood, by
members of the great council, and by knights.
Yet he ftill flattered himfelf, that after the fentence pronounced on thofe records, Robert would
acknowlege his fault, and would come and folicit
his pardon, which he earneftly defired to grant him,
on account of his ancient attachment to his perfon,
as well as becaufe the countefs of Beaumont, his
fifter, had participated in the crime. But the haughtinefs

tinefs of the criminal did not fuffer him to ftoop to this ftep; he continued unconcerned on his lands whilft the proceedings feemed fufpended, and the other culprits remained in prifon.

There were fome ecclefiaftics among thofe who were believed guilty. The king obtained from the pope fome bulls, which directed the bifhop of Paris to enquire and judge them. An act agreeable to the prejudice of the times, and to the little knowledge they then had of the right of the temporal power, and of the principles of our liberty, that is, of the ancient and primitive rules of the church.

There was one ecclefiaftic particularly who was deeply concerned; he was named John Aubery, of the order of Friers preachers. He was able to give the greateft light on the fraud that had been committed, or at leaft to enable them to find out the principal author. Attached to the count de Beaumont, whom he always called his lord, *domino meo*, he had conftantly performed the function of the holy miniftry, and had acquired a reputation, by filling them with zeal and fuccefs; but they could not induce him to fpeak.

Robert of Artois, urged by the king to name the perfon who had fent him the falfe letter of the contract of marriage of Philip his father, fealed with the feal of Philip-le-Bel, the forgery of which was capital, declared that thefe letters had been put into his hands by the frere Aubery. The latter was arrefted and committed to prifon; he had been heard in the depofitions, and he had already

ready informed the magiftrates, that he had been fent by the count de Beaumont into Britanny, to find them in a convent of female religious, in a place which had been pointed out to him. This journey had been fruitlefs; the letters could not be found. Aubery repeated his refearches, and with the fame fuccefs as before: tired with thus loitering away his time in Britanny, he refumed his route to France. But having entered a town of the kingdom, he met a perfon who required of him the fecret of confeffion, who took an oath of him, *fuper pectus*, and who gave him the letters he had been looking for: he deliyered them to Robert of Artois; but thinking himfelf for ever obliged by his oath, and by the inviolable law of fecrecy of the confeffion, he would not declare the perfon by whom thefe letters had been entrufted to him.

Aubery was carried before the bifhop of Paris, to prepare his procefs according to the directions of the apoftolical letters, and a proceeding the moft extraordinary refulted.

We fee appear before Hugh, bifhop of Paris, qualified commiffary-judge and executor, *judici commiffario & executori,* Simon of Buffy, the fame in all probability who was afterwards prefident of the parliament, and who firft took this title. He is ftiled in the whole proceedings the king's attorney, *Simon de Bufiaco procurator fereniffimi principis Philippi,* and it is under this name he makes his appearance before the bifhop of Paris, Saturday af-

ter

ter St. Martin's in the summer, in the month of July 1331; *procuratorio nomine ejusdem regis.*

He presents to the bishop the forged and cancelled records, and requests him to proceed to take information, and pass justice on Aubery: *& procuratorio nomine requiritur per dominum ejuscopum procedi & inquiri summarié, & de ipso justitiam fieri juxta traditam ab apostolica cclesia sibi formam.*

The bishop of Paris assigned a day to Aubery for his defence. The king's attorney pretended that this was an uselefs formality, and that since he confessed having had those forged letters in his hands, and since he was obstinate in concealing the name of the person from whom he had them, it was incumbent to proceed, in consequence of his confession. Notwithstanding this remonstrance the bishop of Paris persisted in the assignation of the day he had given notice of to Aubery.

That day was the Monday after the feast of the Translation of St. Benedict. The king's attorney made his appearance; *procurator prædictus regis,* on one part, *ex una parte,* it is said; and John Aubery on the other, *ex altera parte.*

The latter continued to persist in his former confession, and requested the assistance of a counsel and notary.

The bishop then said, he was perfuaded that the attorney of the king and John Aubery would equally tell the truth, in swearing both on the holy gospels.

This

This kind of invitation to take an oath as a party of the procefs, opened the eyes of Simon de Buffy, on the fingularity of the chara&ter he was going to fill. He protefted againft his being a party to the procefs, but that he a&ed in the king's name, and in the quality of his attorney, and that he was fulfilling for him the office of promotor: *proteftavit quod non faciebat partem in hac caufa, fed erat folummodo nomine procuratorio domini regis, et pro eo* promoter *in caufa prefenti*. Thus, without any authority from the bifhop, who gave up the pretenfion he had juft afferted, Simon de Buffy declared himfelf promoter for the king before the ecclefiaftical judge, and fulfilled the fun&ions during the whole courfe of the affair. It would not be difficult to diftinguifh here the firft feature, if I may ufe the expreffion, the combined proceeding of the royal judge, who prefents himfelf as chief of the officiality, and as ecclefiaftical judge againft accufed clerks, of crimes in a cafe where the common and privileged crimes are found united.

Aubery agreed anew to all he had before declared, but he conftantly refufed revealing the name of him that had delivered him the letter fealed with Philip-le-Bel's feal, maintaining that he heard of perfons (whofe names he mentioned) who hinted that thofe letters could be forged; and that it would be a mortal trefpafs, if he fhould reveal the confeffion.

The bifhop appointed another day (the Saturday following) in order that Aubery might anfwer to the articles produced againft him by the king's attorney

torney; for the bishop constantly gives him this appellation in the acts, and the attorney, in taking it, acts always under the name of promoter (*promotorio nomine*).

He made his appearance on the Saturday, and presented, always *promotorio nomine*, seventeen interrogatory articles. Aubery answered categorically, except as to what concerns the person that had given him the false letters, avoiding all things that might have any direct or indirect relation to him. The king's attorney proposed ninety-four articles of interrogatory, composed with the greatest art possible; so that the accused had need of the utmost circumspection not to let slip in his answers, some indication which might have enabled them successfully to discover the person whose name was searched for.

Aubery answered to the ten first interrogatories that day, and a part of the others on Tuesday following. He continued always immoveable as to the circumstances relative to the desired name; he agreed, however, that he had no power to confess, in the place in which the letter had been consigned to him, asserting that it was not necessary to the object in question. He also confessed that it was a man, and not a woman, that had 'given him the letter; but this latter avowal made him apprehend he might betray his secret if he continued any longer to open himself on such insidious questions. He took the resolution to give no farther answer, notwithstanding the injunction of the bishop of Paris; persisting

fifting in all he had faid, without the leaft addition; and in apology for his refufal, reprefented that he had always enjoyed an unblemifhed reputation; that he had been a long time prieft and confeffor; that he was ready to anfwer to any interrogation, except on this point, on which the king's attorney, or even the bifhop himfelf, could not compel him to an explanation; and he requefted to be difmiffed from the king's attorney's impeachment.

The latter pretended, on the contrary, that the evafions of the accufed, and his perfevering refufal to anfwer, put it beyond doubt that it was through his hands the falfe letter came to the count de Beaumont; and that fo many prefumptions arofe againft him, that his confeffion only was wanting to complete the proof; and that according to the law and nature of the crime, he ought to be condemned and degraded, after having exacted of him the truth, *tormentis et queftionibus*, by the rack and torments; a conclufion which evinces, either the point to which the ecclefiaftical judges then carried their power, which at prefent they can pronounce only on points purely canonical, againft which they proceed officially; or that the king's attorney meant that this part of the information would be made by fecular judges, an object on which he does not explain himfelf in the leaft; but if this latter is the real fenfe, it confirms us the more in our ideas of the combined proceeeding.

The bifhop fixed another day, viz. the Wednefday after the feaft of St. Magdalen; undecided himfelf

himfelf on the part he was to take, he affembled fome canons of the church of Paris, headed by their dean, and attended by doctors in theology in the civil and canonic law, to confult with them. The *procès verbal* was prefented: the bifhop afked of them, whether, in the prefent ftate of the affair, Aubery was obliged to anfwer? They all gave their opinion, one after the other, that he could not forbear.

Aubery himfelf began to deliberate on the definitive part he was to take. Tuefday following the bifhop communicated to him, in judgment, the advices taken of thofe he had called to counfel. A requeft of Aubery was read, by which he fupplicated the prelate to fummon and convoke expert theologians and others to ftate to them the fact, and fee whether he might be permitted to name the perfon that had given him the letters, declaring, that if they fhould be of that opinion, he would, at the bifhop's order, declare, according to their advice, him whofe name was required.

The bifhop of Paris, who had already affembled, the fame day, the fame perfons he had formerly confulted, and an additional number of doctors and learned men, once more put the affair into deliberation. It was difcuffed for a long time in the prefence of the king's attorney. They unanimoufly decided that there having been no facramental confeffion, neither as to the form nor the fubject, the fecret of the confeffion could have no force, and that the oath moft indifcretely taken by the accufed,

far

far from binding him, it would be a mortal fin, if he fhould refufe to anfwer upon his oath before the juftice to the interrogation that was put to him; fo that the bifhop could not command his explanation under the punifhments of the law.

Aubery was immediately fent for; he received notice of the iffue of the deliberations, and the motives of the advice which had been taken by a general counfel. He propofed new evafions; he offered to declare to the king alone the name that was afked of him; which was rejected; to reveal it to the bifhop of Paris alone; this was equally rejected. Then he afked a delay of two days to determine; on which the judge commanded him to give immediate anfwer. Finally, he defired, at leaft, that befides the perfons confulted, who were prefent, the counfellors of the king, and the bifhop's officers, might be called as witneffes of what he was going to declare; this was complied with.

Forced thus from his entrenchments, Aubery drew a declaration from his pocket, which he had written the 30th of July, 1331, and which he read with fear and trembling *cum timore & tremore.*

He at firft confeffed, that he had falfely anfwered to fome of the articles of the interrogatory he had undergone, to paliate and hide the name of the perfon that had delivered him the letters fealed with the feal of Philip-le-Bel, and entreated the bifhop of Paris gracioufly to abfolve him for it. Next he declared, that on his return from Britanny

gerers and falfe witneffes was fentenced, but a long time after Robert of Artois; and the court of peers was not prefent at their judgment, although the crime and the deed were the fame.

We fee by the examination of the proceedings directed againft Robert, that it was then cuftomary to adjourn the accufed perfon to a fixed day, to make his appearance before the king and the court of peers affembled; and if he did not appear, that a default was imputed to him, and that the adjournments and defaults were repeated three, and fometimes four times. Thefe adjournments were ferved either on the perfon itfelf of the peer, or at his houfe, and in the principal places and feats of juftice in his poffeffions. His fortune was feized, if he did not appear, and publications of adjournment were iffued. They were made at the palace, the court fitting at the marble table. The peers received every day information about the action, by letters of the king; but all thefe proceedings, whofe length and multiplicity were only calculated to afford the accufed the means of efcaping the juftice of the laws, are no longer in practice. We only fee the diftant origin of thofe which are now carried on againft the contumacious.

At this prefent time, when an action is to be opened againft a peer of France, the parliament chamber affembled, expofes to the king the fubject of the procefs, and fupplicates him to honour his court of peers with his prefence, at an appointed day, or on fuch other as he might be

pleafed

pleafed to fix. If the king himfelf thinks proper to order the procefs againft a peer to be inftituted, he enjoins his parliament, either by letters patent or verbally, to proceed: in both cafes the peers are equally informed by a bill, which is carried to their dwellings, at Paris, by a fecretary of the court; unlefs the king himfelf choofes to make known his defire to the parliament-court of peers, and he has before fent to defire the peers to attend to receive his commands, in order to proceed in the inftitution of the criminal procefs. The peers of France are every one informed, in the fame manner, of the fealing of the criminal procefs.

With refpect to the proceedings of contumacy, either againft a peer, or any other accufed perfon, (for they are the fame in all cafes) they confift in the making an enquiry for the contumacious; at the place of his refidence, if he has any, or elfe by notices pofted up at the door of the auditory, with intimation of the lift of his feized fortune, and a new affignment for a fortnight. If the contumacious perfon does not make his appearance, he is once more affigned for the eighth day, by a public cry, under the found of trumpet, at the public places, and alfo before his refidence, if he has any. Then a fingle default is taken againft him, which enjoins the re-examination of the witnefs, and that it fhall have the fame effect as if confronted; confidering the abfence of the accufed, they determine the penalty of the default, by the

B b 3   fame

same arret which pronounces on the chief of the accufation.

We fhould read, with a reference to the forms actually fubfifting, what we are going to relate of the proceedings which were directed againft Robert of Artois.

They began by a firft adjournment, to appear at the day and feaft of St. Michael, of the year 1331; it was contained in a refcript of the king, addreffed to Robert of Artois, count de Beaumont, in a direct and perfonal ftile, as were alfo the other adjournments that followed it. The fecond letters of the king contained the injunction of proceeding to the adjournment: they were addreffed to officers of juftice, who performed on this occafion the function of king's ferjeants, and who drew a *procés-verbal* of all their operations, and the ftile of which was directly addreffed to the king's perfon.

The letters of adjournment exprefs the caufe of the action entered againft the count de Beaumont; viz. that he exhibited and produced in judgment againft the duke of Burgundy and countefs of Artois certain letters, found to be counterfeit and bad, (firft head); that he himfelf had contributed to their forgery, and that he had knowingly and treacheroufly affifted in their fabrication, by his counfel, help, and encouragement, (fecond head of accufation.) The king's ferjeants went to Conches, where the refidence of the accufed peer was. He was abfent at the moment they arrived, and they publifhed the firft adjournment at the caftle, in prefence

of

-of the witneffes they had brought with them, and feveral other knights, efquires and burghers. They left a copy behind, in prefence of the countefs d♦ Beaumont, and in compliance with her orders, tô the gentlemen they had found in the caftle: they likewife publifhed it in the town of Conches, in that of Beaumont-le-Roger, the chief place of the county of Beaumont, as well in the caftle, as in the city, at the gaol of the prifon, and in the court of pleas, or the auditory.

The day of St. Michael being arrived, the peers affembled; but Robert did not attend, nor any perfon in his room. They had been convoked that day by letters of the king, fealed, and addreffed to each of them, with commiffion to the provoft to prefent them to every peer, an ufual practice at every adjournment.

The manufcript enumerates the names of all the peers of France who were convoked, viz. ecclefiaftical, the bifhops of Noyon, Laon, Chalons, Beavais, and Langres; fecular peers, the king of Navarre as count of Evreux, the dukes of Normandy, Burgundy, Bourbon, Guyenne; the counts of Alençon, Flanders, and Eftampes; a great number of other lords affifted at the meeting.

The attorney general concluded againft the count de Beaumont for contumacy, that *he fhould be punifhed by us and by our court on life and fortune, according to the nature of his mifdeed,* expreffions which; at that time, implied capital punifhment, and confifcation of fortune; or at leaft, that *he fhould re-*

ceive

ceive fuch civil punifhment as we and our court fhall think proper in juftice to inflict on him; he requefted default againft the count, that another adjournment might be *granted to him, and that the forfeiture for the contumacy fhould be determined.* The court of peers *declared Robert contumacious, and granted another adjournment at the attorney's requeft.*

It was about the time of this arret, that the demoifelle Divion was fentenced; in all probability it was after this arret, having fince been condemned to the flames for the forgery of the king's feal. She was executed the fixth of October following, 1331, perfifting in her avowal, as it has already been hinted in the firft part of this account; but the other forgerers and falfe witneffes were not perfecuted at the fame time.

The fecond adjournment was upon the fourteenth day after St. Andrew's, Dec. 13, 1331; the fame forms were obferved, if we except that the king's ferjeants went alfo to Joy (where the countefs of Beaumont was refiding), and to Orbie, a place which had been neglected or forgotten the firft time.

The count de Beaumont liftened no more to this than to the former adjournment. The attorney general pronounced the firft fentence of default againft him. He faid, according to the arret, that the count de Beaumont, in virtue of his firft abfenting, as well as the fecond, ought to be reputed contumacious ; and he concluded, that *he fhould be looked upon as convicted, and guilty of the crimes and*

had

*bad deeds above-mentioned; and that he should be con-
demned in life and property, according to the nature of
them, and have his right of defence forfeited.*

It is evident that the word *malefeces,* juft employed, can mean here only *malefaɛta, mifdeeds,*
and that it has no relation to forcery or witchcraft. Might not this expreffion, have given room
to the miftake of thofe hiftorians, who attempted
to introduce forcerers and witches in the recital of
this affair ?

The attorney general took, at the fame time,
fecondary meafures, and requefted that in cafe the
count might not be confidered as convicted, or
condemned by any of the faid ways, a new adjournment fhould at leaft be granted to him. This was the
part which the court took, and the third adjournment was fixed on the fortnight after the day of
Candlemas, February 17, 1331; the year began
then at Eafter.

The third adjournment was attended with the
fame forms as the preceding; we fhall only fubjoin
two obfervations on this fubject:

The firft, that the property of the count de Beaumont were put into the hands of the king and
juftice, by means of the firft abfenting pronounced
againft him, at the fecond fetting upon his caufe,
and that the third adjournment was not only publifhed at his dwelling, but alfo publicly announced
in Paris. In fact, the 20th of December, 1331, *the
ferjeants of the king,* repaired to the great chamber
of parliament, and there, *in prefence of our lords in
parliament*

parliament, and thofe *that were met to plead,* they made, read, and divulged the adjournment, declaring, that if there was any there for the count, they would charge them to remit him the adjournment; at the fame time they went and did the fame in the great hall of the palace, at the table of marble, in prefence of the audience, and thofe that flew together to hear it.

The fecond of thefe formalities is that on which the greateft ftrefs was laid. The ferjeants, unable to get admittance to the countefs de Beaumont, who would neither fee nor hear them, pofted themfelves at the windows of the room contiguous to that fhe was in, and publifhed the adjournment *fo near and loud,* that madame the countefs, and all thofe who were in her room, as alfo in other rooms and houfes of the neighbourhood, could *hear and underftand it.*

After this third adjournment, Robert of Artois gave a procuration to the meffengers that came on his part, with other meffengers of the duke of Brabant, to whom he had retired. Their powers were not to appear on Monday, the day appointed, but on Tuefday, one day after; and moreover, they had no commiffion for acting in judgment on the main of the pending caufe, but only to apologize for his abfence, and to propofe the conditions under which he was willing to make his appearance.

This procuration was a letter fealed with his feal, and addreffed to the king *by his humble, loyal, and devoted Robert of Artois, count de Beaumont.* They fignified, that having the ftrongeft confidence in

the

the two perfons he had made choice of, he fent them to prefent themfelves to the king, in order to expofe for him and in his name, the motives of his abfence, and why he could not, for certain juft and urgent caufes, perfonally appear before him in his court at the appointed day, *Tuefday fortnight after Candlemas*, and that he was ready to take his oath for the truth of the reafons of his abfence, and that he would prove it in time and place.

The day was on Monday, and the procuration fixed in its room Tuefday. The agents of Robert prefented themfelves however on Monday at the court of peers, gave in their procuration, and the libel of excufes of the count de Beaumont, faying *that they prefented it previous to judgment.* But the court refufed to receive it, confidering the indication of Tuefday inftead of Monday. There was not even any mention made of it in the arret which was rendered on Monday; we find the proof only in the act I am going to fpeak of, and wherein we read to the following purport:

" It was anfwered to them by the court of the
" king of France, in his prefence, the faid court be-
" ing fufficiently attended with peers and others,
" that they refufed hearing or receiving any thing
" they might fay, propofe, or give in, confidering
" the tenor of their prefent commiffion brought be-
" fore the faid court, by which it appears that they
" could not fay, propofe, or prefent any thing, on
" the faid Monday, which being the day affigned to
" the faid count, they fhould not have prefented
them-

" themfelves on any other day than the faid Mon-
" day, and for many other motives."

Thus the commiffioners of Robert could not find
admittance, and the court of Peers, after having
taken examination of their powers and excufatory
libel, did not pronounce on the count's plea, refpecting his non-obfervation of the appointed Monday, and his having inftructed them with orders for
Tuefday.

This action, which feems at firft a fubtilty, and
a rigour of formality, carried to the laft excefs,
might be fufceptible of an interpretation by a re-
flexion on the nature of the excufes, of Robert of
Artois. They glanced almoft in every article at
the king's perfon that tended to criminate him.
Might not this have been his motive, to cover under the veil of irregularity of proceedings, the incompetency of the court, and the independence of the royal majefty? Thefe latter
words feem at leaft to imply it, *and for many other
motives*.

This decree pronounced, the king's attorney
moved, that contumacy fhould be pronounced
againft Robert, and that in vindication of his abfence, which fufpended the merited rigorous punifhments on his perfon, he fhould be banifhed, and
his property confifcated; a fentence which was
attended with civil death. It was alfo addition-
ally concluded, probably in refpect to the plea
alledged, and the anfwer that was to be made, that
a new adjournment fhould be publifhed. It was
affented,

aſſented to by the court of peers, and the king, fixed upon the Wedneſday before Palm-Sunday of the ſame year, 1331.

The court of peers had not taken judicial cognizance of the excuſes of the count de Beaumont, but the king would not leave them unanſwered. He was not bound to ſubmit himſelf to the judgment of his own court, becauſe he was perſonally attacked, and that they complained ſtrongly againſt his conduct, even imputing to him a deſign of aſſaſſinating Robert. He reſolved to exculpate himſelf, and he aſſembled his court the next day, *independent of the cauſe in agitation.* The deputies of Robert and the meſſengers of the duke of Brabant, were advertiſed to repair thither; and they attended. This act is too ſingular in itſelf not to be related with ſome detail. We ſee here the ſovereign majeſty anſwering the reproaches of a ſubject, confounding his allegations, and facilitating to him, all poſſible means of defending himſelf. This act is called in the proceſs and in the manuſcript, *the plea of Meſſire Robert of Artois, and the anſwers of the king thereto.*

An expoſition is firſt made of what has happened at the ſitting of the preceding day, and what had been pronounced by the king's court; whereupon the king proteſted, that he was not come to the ſaid court with the view to hear in judgment the meſſengers of the count, but for that reaſon only, " that the ſaid meſſengers (of the count and of the " duke) may ſee and hear the good intentions and equity

" equity of the king of France and his council,
" and not with the defign to proceed on this day,
" in the judgment, upon what the faid meffengers
" had given in on the faid Monday; but that the
" king was willing, in perfon, and out of judgment,
" and all proceeding of judgment, to fay and pro-
" pofe what follows."

Here each of the articles of the plea of the count
were fucceffively read, together with the king's
anfwer to each of them, an example unheard of
in this kind, the effect perhaps of the happy fimplicity of mind and juftice of thofe ancient times.

The firft article of the count de Beaumont's
plea confifted in faying, that Peter de Garancieres,
John de Gaillon, and P. de Roys, knights, came
to him on the king's part laft Magdalen's day, and
fignified to him, that the *king was ill fatisfied with
him for the many things he had heard on his account.*

" That he anfwered, if he pleafed that he
" fhould prefent himfelf, he was ready to excufe
" and purge himfelf with refpect to the king, and
" any perfon that fhould have complaints againft
" him; that the faid knights coming before you and
" relate that you did not wifh my calling before you
" unlefs in full council; but he enjoined, that I
" fhould repair before you the fifteenth day, or
" middle of Auguft, at St. Germain-en-Laye; that
" there you would be in your council, and delibe-
" rate, whether I fhould be admitted before your
" council, or no."

The

The king made anfwer, that the faid knights had intimated to him, *that if the king was ill fatisfied with him*, it was not for any averfion to his perfon, but for the end of juftice, *as it becomes a good prince*; for he exprefsly defired, that he fhould come before *him in council, and would know*, "whether the count " may be heard in his advances, or no. For in " fuch an affair he did not think eligible to " confult only his own judgment; but that he " would naturally deliberate in his great council, " and in prefence of the peers and prelates, barons, " clerks, laics, and feveral other competent judges."

In the fecond article of excufes, Robert faid that having known the king had charged the faid knights to arreft him, he was obliged to leave the kingdom; and that he could not prefent himfelf at the firft fummons, as no *fafe conduct* would be granted to him. The king replied, that it was but juft that the knights fhould arreft him, and that he did it by an impulfe of juftice, and for equitable and urgent caufes, having violently fuf-pected him for having made ufe of falfe letters in judgment before the king; which he had re-nounced, and openly declared in judgment, that he would forbear their farther ufe, and which were de-clared falfe; and that he had confented, affifted, and encouraged the forging of thefe letters with a defign to deceive.

The king fuperadded, that he was obliged to order his arreft; that he had too long tarried, and ought to have done it the very fame day the let-
lers

ters had been condemned as false ; that it was only the strong feelings he entertained for him that had suspended his order, and that he had not caused the said knights to lay hold of him. Farther, that, " if it " was said to him, on the king's part, that he should " come before him, it was at his own request ; " and that when a man is suspected of a crime, it " was his duty to lay his cause before the king, " and to deliver himself up to the power of his " lord," to receive justice ; and that if he departs, he cannot be excused for going out of the kingdom, and not appearing on the fixed day.

As to the safe conduct, the king replied, that " he never was, nor is, nor ever will be backward to " bestow those which are requisite and solicited ; " these have always been his offers and promises " to those who have mentioned any thing about " them ; that he was ready to give him a safe con- " duct for the undisturbed security of his journey, " on his coming to judgment ; although it is a " known thing that no good judge is bound to give " safe conducts to those who are prosecuted for " crimes, and that they may be stopped and ar- " rested on their way, if circumstances should ren- " der it necessary : remarkable and important " words these, as they relate to safe conducts in " criminal affairs."

In the third article of these excuses, Robert pretended, that he could not in prudence be present at the second adjournment, in the apprehension he might be arrested or killed, as was the case with

Messire

Meffire Hue of Caumont, knight, who confeffed to creditable perfons, that at the time of his banifhment, he was fearched for to be killed; which many others have attefted, and is a known topic in the country.

The king made anfwer, that in confèquence of the flagrant prefumptions, fufpicions, defamations, and other above-mentioned caufes, and for his having deferted the kingdom and affociated with other exiles and enemies of the kingdom of France, and his violation of the royal majefty; that he had ordered him to be feized, but that he never commanded to kill either him or any other perfon; and that what he had done was from a motive of juftice.

The fourth excufe of Robert for his non-appearance to the third fummons, refted on the fame motives, and moreover, for that the count de Bar, who was a ftrong man, and fo powerful both within the kingdom and without, had challenged him, without his having given him any provocation, and had alfo defied the whole country where he refides on his account, and that he could not depart from thence without evident peril to his perfon.

The king ordered him to be anfwerd, that thefe reafons were not admiffible; and that if he fufpefted the count de Bar, he fhould have made the king acquainted with it, in perfon, or by others; and which the king would have provided for.

In fine, the beginning and the conclufion of thefe pleas, implies no more, than that the king would be pleafed to grant a new adjournment, as it behoveth to be; that he may be affifted by a fafe conduct, he and his attendants, to purge himfelf in a perfect manner, as it ought to be, of all that might be objected or propofed againft him; begging excufe for his leaving the kingdom, and that his abfence and contumacy againft him might be difpenfed with, and that he may have the count de Bar's parole, who was his vaffal.

To this demand the king anfwered, that by all that appeared, the count de Beaumont had no juft pleas to alledge for his abfence, and not appearing to the fummons; that the court had given him a reafonable adjournment, that of Wednefday before Eafter, in the Louvre, at Paris and declared in the prefence of the meffengers, that the faid Wednefday would be the final adjournment.

That, however, he granted him from that moment the fafe conducts to appear to the fummons, and hear fentence; and that he fhall be difmiffed unhurt, if the king and his court did not find him guilty by juftice and reafon, and by the wife and deliberate council of the king and his court; that he might bring with him fuch perfons as he fhould choofe, and that they are permitted free return, provided they are not banifhed people, or enemies to the country; and if he would fignify a defire to the king of proper affiftance, he would fend him fuch, and fo ftrong perfons, as he may depend upon his being conducted in perfect fafety.

Then

Then the king commanded and requested the count de Bar, who was present at the sitting, to give to him and his, and the whole country of Brabant, good and sincere testimonials; which the said count de Bar readily granted *in honour of the king, at his order and request.*

We see by this, that the king commanded the count de Bar as being his vassal, and requested him, in his character of an independent sovereign out of the kingdom, and that the count in this double capacity, has obeyed the command first, and then granted the request of the king.

At last, the king declares, that he will send letters of the whole to the count de Beaumont, if he should wish any; that he would let him have those of the count de Bar, if he solicited for them; and if he should have some others in contemplation that he should signify it to the king, and that he would also provide them. Such was the conclusion of that act, dated the 18th of February, 1331.

Extraordinary as it may appear, still we perceive, on reflection, that it was requisite for ascertaining the legitimacy of the pending judgment; that it run in part on objects which could not be decided by the court of peers; as well for the exculpations, and the plea contained against the king, as for the objects which depended solely on his authority, and not on the judiciary power; and that, far from trenching on the royal majesty, it served, on the contrary, to evince the goodness, loyalty and justice of the king, as well for the past, as the present, and future, and

that

that it put into the hands of Robert all the means permitted by juftice, to enable him to make good his defence. Eu: what defence could an accufed alledge who would never avow his crime, although overwhelmed already under the preffure of evidence, and recently corroborated by the perfevering declaration of the demoifelle Divion, previous to her undergoing her laft punifhment, and by the confeffion of Frere Aubery the Dominican.

No wonder then if Robert, who had only fought means of procraftination, or of embarraffing the caufe with intricacies, which might in time enable him to trump up his claims in fpite of the judgment which condemned him. No wonder, I fay, if he was little folicitous about a fafe conduct, and if he continued in Brabant.

The fourth and laft fummons, which had been granted, was publifhed in the fame manner at Paris, Conches, Orbec, and at Beaumont-le-Roger; and at the appointed day, a firft arret pronounced the abfenting final; and by a fecond arret, directing the confifcation, it was faid and pronounced, *in our prefence the faid Robert fhall be banifhed from our kingdom, and all his property and rights whatfoever be confifcated and forfeited.*

Executory letters were difpatched the fame day, fealed with the king's feal, addreffed to the bailiffs of Rouen, Vermandois, Aix, Touloufe, and Carcaffone, or to their lieutenants, and all others, royal juftices.

They contained the arret publifhed againft Robert of Artois; they enjoin publication on affizes

and

and markets, on the usual days and places, with orders, that if the banished should be found any where, to arrest him, *except sacred places*, (so these asylums were still respected) to bring him, or send him under safe guard to the Chatelet of Paris, to receive due justice. The judgment which had been pronounced against him for contumacy, was therefore not yet final, and the bare representation of the accused was not valid, as it is at present, in fixed prorogations, since Robert was to be brought to the Chatelet to receive sentence.

The same executory letters, prohibit all subjects of the king from receiving the banished person, from lending or giving him, in any manner, assistance or counsel, under pain of being punished in an exemplary manner.

These formalities are now obsolete with respect to the contumacious; but sentences of death are executed in effigy, at the place of execution. With respect to other condemnations, they are inscribed on a board posted in the same manner, and the judgment is noticed at the place of residence of the contumacious culprit. If he should have none, a copy is fixed at the door of the auditory. This form of public execution expresses the term of the time, within which he is permitted to present himself, and notifies of course the same orders and the same prohibitions to the king's subjects, with respect to the condemned person, as are for the most part contained in the executory letters now speaking of.

They

They concluded by ordering all the property and rights, which Robert held and poſſeſſed, to be put into the king's hands.

The manuſcript then enumerates the names of the judges who aſſiſted at the laſt ſealing of the proceſs.

The remainder of the matters contained in this manuſcript, will be the ſubjeƈt of the third and laſt part of this notice.

THIRD AND LAST PART.

IT remains that we ſhould give an account of what concerns the other accuſed in the affair of Robert of Artois, of new events that took place concerning him, and laſtly the king's letter, which declared him guilty of high treaſon.

Among thoſe who had been accuſed for forgery, were Robert Teſſon, who had been royal notary, and who became afterward curate of St. Andrè des Arcs, at Paris, *curato St. Andreæ de Arcubus Pariſiis.* The biſhop of Paris formed his proceſs at the ſame time Robert of Artois was judged. It is related with all its circumſtances in the manuſcript.

He was accuſed for having lent his aſſiſtance to the forgery, and particularly, for having made an eraſement and correƈtion in one of the falſe aƈts, whilſt the inquiſition of theſe aƈts were making in parlia-

parliament concerning their validity. He had been arrefted, and confeffed the whole before the provoft of Paris, Thurfday before St. Magdalen, 1331. He entreated, in the fame time, the king's pardon, who had fent him to prifon. Information was taken againft him, at the requeft of the promoter of the bifhop, *per procuratorum feu promotorium curiæ noftræ epifcopalis ex oficio noftro procedentem*, fays Hugh bifhop of Paris, and he made the profecution in this name, *promotorio nomine*; fo the king's attorney had no fhare in this fecond proceeding againft an ecclefiaftic, and it was the agent of the bifhop who acted alone.

The bifhop nominated for the carrying on of the procefs, two commiffaries, which he had felected from the canons of the church of Paris, *a domino epifcopo fpecialiter deputatis*, whilft he had prefided himfelf at the procefs againft the Dominican; but he referved to himfelf the decifive judgment of the procefs, *decifionem vero & executionem dicte caufa penes nos retinemus.*

Thus the bifhops had no officers at that time with titles; they nominated, by fpecial commiffion, thofe they thought proper in each affair; they entrufted them with the decifion, or kept it for themfelves at their pleafure. It is eafy to fee the danders of fuch a licence to the accufed, and with how much reafon the prelates have been obliged to keep their titled officers in their officialities, as alfo the lords juftices in their temporal courts, without being allowed to affume to themfelves the liberty

of

liberty of judging affairs, either civil or criminal, which formed part of their jurifdiction.

The promoter after the reading of the commiffion from the bifhop, produced the titles, declared falfe by parliament, as alfo the confeffion of Robert Teffon, before the provoft of Paris; propofed the articles of the interrogatory he was to anfwer, and pronounced againft him privation of all benefice: *pænam privationis omnium beneficiorum fuorum incurrit, propter falfitatem ab eo fraudulenter commiffam.* Teffon agreed to the truth of all the articles: he begged pardon again, pretending to have acted by no impulfe of affection or animofity; nor by feduction, fince, in fact, the count de Beaumont had himfelf made the correction almoft in fpite of him; neither by any profpect of hope, or fear of lofs; but merely by ignorance and fimplicity, *per fimplicitatem & ignorantiam.*

The commiffaries of the bifhop of Paris ended their proceedings, by adjourning Teffon to appear before the bifhop to hear his final judgment.

The motives of the bifhop of Paris were,

1ft. That Robert Teffon was a royal fworn notary: *attentis & confideratis quod dictus R. Teffon erat notarius domini regis & juratus.*

2. That he had known from the origin the whole plot of the forgery: *& quod a principio noverat negotium de quo agebatur.*

3. That he had made an erafement in the falfe act even pending the civil procefs: *& quod pendente caufâ*

causâ coram domino rege, raturam fecit in dictâ literâ sigillatâ.

4. Lastly, the nature of so important an affair, where the county peerdom of Artois was at stake, the perils that might have accrued to the king and the nation, and the quality of the persons who were of the royal blood; *attentis etiam quod res magna erat de quâ agebatur, scilicet pariæ & comitatus Atrebatensis, in quo regi & regno poterant magna pericula imminere, tum · quia persona inter quas quæstio erat mota, sunt & erant de majoribus regni, & de genere regio.*

In consequence, the bishop declared that Tesson was a forgerer: *pronuntiavimus & definivimus ipsum Robertum Tesson esse falsarium & falsum commisisse,* which he did not ·do till after having consulted, *de peritorum consilio.*

And he condemns him,

1st. To the privation of all benefices to which he was intitled, with a suspicion, however, of the extent of his powers in this respect; *& privamus eum, quantum in nobis est, ut falsarium, in omnibus beneficiis quæ obtinet, & privatum nuntiamus.*

2. To do penance in prison as long as the bi-·shop should think proper: *ipsum ad agendum pænitentiam in clauso carcere detendi præcipimus per eundem nostram sententiam, quam diu nostræ placuerit voluntati;* a punishment which has not reached the present time, either in itself, neither in its arbitrary duration, but which has probably given room to that which condemns at present an ecclesiastical delin-

delinquent to pafs either the reft of his life, or a time fixed by the fentence of the officiality, in a feminary.

3d. And laftly, the confifcation of all his moveable effects to the profit of the bifhop; *bona ipfius mobilia nobis applicantes ac etiam confifcantes*; an abufe which fubfifts no longer, it being no more permitted to ecclefiaftical tribunals, to pronounce temporal punifhments or confifcation, and ftill lefs to the profit of the bifhops: it is their province to pronounce only canonical punifhments on the culprits.

This fentence was pronounced by the bifhop of Paris, in prefence of fix bifhops and two abbots, among whom there was that of St. Geneviève, two knights of St. John of Jerufalem, and feveral others; namely, Simon de Buffy, the king's attorney, exprefsly invited for this purpofe: *Et Simon de Bufiaco procuratore domini regis Franciæ, & pluribus aliis fide dignis teftibus, ad præmiffa vocatis fpecualiter & rogatis.* Simon de Buffy occupies a better place here than he did in the affair of Aubery, which has been related in the fecond part of this account.

Laftly, this fentence has apparently been delivered in the epifcopal palace, the bifhop being on his tribunal, inftead as at prefent in the officialty, which as a free place defigned for the execution of juflice, can no longer be within the epifcopal palace: *pronuntiata per reverendum patrem & dominum noftrum Hugonem, in aulâ fuâ epifcopali, fuo tribunali fedente,*

dente, anno 1331, *indictione decimâ quintâ menfis aprilis.*

Befides the falfe records which Robert had fabricated, there exifted ftill a fifth of the fame kind; it was a will of Thierry, bifhop of Arras, who bequeathed his whole fortune to Robert, in difcharge of his confcience, and as a compenfation for the wrong he had done him, having been the caufe of his deprivation of the county of Artois. This act had no other aim, but falfely to imply, that this bifhop had concealed, during his life, the rights of the count de Beaumont to the property of the county peerdom of Artois.

Robert had obtained letters in confequence from the king, to take poffeffion of the fortune of Thierry. The countefs of Artois, who had alfo claims to a part of that fortune, judicially attacked Robert, and a firft arret had ordered an enquiry into the truth of the facts; but it may eafily be conjectured that no great light could be thrown on the conteft, the falfity of the principal titles being an incontrovertible proof of that of the will.

After having been compelled by the coincidence of fo many circumftances, to order the profecution and condemnation of his brother-in-law; Philip de Valois, threw off all farther reflection on fo difagreeable an affair. The reft of the forgerers and falfe witneffes continued in prifon without receiving fentence, and Robert might have remained perfectly undifturbed in his retreat, if paffion would have permitted him.

He

He withdrew, as it has been faid, to the court of the duke of Brabant: he was very favourably received at firft, but affairs foon took another turn. The duke of Brabant married his fon to the daughter of Philip de Valois, and having on this occafion paid a vifit to the court of France, he was foon informed of the reality of Robert's crime, and of the juft indignation of a monarch, fo much the more irritated againft him, as he had before loaded him with kindnefs.

The duke of Brabant, on his return, did not think it eligible to expel Robert from an afylum he had firft granted him; but refolving no longer to receive him at his court, he permitted him to continue in his dominions, as it were in concealment. This prince wandered from caftle to caftle, and from town to town, efpecially in the country of Liege, yet always preferring the caftle and city of Namur, which he made his ufual refidence.

His reftlefs imagination grew more and more inflamed, and foon new attempts on his part, or rather fchemes to new crimes were laid, which filled the French court with terror, and brought on the judgment of the remaining accomplices; and laftly the circumftances which irrevocably determined Philip de Valois to iffue the famous declaration againft him. Such objeâs this remaining account treats of.

They did not in France lofe fight of an exile of fuch importance. Loofe reports were at firft circulated of his criminal defigns: attention was
awakened;

awakened; a monk of the order of the Trinita-
rians, and a prieft of Liege, either revealed more
circumftantial facts, or were pointed out as capable of revealing them. Means were found to
feize them; they were put in prifon by the king's
order, thence conveyed to the epifcopal prifon of
Paris, and the bifhop himfelf received their declarations and depofitions, in prefence of John bifhop
of Arras, other counfellors of the kings, and of notaries called for that purpofe, the laft of January,
1334, which, after the modern computation, would
be 1335.

The two witneffes are ftiled king's prifoners, for
motives which concerned the royal majefty, *propter
aliqua tangentia regiam majeftatem.*

They both take their oaths upon the holy gofpels of their falvation, *in animam fuam præftita,* that
they were going to declare, without their being
urged either by folicitation, fubordination, promifes, love, hatred, fear, fraud, or by the effect of
circumvention or deception, or by the compulfion
of ill-treatment in prifon, or terror; but merely
from their own knowledge and fpontaneous will,
fed ex certâ fcientiâ & fpontaneus.

Thefe queftions often preceded the oath then exacted on depofitions and judiciary confeffions, of
which they made part, as we may fee in feveral other
depofitions tranfcribed in the manufcript. They
are now expunged (for good reafons) from criminal proceedings. Witneffes that would depofe
from

from the like motives, would deferve profecution, as culpable ; nor would there refult any thing but reproaches on the part of the accufed in confuting them, if he has reafon to prefume that they have been guided by the like criminal motives. Thefe two depofitions are very prolix; I have felected only the effential part of them, to render the recital as little tedious as may be.

Robert had particularly attached to his perfon, the Avowee of the town of Huy, and Bertholot his equerry, who had given to him Henry Sachebren, of the order of the Trinity, to ferve him in the capacity of a chaplain, at leaft occafionally. Robert pitched upon him as an inftrument to his impious defigns ; but he was fomewhat circumfpect in confiding, and it feems he did not fucceed in corrupting him.

Robert wanted at firft to fend him to France to expedite fome of his affairs ; but Sachebren refufed going, as he could eafily be difcovered by the religious of his own order.

About Saint John Baptift's day, in the fummer, 1333, Robert being at Namur, ftrove to infinuate to him, that the queen of France had made ufe of witchcrafts *briefs ècrits*, whofe virtue was, that if Robert fhould put it on his head, *fur fon chief*, he would fleep as long as he fhould have it upon him, and fo profoundly *that he might be carried off wherever it might be moft convenient.* He afked of him, whether there was any
 *   fuch

such thing poffible, and how a like forcery might be effected.

Sachebren anfwered him, that he believed no-thing of it, and that it was without doubt a con-trivance of fome deceitful people, *de truffleurs*. Robert maintained that the fact was true, and that he wifhed to know how to counteract it. Ber-tholot, who was prefent at this converfation, pre-tended that one, named Henry Fouriau, of Namur, knew how to do it; and as Sachebren was ac-quainted with him, he was defired to converfe with him on the fubject. Fouriau wrote a bill with red and black ink, and brought it to Robert with the inkhorn, in which the reft of the ink he had made ufe of was contained. This firft compliance on the part of Sachebren, matured the confidence which he was gradually prepared to be intrufted with.

The fame day Robert of Artois charged Bertho-lot, in his prefence, to find him out companions for his journey to France, faying, that he would beftow the greateft benefits, on any who fhould have the courage to put to death, thofe who injured him fo infufferably before the king. Then Gilles Nelle offered himfelf to conduct them to France, and afked who thofe were Robert fpoke of?

He anfwered, they were the duke of Burgundy, the chancellor, the count de Bar, and others. Gilles Nelle replied, that he had found fome companions of Namur, who were going with him; that they were banifhed men, and read to affaffinate for money.

Robert

Robert, in the firſt moment, uſed diſſimulation, ſaying, *take brave people like yourſelf, and deſtroy thoſe who hurt you, be it the king, or others.* The ſame time Meſſire Hue Desjardins, knight, who ſhared the fate of Robert, and who was preſent, ſupported this propoſal, ſaying, *It would be the beſt way of any, and I take it to be more honourable to fall in the performance of a good action, than to live with ſhame.*

Then, (ſaid Robert, graſping at what firſt he re-jeĉted) *it is no longer neceſſary to make open war with them; I muſt take the counſel ſuggeſted by Gilles de Nelle;* and a warm diſcuſſion enſued between Gilles and Hue Desjardins. Robert reflected at laſt, that he had often conſidered, " that he ſhould look upon
" himſelf as a mean man, ſhould he ſo ſoon make
" his peace with the king; eſpecially at this time
" when the queen was with child, and would certainly
" in her acute pains and ſufferings bitterly repent
" the wrong ſhe has done me, and be reconciled,
" perhaps, when I ſhall have procured myſelf
" peace, and thereby I ſhall inſure it."

Let us ſee now the manner in which Sachebren deſcribes the ſtate of Robert.

" He is a man ſo fickle and inconſtant, that
" he will have his bed to-day in this place, to-
" morrow in that, and another day in another;
" ſometimes in one ſingle day in different places.
" He will frequently ſtay by himſelf, the door of
" his rooms faſtened behind him, for half a day to-
" gether."

This

This picture of a man, agitated by remorse, fear, fury and vengeance, was interpreted in a manner still more invidious by thofe who had lived with Robert. They thought him to deal in forcery. In fact, one day Robert being in his room, where there was a cage of birds, and where he remained alone, fpeaking aloud to them, without his words being underftood, and whilft dinner was upon the table; Sachebren obferved to the chevalier Hue, how the prince could leave his meat to fpoil, for the fake of fpeaking to birds ? The chevalier touching him by the fhoulder, faid, *why, brother Henry, he does not fpeak to the birds, but to the devil.*

In the mean while the project of fending the murderers to France continued ftill in contemplation. Gilles de Nelle, with a man of the city of Meaux, and with two others whofe names are not reported, departed the day of St. Peter, with the defign of executing, at Paris, the faid *maléfices*, or mifdeeds; for there is no recourfe to forceries as yet, they have only been announced.

They repaired to Cambray to engage fome more companions. They entered France, and remained at Rheims, where the count de Bar was expected to affift at the celebration of a feaft that was to be given to the ladies. He was not arrived when they entered this city; but they were not fuffered to proceed farther. The avowee of Huy, who difapproved this enterprize, fent them word, in a letter, by Sachebren, that they fhould return; which they did.

The flattering profpect of fuccefs more elated the heart of Robert every day. He now on a fudden refolved, at the end of Auguft of the fame year 1333, to repair to France to fee his wife, for whom, however, he did not profefs any regard; but to have in reality an exact account of his eftates. He defired the avowee of Huy to give him his company; but he, after having declined the offer, becaufe of his being known by the king and the whole court of France, where he had been feen, on the occafion of negociating the marriage of the fon of the duke of Brabant, advifed Robert to defift from this journey, the fecret aim of which might alfo be criminal.

Robert, after having fhewn fome attention to his reafoning, returned however to his former refolution of executing his project, as foon as the avowee had left him; and he departed with Golnier, Gilles Nelle, and five or fix well armed men: he was not abfent above a fortnight.

This journey increafed his hopes; and he faid to the avowee of Huy, on his return, " Know that " I am not deftitute of friends at Paris; I am re- " gretted by all claffes of men; and if I could " have put the king to death, and others who mo- " left me, I fhould meet with a general approba- " tion, and receive more affiftance on the part of " the Parifians, than the king himfelf: there are " fome hundred burghers that are ready to ad- " vance me each one thoufand livres, at a mo- " ment's call."

The

The avowee replied, " You are in the wrong
" to fpeak thus, and to believe that you could
" not mifcarry ;" and going to fee Sachebren, who
had not been prefent at this converfation, he reported it to him, and added, " Madame de Beau-
" mont threatens him with many evils. She has
" been the caufe of his lofing his honour in France,
" and fhe will perhaps, fome time or other, find
" means to have his head cut off. Never believe
" that he went to France with any good intent;
" for if he had feen her, he would have done much
" mifchief. When firft he began to be embroiled
" with the king, if he loft his affection, it was
" through her infinuations."

From this epocha it feems, that Robert renounced
his ideas of affaffination, to find refources in magic
and witchcraft, according to the fuperftitious prejudices of thofe times ; and it is here the MS. begins to enter on that fcene for the firft time.

About the day of St. Remis, or All Saints, 1333,
he faid confidentially to Sachebren, that the queen
of France had prepared an image of wax for and
againft him, to injure him and his adherents; but
that fome friends of his had taken their meafures fo aptly, that they obtained poffeffion of the
wax figure, and had fent it to him.

Sachebren feemed not difpofed to credit what
Robert faid to him, who entered into a confidential
difcourfe with him: he took an oath of him,
under the feal of confeffion, by making him

lay

lay his hand on his breaſt *ad pectus*, and diſcloſed to him the ſecret, after having thus enſured his fidelity.

He agreed at firſt that what he had ſaid about the queen of France was totally untrue, but that it was himſelf who had contrived the figure of wax which he ſhewed to him. This figure was one foot 'and an half in length, and repreſented a young man with hair. He declared to him, that it was made againſt John of France, the king's ſon. Sachebren was going to extend his hand on it, but Robert cried: *don't touch him brother Henry, he is quite made and baptized; he has been ſent to me from France completely made and baptized; he wants nothing more, and is againſt John of France, in his name, to diſtreſs him.*

He added, that he would have another figure of a woman not baptized, and Sachebren having aſked of him for whom, Robert anſwered; " Againſt a " ſhe devil; it is againſt the queen; not queen I " ſay; ſhe is a ſhe devil; as long as ſhe lives no " good may be expected; ſhe will not ceaſe tor- " menting me, nor can I hope for peace as long as " there is breath in her; if ſhe and her ſon were " once gone, I would ſoon make my peace with the " king; for with him I can do what I pleaſe, take " my word for it." He ſubjoined that that figure was not yet to be baptized; but that the godfather and godmother were ready, and that in time Sachebren ſhould baptize him.

Sache-

Sachebren loft no time to explain to him that he could not do fuch things; to whom Robert faid: *It is very eafy to do it, you need but to obferve the fame forms as with a real child, and pronounce the names it is to have;* an anfwer which gives an exact notion of the form of that fuperftition.

Then Sachebren fwore that he would never be guilty of fuch an action, *and that a man of his rank fhould not ftoop to fuch things. You intend to act againft the king and the queen, who are the only perfons who can reftore you to honour. I would rather,* replied Robert, *ftrangle the devil, than be ftrangled by him.*

Robert wifhed to engage him at leaft to find out a perfon who could affift him in. his defigns, promifing to heap riches on him; but on his re-fufal he contented with recommending the deepeft fecrecy, which he promifed him anew, and which he pretends to have kept; adding, that had it not been for the evils threatening fo eminent a per-fon, no fyllable would ever have tranfpired from his lips; the more fo, as a girl, named *Jannette*, who made journies to France under a man's difguife for Robert's affairs, had faid to him one day, that a woman who had healed up a wound of the prince's, had communicated to her, that fhe ferved a bad mafter, as in opening a tub one day in his room to fhut up the ointments fhe made ufe of, fhe dif-covered in it a large waxen image, and not unlike a woman; and that Robert flew in fuch a paffion, that

D d 3   he

he would have killed her if she had not precipitately run away.

To these facts were joined those which the priest of Liege attested. They have no direct dependance on those related by the details of Sachebren, but they were of the same purport as to the execution of the project, which was grounded upon forcery, since a French knight propofed him to the country of Liege in 1332, his magic affiftance, *by which the king of France would die foon, and he brought to an end*, and that the following Lent, the avowee of Huy and his equerry having brought him to Namur, wanted him anew to engage, notwithftanding his former repugnance, and upbraided him with his inflexibility in refufing his hand to fuch fervices; his name was *John Aimeri*.

Such incoherent depofitions in many points, which evinced a criminal defign, fupported by means as atrocious as impotent, would excite at this time only the refearches and feverity of juftice, without intimidating any perfon ; but the contrary happened then; the proceedings already entered into in this refpect were interrupted, and the royal juftice neglected taking cognizance; terror alone took poffeffion of the mind.

Meafures little efficacious were called forth againft imaginary dangers, the reality of which they believed.

The fpirit of fuperftition that reigned at that time, had perfuaded people, that figures of wax baptized,

baptized, and pierced for several days to the heart, brought about the death of him againſt whom they were intended; what happened in time of the league, reminds us how long this abſurd and groundleſs opinion has been perceived.

Under Philip, the whole ſtate was thought in danger; and thoſe who, in compliance with their duty, had excited the king againſt Robert of Artois, ſhared the terror with which the royal houſe was ſeized; freſh oaths were exacted from the grandees for their fidelity to the king and his family, and from thoſe who had given him counſel. Theſe oaths were taken not only againſt Robert, but alſo againſt his two ſons, as children of a criminal guilty of high treaſon of the firſt claſs; but this new crime having never been informed againſt nor judged, John of Artois, eldeſt ſon to Robert, was afterwards count of Eu, and Charles of Artois, his ſecond ſon, became count of Longueville: theſe oaths are of the year 1334.

Philip de Valois was then ordered by new letters patent, the parliament to proceed againſt the reſt of the forgerers and falſe witneſſes. I am not going to mention thoſe who had taken their flight, nor thoſe who died either before proſecution, or before having been ſentenced, nor of the witneſſes whoſe depoſitions did not expoſe them to any enquiries, although the manuſcript furniſhes us with the moſt circumſtantial details; theſe are private tranſactions totally ſuperfluous in the hiſtory.

The

The procefs was refumed by virtue of Philip's letters of the 17th of February 1334; he recapitulates, in few words, the preceding tranfactions of the affair, the falfe informations wherewith the witnefses had been corrupted, and *for which no one had received fentence:* we know only of demoifelle Divion, who had been condemned at that time, and of the fentence pafsed againft Robert Tefson, curate of St. André del Arcs, by the bifhop of Paris, and *of which,* it is faid, *fome remain ftill to receive punifhment.* The king orders that thofe who fhall be found guilty, either by their confefsions or otherwife, be condemned and punifhed, *foon and without delay in fuch manner as might be examplary.*

Thefe letters are cited at the head of the arret of parliament, which contains the procefs and fentence.

The attorney general propofed that the falfe witnefses fhould be brought to punifhment. They were interrogated anew upon their former confefsions; they all agreed as to the crimes that were imputed to them, as may be feen by their anfwers and confefsions inferted in the procefs. We are going fuccinctly to notice them, indicating the fentence pafsed on them by the final arret of the 13th of May 1334.

1. Martin de Neufvort was the firft who confefsed the whole manœuvre that had been practifed, and the forgeries that had been committed. His early repentance, and the difcoveries he had made, pro-

procured him his pardon. " The king, by a fpecial grace, has remitted and pardoned him the punifhment, which he had incurred, as appears by the king's letters." The form of thefe letters, granted to the guilty, was then nearly the fame as is obferved at the prefent time.

2. Robert Corbeau and James Rondelle, both ecclefiaftics; *were delivered into the hands of their ordinary judges, to receive fentence according to their malverfations* The manufcript does not apprife us; neither if their procefs has been made afterwards, nor before what ecclefiaftical judge it had been made, nor even to what punifhment they have been condemned; however we may infer from the judgment the bifhop of Paris paffed againft Teffon what was their lot; befides this way of pronouncing fentence, feems to brand them as criminals, and to commit them into ecclefiaftical power, for no other reafons than to inflict the merited canonical punifhments on them, in the number of which, privation of benefice was then reckoned. So the arret feems tacitly to declare, that they lay under no capital fentence, and it only offers to the judge of the church, the option of the punifhment to be pronounced againft them, a very extraordinary formality, which would be rejected at prefent.

3. Gohier de la Chaine, Jean le Blanc, Giraud de Juvigny, and William de la Chambre, all four falfe witneffes, were condemned to ftand twice on the

the pillory, the firſt time at Paris, and the ſecond at Arras, for the three former; and at St. Germain-en-Lay, for the latter: they were declared deprived of their offices, and Giraud de Juvigny, the fourth, was moreover baniſhed from the kingdom for perpetuity. The ſame arret orders alſo, that when theſe culprits ſhall be brought to the pillory, they ſhall be covered with a ſhirt with painted heads on them, *with red tongues iſſuing from their mouths*; an odd cuſtom indeed, of which ſome traces may ſtill be found in the puniſhments inflicted on children in convents and ſchools, to repreſs their propenſity to lying.

4. William de la Planche, another falſe witneſs, was ſentenced to put, at his own expence, and to carry them himſelf to the cathedrals of Paris and of Arras, two baſons of ſilver, three marks weight, with a chain of the ſame metal, for ſuſpending them in the churches as an everlaſting memorial, and to furniſh a wax-taper of three pounds, to burn every day during the celebration of the Great Maſs; and for farther example, that La Planche ſhall depart from the *palais* of juſtice, carrying the baſon, the taper, and the chain, in Arras, as well as in Paris.

5. Jeannette Deſquenes, chamber maid to the demoiſelle Divion, who had applied the ſeal of Phi-lip-le-Bel to the falſe letters, and who had alſo born falſe teſtimony, was not ſentenced in the ſame arret which ordered her to cloſe priſon, in expectation of a more ſolemn puniſhment. She was condemned

at

at laft by a fecond arret, which is not related in the manufcript, where we only find, " that fhe was " burnt in the Swine-place, near the city of Paris ; " and that fhe perfevered, when on the flaming " pile, in her former confeffions and declarations, " humbly and earneftly entreating the attending " people to fupplicate the Almighty for her: that " fhe had upon her falvation fworn fecrecy to the " faid Robert, and fealed the falfe letters with the " king's feal, with ftrings of filk and green wax, with " which Robert had fupplied her. She alfo con- " feffed, fhe had been prefent at the forgery com- " mitted by the demoifelle Divion; whereupon " the faid Jeannette was committed to the flames, " in the year 1335, Saturday before Afcenfion."

All the falfe witneffes underwent the punifhments pronounced againft them, and *procès-verbaux* were drawn of their execution, which are inferted in the manufcript.

The day of the Afcenfion, De la Planche was conducted from the *palais*, on foot, to the church Notre Dame, carrying the bafon, the chain, and the taper. When he had entered it, the caufes of his condemnation were publicly and folemnly declared to the congregation. The fame was repeated in the cathedral of Arras, according to the orders of the *procès-verbal*.

As to Robert of Artois, when he quitted Brabant to pafs to England, Philip de Valois declared him guilty of high treafon, by a declaration of the

7th

7th of March, given at the Bois de Vincennes, We do not think proper to infert the copy, as it is printed entire, and in every refpect the fame as in the manufcript, in the collection of pieces concerning the peerage, by M. Lancelot,

It feems unneceffary to reflect in this place, on a declaration fo uncommon in its nature, fince the crime of high treafon had only been announced, without having been verified, or formally been judged; fo that it feems to prefent a kind of declaration of war againft Robert, and the king of England, a vaffal to the king of France, for what he poffeffed in his kingdom, and who received Robert under his protection, rather than as an act of juftice, as it could not produce, nor did produce, any other fruit but unrelenting reciprocal enmities.

After having examined the manufcript with clofe attention, it feems, one cannot help obferving in the information, the compleateft proofs of the forgery committed by order of Robert of Artois and his wife; that Philip is never unjuft, as Lancelot attempted to prove, in the memoirs of the academy; but that he may rather be afferted to be fometimes too compaffionate to his fifter, and too indulgent to his brother-in-law, whofe haughtinefs had brought on his ruin, by forbidding him to fubmit to an avowal of his crime, or to the afking the king's pardon.

As to the divers proceedings which have been traced, we think it of fome ufe to unite in a

kind

kind of fummary, the principal remarks to which they have given room.

1. The civil and the criminal objects were confounded together in the information, and judged feparately, the civil before the criminal.

2. The accufed were judged feparately for the fame affair, and for the fame fubject. Robert was judged the firft by the court of peers; the demoifelle Divion by the parliament, without the court of peers; the ecclefiaftics by the judge of the church, and the other accufed a long time after by the parliament; and always on the fame proceedings by virtue of new letters patent from the king; an antiquated cuftom, which has not been tranfmitted to this time, as all the accufed for the fame crime ought to be judged together, or at leaft in fucceffive order, and by the fame proceeding, never interrupted or altered by frefh letters patent of the king, in any cafe whatfoever.

3. The depofitions of the witneffes and their confeffions, made at one time, by way of interrogatory; at another by a declaration, written and fealed by the feal of the witnefs, with liberty of adding, at pleafure, to their firft affertions, and deprived at the fame time of re-examinations and confrontations which are indifpenfible at prefent; might often have given birth to great errors, which yet have not been produced in the affair in queftion.

4. It alfo appears, that they condemned an accufed on his avowal, whilft at prefent the avowal

of

of the guilty, conſtitutes in itſelf only one half of the proof demanded by the law, which orders, that for complete conviction, no leſs than two poſitive, uncorrupted, unſuſpected, and above all, (either in themſelves, or among them, in eſſential circumſtances,) uncontradicting witneſſes, ſhould be required.

5. The crime of forgery of royal letters, or the king's ſeal, was then puniſhed with death, and this was inflicted by fire.

6. The puniſhment of falſe witneſſes varied in proportion to the nature of their falſe depoſition.

7. The ancient way of making the proceſs of a peer of France, was attended with tedious, difficult, and arduous forms, which enabled the accuſed to eſcape the ſword of juſtice, whenever authority had not ſecured his perſon in the firſt inſtance.

8. The proſecutions intended againſt them, in caſe of abſenting, were the baſis of theſe obſerved now againſt an outlaw, though even a peer of France; and which, although reduced to great ſimplicity, are ſtill in ſome meaſure exceptionable.

9. The convocation of the peers ſeems to have been no more eſſential in thoſe times than at preſent, as for affairs relative to the intereſt of peers and peerdoms, ſave in criminal caſes; but they could be convoked according to the conjunctures, and the degree of intereſt which the whole claſs of peers might have had in it, *tum maxime ſuper paribus Franciæ*.

10. The

10. The letters of pardon and remiffion, were nearly of the fame form as ours.

11. The privilege of afylum in facred places was refpected even in cafes of high treafon.

12. The royal juftice caufed to be publicly executed in churches, certain penances, fuch as were thought proper to be difcharged to God, whilft at prefent they are done at the doors of the church ; and though public fcandals may ftill be perpetrated in churches, for which public reparations are exacted, yet they are no longer made in the church by the perpetrators in perfon, but at the door of the church.

13. The king, in certain occurrences, advifed with the pope, to obtain delegations or briefs for a bifhop, in order to open a procefs againft ecclefiaftics.

14. The royal judges remitted to the ecclefiaftical judges the criminal affairs of clerks, either for being punifhed or judged.

15. It feems no diftinct idea had as yet been conceived, about what has been called common crimes and privileged crimes.

16. They were fent to the judges of the church, though they had not claimed their privileges ; whereas at prefent this only takes place in cafe it is claimed by the clerk ; or if the bifhop himfelf claims the cognizance of the caufe, to be determined in his officiality.

17. The bifhops made the criminal information themfelves, if they thought proper, or they committed

mitted it to ecclefiaftics, at their option. They fometimes only kept to themfelves the cognizance of the definitive judgment; but at this day they can neither inform or judge the civil or criminal procefs pending at the officiality. They are obliged to nominate officers of juftice, under the name of promotors and vice-promotors, officials and vice-agents, to confult on the affair, and which may not exercife their functions; till after having taken their oath, and being received in that character in the officiality, on provifions delegated by the prelate.

18. The bifhops had the right of pronouncing temporal punifhments, fuch as commitment to prifon; and they referved to themfelves the right of fixing at pleafure, after judgment, the duration of that punifhment; alfo to confifcate all the moveable property of the delinquent for their own profit, when he happened to be judged by them incapable of poffeffing any benefices. Their power at prefent is limited to pronouncing officially canonical punifhments, fuch as the privation of benefices and penitential corrections, with retreats into feminaries, towards the reparation of the fcandal, and reviving in themfelves the fpirit of the ecclefiaftical vocation.

19. The importance of the competence of the royal judge, againft clerks concerning crimes of violation of public order, was not yet felt in its full extent, and ftill lefs that of the joint information of the ecclefiaftical and royal judges. Yet

in

in the midſt of this confuſion of proceedings, we
may ſee the firſt dawn of that part of our laws,
in the articles reſpecting frere Aubery, where the
king's attorney informs, as promoter in the king's
name, with the biſhop as judge. It was at leaſt the
firſt feature of that rule, which was afterwards invi-
gorated and ſanctioned by the laſt laws iſſued on this
matter, under the reign of Louis XIV. for eccleſiaſtics of the ſecond claſs, without any thing being
yet fixed on this ſubject with reſpect to the perſon of
biſhops.

20, and laſtly. The eccleſiaſtical judges, (as we
have ſeen) inſert in their ſentence, at leaſt with reſpect to important affairs, the motives for their
judgment.

The manuſcript we have given an account of,
ends with an extract of the whole proceſs; it is a
kind of report, very much abridged, which tends to
eſtabliſh the deciſion and reaſoning of every part of
the inſtructions and judgment that have been pronounced.

There exiſts alſo other manuſcripts of the criminal proceſs againſt Robert of Artois. D. Porier,
one of the free reſident fellows of the academy, has
undertaken to compare and give a critical account of
them. I have in this confined myſelf to the manuſcript before me, and more particularly to what
could have reſpect to judiciary and criminal proceedings; more was uſeleſs. M. Lancelot has examined

amined to the bottom what concerns Robert of Artois in the memorials inferted in the eighth and tenth volumes of the Collections of the Academy; and I cannot add any thing to the refearches of this learned and laborious Academician.

THE

HISTORY

OF THE

ATABEK PRINCES

In SYRIA.

By Aboulhafan Aly, furnamed Azzeddin, Son of Alathir-al-dgezeri, named Ebn-al-athir, or Ben-al-athir, a Writer in the Thirteenth Century of the Chriftian Æra.

Arabian Manufcript, No. 818, in Quarto, containing 372 Pages, on Oriental Paper, without a Title.

By M. De Guignes.

IN the catalogue of the king's library, this manufcript, which contains the hiftory of the Atabeks, that is, of the princes who have reigned at Mouffoul, in Mefapotamia, from the year 477 to 607 of the Hegira (from 1084 to 1219 of Jefus Chrift), appears to be without the name of its author; and indeed it is not pointed out at the beginning of the book, which is even without a title; but in perufing it, one may eafily be convinced that it cannot be any other than Ebn-al-athir or

E e 2 Ben-

— Ben-al-athir-al-dgezeri, that is, born in Mesapo-
tamia, called by the Arabians Dgezirat, or the
Island. There are two authors of this name, who
are brothers, as M. de Herbelot remarks under the
word Athir. The firſt is Abouſſaadat-al-mobarek
Madgeddin, ſon of Mohammed Aſſcheibani, born
at Dgezirat ben Omar, a city ſituated on the Tyger,
above Mouſſoul. He has written ſeveral works on
the Mahomedan religion. His brother, who is the
ſecond, is alſo called Ebn-al-athir, and equally ſurnamed Al-Dgezeri, by reaſon of his native place,
and his full name is Aboulhaſan Aly Azzeddin.
He has compoſed three hiſtories; the firſt intitled
Kamel, which is a general hiſtory; the ſecond, Ebrat
ouli-al-abſar, that is, Examples for wiſe People; and
third, The Hiſtory of the Dynaſty of the Atabeks.
However, at the word Tarikh Ebn-al-athir, the ſame
M. de Herbelot aſcribes to him two only, taking the
Ebrat to be the ſame with the hiſtory of the Atabeks. This doubt would be removed if the manuſcript we are going to give an account of had a
title. It actually contains the hiſtory of the Atabeks; and what confirms us that it is Ebn-al-athir's,
is, that the author makes mention of his brother Abouſſaadat Madgeddin: he affirms that his
father had been witneſs of the moſt part of the
events he relates; that it is from him he has them;
and adds, "that he did not think proper to give
"his hiſtory too large a ſize, becauſe in his time
"people preferred abridgments." Theſe are his
words. The ſciences had ſhared the fate of the
khaliffs.

khaliffs. It was therefore to conform himfelf to the tafte of his age, which he feems to difapprove, that he had made this an abridgment; but refers to another work, thofe who fhould prefer inftruction to amufement.

Some other works are ftill afcribed to Ben-al-athir: and I find that Ben-el-ouardi makes him the author of a book intitled, *Adgiaïb-el-Makbloucat*; that is, *the Wonders of the Creatures*; but we are ftill in the dark, whether it was his work or that of his brother; however, as the author in queftion has, in this account, written much on hiftory, I fhould be tempted to conjecture that this latter work is one of his productions. If we believe M. D'Herbelot, this writer fettled at Mouffoul, and died in the year 630 of the Hegira (of Jefus Chrift 1232). Under the word *Kamel*, he names him *Azzeddin-ali*, fon of Mohammed, fon of *Abdolkerim Affcheibani*. We are too little verfed in the literary hiftory of the Orientals to pronounce on this head. The examination we are making of the manufcripts of the king's library may of courfe give us the light we defire; I fhall not therefore hazard any affertion on what concerns this hiftorian.

For a knowledge of the events related in this hiftory of the Atabeks, we muft recollect what has already been faid in the hiftory of Mafoudi; that the empire of the khalifs was annihilated, and that thofe monarchs were no more than pontifs of the Muffulman religion. The princes Bouïdes, who had ftripped them of their whole authority, left

them

them but a shadow of respeft and vain honours;
but towards the year 1029, of Jefus Chrift, the
Turks, named *Seljoucides*, in their turn, difpoffeffed
the Bouïdes of their dominions, and made themfelves mafter of Perfia, of Bagdad, and feveral other
countries, which formed them a moft confiderable
empire, in thofe tracts which had been before under
the jurifdiction of the khalifs. The Seljoucides,
who continued to regard thofe as fimple pontifs,
bore the title of *fultan*, then more eminent then that
of *malek* or *king*, which they left to thofe of their
attendants, who had principal offices about them,
and on which they beftowed large governments,
which formed a kind of fiefs. Thofe fiefs were
tranfmitted to the iffue of thofe who had obtained
them, provided the fultan had confirmed them.
Thefe governors may be called as many fovereigns,
who made war againft one another, without the fultan's taking much concern in it; of this clafs were
the Atabeks, of which Ben-al-athir gives us the
hiftory. There were, however, fome other petty
princes in Syria who had fubfifted there before the
conqueft of the Seljouc Turks. The Greeks, the
Franks, and the Crufaders, were alfo mafters of
fome parts of it, and the Atabeks had frequent
quarrels with them. The recital Ben-al-athir makes,
muft therefore greatly contribute to elucidate the hiftory of our Crufades; and it is in this view I am going
to give an account to fome extent. In our hiftorians the names of the Oriental princes and towns
are very disfigured; here we may diftinguifh them
with

with certainty. Befides, it may not be amifs to produce the fentiments of the Muffulman hiftorians on thofe wars, which are fo much the fubject of cenfure at prefent, though in the different motives which have occafioned them, we fhould not overlook the commerce to India, and the benefit that has accrued to the arts.

Malekfchah, fultan of the Seljoucides, had in his fervice a Turk, named *Cafim eddoulet Acfancar*, who had rofe himfelf at court, where he enjoyed fo confiderable a credit, that the firft vizier, Nedham Almoulk, one of the great men of his age, took umbrage. This vizier found no other expedient to difcard the favourite, than to prevail on the prince to fend him with an army towards Aleppo. Cafim Eddoulet Acfancar, charged with this expedition, departed with his troops, and accompanied by another vizier, marched towards Diarbekr, in the year 477 * of the Hegira, (of Jefus Chrift 1084.) He came up on his way with the emir Ortok, king of Moffoul, who voluntarily fubmitted to the fultan, and obtained thereby the reftitution of his country †.

* This year 477, begun the 9th of May 1084, and ended the 27th of April 1085. In what concerns the Franks, I point out the beginning and the end of the Hegira, as this year may often be applied to two years of the Chriftian æra, which might make an apparent difference in the hiftorians.

† Ben-al-athir, fpeaking of this expedition, fays, " *As I have* " *related it in the Tarikb, or the chronicle under the reign of Mouf-* " *taedi.*" this is likely that Univerfal Hiftory, intituled, Kamel, of which M. D'Herbelot fpeaks.

E e 4   The

The city of Aleppo was then under the com‑
mand of Scharfed-doulet Mouſlim, of the Arabian
family named the Merouanides, or the Ocaïlites;
and that of Antiochia, dependant on the Greeks,
annually paid him a tribute. The inhabitants dif‑
contented a ſhort time ſince with their governor,
named Phardrous, happened to call in Soliman, ſon
of Coutholmiſch, one of the Seljouc princes; the
latter immediately ſet off, took poſſeſſion of the city,
put ſeveral inhabitants to the ſword, and ſtripped
them of all their riches. Scharfed-doulet then im‑
poſed on Soliman, now maſter of Antiochia, the uſual
tribute, but he refuſed to pay it, and they came to
action in the year 478, (of Jeſus Chriſt 1085,*) but
Scharfed-doulet abandoned in the heat of battle by
the Arabians and the Turkomans, was worſted and
killed in his flight. This prince poſſeſſed the coun‑
try from Sindia in Erac, on the river Iſſa, down to
Manbedge; all the intermediate countries along
the Euphrates, ſuch as Mouſſoul, Diar-rabia, Diard‑
gezira, Aleppo, and other places, which were all
under his dominion. The inhabitants of the latter
of theſe cities meditated their return to Soliman,
who was killed not long after, and then they ſub‑
mitted to the ſultan Malekſchah, who by the ad‑
vice of the great vizier, Nedham Almoulk, gave
this city, together with thoſe of Hama, Manbedge,
and Ladikia, to the emir Caſim Eddoulet Acſancar;

* In the month Sepher, this year has begun the 28th of
April 1085, and ended the 16th of April 1086.

thus

thus the author eftablifhes the firft introduction of the emir to power.

In the year 485, (of Jefus Chrift 1092 *,) the grand vizier was killed, and the fultan Malekfchah died a fhort time after, aged thirty-eight years and fix months, of which he had reigned about twenty. His empire was of an immenfe extent, the khothba, or public prayers, were made under his name, from the frontiers of China to thofe of Greece. Yemen and Hedgiaz, countries which had always maintained their independence, acknowledged his fovereignty, as the author obferves. We have hinted already, that public prayer, in which mention of the prince was made, independent of the prayer for the khalif, was the greateft mark of fovereignty. The emperor of Conftantinople, the kings of Tharaz, of Efphidgian, of Khafchgar, of Balafgoun, of Samarcand, and of Maouarennahar, paid annually a tribute to Malekfchah; it was, as we fee, another empire formed on the ruins of that of the khalifs, who were not reftricted within the limits of their ecclefiaftical functions. Malekfchah was a prince of a mild and generous difpofition towards his enemies; he ordered cifterns to be made on the way to Mecca for the ufe of the pilgrims, which in thofe dry wildernefles is of the greateft benefit; he opened channels in different places, and conftructed a college near the tomb of Imam Abouhanifa, a fump-

* This year begun the 11th of February 1092, and finished the 30th of January 1093.

tuous mofque at Bagdad, a minaret in the environs of Koufa, and another at Samarcand.

After the death of this fultan, there were, during twelve years, contefts for the fucceffion to the empire, which the author relates, and which were only put an end to, by the death of Barkiaroc, fon of Malekfchah. It was during that fpace that the Franks came to make themfelves mafters of Lahel, or of Phenicia, of Antiochia, and feveral other places, which the author fays he has related in his great chronicle. Cafim Eddoulet Acfancar, mafter of Aleppo, though dependant on the fultan, who did not interfere with the difputes of the emirs for fmall cantons, made peace with his neighbours; afterwards being defeated in another action and made prifoner, was killed in the year 487, (of Jefus Chrift 1094 *), in which alfo died the khalif Moctadi, who had for fucceffor Moftadher Billah; for the proclamation of this khalif the fultans ratification was firft neceffary; but Moftadher was proclaimed before they had publifhed the death of Moctadi; they then made Barkiaroc, who was then at Bagdad, acquainted with it. This prince fent immediately fome of his officers who proclaimed the new khalif; they next proclaimed the fultan himfelf, and deputed feveral perfons to ufe the fame ceremony at Ghazna, in Maouarennahar, in Kirman and in Syria. In the prayers they comme-

* This year has begun the 20th of January 1094, and finifhed the 9th of January 1095.

morated

morated the khalif, and next to him the fultan. Such was the cuftom of the Muffulmans; and in places where there was a vaffal, in the fultan's dependence, they alfo added to the prayer, the name of that petty prince, a cuftom which fubfifts alfo among us. We relate thefe circumftances, to enable us to form a judgment of the real ftate of the khalifs.

After the death of Cafim Eddoulet Acfancar, his fon Emadeddin Zenghi, aged ten years, fucceeded nim; but was forced, in order to maintain himfelf, fervilely to court the different emirs, who were then contefting the different countries of Syria. He attached himfelf to the moft powerful, at firft to Dgiouli Sacaou, who had conquered Mouffoul, then to the emir Albourfki; and in the year 511, (of J. C. 1117*,) he began to fix his reputation to advantage. The Sejouc princes quarrelled for the empire, and the author relates the details of their diftractions. At laft, Zenghi obtained from the fultan the government of Mouffoul, which was to be taken by force, as in thofe times, thefe princes often diftributed governments which were to be conquered.

The Franks, fays the author, were then moft powerful in thofe countries, and kept up numerous armies, were mafters from Maredin and Schekhanau to Arifch in Egypt; there remained to the Muffulmans only Aleppo, Hemeffa, Hama, and Damaf-

* This year began the 4th of May, 1117, and finifhed 22d April, 1118.

cus:

cus: they poffeffed the tract between Diardged-
zira, Nefibin and Ras Alaïn. In the year 521 of
the Hegira, (1027 of J. C.) Zenghi expelled the
enemy from Mouffoul, conquered Diardgezira, and
Nefibin, which had belonged to the emir Albourfki;
he obtained the fultan's agreement for his keeping
them, took afterwards feveral other cities, and pur-
fued his victories as far as the country of Haran:
the Franks poffeffed Roha, or Edeffa, Saroudge,
and other places of Diardgezira. The inhabitants of Haran, little fatisfied with their neighbourhood, folicited Zenghi to approach to their fuccour; he flew without lofs of time, and took poffeffion of that place. Then this prince wrote to
Joffelin, to inform him of his fuccefs, as alfo of the
defign he meditated againft Aleppo. They made
peace together in the year 522 of the Hegira, (of
J. C. 1128 *,) he entered that city at the requeft of its inhabitants, after having taken Manbedge and the caftle of Bouzaa. In the year 524
of the Hegira, (of J. C. 1130†,) he carried his
arms againft the Ortokide princes: took feveral
of them, and then concluded a peace with them;
but as our limits do not permit us to follow this
author in his various details, we fhall particularly
felect for this account, what has any relation to the
Franks. It is known, that this prince, under the

* This year began the 5th of January, 1128, and ended the
23d December of the fame year.

† This year began the 14th of December, and ended the 2d
of December, 1130.

name

name of Sanguin, is famed in the hiftory of our
crufades. After having made peace with the Ortokides, he marched againft the Franks, who, from
the fortrefs of Athareb, greatly molefted the Muffulmans of Aleppo. Zenghi made himfelf mafter
of the caftle, levelled it to the ground, and haftened to lay fiege to Haran; but as he had a
number of wounded in his army, he made peace,
and returned without taking that important place.

Zenghi took part the following year, 525, (of J.
C. 1131*,) in the contefts which originated in the
family of the Seljoucide fultans. Mahmoud, aged
28 years, happened to die, and Mafoud had been
nominated fultan, a war broke out between the
princes of that family, in which Zenghi acted a
confiderable part, according to the author. He
embraced the intereft of Mafoud, and marched toward Bagdad, where the khalif Moftarfched hearing
that Mafoud had juft been beaten, had affembled
fome troops, and entered the city, to defend it
againft Zenghi. About the end of Redjeb, of the
year 526, (of J. C. 1132†,) the armies found themfelves in prefence of one another. The khalif was
encamped under a black tent, which was the colour of the Abaffides. At the fight of this pontiff
of their religion, at the head of his army fword in
hand, his enemy feized with fear and refpect, took

* This year began the 3d of Dec. 1130, and ended the 22d
Nov. 1131.

† This year began the 23d of Nov. 1131, and ended the
10th of Nov. 1132.

to

to flight, and Zenghi retreated to Mouſſoul. The khalif, who ſeemed now to reacquire ſome authority, declared himſelf for the party of Maſoud; but new diviſions between the Seljoucides induced him to alter his inclination: he put a ſtop in Bagdad to public prayers for this ſultan, and quitted the city. Maſoud came up to him, routed, took him priſoner, and ſeized on all his goods, which cauſed a violent ferment in Bagdad.

When the khalifs were employed in ſtipulating the articles of peace among them, the khalif detained priſoner was aſſaſſinated by a troop of Bothenians, who ſtruck off his head, and left him uncovered. Succours was brought to him, but too late; ſome Bothenians were put to death, others eſcaped, and the body of the khalif remained extended on the ground the remainder of the day and the enſuing night. The inhabitants of Maraga, a city in whoſe vicinity the cataſtrophe had happened, performed his obſequies, and the ſultan Maſoud ſent an officer to Bagdad, with power to nominate another khalif. It was Raſched Billah, who was proclaimed. Such was the ſtate of the ſucceſſors of thoſe who had erected the empire and the religion of the Muſſulmans. The Bothenians here in queſtion, are thoſe which we call *the aſſaſſins*, who had at their head the *old man of the mountain*. This happened in the year 529 of the Hegira, (of J. C. 1135 †). Zenghi once

---

* This year began the 21ſt of Oct. 1134, and ended the 9th of Oct. of the year 1135.

more

more intermeddled in the troubles which arofe between the fultan and the new khalif, and was conftrained to return to Mouffoul, whilft the fultan made
himfelf mafter of Bagdad. After thofe details, let
us now pafs to tranfactions of a nearer and more
interefting nature to us.

In the year 532 of the Hegira, the emperor of
Conftantinople, which our author calls *fimply the
king of Roum*, followed by the Franks, paffed into
Syria with a numerous army, and fpread a general
terror. As Zenghi could not then leave Mouffoul,
the Greeks firft made themfelves mafters of Bouzaa,
near Aleppo, where they did not even fpare the
children; then laid fiege to Schizour, from before
which they carried off eighteen engines. The emir
Aboulafaker, to whom it belonged, fent for fuccours to Zenghi, who did not delay to repair with
his army to Hama, where he found the enemy encamped on a mountain at the eaft of that place.
He propofed to them to defcend, and make proof
of their ftrength on the plain, offering to abandon
to them Schizour if he fhould be vanquifhed;
provided in cafe he fhould obtain the victory, they
would confent to withdraw, and defift from difturb-
ing the Muffulmans. He only wanted to intimi-
date them, as he was not ftrong enough to cope
with them. The Franks urged the emperor to
meet him. Zenghi, on the other hand, infinuated
to thofe of the Franks who had formerly fettled in
Syria, that the emperor waited only for an occafion
of deceiving them, and that if he fhould take one
single

single fortress in that country, he would invade all they were in possession of. He succeeded by this stratagem to create so much distrust among them, that the emperor of Constantinople was obliged to raise the siege, after an attack of twenty-four days, leaving all his machines behind. Zenghi set out on his pursuit; he defeated his rear guard, plundered his baggage, and took him, with a great many prisoners. If the Greeks, observes the author, had taken Schizour, nothing would have remained to the Muffulmans in that region. The poets celebrated this victory, and Zenghi went to take the castle of Arca in the environs of Tripoli, made the Franks who held out in it prisoners, demolished the place, and returned rich with booty.

All the emirs of that tract were then warring against each other; dominions were taken and retaken, without the sultan's interfering in the divisions of vassals. In the year 533*, Zenghi laid siege to Damascus, which surrendered; he took Baalbek sword in hand, next he made his way into the country of the Franks, and after a bloody combat, he forced them to fly into the castle of Barin, which he laid siege to. The Franks were too hasty in capitulating; if they had kept firm but two days longer, Zenghi, in consequence of the succours that were near for them, would have been compelled to raise the siege; he had been informed of it,

---

* Began the 27th of August of the year 1139, and ends the 15th of August 1140.

and

and he made all the hafte he could to take poffeffion of the place. Barin was fituated on the extremity of the country of the Franks; from thence they made excurfions between Hama and Aleppo; inceffantly diftreffing the Muffulmans. After this important reduction, he fent to take Maara and Kafartab, cities whofe environs were at once very populous and very fertile.

The Franks and the Roums, newly landed in Syria, not having been in a capacity to carry fuccours to Barin, turned towards Aleppo, of which they formed the fiege. At the fight of fuch an innumerable army, Zenghi, terrified, gave advice to the fultan Mafoud, and requefted him to fend the neceffary fuccours. Ben-al-athir affures us he had heard it of his father, who was then living, and who was informed by the cadhi, the carrier of the letter to Zenghi, what he is going to relate. Notwithftanding the danger menacing Syria in that conjuncture, the fultan paid little attention to the letter and command of Zenghi, and the cadhi, obliged to recur to artifice, to engage this prince in the defence of his ftates, threw fome pieces of gold among the people, and perfuaded the *khatib*, that is, him who recited the difcourfe, or prayer from the tribunal, to advertife the people of what was paffing in Syria; which he exactly complied with. In fact, when the other afcended the tribunal, he exclaimed, in a lamentable voice, *Ob. iflamifur! O religion, O Mahomet!* The people, in a crowd, thronged out of the mofque, and furrounded the fultan's palace, intreating him to fend the defired fuccours; the fame art was practifed in the other mofques, and was attended with equal fuccefs. From this recital we may infer, how much the Muffulmans thought themfelves endangered on the arrival of their new foes, and to what an extremity the infenfibility of the fultans, to the prefervation and defence of their ftates arofe. It is true as we remarked already, that the emirs, like our grand vaffals, bound to fome marks of obedience towards the fultan, were uncontrouled as to their power. The fultan, frightened by the tumult, ordered the cadhi before him, and reproached him for having ftrove to excite a fedition. The latter gave for anfwer, that the enemy was at a fmall diftance, and that if he took Aleppo, Bagdad would foon fall into his power, as there was no intermediate place which could retard his progrefs. Here the fultan ordered, that twenty thoufand men, cavalry, fhould immediately be put under arms; but as this troop was upon the point of departing, frefh letters were received by Zenghi, importing that the Greeks and Franks had raifed the fiege of Aleppo, and were retreating.

Zenghi, free from fuch formidable enemies, went in 537* to make incurfions into the country of the Kurdes. In 538†, he had different mifunderftand-

* Began the 26th of July of the year 1142, and end the 11th of July 1143.

† This year began the 15th of July, 1143, and end the 2d of July, 1144.

ings

ings with the fultan, and re-ingratiated himfelf by
certain fums of money he paid. Then he reduced feveral places of the Diarbekir, and in
539, advanced to form the fiege of Roha, or
Edeffa, then in the hands of the Franks. It was
count Joffelin who was then mafter of it. He
was, fays the author, the braveft and moft valiant
of the Franks. After a fiege of twenty-eight days,
Zenghi took poffeffion of the city. Ben-al-athir
gives a diftinguifhed eulogium of that prince, on
the fubject of this conqueft, which was looked
upon as one of the moft important obtained over
the Franks. By thefe details, which we abridge,
may be collected how far the hiftory of our crufades may be affifted. Zenghi then proceeded to
take the caftle of Barin, which was ftill under the
command of Joffelin, and thence to befiege the
fortrefs of Dgiaber; but during his fleep, a troop
of his own flaves fell upon him, cut his throat, and
took refuge in the caftle: it was the befieged garrifon who apprifed the army of his death.

We muft not always judge of thofe princes
agreeable to the defcriptions of our own hiftorians
of crufades. Zenghi, according to Ben-al-athir,
was one of the greateft men of his age. He rendered himfelf commendable by his wifdom, prudence, and courage: all his fubjects lived in fecurity; he was always the defender of the weak,
knew how to reprefs the violence of his emirs, and
never fuffered them to invade the property of

F f 2   others;

number in the city, where he had collected an immenfe booty.

Edeſſa remained then in his poſſeſſion.

After that conqueſt he concluded a peace with
his brother the king of Mouſſoul, which formed two
principalities of Atabeks. It is thus that thoſe
petty ſovereigns were called; the one was at
Aleppo, and the other at Mouſſoul. Atabek ſignifies the father of the prince; it is the title which
the ſultans gave to ſome of their emirs. The
princes of Mouſſoul, more diſtant from the poſſeſſions of the Franks, had in conſequence leſs inter-
courſe with them; and as we give only an account
from our author, we ſhall paſs in ſilence the broils
that broke forth between theſe princes of the ſame
family. The details we meet with in this work form
no part of our plan, and we ſhall confine ourſelves
to ſuch as may concern our cruſades, and even thoſe
we ſhall abridge.

We ſhould here call to memory, that about the
years 1146 and 1147, the emperor Conrad III. with
ſeveral German princes, Henry of Suabia, and others,
undertook a new cruſade. Lewis VII. king of
France, attended by a great number of French
lords, ſet out with the ſame intention. It was in the
year 843*, according to Ben-al-athir, that information was given, that the *king of the Germans* was
arrived with an innumerable army in Syria; that he
had united with the Franks of Sakel or Phenicia;

* Began the 21ſt of May, 1148, and end the 9th of May,
1149.

and

and that they were jointly approaching to befiege
Damafcus. This city was then poffeffed by Mod-
girredin-ibk; but the whole authority lay in the
hands of one of his flaves, named Moïn-eddin, a
wife and prudent man. The moft part of the Afi-
atic princes had in the fame manner always flaves
who governed for them; the eaftern effeminacy did
not permit them to take the government of their
ftates into their own hands. It is by the like conduct that the khalifs have been overthrown, and
that the power of the Seljouc fultans, and even their
great vaffals has been undermined, and by which
fo many revolutions have happened in the eaft.
It was the 16th of Rabi-al-aoul that the Franks
arrived before Damafcus, Moïn-eddin gave immediate notice thereof to Seïf-eddin, king of Mouffoul. The latter intimated to the foreign Franks
that he would make war againft them if they would
not retire, The author diftinguifhes thefe Franks
by the epithet *foreign,* which denotes thofe lately
arrived from Europe; and by *Franks of Sakel,*
which marks thofe who had been eftablifhed a long
time on the coafts of the fea and in Syria. On
his fide, Moïneddin fpread a rumour, that the
fultan of the eaft was advancing with his powerful
armies. At the fame time he wrote to the Franks
in Syria, to infpire them with fear and jealoufy
againft thofe foreign Franks. " If they," fays
he, " obtain poffeffion of Damafcus, nothing re-
" mains for you in this country; and if I am com-
" pelled to put the place into the hands of Seïf-

F f 4   " eddin,

" eddin, you will never be able to hinder him from taking Jerusalem." He offered them, at the same time, the city of Paneas, if they could prevail upon the king of the Germans to retire. The Franks of Syria, who were not averse to these proposals, frightened the foreign Franks with the arrival of Seïf-eddin; and gave them to understand, that if this prince should happen to open his way into Damascus, nothing of what they possessed in Syria, would be spared or left them. Then the king of the Germans raised the siege and retreated. Moïn-eddin, on his side, remained faithful to his promise with respect to the Franks of Syria, and resigned to them the city of Paneas.

Such was the conclusion of this crusade, which had no success, owing to the jealousy which the Franks of Syria entertained against those of Europe, who appeared to come to their assistance, whilst in truth they made it their endeavours to establish themselves on the ruin of the former. It was an extensive colony we had planted, and which attracted the envy of all the Europeans who crouded thither, either to plunder the former colonists, or to make new conquests. As in those times nothing was transacted without the pope's influence, we have considered those wars as wars of religion.

After the Franks had abandoned Damascus, (continues the Arabian historian) the two brothers Noureddin and Seïf-eddin, who repaired to Baalbek, received a letter from the count of Tripoli

(Raimond)

(Raimond) to enduce to come and take the caftle of Arima, which belonged to the foreign Franks. It was the fon of Alphonfo, king of Sicily, newly arrived, who had defpoiled him of this place, and was inclined to difpoffes him even of Tripoli. Noureddin immediately marched towards the caftle, and notwithftanding the vigorous refiftance of the befieged, made himfelf mafter of it by a capitulation; by which it was agreed, that the men, women, and children fhould quit it, which was executed: the fon of Alphonfo was of the number. Afterwards Noureddin caufed the place to be demolifhed.

I omit fome other expeditions againft the Franks, and the narrative of the death of Seïf-eddin, king of Mouffoul, which happened in 544*. In the fame year Noureddin went with a defign to befiege the caftle of Harem, which belonged to the Franks; but he only pillaged the environs, and then marched againft the caftle of Anab. The Franks affembled immediately, having at their head Albornos, or Brins, mafter of Antiochia (Raimond prince of Antiochia). The two armies fought a bloody battle, in which the prince of Antiochia loft his life. He left an infant fon behind him, named Boemund, who remained with his mother in that city, where this princefs married another prince, who commanded until Boemund was of age to govern.

* Began the 10th of May, 1149, and end the 28th of April, 1150.

In

In courfe of time, Noureddin gave battle feveral
times to the Franks : in one of them he took captive the prince whom the princefs of Antiochia had
married, and Boemund reigned alone, until he was
alfo made prifoner by Noureddin in 559. The
poets made verfes on the fubject of this victory,
which Noureddin obtained over the army of Antiochia.

In the fame year 544 (of Jefus Chrift 1149) he
marched towards Arphamia, or Apamea, one day's
journey from Harem. It was ftill in the poffeffion
of the Franks, and reputed a ftrong place, being
fituated on an eminence, whence they made excurfions into the territories of Hama and of Schizour.
Noureddin gave the garrifon no breath, and took
the place before the arrival of the fuccours, which
the Franks were expecting. He found provifions
and ammunition in great abundance; thence he
marched towards the Franks, whom he forced to
retreat. The poets alfo fung this expedition.

He then turned his arms towards the dominions
of Joffelin, which confifted of feveral caftles, fituated north of Aleppo, fuch as Tellbafcher, Aïntab,
Ezaz, &c. but he was over-powered, and his efquire,
who was made prifoner, was fent by Joffelin to Mafoud, fultan of Iconium and of Acfara, whofe daughter
Noureddin had taken in marriage. Joffelin fignified to this prince, that he had fent him the arms of
his fon-in-law, and that he would foon fend him in
perfon. Noureddin, irritated at this defeat and af-

front

front, only ftudied to revenge himfelf. He engaged
a troop of Turkomans, to whom he made great
promifes, if they would deliver him Joffelin alive
or dead. They took advantage of a hunting
party which the count went to, with a few attendants, and feized him. They were on the point
of letting him go again for fome prefents, but one
of them having given notice to the governor of
Aleppo, the latter informed Noureddin of it, who
was at Emeffa, and immediately fent fome troops,
who carried Joffelin off to the Turkomans. This
was looked upon as equal to the greateft victory
the Muffulmans had gained. This Joffelin (fays
the author) was the moft terrible of devils, and the
greateft enemy to the Muffulmans. In every battle
he was at the head of the Franks, who knew his
bravery, his intrepidity, his prudence, and his hatred
to Iflamifm.

By this capture the country remained without defenders, and it was eafy to get poffeffion of moft of
the fortreffes, as Tellbafcher, Aïntab, Ezaz, Cou-
ros, Ravandan, the caftle of Bada, Tell-Khaled,
Kafarlatha, Rafarfoud, the caftle of Sarphout, Dalouk, Maráfch, Nahar-al-Dgiouz, and Bourge-er-
Raffafs. I name them all here, becaufe moft of
their names are disfigured in the hiftorians of the
Crufades. Noureddin fortified and placed good
garrifons in them. At this news the Franks re-
affembled their armies, and having begun their
march to prevent them from taking reft, they met
them near Dalouk, came to action with them, and
after

after a violent engagement, they were obliged to take flight, and Noureddin made himself master of Dalouk, and other places.

We shall not here detain our readers with the death of sultan Masoud, which happened at Hamadan, nor of a new sultan being proclaimed, who was, as we have said, the sovereign of all Asia. Noureddin himself was only one of his principal vassals.   In the year 549 *, this prince made himself master of Damascus, which belonged to Modgireddin-ibk; the Franks the year before had taken Ascalon, one of the strongest places in Palestine, without his being able to prevent them, because the city of Damascus lay in his way.   The Franks equally endeavoured to seize it, and kept up a correspondence in the place.   The citizens of Damascus, seeing themselves besieged by Noureddin, demanded succours from the Franks, promising them a sum of money, and the castle of Baalbik, if they would raise the siege, which they could not effect. Noureddin entered Damascus and recovered Hemasca, whither the king of Damascus had retired.

The Franks and Noureddin were too near neighbours to live in peace.   Each sought to extend their territories, and Noureddin again besieged the castle of Harem, as he had done several times before.   This castle, which belonged to Boemond prince of Antioch, was in the vicinity of that place, and west of Aleppo: it was very strongly fortified, and commanded by one of the bravest captains

* This happened in 546 of the Hegira; of Jesus Christ 1157.

among

among the Franks, who defended himself so courageously, that Noureddin was compelled to retire.
In the year 552 the country was laid waste by an
earthquake. Noureddin was very active to protect the places that had suffered by it from the attempts of the Franks, and made himself master of
Schizour, a castle belonging to the Monkadites,
situated on a steep rock half a day's journey from
Hama. The only way to this castle was by a path
cut in the rock at the side of the mountain: this
path was interrupted in the middle, by a moveable
wooden bridge, which, when taken away, rendered
it impossible to proceed. This castle was laid in
ruins by the earthquake, and Noureddin, by his
activity, prevented the Franks from making themselves masters of it as they had intended.

I shall take no notice here of the troubles which
took place in Bagdat in 553, and which gave full
employment to Zeineddin prince of Mouffoul; I
shall also pass over the death of the khalif Moctafi,
who was succeeded in 555 (A. D. 1160) by Mof-
tandjed; and the divisions in the sultan's family;
and shall return to the expeditions of Noureddin
against the Franks. In 557 this prince again af-
sembled his troops to besiege the castle of Harem:
but he still found it so well fortified and defended
that he could not take it. After having in vain offered battle to the Franks, who had assembled their
forces, he returned to Aleppo.

The year following, 558, Noureddin, always an
enemy to the Franks, assembled all his forces, entered

tered again into their territories, and encamped in
a plain (Rakia) at the foot of a caftle belonging to
the Kurdes (Hifn-el-akrad). His defign was to
march thence to Tripoli; but, whilft he leaft expected it, he was furprifed in his camp by the
Franks, fo that his troops had not time to mount
their horfes, or even to take arms. The carnage
was terrible, and the Franks took many prifoners,
and all the baggage. A Greek, named Ducas, was
the moft violent againft the Muffulmans on this
occafion. Noureddin made his efcape in the utmoft diforder towards Hemeffa, and encamped at
Bahirat-couds, one parafang from that city, and
four from the field of battle. It was fuppofed he
would have gone as far as Aleppo, but he was too
brave. " Let me have but a thoufand horfe," faid
he, " I fhall not be afraid of the Turks, whatever be
" their number." He wrote immediately to Damafcus and Aleppo for money, provifions, tents and
arms. The Franks intended to purfue him, but
learning that he halted near Hemeffa, they did
not think proper to attack him there, and propofed a truce, to which he refufed his confent.
They then fortified the caftle of the Kurdes and
returned.

On his part, Noureddin meditated an expedition
of more importance than the, taking a few caftles
from the Franks; it was the conqueft of Egypt.
He fent one of his principal emirs, named Schirkouh, with an army to fubdue this country, in the
year 559. This emir and his brother Nodjmed-

din

din-Ayoub, both fons of Schadi, were from the country of Douïn, and Kurdes by birth, being of the tribe of Kouadia, the moft noble and illuftrious amongft the Kurdes. This is worth remarking,. for the purpofe of afcertaining the origin of Saladin, the fon of Nodjmeddin-Ayoub, and confequently nephew to Schirkouh. Thefe two Kurdes had come to Erac, where they entered into the fervice of Moudgiahdeddin, who, finding in Nodjmeddin much fenfe, prudence, and good conduct, gave him the poft of dizdar at Tekrit. Schirkouh accompanied his brother ; but killing a man fometimes afterwards, Moudgiaheddin expelled them both from the city. They then repaired to Emadeddin Zenghi, who gave Nodjmeddin the place of dizdar in the caftle of Baalbek. After divers events, and particularly the death of Zinghi, Schirkouh was compelled to quit this city alfo. The two brothers followed Noureddin; he employed them in his troops, and at length gave Schirkouh the command of the expedition againft Egypt.

Noureddin was induced to fend an army into Egypt by Schaour, vizir of Adhedledin-allah, khalif of Egypt, who, having been depofed, had retired to Noureddin the year before, and pretended it was to be feared, that the Franks would make themfelves mafters of that country. In fact, they had conftantly endeavoured to eftablifh themfelves there; Noureddin therefore fent Schirkouh at the head of an army, in the month Dgiou-madiel-aoual

el-aoual of the year 559 (of Jefus Chrift 1164),
with orders to reftore the vizier to his office. He
accompanied him with another body of troops as
far as the frontiers of the Muffulman territories.
Schirkouh arrived in Egypt, re-eftablifhed. the
vizier, and remained encamped in the neighbourhood of Caïro.. But Schaour, far from keeping the
promifes he had made to Noureddin and Schirkouh, wrote to the latter, to induce him to return
into Syria. Schirkouh perfifted in remaining, put
him in mind of his promifes, and finding that Schaour no longer gave him any anfwer, he detached
one of his officers to feize the city of Bilbeïs.
Schaour, on his fide, demanded fuccour from the
Franks, informing them that Noureddin wanted to
get poffeffion of Egypt, which the Franks feared
above all things: they haftened therefore to anfwer
him, and prepared to go to his affiftance, as their
intention was to make themfelves mafters of the
country. Noureddin, who was informed of this,
affembled his forces, and approached their frontiers
to make a diverfion. The king of Jerufalem
(Amauri) left a part of his troops to guard his territories, and marched with the reft towards Egypt.
At the fame time a great number of Franks, newly
arrived by fea to vifit Jerufalem, joined the king.
Schirkouh was foon befieged in Bilbeis, where he
had retired with his army. Though the walls of
this city were in a bad ftate, and there was no ditch,
the Franks remained before the city three months.
During this time Noureddin prepared for laying

fiege

ſiege to the caſtle of Haram, in Syria, a place of importance, and which he had often endeavoured to take. The Franks, informed of this, and fearing he would then go to Paneas, propoſed to Schirkouh to reſtore to the Egyptians what he had taken from them, and to return into Syria, aſſuring him that they alſo would retire on their ſide. Schirkouh, ignorant of what paſſed on the part of Noureddin, accepted theſe propoſals and evacuated Bibleïs.

Noureddin, after the defeat we have mentioned above, had aſſembled all his forces, and thoſe of his neighbouring allies, and ſat down before Harem with a great number of engines of war. The Franks had at their head Al-brins, (the prince) governor of Antioch, and Coms (the count) governor of Tripoli: the ſon of Joſſelin, who was one of the moſt brave and illuſtrious of the Franks, al Douk (the duke) who commanded the Greeks, haſtened to their aſſiſtance. Noureddin defeated them in a general engagement, killed ten thouſand, and took many priſoners, amongſt whom were their chiefs: after this victory he marched towards Harem, and made himſelf maſter of it the 21ſt of Ramadhan. He was adviſed to go and take Antioch alſo, but this new expedition he would not undertake, and contented himſelf with a ranſom for the priſoners.

In the year 560, Noureddin took the caſtle of Paneas, the Franks being too much weakened by their late defeat to ſuccour that place: he found in it immenſe riches. In the year 561, he made himself master of Mounaidhara, (the castle of Mirabel) which belonged to them, took it by assault, and killed or made prisoners all that were in the place.

The following year, 562, he sent Schirkouh into Egypt, of which he was extremely desirous of becoming master. Schaour, who commanded there under the authority of the khaliff, being informed of the arrival of Noureddin's troops, acquainted the Franks with his situation, and demanded assistance. They immediately marched to join Schaour: Schirkouh met them at Babaïn, and, giving battle, defeated them. This, says the author, was one of the most surprising actions mentioned in history, a thousand horse having put to flight the combined army of the Egyptians and Franks. After this victory Schirkouh took possession of Alexandria, the command of which he gave to his nephew Saladin, and took the road to Saïd. The Franks and Egyptians had retired to Cairo, from whence they went to besiege Alexandria. This place was in want of provisions: Schirkouh returned, peace was proposed, and he agreed to it, on condition that they gave him fifty thousand dinars, or pieces of gold, that he should keep what he had taken, but that Alexandria should be restored, and that the Franks should not remain in Egypt, nor possess any place in that country. After signing the treaty Schirkouh returned into Syria, and arrived at Damascus in the month Dhoulhedge.

On

On the other hand the Franks secretly agreed with Schaour that they should have a body of troops in Caïro, to guard the gates, to prevent Noureddin from making himself master of it, and that he should be paid a hundred thousand dinars a year. Adhed, khalif of Egypt, was ignorant of all these treaties between the Franks and his vizier.

We shall not here speak of some particular events concerning Mouffoul, nor the taking the castle of Dgiaber from the Oeaïlites by Noureddin, but return to the history of Egypt, of which the Franks were always endeavouring to get poffession. This country was the magazine of all the commerce of India, and our Crusaders left no method untried to establish themselves there, in order to render themselves masters of this commerce: their ideas on this subject may be read in Sanute. The Muffulmans were jealous of its preservation, and, disturbed at seeing these Franks in Cairo, solicited Noureddin to send new troops thither. The Franks, who had a party in Egypt, laid siege to Bilbeïs (Pelusium), in order to prevent this, and took that place, which they pillaged, and made the inhabitants prisoners. Thence they marched to Cairo. Schaour set fire to that part of the city called Meff, which continued burning fifty-four days. The khalif Adhed, who did not approve of all the steps of his vizier, wrote to Noureddin for assistance, informing him that the Muffulmans could no longer refist the Franks. He inclosed in his letter some hair of the women, to shew that

they

they implored his help. The Franks preffed hard
on Caïro: Schâour wrote to them, and, reminding
them of their ancient connections, acquainted them
with his fears. from Noureddin; who had been engaged to come thither: on this account he demanded peace, offering a million of Egyptian dinars.

: The khalif Adhed, on his part, in order to
drive out the Franks, offered Noureddin the third of
Egypt, on. condition that Schirkouh repaired thither
with an army, and remained at Caïro; the Egyptians were not lefs eager in their folicitations:
Noureddin hefitated no longer, and fent Schirkouh with a powerful army. The Franks, informed that Schirkouh was approaching, retired.

, Schirkouh entered Cairo the 7th of Rabi-alkher,
where he was received by the khalif, who made
him confiderable.prefents.. Schaour diffembled his
difcontent, and propofed to arreft Schirkouh; but
his fon Kamel;diffuaded him, by fhewing him that
it would be taking the country from the Muffulmans to deliver it to the Franks. On the other
hand, Saladin, who miftrufted Schaour, had with
fome others concerted his death, and, though this
ftep was not agreeable to Schirkouh, perfifted in
his defign, arrefted the vizier, and Schirkouh fent
his head to the khalif Adhed, who had demanded
it of him: he then.entered.Caïro, and faid to the
people, who appeared alarmed, that the khalif
ordered the palace of. Schaour to be pillaged;
the people.executed it immediately.. Schirkouh

was

was made vizier of Egypt in the place of Schaour; but this emir did not long survive his elevation and conquest; he fell ill and died on Saturday, the 22d of Dgioumadi-alkher. Selaheddin Yonsouf, or Saladin, his nephew, son of Nodjmeddin-ayoub was with him, with many other emirs, Kurdes, of his family. After the death of Schirkouh, the khalif Adhed persuaded that he had not much to fear from a man without power and without troops, resolved to promote Saladin to the dignity of vizier, whose ambition had not prompted him to solicit that place. The khalif gave him the title of Maleken-naser, that is, the victorious king. The new vizier, returning to the palace of his uncle, and perceiving that the other emirs Kurdes, of his family paid no great respect to his person, and that none of them were pleased at his promotion, distributed the treasures of his uncle with profusion, conciliated the people by his liberality, made himself beloved by them, and acquired so great a credit as to weaken the party of the khalif Adhed.[1] Noureddin was equally displeased at this promotion.

The Franks, who in all their expeditions never lost sight of Egypt, where they wished to establish themselves, assembled at this time to make an incursion into that country. Noureddin sent fresh troops to their assistance, among whom was an elder brother of Saladin, called Schamseddoulet Tourankhah. Noureddin considered Saladin only as his lieutenant in Egypt; and, whilst this prince was

alive

alive, Saladin dared not declare himself king of Egypt.

It was in the year 565, at the beginning of Sepher, that the Franks, who were alarmed by the success of Schirkouh in Egypt, appeared before Damietta: they had written to the Franks of Andalusia, Sicily, and other places, to demand assistance, informing them that Jerusalem might be attacked. The priests and monks encouraged the Franks to take arms to besiege Damietta, hoping, if that place was taken, they should soon become masters of all Egypt. Saladin sent to that place all the succours he could assemble, and imparted to Noureddin his fears, and the mistrust he had of the Egyptians. Noureddin sent him fresh troops, and prepared on his part to lay waste the country of the Franks, in order to make a diversion, which obliged them to raise the siege of Damietta, after fifty days, leaving behind them their provisions and baggage.

Noureddin laid siege to the fortress of Krak, to protect the convoy which he sent into Egypt; but he did not remain long before that place. Being informed that two generals of the Franks were come with troops, he retired, ravaging the country, and encamped at Aschtara, to observe them. While he was there, a violent earthquake, in the environs of Aleppo, and throughout all Syria, obliged him to go to succour the places whose walls had been thrown down, and which it was necessary to rebuild. The Franks were not less employed in
repairing

repairing the diforders occafioned in their territories by this event. They were again defeated by Schehabeddin Mahmoud, a prince of the Ortokides, who joined Noureddin, and were put to flight with the lofs of many of their principal officers; amongft others the mafter of the hofpitalers, who poffeffed the caftle of the Kurdes, (Kin-elakrad) and who was one of the braveft of the Franks.

At this time died Cothbeddin Maudoud, brother to Noureddin, who reigned at Mouffoul. The author beftows great encomiums on this prince, as he does under the year following, 566, on khalif Monftandged Billah. Noureddin informed of the death of his brother, and the divifions refpecting his fucceffion, went to the Racca, Khabour, Nefibin, and other places, to guard them from the invafion of the Franks. He then befieged Sandgiat, of which he made himfelf mafter: thefe places belonged to his brother. He advanced thus to Mouffoul, which fubmitted to him: he did not keep all thefe cities, but reftored them to his nephew Saïfeddin, who was declared king of Mouffoul.

In the year 567, the Franks having refufed to give up fome veffels which they had taken on their paffage from Egypt to Syria, Noureddin fent to make an incurfion towards Antioch and Tripoli; he befieged the fortrefs of Arca in perfon, whilft another divifion of his troops took Saphet and Arima; he then went towards Tripoli, ravaging and burning all that came in his way, whilft other

troops

troops did the fame towards Antioch. The Franks then offered to deliver up the veffels, and peace was made: They were like the Jews, fays our author, who will pay no tribute till they are beaten; he at the fame time complains how little faith was then to be met with, even amongft the Muffulmans. His father was concerned in the cargoes of thefe veffels. Noureddin ordered all the goods to be reftored, but many took what did not belong to them.

It was in the fame year 567 (A. D. 1171) in the month Mouharram, that the great revolution happened in Egypt, and which was the confequence of all the events that had previoufly taken place. Noureddin's defign in fending armies into that country, was to be before the Franks, and to make himfelf mafter of it. Saladin, his lieutenant, had eftablifhed himfelf there, and acquired a formidable party. Noureddin then ordered him to caufe the name of the khalif of Bagdad to be fubftituted to that of Adhed khalif of Egypt, in the public prayers. Saladin, who feared fome infurrections would follow fuch a ftep, for it was in fact to declare the khalif of Egypt dethroned, excufed himfelf, under pretence that the Egyptians were ftrongly attached to the Alides, from which family thefe khalifs pretended to be derived, whilft they detefted thofe of Bagdad. Noureddin perfifted: Happily the khalif Adhed fell fick; Saladin profited by this occafion, affembled all the emirs, and held a council to determine how the order of Noureddin

reddin fhould be executed. They were yet uncertain what part to take, and Saladin began to fear he fhould not fucceed, when a Perfian, named emir 'Alem, " whom, (fays the author) I have many times feen at Mouffoul," offered to pray in the name of the khalif of Bagdad.". The firft Friday in Mon-harram, he mounted the pulpit, placed himfelf be-fore the khatib (or preacher,) and prayed for the khalif Moftadhi Bamrillah, of Bagdad.   No oppo-fition was made to it, and the Friday following Saladin ordered all the khatibs of Mefr and Cairo to do the fame, which they did without the leaft difpute; the fame was then done throughout all the provinces, Adhed, who was dangeroufly ill, being unacquainted with what paffed. If he die, faid they, it is of no fervice to difturb the few days he has to live.   In fact, he died without being informed of it.   Saladin immediately took poffeffion of his pa-lace, and all the riches it contained; fent all the family of Adhed to another place, where they were kept under a ftrong guard; fet many of his flaves at liberty, fold others, and thus cleared the whole palace.

Such was the end of the khalifs of Egypt: they had commenced in Africa, in the month Dhoul-hedge, in the year 299, (of the Chriftian æra 911.) The firft was Mahadi Abou Mohammed Abdallah, who built the city of Mahadia (on the coaft of Bar-bary.) 'He reigned over all that part of Africa.

2. His fon, Caim-bamrillah Aboulcafem Mo-hammed, fucceeded him.

3. Next

3. Next reigned Almanfour Billah Abonthaher Ifmaël, fon of Caïm.

4. The fourth was Moezzeddin Allah Ahoute-mim Maad, fon of Manfour. He fent an army into Egypt, under the conduct of one of his gene-rals, named Dgiouhar, who conquered it in the month Schaban, 358, (A. D. 968,) and built Cairo. Moez then quitted Africa, and came to refide in Egypt, where his defcendants reigned after him two hundred and eight years.

The fucceffors of Moez were ; .5, Aziz-billah, 6. Hakem-bamrillah. 7. Dhaher-l'ezaz-eddin-illah. 8. Mouftanfer-billah. 9. Haphedhledin-illa. 10. Dhapher-billah. 11. Phaïz-billah. 12. Adhedledin-illah, who was the laft.

Our author omits two khalifs between Mou-ftanfer and Haphedh, which is doubtlefs an error of the copyift. This hiftory, he fays, he has related more circumftantially in his chronicle, under the reign of khalif Mouftaçdhi.

Saladin became mafter of all the treafures of the khalifs, took what he chofe, diftributed a part to his relations and emirs, and caufed the reft to be fold. " No king in the world, (fays the author) had collected fo great a number of precious ftones and pearls as were found amongft this treafure." Among other curiofities were a rod of emerald, and a mountain of yacout, befides about a hundred thoufand chofen volumes, remarkable for the beau-ty of their writing. Noureddin fent to the khalif
Moftadhi,

Moftadhi, at Bagdad, the important intelligence of his name being inferted in the prayers in Egypt. This gave great joy to Moftadhi, who fent a robe of honour to Noureddin, and black covering, (the colour of the Abafides) to put on the pulpits in Egypt.

After this conqueft, Noureddin ordered Saladin to return into Syria with his troops, to join him in the fiege of Krak, belonging to the Franks. Saladin began his march, and Noureddin waited for him at Damafcus, where he foon learnt that Saladin had re-entered Egypt, under pretence, as he wrote him, that the Egyptians might rife in his abfence. Fears and fufpicions of Noureddin had been inftilled into the mind of this emir, which was the reafon of his difobedience. Noureddin, difpleafed at this conduct, determined to go into Egypt and drive out Saladin. The latter, who was informed of it, affembled all his relations and emirs, to afk their advice: in this, they by no means agreed; feveral faid they were the flaves of Noureddin, and that his orders muft be executed; they then wrote him word what had paffed. The father of Saladin, not pleafed with his fon, called him an inexperienced boy, blamed him for having difclofed his fentiments before fo many people, and advifed him to write immediately to Noureddin, to induce him to lay afide his defign: with this advice Saladin complied. It appears, that this emir afpired to the throne of Egypt, at which he afterwards arrived.

In

In the same year 567, (of Christ 1171,) Noured-din established post pigeons (hemam al-haouadi); these are a particular kind of pigeons that return to their nests from a very great distance. At that time his dominions were so extensive that he could not be informed of the incursions made by the Franks soon enough to send succours to the places attacked. Men, with these pigeons, were stationed every where, from city to city, and at the first dis-covery a letter was written and fastened to the pigeon, who was dispatched to the next city; there another pigeon was charged with it; and thus in one day the news was conveyed to Noureddin. Thus they were enabled to surprise the Franks in their expeditions.

In 568, A. D. 1172, Dhoulnoun, son of Da-nischmend, king of Malathie and Siouas, requested the aid of Noureddin against Kilidge Arslan, sultan of Iconium, who had just seized on his dominions. Noureddin, who was not accustomed to make war on Mussulman princes, but, on the contrary, to defend them against the enterprizes of the Franks, wrote to Kilidge Arslan, to induce him to restore to Dhoulnoun what he had taken from him. But Kilidge Arslan returning no answer, Noureddin seized Bahsna and Marasch, whilst another body of his troops took Sionas. This war, however, was attended with no other consequences. Noureddin, after several letters, wrote one in which he confined his demands to three conditions. Kilidge Arslan, says the author, was attached to *the philosophic sect*;

as

as he expreffed it : on this account Noureddin required him firft to make a new profeffion of faith
in the prefence of his envoy, a remarkable circumftance, as the Muffulmans and Chriftians treated
together confidentially ; in the next place, to furnifh troops whenever they were wanted to make
war on the Franks ; and laftly, to give his daughter in marriage to· his nephew Seïfeddin Ghazi.
Kilidge Arflan accepted thefe conditions ; the peace
was concluded, and Noureddin returned, leaving a
body of troops, commanded by one of his emirs,
at Sionas, for the fervice of Dhoulnoun.

In the year 569 (of Chrift 1173) Noureddin was
at Damafcus, preparing to go into Egypt with an
army, after leaving in Syria a fufficient number of
troops to refift the Franks, in cafe of an ·attack.
He was ·difpleafed with Saladin, and refolved to
make him quit that country. But when the latter
faw himfelf on the point of being obliged to yield
himfelf up to Noureddin, he heard, that he died
at Damafous, on Wednefday the 11th of Schoual.
This unexpected event produced great changes in
thefe countries. Noureddin had ordered an army
to go from Egypt into Yemen, under the command
of Schamfeddoulet, brother to Saladin. This
emir fubdued that province, and caufed public
prayers to be made in the name of Noureddin, in
the two mofques of Mecca and Medina : but this
prince did not enjoy the conqueft, and Schamfeddoulet became afterwards king of Yemen.

Nou-

Noureddin was succeeded by his son Malek-effaleh, who was yet a youth. All the emirs took the oath of fidelity to him, and in Egypt, Saladin caufed the public prayers to be made, and money to be coined, in his name. There were however fome difturbances in Noureddin's family; but it is ufelefs to notice circumftances of fo little importance. Let us proceed to the portrait our author gives of this prince, who became fo formidable to our crufades.

Noureddin was fair, ftout, and well made. Except the firft khalifs, and Omar, fon of Abdolaziz, there never was fo great a prince as Noureddin, according to our author, whether we confider his conduct, his prudence, or his juftice. Though extremely rich he was fimple and modeft in his drefs, never wearing either filk, gold, or filver, which the law prohibited: he neither drank wine, nor would he permit it to be fold in his dominions. He was exact in the duty of prayer, and rofe early to perform it: the reft of the day he employed himfelf in ftate affairs. He was not prodigal of his treafures to thofe who requefted favours of him: " What is in my hands, (faid he) belongs not to me; I am but the treafurer of the Muffulmans." He attended to the complaints of every one, and was fpeedy and ftrict in adminifter-ing juftice. It is related, that a man, full of confidence in his juftice, came to fettle at Damafcus; but, after the death of Noureddin, Saladin having taken poffeffion of that city, his foldiers and emirs com-

committed many exceffes, which he took no care to
fupprefs. This man, who had made complaints, in
vain, came down from the caftle one day, tearing
his cloaths, and crying, *O Noureddin, where art
thou! if thou wert witnefs to the injuftices we fuffer,
thou wouldeft have pity on us: where is thy juftice!*
He repaired to the tomb of Noureddin, followed
by the people, and they fhed tears together over
his body. At length, the fear of a revolt obliged
the conqueror to indemnify the man, who, continuing to weep, faid to Saladin, by whom he was
afked the reafon, " I weep becaufe the juftice of
Noureddin has deferted us."

Noureddin built a court of juftice, where he fat
twice a week with the judges. He was brave and
experienced in war: in peace he exercifed himfelf
at the mallet and the bow. He built the walls of a
great number of cities, of Aleppo, Hama, Hemeffa,
Damafcus, Maredin, Schizour, Manbedge, and
feveral fortreffes: at Aleppo, Hama, Damafcus,
and other places, he founded colleges, in which
were taught the doctrines of Schafi and Hanifa; he
built and endowed mofques at Mouffoul and Hama;
and Bimareftem, or hofpitals for the poor, the moft
confiderable of which is at Damafcus. On the frontiers he erected towers for obferving the motions
of the Franks, in which he placed pigeons: he
built religious houfes for the retreats of the fophis,
and gave them funds for their fupport, places for
teaching religion, fchools for orphans, and places
where

where these orphans had pensions for reading the Alcoran. He expended prodigious sums on these foundations. In Syria alone, the author says, they amounted, in his time, to nine thousand Sourien dinars (or dinars of Tyre) a month.

This prince received men of learning, doctors, and sophis, with the greatest distinction: he arose, went to meet them, and made them sit down, favours which he did not grant to his emirs.

The author considerably abridges the continuation of the history of Noureddin's successors, and it grows less important. Seïfeddin Ghazi, who reigned at Moussoul, took possession of many places. Saladin, who only aspired to become king of Egypt, made himself master of Damascus; but did not set aside the public prayers for Saleh, Noureddin's successor, in that city, a circumstance that deceived no one. *What happened, happened,* says the author, *doubt not but it was right, and enquire no further.*

The author mentions also the death of Moftadhi-billah, khalif of Bagdad, in the year 575, of Christ 1179; and that of Seïfeddin Ghazi, grandson of Emadeddin Zenghi, who was succeeded by his brother Azeddin.

Malek-effaleh Ismaël, who succeeded his father Noureddin, at Aleppo, died in that city in 577, not being then twenty years old. He named Ateddin, whom we have just mentioned, for his successor; he thus succeeded to the possessions of all the Atabek princes, at least what Saladin left them.

them. This prince, indeed, delayed not to go into Syria, where, favoured by the divisions that arose in the family of the Atabeks, he took several princes.

This ambitious prince died in the month Sepher of the year 589 (A. D. 1193). Azeddin, upon receiving information of this event, was desirous of retaking some of these places, but was prevented by death, on the 27th of Schaban, in the same year: he was succeeded by his son Noureddin. These Atabeks began to grow very weak, and Saladin's successor in Egypt took from them their ancient patrimony, so that their possessions were soon reduced to a few places, and they were no longer able to play an important part in this country.

Noureddin II. who also reigned at Mouffoul, died in the year 607, (A. D. 1210) in the month Redgeb: Malek-el-caher Azzeddin was his successor. Our author, who lived in his time, gives him the pompous titles of king, conqueror of the world, just, protector, victorious, brave, and pious: he stiles him the glory of the world, and of religion, the sultan of Iflamifm, and of the Muffulmans, and the protection of Aboulmodhaffer-mafoud, commander of the faithful. All these pompous titles suit but little with the feebleness of his actual taste; but it is the custom of the eastern princes to assume a multitude of empty titles. After having made the eulogium of this prince, the author finishes this abridgment of the history of the Atabeks, with faying, that it is more amply recorded in his great chronicle.

This manufcript is in good condition, the writing very elegible; but it is not mentioned at what time it was copied. In the latter pages fome places were left blank, to have been filled up with titles, in red letters, as there are in the preceding part of the volume.

END OF THE SECOND VOLUME.

E R R A T A.
VOL. II.

PAGE 15, line 22, for *Hamzabay,* read *Hamzabeg.* P. 46, l. 13, for *it,* read *him.* P. 47, l. 1, for *caftan,* read *caftan.* P. 60, l. 15, dele *had.* P. 62, note, for *cafting,* read *cannon.* P. 93, l. 4, for *ratio,* read *rations.* P. idem, l. 27, for *port,* read *poft.* P. 101, l. 23, dele *of.* P. 106, firft note, l. 1, after *this,* infert *is.* P. 130, l. 19, for *faddam,* read *faddan.* P. 131, l. 28, for *confift,* read *confifts.* P. 135, l. 15, for *fcaifes,* read *fcarfes.* P. 167, l. 3, after *rather,* infert *than.* P. 214, l. 26, after *it,* infert *is.* P. 248, l. 13, infert *Armagnac.* P. 256, l. 6, for *Purelle,* read *Pucelle.* P. 291, l. 27, for *ruined,* read *rhimed.* P. 295, l. 10, dele *one,* and for *arm,* read *armour.* P. 297, l. 1, for *each and,* read *each with.* P. 306, l. 17, for *for,* read *of.* P. 312, l. 3, for *Pettria,* read *Petri.* P. 313, l. 18. after *peace,* infert *his;* l. 29, dele *the.* P. 321, l. 21, for *Chriftiany,* read *Chriftianity.* P. 335, l. 6, dele *were;* l. 11, dele *to.* P. 342, l. 4, for *fuppor,* read *fupport.* P. 400, l. 30, for *behind,* read *upon.* P. 412, l. 11, for *nim,* read *him.* P. 414, l. 1, after *induce,* infert *them.* P. 447, l. 13, for *fometimes,* read *fometime.* P. 455, l. 11, dele *under.*